# THE HISTORY OF
# N.V. PHILIPS'
## GLOEILAMPENFABRIEKEN

VOLUME 1

*The origin of the
Dutch incandescent lamp industry*

A. HEERDING

*Translated by*

DEREK S. JORDAN

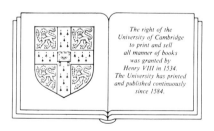

The right of the
University of Cambridge
to print and sell
all manner of books
was granted by
Henry VIII in 1534.
The University has printed
and published continuously
since 1584.

CAMBRIDGE UNIVERSITY PRESS

*Cambridge*
*London    New York    New Rochelle*
*Melbourne    Sydney*

Published by the Press Syndicate of the University of Cambridge
The Pitt Building, Trumpington Street, Cambridge CB2 1RP
32 East 57th Street, New York, NY 10022, USA
10 Stamford Road, Oakleigh, Melbourne 3166, Australia

Originally published in Dutch as *Geschiedenis van de N.V. Philips'
Gloeilampenfabrieken, Deel 1, Het Ontstaan van de Nederlandse
Gloeilampenindustrie* by Martinus Nijhoff, The Hague 1980 and
© N.V. Philips' Gloeilampenfabrieken, Eindhoven, 1980

English translation © N.V. Philips' Gloeilampenfabrieken, Eindhoven, 1985

First published in English by Cambridge University Press 1986 as *The
History of N.V. Philips' Gloeilampenfabrieken, Volume 1, The Origin of the Dutch
Incandescent Lamp Industry*

Printed in Great Britain at the University Press, Cambridge

*British Library cataloguing in publication data*

Heerding, A.
The history of N.V. Philips' gloeilampenfabrieken.
Vol. 1 : The origin of the Dutch incandescent
lamp industry
1. Philips Gloeilampenfabrieken – History
I. Title  II. Geschiedenis van de N.V. Philips'
Gloeilampenfabrieken. *English*

338.7'621381'09492  HD9696.A3N4

*Library of Congress cataloguing in publication data*

Heerding, A.
The origin of the Dutch incandescent lamp industry.
(The History of N.V. Philips' Gloeilampenfabrieken; v. l)
Translation of: Het onstaan van de Nederlandse
gloeilampenindustrie.
Bibliography: p.
Includes index.
1. Philips' Gloeilampenfabrieken – History.
2. Electric lamp industry – Netherlands – History.
I. Title  II. Series: Geschiedenis van de N.V. Philips'
Gloeilampenfabrieken.  English ; v. 1.
HD9697.L334P48313 vol. 1 338.4'7621322'09492 s 85–19059

ISBN 0 521 32169 7  [338.4'7621326'09492]

# CONTENTS

# ILLUSTRATIONS AND ACKNOWLEDGEMENTS

# LIST OF TABLES

ix

# PREFACE

A study based on historical research tracing the development of N. V. Philips' Gloeilampenfabrieken has been urged on a number of occasions, both within the Company and without. By the end of the 1950s the concept of such a study had gained ground among the Board of Management. The decision taken in 1960, to place relevant portions of the Company archives under central control in fact marked the first step in this direction. In 1973 the earlier proposal to commission and publish a history of the Group was revived, and the realization that the Group could thereby contribute to the historiography of Dutch industry, and had a duty to do so, encouraged a positive decision.

The plans were developed under the guidance of Mr J. R. Schaafsma, who at that time was about to retire from the Board of Management and who for many years had been the principal advocate of the project. In association with Jonkheer H. A. C. van Riemsdijk, now Chairman of the Supervisory Board, he drew up the formal plan and the terms of reference. Final preparations began during 1974.

This volume is the first of several which will embrace the history of the Philips' Group until the 1950s. It deals with events leading to the establishment of the enterprise and, as a necessary background, it outlines the origins and development of the electrical industry in the Netherlands in the 1880s.

As a starting point for this study, I opted to explain the birth of the enterprise in terms of economic, technical and social factors, in the context of the rise of the electrical industry. Certain received traditions were thus subjected to renewed investigation. As a consequence a number of preliminary studies had to be carried out, which frequently developed into independent research projects. Government and industrial archives at

home and abroad, and English, French and German technical literature dating from the first decade of electric lighting filled the gaps in the Group's own records.

Thus a historical picture gradually emerged in which the establishment of the Philips incandescent lamp works stood out against contemporary developments within the international incandescent lamp industry. Moreover, Company founders Frederik Philips and his son Gerard now emerge in a clearer perspective than had originally seemed possible.

The resulting book records not only the genesis of a company, but also the origins of the electric lighting industry, both in the Netherlands and abroad. From a historical point of view, the present approach appears to be justified by the pioneering work of the many who contributed to that new era of national industrial development which commenced with the introduction of electric lighting in the Netherlands a hundred years ago.

I am grateful to the former President of the Company, Dr N. Rodenburg, for the trust which he has placed in me. I also acknowledge a debt of gratitude to his successor Dr W. Dekker whose keen interest both in the publication of this English language edition and in the progress of the second volume was a welcome stimulus. To Dr Joh. de Vries, professor of Economic History at the Catholic University of Tilburg, who agreed to act as external adviser to the project, I am greatly indebted.

I met with interest and co-operation elsewhere: and foremost I would thank those persons, too numerous to mention individually, who supported me by making available important information. The generous assistance which I was privileged to receive from government archives and libraries and from those of industry was invaluable to my work; a list of sources can be found at the end of the book.

To my assistants, Mr I. J. Blanken and Mr P. H. Hurkmans, I am indebted for their joint efforts which contributed to the publication of this book. I would also express my gratitude for the co-operation of Mr C. F. M. Jansen, archivist of N. V. Philips' Gloeilampenfabrieken, whose researches in the interest of this book extended to Germany, and of Mr P. I. Nicholson of Mullard Limited, London who provided valuable supplementary information from English and Scottish sources.

Finally, I am sincerely grateful for the commitment and interest of Willem G. Ph. van der Heyden, former secretary of the Company, who, as a friend,

guided me through the extensive Philips organization and who played a
great part in the realization of the English edition.

*Wintelre, July 1985*                                          A. Heerding

### NOTE ON THE TRANSLATION

Quotations in foreign languages have been translated, as has source
information, with the exception of the names of institutions and titles of
books and other publications.

### NOTE ON CURRENCY

Approximate rates of exchange at the end of the nineteenth century.

£1 = 12 guilders (*f*)
£1 = 20 German marks
£1 = 24 French francs
£1 = 4.8 US dollars
£1 = 24 Swiss francs

US $ 1 = 2.5 guilders (*f*)
US $ 1 = 4.2 German marks
US $ 1 = 5 French francs
US $ 1 = 0.2 £ sterling
US $ 1 = 5 Swiss francs

Extract from the minutes of the meeting of the Board of Brush, 23 October 1889

*Chapter 1*

---

# AN INTERNATIONAL
# RECONNAISSANCE

The name 'Philips' first appeared in the annals of the electrical industry on
23 October 1889. The agenda for that day refers to a proposal by the
Anglo-American Brush Electric Light Corporation Limited of London to
establish an incandescent lamp factory in the Netherlands in association
with Messrs Philips of Zaltbommel. The brief report ends with the words:
'the policy of continuing these negotiations was approved.'[1]

Brush[2] and its main rival, the Edison & Swan United Electric Light
Company Limited, had been engaged in the manufacture of incandescent
lamps in Great Britain since 1881. The company had exclusive rights to the
incandescent lamp patents granted to the English inventor, St George Lane-
Fox and, for the countries of Europe and the British dominions, to those
covering the arc lamp and the dynamo machines developed by the American inventor, Charles F. Brush, the founder of the Brush Electric Light
Company of the United States. The Brush company in England,[3] which
operated independently, was established by London financiers in 1880 with
an authorized capital of £800,000, of which half of the shares were issued.
By combining the above-mentioned licences, the company itself proposed
to carry out complete electric lighting projects in towns and factories. For
the financial year 1881 – the year of the first international electricity
exhibition, held in Paris – the company paid a dividend of 100%. In the
mind of the public, the name Brush was synonymous with the earliest and
most successful lighting installations, which had principally been carried
out in England and Scotland but included a number in capital cities on the
Continent. Like the English gas manufacturers half a century earlier, the

---

[1] Minute Book No. 1, meeting of 23.10.1889, Board of Anglo-American Brush Electric Light
  Corporation Ltd, Archives of Brush Electrical Engineering Company Ltd, Loughborough, England.
[2] Where the name 'Brush' is used hereafter, it refers to the Anglo-American Brush Electric Light
  Corporation Ltd.
[3] I. C. R. Byatt, 'Electrical Products', in D. H. Aldcroft, *The Development of British Industry and
  Foreign Competition 1875–1914*, 244 ff.

Board of Brush, convinced that the country had a technical lead, hoped to modernize the lighting of the towns and cities of Europe, or at least to secure an important share of the market there.

To obtain a firm foothold on the Continent, where the market was dominated by Siemens & Halske, Brush in 1882 established an operating company on the lines adopted by the English gas companies. The activities of the Anglo-Austrian Brush Electrical Company,[4] as it was known, comprised the installation of electric lighting systems in Austria-Hungary and Roumania, and the manufacture of electrical products. It also issued manufacturing licences on behalf of Brush and supplied materials. In 1884 the company installed electric lighting in the Hungarian town of Temesvar; this completely replaced gas for street lighting.[5] In 1885, Brush set up an agency for the German Empire, in Berlin, which initially prospered under the influence of the rapid expansion of electric lighting in Germany.[6] The subsequent establishment of the Anglo-Spanish Brush Electric Light and Power Company further enhanced the group's international image.

The promising nature of this continental business in the 1880s and the expectation on the part of the Board that it would assume far greater proportions in the future were revealed in an optimistic report presented to the shareholders in March 1889.[7] The tripling of the turnover and profit in the preceding years justified expansion of the activities in the widest sense. The plans provided for an increase in the capacity of the Brush incandescent lamp works in Vienna, which operated under the name Kremenezky, Mayer & Co. It was the possible enlargement of this existing plant in Austria which conflicted with the pending decision to set up a new incandescent lamp factory in the Netherlands in partnership with Frederik and Gerard Philips. For the manufacture of incandescent lamps was – and still is – an international affair. This had been true from the onset, which had occurred simultaneously in the United States and England ten years earlier.

On 21 October 1879, Thomas Alva Edison (1847–1931) lighted an incandescent lamp having a burner of carbonized cotton thread,[8] which he

4  *The Electrician*, A Weekly Illustrated Journal of Electrical Engineering, Industry and Science, 17.6.1882, 118.
5  *The Electrician*, 29.12.1883, 168 ff; 5.1.1884, 190 ff.
6  Historical review, 'The Anglo-American Brush Electric Light Corporation, Ltd', unpublished, Brush Archives, Loughborough.
7  *The Electrician*, 8.3.1889, 521 ff.
8  John W. Howell and Henry Schroeder, *History of the Incandescent Lamp*, 1927, 58.

called a 'filament'. This was contained in a glass bulb from which the air had been exhausted. The lamp burned for two days, giving a bright and constant light. Edison, who had commenced his experiments at the end of 1877, realized that he was on the right track and proceeded to carbonize every material which was amenable to the process. After a few weeks he discovered that Bristol board (visiting-card paper) produced a filament which would burn for several hundred hours. On 4 November 1879 he submitted an application to the United States Patent Office, and on 27 January 1880 he was granted Basic Lamp Patent No. 223 898.[9] This was to become the most controversial patent in the history of the incandescent lamp industry. Edison also lodged applications in Canada, France and Great Britain; the last-named country responded promptly by granting him a patent on 10 November 1879 (see Appendix 1). In the ensuing year he obtained thirty-four supplementary patents in the United States, all of which concerned the incandescent lamp.

The basic patent was in respect of: (1) a high-resistance filament of carbon, in (2) a chamber made entirely of glass and closed at all points by fusion of the glass, which contained (3) a high vacuum and through which (4) platinum wires passed to carry the current to the filament. It was a patent based on a combination of known principles which produced a new object: a lamp which could be manufactured in large quantities and which lent itself to wide application in many fields. In the light of technological developments and the pattern of consumption, it seemed that the time was ripe for the incandescent lamp.

The most common sources of artificial light in 1880 were gas, paraffin and candles.[10] Gas lighting, the first modern source of illumination, was followed by the electric arc lamp, which reached the commercial stage round about 1877. The new feature, and at once the attraction, of this type of lamp lay in the intensity of the light; but this limited its range of applications. The arc lamp was mainly suitable for streets and squares, but for indoor lighting it could be used only in very large spaces. Its limitations encouraged a series of inventors to search for a source of electric light which, like gas lighting, was suitable everywhere and could be distributed over a large number of low-intensity lamps. It was with the latter object in view that the Edison Electric Light Company was established on 17 October 1878, with a capital of $300,000. This, it was considered, would

[9] A. A. Bright, *The Electric-Lamp Industry: Technological Change and Economic Development from 1800 to 1947*, 1949, 66.
[10] E. Rebske, *Lampen, Laternen, Leuchten*, 1962.

enable Edison to develop 'the complete lighting system'.[11] Others followed more individual paths which were less smooth in financial terms. But all fell back on earlier researchers, whose work had suddenly assumed new significance.

One of the earliest experiments with electric light was carried out by Humphry Davy, a lecturer at The Royal Institution in London, in 1802.[12] His first filament was a platinum wire, but he later used a thin stick of charcoal, which he connected to the terminals of a galvanic cell. The stick glowed for some time before failing due to oxidation. In one of his experiments in 1810, Davy placed two carbon rods with their ends close together in conditions of vacuum in a glass dome, thereby demonstrating for the first time the bright arc flame (the Davy arc). The two fundamentally different systems, incandescent light and arc light, thus both originated from the work of one man.

The first continuous source of current, the Voltaic Pile, invented in 1800, laid the foundations for these experiments. Decades were to pass before the principle which Volta developed assumed practical significance. The current source was too costly, and the aids and materials too primitive, for this to be an efficient source of power for lighting.

A sudden wave of experiments involving both arc and incandescent lamps is seen to have occurred round about 1840. The famous zinc–copper cell invented by J. F. Daniell in 1836, the one developed by W. R. Grove a year or two later and the Bunsen cell of 1842 raised hopes of a source of electricity which would be practical in terms of cost.[13] In 1838, inspired by Davy's concept, Professor J. B. A. M. Jobard, the curator of the Musée Industriel in Brussels, carried out an experiment in which he placed a thin carbon rod in a vacuum. One of his students, the mining engineer J. De Changy, constructed a similar lamp employing coke, with which he achieved a significantly better result. Two years later, Grove appeared before the Royal Society in London, where in a demonstration of his batteries he illuminated the auditorium with incandescent lamps with platinum filaments. Another Englishman, F. de Moleyns, obtained a British patent in 1841 for a vacuum lamp, the filament of which consisted of a combination of platinum and powdered charcoal. The American inventor,

[11] Bright, *Electric-Lamp Industry*, 60.
[12] J. Escard names the Frenchman Thénard as the inventor of the incandescent lamp and puts the date of the invention at 1801; cf. *Les Lampes Electriques*, 1912, 67.
[13] P. v. Cappelle, *De electriciteit, hare voortbrenging en hare toepassing in de industrie en het maatschappelijk verkeer*, 1893, 29 ff.

J. W. Starr of Cincinnati, travelled to England in 1845 and in the same year obtained a British patent for two incandescent lamps, one of which had a strip of platinum as the filament, the other a carbonized thread.[14] He used platinum because this metal, although having a lower melting point than iridium, was less prone to oxidation. His description of an alternative construction, using carbonized thread in a torricellian vacuum, was of far greater significance, however. This was a potential application which others, notably the later English researcher J. W. Swan, were to recognize,[15] and of which, according to the corresponding Dutch patent application of 1845, the technical principle was described as follows:

In certain cases carbon worked into very thin strips may be employed instead of platina; but it should be enclosed in a torricellian vacuum, care being taken to exclude moisture. This method requires a glass tube with platina wires passing through its upper end to hold the carbon, the vacuum being obtained as in a barometer.[16]

Although this was in fact an experimental lamp, Starr at that time came closest to the principles of the later incandescent lamp with a carbonized thread filament. It is reported that in 1845, in the presence of Faraday, he gave a successful public demonstration with twenty-six such lamps. Legend adds a distressing rider: Starr's patent agent, E. A. King, is said to have taken possession of the discovery, and Starr died mysteriously while returning to the United States.[17] Whatever the truth may be, the fact is that the Dutch patent covering the lamp described above (see p. 000) is not in the name of the inventor, Starr, but of E. A. King of London.

The lamp developed in 1854 by the German, H. Göbel (here we pass over W. E. Staite and numerous others), is said to have differed from all others in having a fine filament, which was also in a relatively high vacuum; this, however, is disputed.[18] The same applies to the vacuum lamp developed by the English researcher De la Rue, which had a platinum filament and is believed to date from 1809. Not only are there no authentic descriptions of the De la Rue lamp, but it would not have been possible to obtain a high vacuum with the mechanical air pumps which existed at that time. De Changy probably came closest to an operational incandescent lamp. He

[14] G. Basil Barham, *The Development of the Incandescent Electric Lamp*, 1912, 12, 22.
[15] M. E. and K. R. Swan, *J. W. Swan – A Memoir*, 1929, 22, 58.
[16] Patent application submitted by A. S. Preston on behalf of Edward Augustus King, dated Rotterdam, 22.11.1845; Government Archives, The Hague, Education section, No. 4813, 20.12.1845, No. 75.
[17] A. Gelyi, 'A short history of incandescence lamps', in *The Telegraphic Journal and Electrical Review*, Vol. 16, No. 375, 1885.
[18] E. A. Krüger, *Die Herstellung der Elektrischen Glühlampe*, 1894, 1 ff.

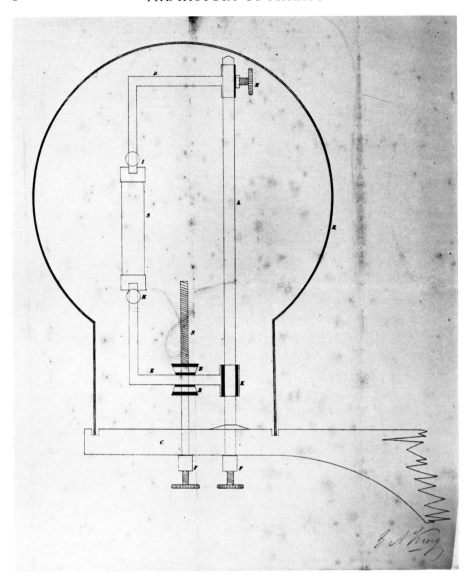

Platinum incandescent lamp developed by J. W. Starr
(This was the subject of Dutch patent No. 1513, granted in 1845 in the name of
E. A. King.)

had resumed his experiments in the 1850s under Jobard in Brussels, and in 1851 applied for a patent for his 'system of regulating and distributing electric current for electric light by incandescence'.[19] De Changy worked impure platinum with carbon and drew this to form a wire, which he wound round a carbon rod and gradually heated it to glowing point, 'in order that this material might become accustomed to the services demanded of it'. The current was kept within close limits by means of a regulator which he had designed for the purpose. Eye-witnesses spoke of several lamps, fed by twelve Bunsen cells, which could be lit simultaneously, individually or in groups, yet with no discernible variation in the intensity of any lamp. De Changy, who as a mining engineer was aware of the practice of patenting inventions in England, was unwilling to publish details of his system without adequate safeguards, and this evoked criticism on the ground that he sought financial reward from scientific work. This led the Academy of Sciences in Paris to sever relations with him, and De Changy was left a disillusioned man.

The ensuing fifteen years produced few noteworthy events in the development of the incandescent lamp. Then in 1873 the work of the Russian physicist Lodyguine, which had earned him a high award from the Academy of Sciences in St Petersburg, attracted international attention.[20] The event served to revive interest in an important problem in the development of the incandescent lamp, namely whether the filament should be of carbon or metal. This, indeed, was the greatest single problem. The next generation of researchers would make a further attempt to solve it.

Similarly, many scientists had concerned themselves with the development of the arc lamp. Léon Foucault pointed the way to a more durable electrode made from coke, and constructed a device which kept the points of the rods the desired distance apart. Between 1840 and 1860, various new systems were devised, mainly by French and English researchers. The lamp developed by the Belgian inventor, Jaspar, in Liège deserves mention. But most widely used was the ingenious lamp produced by the Frenchman, Serrin (see p. 8), which was usually fed from a battery of Bunsen cells, because 'mechanical current' – current generated on the electromagnetic principle – was still in its infancy. There was thus no real breakthrough in arc lighting. Here, too, the cost of energy was the limiting factor. The result was that most of the inventors abandoned the field round about 1860.

[19] Louis Figuier, *Het Elektrisch Licht*, Dutch-language adaptation by A. van Oven, 1886, 64 ff; further references are to this edition.
[20] Cf. Chapter 4, page 140.

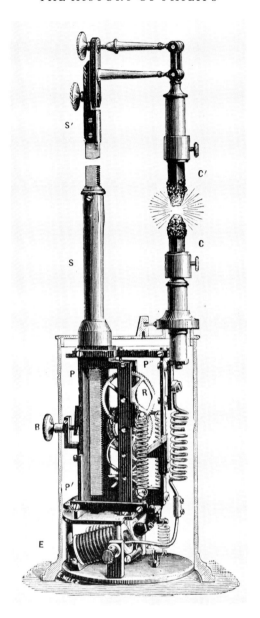

The Serrin arc lamp

Although substantial progress had been made in the construction of the arc lamp itself, and wide interest aroused by the appearance of the phenomenon – albeit only at public events – its application proved to be too restricted.

As stated, the earliest incandescent lamps burned in the atmosphere or in a partial vacuum, or in a space filled with nitrogen. Of the metals which lent themselves for use as filaments, platinum and iridium, with their comparatively high melting points, were the best. Carbon was chosen because its melting point was higher than that of any metal, added to which its resistance was high enough – but not too high – for the purpose. The material did, however, have the disadvantage of evaporating or combining chemically with a gas, reducing the life of the filament. But at the time no materials with superior mechanical properties existed, added to which the optimum shape of the filament had yet to be determined. Moreover, the existing method of generating current would have been an obstacle even if a more practical incandescent lamp had been devised. The fundamental step towards the solution of the vacuum problem, and which made possible such a lamp, came in 1865 with the invention of a new type of pump by the German chemist, Hermann Sprengel, who was then working in England. In the area of dynamo machines, Werner Siemens' earliest model, which dated from 1866, and those of Wilde, Wheatstone and others passed beyond the experimental stage in 1870, after Gramme had built an exceedingly practical dynamo with a new feature, a ring-wound armature. With this dynamo, a higher current than ever before could be generated. Although there was considerable room for improvement in its efficiency, the new source of energy, in principle, brought electric lighting within the realms of feasibility in technical and economic terms. With this discovery, researchers were henceforth able to concentrate their efforts on the incandescent lamp itself. They received a fillip in 1875, when William Crookes, an English chemist and physicist, published a description of his radiometer and also gave details of the perfected methods whereby an almost complete vacuum could be obtained with the aid of the Sprengel pump.[21] To J. W. Swan, one of the leading pioneers of the incandescent lamp, this was a direct incentive to devote himself to renewed research in this field.

Joseph Wilson Swan (1828–1914) was born in Sunderland and acquired an elementary knowledge of chemistry while serving an apprenticeship with a

---

[21] *The Telegraphic Journal and Electrical Review*, Vol. 16, 14.2.1885, 139 ff.

Table 1. *History of the incandescent lamp. Developments up to 1878*

| Year | Researcher | Country | Filament | Atmosphere | Enclosure |
|---|---|---|---|---|---|
| 1838 | Jobard | Belgium | Carbon rod | Vacuum | Glass |
| 1840 | Grove | England | Platinum helix | Air | Inverted glass beaker in a dish of water |
| 1841 | De Moleyns | England | Powdered charcoal between two platinum helices | Vacuum | Glass sphere with stopper |
| 1845 | Starr | U.S.A. | (1) Platinum strip | Air | Glass sphere with stopper |
| | | | (2) Graphite stick | Vacuum | Glass sphere above column of mercury |
| 1848 | Staite | England | Platinum and iridium rods | Air | Glass sphere with stopper |
| 1850 | Shepard | U.S.A. | Charcoal cylinder against sphere of the same material | Vacuum | Glass sphere with stopper |
| 1852 | Roberts | England | Graphite stick | Vacuum | Glass sphere with stopper |
| 1854 | Göbel | Germany | Carbon wire (?) | Vacuum | Glass sphere with stopper |
| 1858 | De Changy | Belgium | (1) Platinum helix (2) Carbon rod | Vacuum | Hermetically sealed glass sphere |
| 1860 | Swan | England | Strips and helices of carbonized paper and cardboard | Vacuum | Jar or bell on copper baseplate |
| 1872 | Lodyguine | Russia | (1) Carbon rod (2) V-shaped piece of graphite | Vacuum Nitrogen | Hermetically sealed glass sphere Glass sphere with stopper |
| 1873 | De Khotinsky | Russia | Carbon rod | Vacuum | Hermetically sealed glass sphere |
| 1875 | Kosloff | Russia | Graphite rod | Nitrogen | Hermetically sealed glass tube |
| 1876 | Bouliguine | Russia | Graphite rod | Vacuum | Hermetically sealed glass tube |
| 1878 | Edison | U.S.A. | Platinum helix | Air Vacuum | Glass sphere |
| 1878 | Lane-Fox | England | Platinum iridium Asbestos carbon | Nitrogen | Glass sphere |

*Note:*
The principal types of incandescent lamp developed in the experimental period are listed above. The second stage of the development of the incandescent lamp commenced round about 1878 and culminated in the commercial lamps of 1880 and following years.

druggist. Upon the completion of his apprenticeship, he was employed in the laboratory of Messrs John Mawson of Newcastle upon Tyne, manufacturers and traders in chemical products; he was later to become a partner in this firm. His earliest researches were in the field of photography and led to the development of a highly sensitive dry photographic plate, a practical carbon printing process and bromide paper for photographic prints. These and other inventions, including a cellular battery plate and, in the field of electrochemistry, a process for the accelerated precipitation of copper, represent a modest proportion of the more than sixty patents which this scientist was to obtain.[22]

Swan's particular interest in the incandescent lamp dated from 1848, when in his home town he witnessed a demonstration by Staite of lamps with platinum and iridium filaments. He was later to discover for himself that these materials did not hold the solution to the problem of the incandescent lamp.[23] In 1860 he succeeded in constructing a lamp which suggested that carbonized thread was the most successful filament material. He took strips and helices of paper and board, as thin as possible, covered with powdered carbon and impregnated with a fluid which would leave a carbon residue, placed these in a crucible and slowly heated them to a high temperature. In this manner he obtained a number of filaments which were fairly satisfactory in terms of strength and conductivity, but which failed after glowing for a short time. The principal cause of the rapid failure lay in the difficulty in obtaining the desired degree of vacuum, and this led Swan temporarily to abandon his researches. In 1864 he obtained a patent for his carbonization process.[24] Although at first sight a meagre reward, this marked a significant advance in the right direction; his concept did not amount to the first practical incandescent lamp, but it was the most universal forerunner of this.

After learning of the results obtained by Crookes with the Sprengel pump to obtain vacuum, Swan, now assisted by Charles H. Stearn, resumed his work in 1877. With the solution of the incandescent lamp problem as his primary objective, he repeated his experiments with carbonized paper and board. When it became clear to him that the 'low-resistance lamp' was not satisfactory, he switched his attention to one of high resistance.[25] Two important problems remained to be solved: early combustion and conse-

[22] *The Electrician's Directory*, 1905; a biography of J. W. Swan.
[23] Kenneth R. Swan, *Sir Joseph Swan and the Invention of the Incandescent Lamp*, published for the British Council, 1946.
[24] Ibid., 11.          [25] Bright, *Electric-Lamp Industry*, 54.

quent fracture of the very thin filament, and blackening of the bulbs. The fact that both phenomena invariably occurred showed that the cause of the failure must be attributed to evaporation of the carbon at high temperature under the influence of the current. This was the final obstacle which confronted Swan, and we can do no better than repeat his description of the manner in which he overcame this:

If this idea of carbon were founded in fact, any further attempt to render incandescent carbon lamps durable by means of a vacuum were mere waste of time, and durable they must be if they are to be of any practical value. Fortunately I did not accept as conclusive the experiments which seemed to show that carbon was volatile, and that the blackening of globes of incandescent carbon lamps was an inevitable result of the carbon being very highly heated. I know that the conditions under which, without exception, all previous experiments had been tried, were such as did not allow to be formed anything approaching a perfect vacuum within the lamp. Screw fittings had invariably been employed to close the mouth of the lamp, and the ordinary air-pump to exhaust the air. Under such circumstances it was certain that a considerable residuum of air would be contained within it, and also that it would leak. Then, there had never been any thought given to the gas occluded in the carbon itself, and which, when the carbon became hot by the passage of the current through it, would be evolved; nor had sufficient care been taken to make the resistance at the points of fixture of the carbon, less than in the carbon to be heated to incandescence. It was evident to me that before any definite conclusion could be arrived at as to the question of the volatility of carbon, the cause of the blackening of the globes and the wearing away of the incandescent rods, we must first try the experiment of heating the carbon to a state of extreme incandescence in a thoroughly good vacuum [...] and under more favourable conditions as to the contact between the incandescent carbon and the conductors supporting it than had hitherto obtained. Accordingly, in October, 1877, I sent to Mr. Stearn a number of carbons, made from carbonised cardboard, with the request that he would get them mounted for me in glass globes by a glass blower, and then exhaust the air as completely as possible. [...] In order to produce a good vacuum it was found necessary to heat the carbon to a very high degree by means of the electric current during the process of exhaustion, so as to expel the gas occluded by the carbon in its cold state, for, otherwise, however good the vacuum was before the carbon was heated, immediately the current passed and made it white hot, the vacuum was destroyed by the out-rush of the gas pent up in the carbon in its cold state. In order to make a good contact between the carbon and the clips supporting it, the ends of the carbon were thickened, and, in some of the early experiments, electrotyping and hard soldering of the ends of the carbons to platinum was resorted to. [...] the prescribed conditions having been rigorously complied with, it was found, after many troublesome experiments, that *when the vacuum within the lamp globe was good, and the contact between the carbon and the conductor which supported it sufficient, there was no blackening of the globes, and no appreciable wasting away of the carbons.* Thus was swept away a pernicious error,

which, like a lying finger post, proclaiming 'No road this way', tended to bar progress along a good thoroughfare. It only remained to perfect the details of the lamp, to find the best material from which to form the carbon, and fix this material in the lamp in the best manner. These points, I think, I have now satisfactorily settled; and you see the result in the lamp before me on the table.[26]

On 19 December 1878, Swan appeared before the Newcastle Chemical Society where he described an experiment for the production of light by electricity. On 4 February 1879 he lectured again on the same subject at Newcastle, illustrating his lecture by experiments exhibiting his electric lamp.[27] While a gathering of chemists among whom the gas industry, with its fear of competition, was strongly represented, could scarcely be expected to display exuberance towards the incandescent lamp, some reservation was certainly justified following the premature report that Edison in America had invented an economically viable lamp. In October 1878, in the wake of this announcement, gas shares fell sharply, but in the European press anxiety turned to ironic laughter[28] when it transpired that the platinum-filament lamp in question was after all impractical; now the shares of the Edison Electric Light Company were under pressure, falling to $20. In the Netherlands the affair was attributed to unfounded speculation 'with no cause other than a false alarm', according to P. Polt, director of the municipal gasworks in Helmond, who thus interpreted the indignation felt in professional circles, even on a regional level.[29] The fear, however, remained.

Edison was the last in the series of researchers who attempted to manufacture an incandescent lamp with the aid of platinum.[30] It is probable that he obtained better results, and came closer to a practical lamp of this type, than any of his predecessors. 'I had tried carbon and carbon would not do', he said in an article which appeared in the *New York Sun* of 25 November 1878;[31] but in the autumn of 1879, having once again prematurely announced success with a high-resistance platinum lamp, he reverted to carbonized thread for the filament. Within a matter of weeks he

[26] Paper presented by Swan to the Institution of Electrical Engineers in London, in *The Engineer*, 29.10.1880, 325.

[27] *The Electrician*, 17.9.1881, 283 ff.

[28] A. Gelyi, 'A short history of incandescence lamps', in *The Telegraphic Journal and Electrical Review*, Vol. 16, No. 376, 1885.

[29] *Provinciale Noordbrabantsche- en 's-Hertogenbossche Courant*, 24.10.1878.

[30] J. W. Swan, *Electric Lighting*, a lecture before the members of the Literary and Philosophical Society of Newcastle, 20 October 1880.

[31] J. W. Swan, *New York Herald*, 11.12.1878: 'I use no carbon'.

achieved the end result described earlier – the high-resistance lamp with a filament of carbonized thread. The widespread scepticism which greeted Edison's third announcement of success, in the *New York Herald* of 21 December 1879, turned to infectious enthusiasm when on New Year's Eve, at his laboratory in Menlo Park, New Jersey, he publicly demonstrated an incandescent lighting system consisting of forty-five lamps powered by three small dynamos. This was a turning point, and it was also reflected on Wall Street, where 'electricals' rose to more than $3,500. The name Edison, already famous in connection with the stock ticker, the gramophone and other inventions, would henceforth be associated primarily with the incandescent lamp.

The lamp in question was still of an experimental nature and was not manufactured in any significant quantity. The filament of Bristol board was not sufficiently strong for commercial production, and the average life of the lamp was too limited. In his search for a material offering greater resistance to fracture, Edison received from Harvard University fifty different types of grass and wood fibres, with which he embarked on a new series of experiments in 1880.[32]

In 1881, after numerous tests, Edison replaced the porous and vulnerable carbonized paper filament with one made from the stem of the *madake*, a variety of bamboo found in Japan. In terms of hardness and strength, this proved superior to any other material that was available. But before the bamboo could be carbonized it had to undergo eight separate operations, all of which were performed by hand:

Men sat for weary hours at workbenches handling bamboo. The cane, received in long strips, was slit with a knife over and over until the smallest possible diameter was obtained. One piece of cane yielded five filament strips, each of which was planed on one side before it was baked. Next it was finished in straight form, then bent into horseshoe shape.[33]

Having perfected his working methods, Edison went on to produce lamps with a carbonized bamboo filament for more than ten years.[34] The early preparations for production were made in a small workshop near Menlo Park. The factory, which was operated by a new Edison company, the Edison Lamp Company of Harrison, New Jersey, opened in 1882. Its

[32] *The Electrician*, 17.4.1880, 261 ff: 'Electric lighting in America'.
[33] John Winthrop Hammond, *Men and Volts, The Story of General Electric*, 1941, 93.
[34] Bright, *Electric-Lamp Industry*, 66.

planned capacity was 1,200 lamps per day with a work force of 150. Sales in 1883 and 1884, however, totalled only 70,000 and 125,000 lamps respectively.[35] In 1885, by which time the early production problems had been solved, sales rose to about 300,000 units.

Two types of lamp were produced, the 'A' lamp of 16 c.p. for a supply of 110 volts D.C. and the 'B' lamp of 8 c.p. for a 55-volt supply; the latter were connected in pairs in series and fed from a 110-volt supply.[36] The letters c.p. stood for candlepower, a unit of luminous intensity which at that time was employed as a standard for gas lighting and which was equivalent to the light emitted by a wax candle 2 cm in diameter and having a 50 mm high flame. Edison's earliest lamps were designed to give 1.68 lumens per watt when new; improvements to the filament increased this to 2.25 lumens per watt in 1881.[37] After a very long life, which in some cases was between 2,000 and 3,000 hours, the intensity was less than 1 lumen per watt. In the interests of lamp efficiency, i.e. the optimum combination of light intensity, useful life and current consumption, it was desirable to replace the lamps after 600–1,000 hours of use.

Edison's first carbonized-filament lamp thus had a filament of carbonized paper, the same material as had been employed by Swan in his experimental lamp. The American researchers William E. Sawyer and Albon Man, with whose work Edison was acquainted, had also used horseshoe-shaped filaments of carbonized paper in their experiments since early in 1878. But they omitted to patent the application of this material in their lamps; moreover, the *low-resistance* filament which they developed was of a much greater diameter than Edison's successful high-resistance filament. In 1880 Edison revealed the composition of his filament, and when Sawyer and Man realized the significance of their earlier work they contested Edison's second patent application (dated 11 December 1879) for an incandescent lamp with a paper filament. After very protracted litigation, and notwithstanding the priority of Edison's application, the plaintiffs succeeded in demonstrating that they had anticipated Edison in the practical use of the disputed material. On 12 May 1885, the United States Patent Office granted them the relevant patent. The comparatively unsuccessful low-resistance lamp developed by Sawyer and Man had by then given way to one of the type

[35] Hammond, *Men and Volts*, 92.
[36] Howell and Schroeder, *Incandescent Lamp*, 65.
[37] The term 'watt' was not introduced until several years after the international conference held in Paris in 1882 for the purpose of establishing units of electricity. At the time, the term 'eight to the horse power' was used to describe the 'A' lamp: this type consumed just over 93 watts.

produced by Edison, Swan and others. In 1882 the incandescent lamp patents granted to these researchers – which embodied the *flashing process* which they employed and which came to be of immense importance for the incandescent lamp industry – were vested in the Consolidated Electric Light Company, which was destined to become a major producer. The flashing process, by which the filament was rendered homogeneous, entailed placing it in a hydrogen atmosphere and causing it to glow by the application of an electric current. The gas decomposed, causing a thin layer of carbon to be deposited at the point where the resistance was greatest, i.e. where the filament was thinnest.[38] This process had been patented by Sawyer and Man in the United States on 7 January 1879. It had already been patented in England in 1878, but only as a detail of a specification for an incandescent lamp which proved impractical.

In 1880, two other American researchers, Moses G. Farmer and the famous inventor Hiram S. Maxim – who had also failed to produce a practical incandescent lamp in advance of Edison, but succeeded in doing so a few months afterwards – entered into discussions with the United States Electric Lighting Company on the subject of their patents. The latter had been established in 1877 to manufacture arc lamps[39] and in due course was to join the ranks of larger producers. As early as 1881 the company sought contact with Siemens Bros. & Co. in London, whom it desired to represent in the United States in the areas of dynamos and electric trams. The Siemens negotiator, G. von Chauvin, a director of the company, paid a visit to the American newcomer in the electrical industry. The following is an extract from his report on their discussions:

This company has its seat in New York. Its president is Mr. Flint and I doubt not that he has a large amount of its shares. They have a set of works at 6th avenue and 25th street corner. Another shop close by, provides the larger quantity of the Maxim incandescent lamps. [...] These works will be retained as an experimental station and will be under the orders of Mr. Maxim as the new works of the company are finished. Mr. Maxim will not be allowed to come to the works (to be put up) where the manufacturing goes on, as he evidently has impressed those in charge of the company no more favorably than he has me and they do not desire to let him disturb their manufacturing arrangements.

The general manager Mr. Francis told me they had ordered for $60,000 tools to fit up these works. Mr. Flint assured that they had retained all the best patent lawyers in America and altogether I have never seen any more extravagant waste of money in every conceivable direction than takes place in this company, which

---

[38] *The Electrician*, 1887, 346, 368, 418, 462: 'Incandescent lamp manufacture – flashing'.
[39] Figuier, *Het Elektrisch Licht*, 102 ff.

seems to count upon its profits from some vague notion that there is a grand future for the electric light.[40]

The Weston Electric Light Company and the Brush Electric Light Company, both established manufacturers of arc lamps, added their 'own' incandescent lamps to their range of products in 1882 and 1883 respectively; this was made possible by acquiring patent licences from others, including Lane-Fox. Finally, the earliest competitors of the Edison Electric Light Company included the Swan Incandescent Electric Light Company of New York, founded in 1882 to introduce the Swan system in the United States.

During the early years of the incandescent lamp industry, it was the Edison company's financial strength and its commercial lead which enabled it to secure three-quarters of the American market.[41] Round about 1885 the manufacturers of incandescent lamps in the United States numbered twelve. From then on, the prelude, the period of 'live and let live', gradually drew to a close, whereupon the Edison Electric Light Company proceeded, by patent litigation, to put its affairs in order.[42] Edison opened its campaign against infringement of its basic patent in 1885 with a suit against the United States Electric Lighting Company, its main competitor.

Swan was granted two patents in the United States in 1880, the first for a lamp with a paper filament, the second for a 'parchmentized' cotton thread. In his applications, Swan did not claim to have invented an incandescent lamp, but merely new means to increase the life of such lamps. According to Swan, the incandescent lamp, like the arc lamp, was *not* the result of a discovery but the product of a gradual development, and was therefore capable only of partial improvement.

His replacement of paper by a natural fibre as the substance for the filament was of dramatic significance in relation to the technique of making incandescent lamps. The best material was cotton thread which, after impregnation with sulphuric acid, lost its fibrous structure, and after a drying period provided a strong, transparent thread. This thread, which was flexible and could be worked to a uniform thickness, maintained its given shape after carbonization; Swan named it 'parchmentized thread'. The process, which enabled an extremely homogeneous filament to be

---

[40] Letter from G. von Chauvin, New York, to Siemens Bros. & Co., Ltd, London, 17.5.1881; Siemens Archives, No. 36 Lh 816, Munich.
[41] Exports of lamps from the United States in this period were of negligible proportions.
[42] Bright, *Electric-Lamp Industry*, 84 ff.

obtained, was to be adopted by a number of lamp manufacturers. It was introduced by Swan in the early months of 1880, and on 27 November it became the subject of a British patent. The same process, but employing paper as the basic material, had been patented by Swan earlier in the same year, as had his well-known method of obtaining a more permanent vacuum in bulbs, developed in 1878, of which the essence lay in exhausting the air while the filament glowed.

In contrast to Edison, who as early as 10 November 1879 had obtained a British patent on the invention of his incandescent lamp, including the basic elements, Swan was slow to patent his lamp. His slowness stemmed from a conviction that the incandescent lamp, like the arc lamp, existed already and only required to be perfected. In spite of warnings from his assistant, Stearn, Swan relied upon the published results of his earlier work[43] as evidence of his having anticipated the claims made by Edison. Although the latter, from a legal point of view, had a lead, the electrical industry in England maintained its defence of the origin of the incandescent lamp for as long as this was of practical significance: 'Our glowlamp is the outcome of Swan's further work.'[44] This was long to remain a bone of contention, with American opinion as a whole attributing considerable credit to Swan – 'the man whom the English people believe to have invented the incandescent electric light'[45] – for having developed the most suitable filament materials, but not the system of connecting lamps in parallel, or a high-resistance lamp with its associated components. Leaving aside the fact that Edison, too, originally worked with lamps in series, this presumption, to say the least of it, takes no account of the direction of Swan's research into carbonized thread as a filament; in contrast to the platinum incandescent lamps which Edison produced in 1873 and 1879, this did not merely tend towards a high-resistance lamp, but had actually been elaborated by Swan. It enabled him to market a lamp of high resistance and with extremely good illuminating properties at the same time as Edison. According to the American author H. C. Passer, cited earlier, the only inventor who, like Edison, based his work on the concept of high resistance coupled with the system of parallel connection was the Englishman, Lane-Fox. In the view of this author, however, he failed to produce a high-resistance filament in time. It is an incontrovertible fact that Lane-Fox was the first to include the principle

[43] *Electrical Review*, 23.9.1882, 251.
[44] *The Electrician*, 26.6.1891, 216 ff: 'The Edison lamp patent'.
[45] Harold C. Passer, *The Electrical Manufacturers 1875–1900 – A study in Competition, Entrepreneurship, Technical Change and Economic Growth*, 1953, 190.

of the parallel circuit in a patent application; this he did in 1878, putting him ahead of Edison. Closer examination shows that not only the development of 'the complete electric lighting system', but also the process of creating the incandescent lamp itself consisted of several unconnected elements, which were the products of the creative imagination of various independent researchers who preceded Edison. It was a repetition of the situation which until then had accompanied the perfection of the arc lamp in Europe and in which no single inventor or manufacturer had mustered the courage to claim exclusive credit. In some countries, the sole right to manufacture a high-resistance lamp would ultimately be decided not so much on technical and historical grounds[46] as on the basis of legal arguments, a state of affairs which at the time was regarded as extremely arbitrary. With his existing reputation, and aided by a great deal of publicity, no one but the seasoned man of practice, Edison, could better be identified with the advancement of this invention. In the United States, between 1885 and 1901, the Edison Company and its successors were to spend some two million dollars prosecuting more than two hundred lawsuits in which the incandescent lamp and the electric lighting system formed the subjects of dispute.[47]

In 1881 Edison's applications for British patents numbered twenty-four, compared with seven by Swan – the same number as were applied for in that year by his compatriot, St George Lane-Fox, who in 1878 had obtained British Patent No. 3988 in respect of his experimental high-resistance lamp with a platinum filament. Lane-Fox who, like Swan, worked unobtrusively, made his first filament from a fibre of flax which, after being subjected to the flashing process – which he had developed independently of Sawyer and Man[48] – provided a strong, uniform filament. He was also the first to patent a carbonized filament made from cellulose, which he 'parchmentized' with the aid of zinc chloride.[49] These experiments paved the way for the extruded filament of colloidal cellulose, an invention by the British scientists F. Wynne and L. S. Powell, which could be more satisfactorily produced on an industrial scale than, say, filaments of bamboo. In 1881 the Anglo-American Brush Electric Light Corporation paid £50,000 for the rights to Lane-Fox's incandescent lamp patents, thereby, in the words of its chairman, obtaining 'the best patents' and 'the best incandescent lighting

---

[46] *The Electrician*, 26.11.1886, 61; 21.12.1888, 202.
[47] Bright, *Electric-Lamp Industry*, 86.
[48] *The Electrician*, 20.7.1888, 341: 'flashing was also independently devised by Lane-Fox'.
[49] *The Electrician*, 17.12.1886, 121.

system'.[50] Brush had been established a year previously with the object of manufacturing and selling arc lamps. The company therefore lacked the equipment to produce incandescent lamps and the related lighting system immediately and in large quantities, and needed time for preparation. The situation was not improved by the fact that the Brush dynamo, which had been developed for arc lighting, was not a suitable source of power for incandescent lamps. Moreover, the sudden arrival of the incandescent lamp demanded the development of new installation materials and new and divergent technical specifications. By 1883 these difficulties had largely been overcome. A year later, Brush characterized both its dynamo and its incandescent lamp as 'leaders of the market',[51] and from that time the Lane-Fox lamp found acceptance in Great Britain and to an even greater extent on the European continent. In the area of policy, however, Brush accorded priority to its role as a licenser and manufacturer of dynamos and arc lamps. The principal reason for this lay in the need to achieve a return on the investment – £100,000 in cash and a similar sum in fully paid-up shares – in the arc lamp patents of Charles F. Brush.[52] In this situation, which dated back to the origin of the company, the manufacture of incandescent lamps was a supplementary, departmental activity which accounted for a relatively small portion of the total turnover and was therefore of secondary importance. Brush thus differed, for example, from Deutsche Edison Gesellschaft, which was founded in 1883. Given this situation, the inventor Lane-Fox and his valuable contribution to the incandescent lamp industry merit closer examination, the more so by reason of the fame which his lamp achieved.

St George Lane-Fox (1856–1932)[53] was the second son of Augustus Lane-Fox, a general in the British Army who, alongside a chequered military career, devoted himself to matters scientific. From 1852 he was in contact with evolutionists like Thomas Huxley and Herbert Spencer; he did a great deal of spadework in the field of archaeology and also developed a theory about the diversity of cultures. In 1875, before the members of the Royal Institution, he expounded his 'Theory of Cultural Evolution', and in the following year, partly at the instigation of Darwin, he was put forward for membership of the Royal Society.[54] General Lane-Fox's large family (there

50  Sir Henry Tyler, addressing the Annual General Meeting; *The Electrician*, 28.1.1882, 174 ff.
51  Unpublished review of the history of Brush.
52  Ibid.
53  Obituary of Mr Fox-Pitt, inventor and psychic student, *The Times*, 7.4.1932.
54. M. Pitt-Rivers, 'Cultural General', in *Books and Bookmen*, June 1977.

Thomas Alva Edison
(1847–1931)

Joseph Wilson Swan
(1828–1914)

St George Lane-Fox
(1856–1932)

were nine children) lived in conspicuous style on the family estate at Rushmore. The philosopher Bertrand Russell, a nephew, observed this turbulent household and, with a touch of derision, expressed the view that, with the exception of the general, 'most of the family were more or less mad'. He also excepted St George, for whom he had a manifest regard: 'the most interesting member of the family and one of the earliest inventors of electric lighting'.[55]

After several years of study and practical research in the field of electricity, during which, among other things, he constructed an electric lighter for gas lamps,[56] St George Lane-Fox obtained Patent No. 3988, to which reference has already been made. The date was 9 October 1878. Like Swan, he regarded his invention as a contribution to the improvement of electric lighting and of the transmission, distribution and regulation of electric current. The lamp described in the patent document had a platinum–iridium filament (or bridge, as Lane-Fox called it) and, like Edison's first platinum incandescent lamp, must be viewed as experimental. Although this was not embodied in the conclusions pertaining to the patent, the filament was required to be of high specific resistance, a condition, here formulated for the first time ('Lane-Fox recognized the economical import-ance of high resistance before Edison did'),[57] which was soon met by almost every incandescent lamp manufacturer. This technical criterion was a logical consequence of the current distribution system which he had proposed in the same patent application and which was based on the principle of parallel connection. The electricians and physicists of the day had, however, considerable doubts as to the feasibility of such a distribu-tion system and thus of electric lighting. When in the spring of 1881 Lane-Fox gave a lecture on his lighting system to the Society of Telegraph Engineers and Electricians,[58] he encountered particular criticism on this point. His chief critic – and later rival – was the highly respected engineer and manufacturer of arc lighting systems, R. E. B. Crompton,[59] who dismis-sed the introduction and use of parallel circuits as wasteful. A no less noteworthy fact is that in 1881 Lane-Fox already considered a daily output of 50,000 lamps to be feasible in technical terms and, like Edison, thought in terms of a complete electric lighting system, i.e. the Brush dynamo

55  B. Russell, *The Autobiography of Bertrand Russell, Vol. 1, 1872–1914*, 1971, 135–6.
56  *The Electrician*, 3.8.1878: 'Gas lighting by electricity'.
57  Ibid., 26.6.1891, 217.
58  *Journal of the Society of Telegraph Engineers and of Electricians*, May and June 1881.
59  Byatt, *The British Electrical Industry 1875–1914 – The Economic Returns of a New Technology*, 1979, 16: in 1882 Crompton designed a dynamo for Swan.

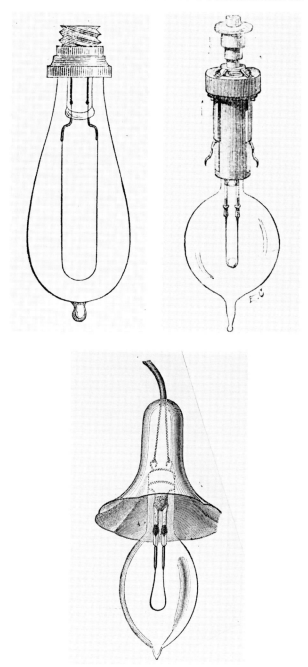

Incandescent lamps of Edison, Swan and Lane-Fox, as demonstrated at the International Electricity Exhibition held in Paris in 1881

machine in conjunction with the Lane-Fox lamp and apparatus for regulating and conducting the current. In later years it would become evident that the Brush management, a prisoner of its own policy, had lacked the courage to throw its whole weight behind the development of Lane-Fox's incandescent lighting system from the outset. By issuing licences to others, the company principally made *commercial* use of the patent rights which it had acquired.

The extent to which Lane-Fox regarded the expansion of incandescent lighting as a personal goal is in part revealed by his collaboration with the British Electric Light Company and his involvement in the establishment of the Electrical Power Storage Company, which employed the secondary battery patents obtained by Sellon, Volckmar and Swan.[60] He also played a part in the founding of the Anglo-Austrian Brush Electrical Company in 1882. At the international electricity exhibition in Vienna in 1883, this company, which had acquired from its parent company at a cost of £44,000 the rights granted to C. F. Brush and Lane-Fox for Austria-Hungary and Roumania, gave an impressive demonstration with eighty Brush arc lamps and four hundred Lane-Fox incandescent lamps, among other products. In the same year, the company signed a contract to illuminate the Imperial Opera House in Vienna and installed 1,400 incandescent lamps in the royal palace in Bucharest.[61]

The end of 1883 heralded a lengthy suspension of Lane-Fox's work in the field of electric lighting. His firm conviction that the incandescent lamp would soon displace the 'obsolete' arc lighting, and his persistent urging that the complete electric lighting system, as specified in his first patent of 1878, be elaborated, led to differences of opinion between the inventor and the directors of Brush. His profound interest in the spiritual life – 'he combined saintliness and company promoting in about equal proportions'[62] – took him to Tibet in the search for his mahatma. On his return to England at the end of the 1880s he must have been struck by the progress which the electric lighting industry had meanwhile made and which confirmed his earlier predictions. In its issue of 4 July 1890, *The Electrician* honoured him as one of the three men who had pointed the way towards electric lighting by means of incandescent lamps.

Edison's incandescent lamp was the product of 'organized invention' and had come about under the energetic leadership of a professional inventor.

[60]  *The Electrician*, 4.3.1892, 465 ff.
[61]  *The Electrician*, 29.12.1883, 168; 5.1.1884, 190 ff.     [62]  Russell, *Autobiography*, 136.

Whereas at the outset Swan and Lane-Fox had principally devoted their energies to the perfection of their respective lamps, Edison's objective – supported by the prospect of ample funds[63] and by a well-equipped laboratory and a team of specialists – had also embraced the immediate realization of the so-called complete lighting system, with the incandescent lamp as a component part. Supplementary patents covering, among other things, a modified principle for parallel circuits and the three-wire distribution system,[64] the development of measuring and control apparatus, a dynamo, cables and wiring, lamp bases and holders, electricity meters and fuses, connectors and all other items necessary for the practical application of the incandescent lamp: these improvements and products, most of which were new, determined the overwhelming range of goods produced by the rising electrical industry. They also laid the foundations for three more Edison companies.

In the United States, the construction of central generating stations and the distribution of electricity was pioneered in 1879 by Charles F. Brush with the installation of street lighting in San Francisco. Other arc lamp manufacturers followed his example. Edison was a strong supporter of the communal system, which obviated the necessity for a dynamo installation in each individual building. It was with such a system in mind that the Edison Electric Illuminating Company undertook a study of indoor electric lighting in New York in 1880. The outcome of this was that a central station in Pearl Street, with a capacity of 7,200 incandescent lamps, or 540 kilowatts (720 horsepower), was put into operation on 4 September 1882. By the end of that year, 153 smaller Edison installations, together involving 29,000 lamps, were in operation or under construction.

On the European continent, where the Compagnie Continentale Edison, in Paris, was engaged in putting the Edison patents to practical use (the company built an incandescent lamp factory in the French capital), the figures in 1883 were:

France, 98 installations with 10,240 lamps; Germany, 44 installations with 5,220 lamps; Austria, 12 installations with 4,440 lamps; Italy, 21 installations with 2,110 lamps plus a central station for 6,000 lamps in Milan (this was the first to be built in Europe); Russia, 25 installations with 2,900 lamps; the Netherlands, 12 installations with 2,930 lamps; Spain, 4 installations with 760 lamps; and Belgium, 11 installations with 620 lamps. In addition, 8,580 lamps were installed aboard ships of various nations.[65]

---

[63] Bright, *Electric-Lamp Industry*, 60: 'Edison's long record of success had gained for him the almost unlimited financial support of his backers.'

[64] This system afforded a saving on copper of 60% compared with the two-wire system.

[65] *Zeitschrift für angewandte Elektricitätslehre*, 1884, 220.

In England, where Edison's position in terms of competition differed from that on the Continent by reason of the presence of the Swan Electric Lamp Company, Ltd, and the Anglo-American Brush Electric Light Corporation, Ltd, the year 1882 saw the establishment of the Edison Electric Light Company, Ltd, which immediately proceeded to contest the patents held by Swan[66] and Lane-Fox.[67] A number of smaller producers of incandescent lamps, such as Woodhouse & Rawson, Pilsen-Joel and Bernstein, each of whom had an output of about 10,000 units per year, had also appeared on the British market. The price of a lamp, which was initially twenty-five shillings, fell during the second half of 1882 to five shillings. The reduction stemmed not only from increased competition, but also from rising sales and improvements in company organization. The manufacturing process lent itself to sub-division in terms of labour, and girls were preferred to men.[68]

The Swan Electric Lamp Company, Ltd, of Newcastle upon Tyne, which had been established in 1880 to manufacture the Swan Lamp, was transformed into a more powerful organization in the following year. It became the Swan Electric Light Company, Ltd, with an authorized capital of £100,000. The new company was able to undertake manufacture on a larger scale, actively promoted the Swan lamp at the international electricity exhibition in Paris in 1881 and patented the Swan lighting system in Germany, France and other countries. Swan, who had received a sum of £50,000 in consideration of his inventions,[69] was appointed to the post of technical director. In the ensuing year the financial basis was again strengthened by the founding of the Swan United Electric Light Company, Ltd, with a share capital of £1,000,000 and headquarters in London. The birth of the new enterprise coincided with the promulgation of the Electric Lighting Act, 1882, which put an end to the speculation and abuses which had accompanied the introduction of electric lighting in Great Britain. This piece of legislation, however, was not without a reverse side, and until its revision in 1888 it was a serious obstacle to the construction of central stations and thus to the process of electrification.[70] In 1883 it put the Swan company, which was geared to large-scale expansion, in the position of

---

[66] *The Electrician*, 25.5.1888, 79.      [67] *The Electrician*, 8.4.1882, 331.

[68] *The Electrician*, 24.3.1883, 443: 'The processes of manufacture are consecutive, and almost all performed by girls, who are preferred by the makers as being cheaper, and having better eyes and more delicate hands for the work than men.'

[69] *Zeitschrift für angewandte Elektricitätslehre*, 1881, 126.

[70] Bright, *Electric-Lamp Industry*, 106 ff.

playing a waiting game[71] and as a result British lighting manufacturers as a whole, and Brush in particular, were obliged to redouble their efforts to expand their continental interests.

Following the international electricity exhibition of 1881, the Swan United Electric Light Company built a lamp factory near Paris; this was moved to Lille a few years later. In Germany, Siemens & Halske, after the failure of their efforts to manufacture an incandescent lamp of their own design, acquired a licence to produce the Swan lighting system.[72] But in 1884 the Swan United Electric Light Company set up its own lamp factory at Kalk, near Cologne, the management of which was entrusted to Stearn.[73] The reason for this step lay in the discovery that Siemens & Halske had close ties, and had entered into a commitment, with Deutsche Edison Gesellschaft (established in 1883 and later to become AEG), after which both companies had commenced to manufacture incandescent lamps on the basis of the Edison patents. These two companies – which, moreover, had acquired the incandescent lamp patents of the American researchers Weston and Maxim – now claimed the sole right to manufacture incandescent lamps and install lighting systems in Germany. The resulting break with the Swan United Electric Light Company heralded a series of bitterly contested patent lawsuits[74] which ended only with a ruling by the German Supreme Court in 1891 that the Edison patents were admittedly valid, but that Swan's lamp did not contravene them.

In Great Britain, the interests of the Swan United Electric Light Company, Ltd, and those of the Edison Electric Light Company, Ltd, had been merged in a single enterprise, the Edison & Swan United Electric Light Company, Ltd (hereafter Edison & Swan), since 26 October 1883. The principal motive for this, the first large-scale merger in the incandescent lamp industry, was the threat of a long and costly struggle in the areas of competition and patents between two parties, each of whom was capable of seriously harming the other, while neither had any certainty of benefiting in the long run: 'All patents relating to electric lighting appliances ... are just insecure enough to tempt an assault, but not sufficiently so to be certain of falling when assailed.'[75] In order to avoid the losses which ensue from conflict, and at the same time to achieve a very strong joint position, the shareholders of the Swan United Electric Light Company, Ltd, opted for a merger. The Edison Electric Light Company, Ltd, was staking everything,

[71] *The Electrician*, 5.1.1884, 182.       [72] *50 Jahre AEG*, 1956, 28.
[73] *The Electrician*, 26.5.1885, 112 ff.
[74] *Zeitschrift für angewandte Elektricitätslehre*, 1886, No. 26.
[75] *The Electrician*, 6.10.1883, 492 ff: 'Amalgamation'.

for it had simultaneously initiated proceedings against its partner.[76] To some extent, therefore, the merger was the result of an ultimatum – a fact which was later confirmed by Swan.[77]

But whereas in England the two had amalgamated to form a combine which in the ensuing decade was to sweep away almost all competition, on the Continent the situation was different: 'The Edison & Swan interests were happily united in England, but they were equally unhappily disunited on the Continent, and they were cutting each other's throats in France, Belgium and Germany and other places.'[78] The reason for this lay in the continued existence of the parent companies of Edison and Swan, each of which was free to pursue its activities outside the United Kingdom. Not until 1894 did the Swan factory in Germany become an operating company controlled by the holding company in Britain. This structure had been adopted by the two rivals in France in 1888 in a joint bid to protect themselves against growing competition from foreign manufacturers in the attractive French market. They joined forces in the Compagnie Générale des Lampes Incandescentes, of Paris, the French subsidiary of Edison & Swan, which had an authorized capital of Fr. 2,000,000.

In 1884 Edison & Swan proceeded against Woodhouse & Rawson of London, manufacturers of incandescent lamps. The subject matter of what on the surface appeared to be a minor case against Woodhouse & Rawson alone was Edison's basic patent on the carbonized filament and the flashing process devised by Sawyer and Man,[79] the British patent for which had been purchased by Edison & Swan. The validity, or tenability, of Edison's basic patent was at first not taken very seriously, especially in Britain, and the claim to exclusive rights in respect of the flashing process, which up to then had been regarded as no more than a scientific experiment relating to an impractical lamp dating from 1878, was not seen by lamp manufacturers as a threat. When in 1886, after what was judged to be an extremely weak defence – 'the case was almost a *reductio ad absurdum* of the expert farce'[80] – the court, amid widespread and sharp criticism, found in favour of Edison

[76] *The Electrician*, 6.10.1883, 501 ff; cf. D. Moralee, 'The electric lamp business', in *Electronics and Power*, February 1979, 106.

[77] *The Electrician*, 25.5.1888, 78.

[78] *The Electrician*, 12.8.1887, 303: according to the chairman of Edison & Swan.

[79] Cf. page 16; in Great Britain the flashing process was commonly referred to as the Cheeseborough Patent, named after the patent agent F. J. Cheeseborough.

[80] J. Swinburne, 'The Edison filament case', in *Electrical Review*, Vol. 19, No. 454, 6.8.1886; and several articles in *The Electrician*, 1886 and subsequent years.

Table 2. *Quantities of lamps produced by AEG, Edison & Swan and Siemens & Halske in the period 1883–90*

| Year | Allgemeine Elektricitätsgesellschaft | Edison & Swan[a] | Siemens & Halske |
|------|------|------|------|
| 1883 | — | 150,000[b] | 10,000 |
| 1884 | 30,000[a] | 200,000[b] | 12,000 |
| 1885 | 60,000 | 290,000 | 50,000 |
| 1886 | 90,000 | 160,000 | 200,000 |
| 1887 | 300,000 | 220,000 | 275,000 |
| 1888 | 450,000 | 290,000 | 350,000 |
| 1889 | 650,000 | 440,000 | 650,000 |
| 1890 | 800,000 | 500,000[b] | 700,000 |

*Notes:*
[a]In Great Britain alone.
[b]Estimated.

& Swan. The verdict was upheld by the Court of Appeal in January 1887, whereupon virtually every manufacturer in Great Britain was confronted with the choice between the production of incandescent lamps with considerable risks in his own country or transferring the activity abroad. For nearly all those concerned made high-resistance lamps with a carbonized filament, which implied the use of the flashing process.

As we shall see, the outcome of the case was the immediate cause of, and indeed set in train, the departure of the younger and most vital element in the British incandescent lamp industry for fresh pastures, including the Netherlands, Austria and Switzerland, following the closure by Pilsen-Joel, the Maxim–Weston Company and others of their factories. In the Netherlands, where the suspension of the Patent Law in 1869[81] had removed all obstacles to production, an incandescent lamp works was established at Middelburg in 1887 and another at Venlo in 1889; these were managed, respectively, by the knowledgeable and experienced Englishmen, C. J. Robertson and F. R. Pope, and the money was provided by local financiers. When in 1889, after a long and costly lawsuit, the Anglo-American Brush Electric Light Corporation, Ltd, the last competitor to threaten Edison & Swan, decided to cease production of incandescent lamps in Great Britain,[82] it, too, was obliged to seek a new location in order to continue the activity. Austria was the first choice, but the Netherlands were also high on the list.

[81] G. Doorman, *Het Nederlandsch Octrooiwezen en de Techniek der 19e eeuw*, 1947, 46 ff.
[82] *The Electrician*, 19.7.1889, 285 ff: 'Report to shareholders'.

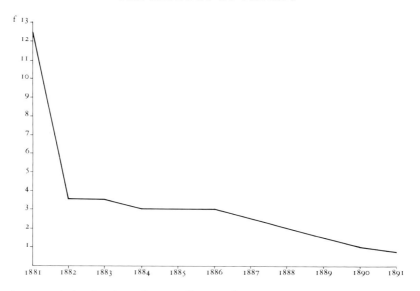

Average wholesale prices of 16-candlepower lamps in the Netherlands, 1881–91[a]

[a]  Compiled from various sources including price lists and articles appearing in journals. Bright quotes
the following prices for the U.S.A.: 1880–6: average $1.00; 1888: 80 cents; 1891: 50 cents.

Transferring the production from England to Austria would simply involve
enlarging the factory in Vienna, where Brush, operating under the title
Kremenezky, Mayer & Co.,[83] had been manufacturing incandescent lamps
since 1884. Employing the Lane-Fox patents, the company had established
a continental production line in Vienna, with highly favourable results in
both technical and commercial terms, for 'the excellent lamp produced by
Kremenezky was greatly in demand in foreign markets'. Even in the most
difficult times the company exported its products, and then principally to
countries which had their own incandescent lamp industries.[84] Thus L.
Bernard in his history of the birth of the Austrian electrical industry, in
which the author also describes the country as the source of the high quality
incandescent lamp. This was indeed high praise for Lane-Fox's lamp, the
manufacture of which in Great Britain was eliminated by the outcome of a
legal jousting match.[85]

Another established manufacturer forced to seek a new base was Alex-

[83]  *The Electrician*, 24.2.1888, 418: 'Kremenezky, Mayer & Co., under which title the Corporation are
there trading'; cf. W. Meinhardt, *Entwicklung und Aufbau der Glühlampenindustrie*, 1932, 53.

[84]  Louis Bernard, *Die Entwickelung und Bedeutung der elektrotechnischen Industrie in Oesterreich*,
1908, 42 ff.

[85]  Cf. Chapter 2, pages 73 ff, for more information on this subject.

ander Bernstein. In 1888 he transferred his lamp works from London to Hamburg. A spectacular feature of this exodus, and one which was more than merely the loss of an individual for the British lamp industry, was the departure of Swan's partner, Charles H. Stearn (1844–1919), who set up as a manufacturer in Switzerland, where incandescent lamps were not protected by patents.[86] Stearn had been in charge of the Swan United Electric Light Company's factory at Kalk, near Cologne, since 1884. He communicated his momentous decision to his closest associates in the following announcement:

I would take this opportunity to inform you that I have resigned my position as a director of the Swan Company, and that as from the 31st instant I shall no longer be connected with the company in either a technical or commercial capacity. As the Swan lamp was a joint invention on the part of Mr. J. W. Swan and myself, and as I have been in charge of its manufacture from our earliest tests in 1877 until now, I shall watch its further development with interest, and it is my hope that the good reputation which it has so far enjoyed will be maintained in the future.[87]

The Zürich Incandescence Lamp Company was formally established at Birmensdorf on 28 February 1890. Stearn himself provided the greater part of the authorized capital of Sw. Fr. 250,000,[88] and in doing so laid the foundations not only for a factory of significance, but indeed for the Swiss incandescent lamp industry. He took with him to Switzerland engineers and others with whom he had worked in England. He was, in the words of *The Electrician* of 9 October 1891, engaged in training the 'Zürich natives' in the skills of lamp manufacture. Stearn appointed agents in Paris, Brussels, Milan, Hamburg, Madrid and, in due course, London.

Only after the expiry of Edison & Swan's basic patent in November 1893, and with this the company's monopoly in Great Britain, did some English manufacturers – having meanwhile successfully developed a large number of lamp factories on the European continent – return to their native land, which with good reason claimed to be the cradle of the incandescent lamp. Work on developing the filament had virtually come to a standstill between 1886 and 1893,[89] and up to the latter year the price of lamps had remained three times as high as on the Continent.[90] The domestic market of

[86] E. Schiff, *Industrialization without National Patents*, Part 2, 1971.
[87] C. H. Stearn, Hotel du Nord, Cologne, 26.8.1889, memorandum to his staff; Siemens Archives, No. 35-16 Lh 474, Munich.
[88] Report Auskunftei W. Schimmelpfeng, Berlin, 14.10.1893; archives of the Vitrite Works, Middelburg.
[89] Bright, *Electric-Lamp Industry*, 138; *The Electrician*, 21.6.1895, 271.
[90] Byatt, *British Electrical Industry*, 155.

the British lamp industry, which would not regain its early lead, was flooded with lamps bearing foreign trademarks, including PHILIPS. A large English user summed up the situation as follows:

In November the Edison and Swan patent came to an end, and the lamps which they used to supply to their customers at 3s. 6d. they were now supplying at much lower prices. They had a new lamp which he was sorry to say was a foreign lamp, and made in Holland. They gave a good lamp for 1s., and the light from it was much superior to that of the old lamp. They had thus saved to their customers an amount of something like £1,500.[91]

During 1889, four incandescent lamp factories were in operation in the Netherlands, the products of which were mainly exported to Germany and France. The oldest of these, the De Khotinsky works, situated in Rotterdam and having a large branch at Gelnhausen, near Frankfurt am Main, increased its output to 1,000 lamps per day in that year. Simultaneously it was decided to raise this to 2,500 lamps daily. The man behind this enterprise was L. W. Schöffer, a Rotterdam coffee merchant, who in 1883 had succeeded in interesting prominent businessmen in the city in providing finance. The second Dutch lamp works, owned by Johan Boudewijnse of Middelburg, had been established in 1887, the backers having included the Boudewijnse brothers, installers and ironmongers. A sharp rise in foreign demand, coupled with growing sales at home, led in 1889 to a decision to double the capacity of the works, which was then 350 lamps per day. In the same year, the lamp works owned by Messrs Roothaan & Alewijnse of Nijmegen went into production. This company and the two previously mentioned are dealt with in detail in Chapter 4. Equally worthy of further study is the lamp works established in Venlo by Emile Goossens, Pope & Van der Kaa, a company financed by Messrs Goossens, who added banking to their principal occupation of coffee and tobacco merchants.

The large number of incandescent lamp works in the Netherlands thus reflected the producers' expectation that this new product could be profitably manufactured and sold. Moreover, consumer reaction, and to an even greater extent that of the emerging purchasers – the central generating stations – indicated that the product had a promising future. In the Amsterdam of 1889, while the idea of electric lighting was difficult to grasp by reason of its technical complexity, its desirability was a non-controversial subject in the Council Chamber. Rotterdam showed itself to be ahead of

---

[91] *The Electrician*, 2.3.1894: 'Annual meeting of the Liverpool Electric Supply Company, Ltd'; the reference is to a sixteen-candlepower standard lamp from the factory in Middelburg.

the times when, in 1889, the Municipal Gasworks Committee concluded that: 'the electric light industry has now achieved such a degree of perfection that there is no longer any technical objection to the widespread application of this new source of light'.[92] Ten years after the Menlo Park lamp, incandescent lighting was already spreading rapidly in the Netherlands, as elsewhere in Europe. A few years later, the manufacturers would be obliged to switch to mass production.

The incandescent lamp industry in the United States produced about five million lamps in 1890.[93] It had no demonstrable lead over its European counterparts, in terms of either output or product quality. Owing to a different approach to the concept of lamp efficiency, the standard American lamp consumed on average 4.5 watts per candlepower against the 3.5 watts of European lamps, giving it a longer life but increasing the running cost.[94] The total production in Europe in 1890 was also of the order of five million units,[95] of which just under half were made in Germany. 'If one studies the spread of electric lighting,' a former colleague of Gerard Philips, the German lamp expert J. Zacharias, observed in 1890, 'the production of incandescent lamps must increase tenfold within a few years.' It therefore seemed to him to be a highly remunerative activity in which to engage, certainly in the near future: 'as the prospects of those holding the Edison patents recede, the more are others encouraged to set up new factories'.[96]

It was the tide of history outlined above, which was governed by forces in the Netherlands and abroad, that encouraged in the minds of the entrepreneurs Frederik and Gerard Philips the idea of entering into an association with the Anglo-American Brush Electric Light Corporation, Ltd, for the purpose of carrying on in the Netherlands the production of the Brush lamp, which had been brought to a standstill in Great Britain.[97] To approach this international concern was an audacious step and one which for the Messrs Philips did not progress beyond exploratory discussions, but which certainly stimulated them to achieve their goal by their own efforts and with their own resources.

---

[92] Report to the Municipal Gasworks Committee following an inspection of gas and electric lighting at the World Exhibition in Paris in 1889; Municipal Archives, Rotterdam.

[93] *General Electric Review*, Vol. 23, No. 1, 1920, 49; Bright, *Electric-Lamp Industry*, 4, presumes the output in the United States in 1891 to have been 7.5 million lamps.

[94] 'Life and efficiency tests', in *The Electrician*, 29.7.1892, 16.9.1892 and 25.11.1892.

[95] J. Zacharias, *Die Glühlampe, ihre Herstellung und Anwendung in der Praxis*, 1890, 137.

[96] Zacharias, *Die Glühlampe*; for the relationship between Gerard Philips and Zacharias, see Chapter 2, pages 67 and 79.

[97] Cf. pages 1 and 2.

## Table 3. *Incandescent lamp manufacturers in Europe in 1890*

| Domicile | Company | Type of filament |
|---|---|---|
| Austria | | |
| Vienna | B. von Berndt & Co. | Berndt |
| Vienna | Kremenezky, Mayer & Co. | Lane-Fox |
| Vienna | Wiener Elektrische Glühlampenfabrik, Sturm & Co. | Sturm |
| Belgium | | |
| Brussels | S.A. Belge pour la Fabrication das Lampes à Incandescence | Seel |
| France | | |
| Paris | Compagnie Générale des Lampes Incandescentes | Edison & Swan |
| Paris | Philippart Frères[a] | De Changy |
| Paris | Société de Soudure Electriques des Métaux | Cruto |
| Germany | | |
| Berlin | A.G. für elektrische Glühlampen, Patent Seel | Seel |
| Berlin | Allgemeine Elektricitäts-Gesellschaft | Edison |
| Berlin | Elektrotechnische Industriegesellschaft | Langhans |
| Berlin | Fritsche & Pischon | Fritsche |
| Berlin | Siemens & Halske | Edison |
| Gelnhausen | Electriciteits-Maatschappij, Systeem 'De Khotinsky' | De Khotinsky |
| Hamburg | Elektrische Glühlampenfabrik, Alexander Bernstein | Bernstein |
| Hamburg | Glühlampenfabrik und Elektrizitätswerke, Müller | Müller |
| Great Britain | | |
| Gateshead | Sunbeam Lamp Company, Clarke, Chapman & Co.[a] | Edmundson |
| London/Newcastle | Edison & Swan United Electric Light Company, Ltd | Edison & Swan |
| Hungary | | |
| Budapest | A.G. für elektrische Glühlampen, Budapest | Seel |
| Budapest | B. Egger & Co. | Bernstein |
| Italy | | |
| Milan | Rivolta & Co. | Cruto |
| Milan | Tecnomasio B. Cabella & Co. | Cabella |
| Turin | Società Italiana di Elettricità, Sistema Cruto | Cruto |
| Netherlands | | |
| Middelburg | Johan Boudewijnse | Robertson |
| Nijmegen | Roothaan & Alewijnse | De Khotinsky |

| Domicile | Company | Type of filament |
|----------|---------|------------------|
| Rotterdam | Electriciteits-Maatschappij, Systeem 'De Khotinsky' | De Khotinsky |
| Venlo | Goossens, Pope & Co. | Pope |
| Sweden | | |
| Stockholm | Bergström & Taxen, Glödlampenfabriken Svea | Bergström |
| Stockholm | Strehlnert & Co., Svenska Glödlampenfabriken | Strehlnert |
| Switzerland | | |
| Birmensdorf | Zürich Incandescence Lamp Company | Stearn |

Note:
[a]Manufacturer of low-resistance lamps.

It is to the events leading up to the establishment in 1891 of Philips & Co. of Eindhoven, which was favoured by the same conditions of existence as the aforementioned Dutch incandescent lamp works, that our research is particularly directed in this first volume of the history of N.V. Philips' Gloeilampenfabrieken. It is an analysis of the first steps on a steep upward path in the international incandescent lamp industry, a path which was to reach its symbolic high-point in England in 1920, when the technical management of Edison & Swan's lamp manufacturing activities was entrusted to Philips of Eindhoven. Gerard and Anton Philips were thereupon given seats on the Board of Edison & Swan, for, in the words of the chairman, C. J. Ford:

The Philips' Glowlampworks, Limited, is acknowledged to be the premier lamp manufacturing concern in Europe, possessing processes, plant and machinery, which have hitherto enabled it to manufacture lamps on the most economical basis and of the very highest quality. Similar plant, machinery and processes have now been installed at the works of the Edison–Swan Company.[98]

The Messrs Philips distinguished themselves from others, not only by their achievements in the field of incandescent lamp manufacture – which was among Gerard Philips' most outstanding merits[99] – but equally by their commercial skill.

---

[98] Thirty-Seventh Annual Report, for the year ended 30 June 1920, The Edison–Swan Electric Company, Ltd, London; *The Electrician*, 7.1.1921.

[99] Meinhardt, *Glühlampenindustrie*, preface: 'Holland wegen seiner verdienstvollen Entwicklung der Fabrikation'.

Frederik Philips (1830–1900)

*Chapter 2*

# FREDERIK AND GERARD PHILIPS: THE BIRTH OF A PARTNERSHIP

Benjamin Frederik David Philips (1830–1900), who was known as Frederik Philips, was respected as an enterprising merchant. On 15 May 1891 he entered into a private agreement[1] with his eldest son, Gerard Leonard Frederik, to establish a company with the object of 'manufacturing incandescent lamps and other electrical articles, and engaging in trade in the same'. Frederik Philips was, moreover, familiar with the affairs of banking, and possessed of a fortune. As the owner of large estates in and around the Bommelerwaard region, he was counted among the principal landowners. The W. Schimmelpfeng Institute for International Commercial Intelligence, with which Frederik Philips maintained contact, estimated his fortune at that time to be half a million guilders.[2] As a young man he had been introduced to the commercial activities of Peletier & Philips Bz. of Zaltbommel, a company founded in 1815 by Gerlachus Ribbius Peletier (1790–1872) and Lion Philips (1794–1866), his father. The two partners, who also owned a tobacco-cutting factory, are reported to have been licensed as manufacturers of smoking tobacco and snuff, and sellers of 'First Class' wares.[3] Their activities embraced the processing of tobacco and the wholesaling and retailing of the finished products, which bore the trade name 'De Eenhoorn' (The Unicorn).

It is clear from the volume of their business that the trade in tobacco – in which the Philips family had been engaged for at least two generations – was flourishing at that time, and offered prospects for expansion. In 1817, Lion's brothers Joseph and Philip, as De Gebroeders Philips, established a tobacco-processing works at Maastricht with the title 'De Dubbele Een-

---

[1] This private deed cannot be traced. Cf. Chapter 6, page 283.
[2] Report by Schimmelpfeng, Amsterdam, 14.2.1896; archives of the Vitrite Works.
[3] Deed dated 24 February 1815, executed before Paulus van Essen, notary of Zaltbommel; Philips Archives, Eindhoven.

hoorn' (The Double Unicorn). The two companies maintained a close relationship, especially in the purchase of tobacco.[4] In the course of time, Lion's five other brothers earned a living in the same branch of industry as their father and grandfather, thereby adding to the power and scope of this family business. Favoured by the revival of trade in the period which followed the ending of the Continental System, they established tobacco factories at Aachen, Offenbach, Liège and Budapest alongside the businesses at Zaltbommel and Maastricht. In the ensuing decades, these prospered and expanded, and to them was added a cigar factory at Eitorf/ Sieg belonging to Louis Philips, a son of Isaac Philips, who had earlier established the Gebrüder Philips Juniores tobacco works at Aachen.[5]

In 1820, Peletier & Philips – the *Stammhaus* in Zaltbommel – set up a company trading in tea,[6] and this was followed some years later by a coffee-roasting establishment. In addition to their joint activities, each of the partners engaged in trade on his own account. It is said that Lion or Frederik Philips had a small works in Zaltbommel which produced cotton wool, but there are no details of this.[7] A register maintained in accordance with the licensing laws and bearing the name of Lion Philips Bz.[8] shows that in the period 1820–59 he employed the following numbers of people: 1820 three, 1830 four, 1840 six, 1850 six, 1859 thirteen.

Concerning Gerlachus Ribbius Peletier, it is known that he and his son established a cigar factory at Utrecht in 1844. The company, which enjoyed great prosperity, produced more than two million cigars in 1856. At that time the work force numbered seventy-five and their wages amounted to some 25,000 guilders per annum. In 1859, father and son set up a second cigar works in Utrecht, this time with an entirely female work force (just over one hundred girls). Four years later, the two factories were together producing something like ten million cigars annually.[9]

Although it may be assumed that neither Lion Philips nor, subsequently, his son had any direct interest in the cigar manufacturing company in Utrecht, they maintained important commercial ties with it through Peletier & Philips. To this end, among others, the partners each had a half-share in a tobacco warehouse situated in the Gamerschestraat in Bommel. In 1895,

[4] *Weekblad Zaltbommel, Bommeler- en Tielerwaard*, 1.3.1935: 'Peletier & Philips 1815–1935'.
[5] Cf. summary of the business activities of the Philipses, page 53.
[6] Deed dated 26 October 1820, executed before Paulus van Essen, notary of Zaltbommel; Philips Archives, Eindhoven.
[7] P. J. Bouman, *Growth of an Enterprise: The Life of Anton Philips*, 1956, 15.
[8] Register of Employees of Mr Lion Philips Bz.; Philips Archives, Eindhoven.
[9] Archive research by H. Coelingh Bennink, Municipal Archives, Utrecht, 6 January 1977; Philips Archives, Eindhoven.

Trademark of Peletier & Philips

Table 4. *Quantities of tobacco and coffee (in half kilogrammes) processed by Peletier & Philips in the period 1859–69*

| Year | Tobacco | Coffee |
|---|---|---|
| 1859/60 | 87,170 | 55,813 |
| 1860/1 | 81,856 | 57,270 |
| 1861/2 | 80,532 | 54,380 |
| 1862/3 | 71,804 | 52,000 |
| 1863/4 | 72,172 | 52,391 |
| 1864/5 | 74,491 | 57,722 |
| 1865/6 | 81,415 | 64,630 |
| 1866/7 | 80,068 | 67,041 |
| 1867/8 | 80,646 | 75,574 |
| 1868/9 | 79,800 | 67,632 |

fifty years after its establishment, the company – which was then among the largest and oldest in its field in the Netherlands – was transformed into a limited liability company[10] with an authorized capital of one million guilders.[11]

When Lion Philips retired from Peletier & Philips in 1856 for reasons of health, Frederik Philips succeeded his father. In 1870, Gerlachus Ribbius Peletier, then quite elderly, transferred his share in the firm to his 'friend'[12] Frederik Philips. From then onwards, Frederik, who for years had been the driving force, carried on the business under the original name but entirely on his own account. A survey of the quantities of tobacco and coffee processed, which was drawn up by Frederik Philips, provides an indication of the volume of business transacted at Zaltbommel between 1859 and 1869. This is reproduced as Table 4. Based on the raw material prices of the time, the annual turnover in these two commodities averaged 50,000 guilders.

The fourth and fifth decades of the previous century had witnessed an exceptional increase in the smoking of cigars in Europe. Prof. S. Bleekrode (1814–62), who is renowned for his manual of technology,[13] among other works, estimated in 1860 that in Paris, where tobacco was the subject of a government monopoly and its consumption was accurately recorded, sales of cigars had risen from $13\frac{1}{2}$ million in 1839 to 63 million in 1854. Against

---

[10] Koninklijke Tabak- en Sigarenfabriek voorheen G. Ribbius Peletier Jr.
[11] *De Nederlandsche Handel en Industrie, 1913,* commemorative issue, 244.
[12] Circular letter issued by G. Ribbius Peletier, 18.5.1870; Philips Archives, Eindhoven.
[13] Doorman, *Het Nederlandsch Octrooiwezen,* 303.

the background of this general phenomenon, he stressed the desirability of the national cigar industry mechanizing its production processes.[14] The snuff industry had by this time ceased to be of importance, and pipe tobacco was losing ground to cigars. Bleekrode was moved by this situation to bring to the notice of manufacturers the advantages of some new machines for the purpose, including those developed in 1856 by the American, W. Dawson of Huntington, Conn., and by A. Hirschfeld and H. Jander of Hamburg.

Evidence of Frederik Philips' enterprising spirit and receptiveness to the most up-to-date manufacturing methods is seen in the fact that in 1857 he obtained from the above-mentioned inventors an exclusive concession to introduce the machine in the Netherlands. In the notes which accompanied his application for a patent[15] – which was submitted to King William III and contained a full explanation and technical drawings – Frederik Philips stated, *inter alia*:

The machine is operated by two persons and rolls 7–8 cigars per minute, as perfectly as they could be made by the best cigar maker. It therefore manufactures between 4,200 and 4,800 well-made cigars in ten hours. Three or four people form the tips, or heads, and seal these.

If it is desired only to manufacture bunches from fine waste or cut veins, the machine will produce 6,000 of good quality in ten hours. It has the advantage that the cigars are made in the same manner as in Havana, namely without binder or filler.

Twelve machines, operated by 60–80 persons, including those who make the heads, will do the work of at least 320 workpeople rolling by hand; and in addition to the great saving of space, wages and time, they have the significant advantage that waste and veins, which have no value, can be made into cigars.

Frederik Philips lodged his request for a fifteen-year patent with the Clerk of the Provincial States in Gelderland at 6 p.m. on 22 July 1857. On 12 November of that year, it having meanwhile been verified in Delft that the invention in question had not appeared in print in the Netherlands, he received a patent for a period of five years. Earlier, on 28 July, the King's Commissioner in the province of Gelderland had informed the Minister of Home Affairs that the applicant, Frederik Philips, enjoyed confidence as a merchant and 'has sufficient means to effect the introduction'.[16]

The introduction of the machine in the Netherlands was not long

[14]  *Nieuw Tijdschrift qewijd aan alle taken van Volksvlijt, Nijverheid, enz.*, Vol. 4, 1860, 187 ff.
[15]  'Beschrijving van het werktuig enz', dated 21.7.1857, and various letters on this subject, included in the Nationale Nijverheid collection; Government Archives, The Hague; cf. Doorman, *Het Nederlandsch Octrooiwezen*, 378.
[16]  Cf. correspondence referred to in note 15.

delayed. It resulted from the decision by Ribbius Peletier 'to have built, in addition to the workshops earlier equipped for male employees, an extensive building for female employees, *the like of which does not yet exist in this country*, which factory, when in production, will provide a decent living for a number of girls'.[17] Thus the 'Introduction' to the regulations pertaining to the factory, in which the wages and conditions of employment were set out in detail. The working week was fixed at sixty hours, and the corresponding weekly wage was seventy cents at the commencement of the first year of training, rising to 2.75 guilders in the fourth year. Girls below the age of twelve years were not accepted, and preference was given to applicants who were literate and numerate.

This was the cigar factory established by Ribbius Peletier in Utrecht, to which reference was made earlier in this chapter and which commenced production in 1859. It was here, shortly after the 1856–7 boom in the tobacco industry, that mechanization, based on the patent obtained by Frederik Philips, was first introduced. Whether the tobacco and cigar manufacturing processes at the Zaltbommel works of Peletier & Philips were mechanized, it is impossible to ascertain; but this seems improbable. It is also known that in 1856 Philip Philips, in Maastricht, obtained a patent for the introduction of a tobacco drying machine.[18] These facts confound the assumption, which has existed up to now, that the replacement of labour by machines in the Dutch tobacco industry did not commence until the 1870s.[19]

Zaltbommel, which was favourably situated on the River Waal, was the centre of Frederik Philips' business activities. In the surrounding provinces of Gelderland, North Brabant and Utrecht, tobacco and cigar manufacture in the 1850s was in the hands of about one hundred firms, the majority of which were very small.[20] They depended upon middlemen for their supplies of tobacco and for the sale of their products. In addition to the Peletier & Philips works, Zaltbommel in 1858 boasted five tobacco and cigar factories, the owners being J. van de Grunt, G. W. Nouhuys, C. H. Ribbius, the Van de Water brothers and P. Wigels.[21]

Prior to the arrival of Sumatran tobacco, supplies of which commenced

[17] 'Reglement voor eene, door G. Ribbius Peletier, Jr. binnen de stad Utrecht op te rigten tabak- en sigarenfabriek voor vrouwelijk personeel, vastgesteld 1 juni 1859'; Municipal Archives, Utrecht.
[18] Doorman, *Het Nederlandsch Octrooiwezen*, 360.
[19] J. A. de Jonge, *De industrialisatie in Nederland tussen 1850 and 1914*, 58.
[20] *Staat van de Nederlandsche Fabrieken volgens de Verslagen der Gemeenten*, published in 1859 by the Maatschappij van Nijverheid.
[21] Cf. summary referred to in note 20.

in 1864, the cigar industry chiefly used the well-coloured leaf grown in the Betuwe and Land van Maas en Waal regions of Holland. This was bought from local growers by knowledgeable traders, such as Messrs Peletier & Philips, who resold it. Substantial consignments of this tobacco were often shipped to central Europe by way of the major rivers. For example, a large portion of the 1852 crop was sold to the Austrian tobacco monopoly.[22]

The increase in the numbers employed in the manufacture of cigars in Holland between 1850 and 1870, from about 2,000 to 12,000, is a measure of the growth achieved by this branch of industry. In Eindhoven, where in 1858 the tobacco, cigar and snuff factories together employed 278 persons, the figure for the cigar industry alone rose to more than 1,000 in 1875, while production increased from seven million to sixty million cigars. At 's-Hertogenbosch, a town which also lay within the mercantile realm of Peletier & Philips, the cigar industry steadily expanded during this period. In the years which followed the introduction of East Indian leaf, the tobacco trade as a whole obtained good prices and the merchants prospered, especially as a result of the system of selling by tender. The tobacco cutting branch, in contrast, declined. During the 1870s and 1880s the trade in tobacco and cigars continued to be the mainstay of Peletier & Philips' business; this they combined with a relatively small tobacco cutting works and a coffee-roasting establishment at Zaltbommel. When, between 1887 and 1889, the government-appointed engineers H. W. E. Struve and A. A. Bekaar were assembling data on the equipment of factories and workshops in the Netherlands and the health and safety measures for the benefit of workers,[23] their sole entry for Zaltbommel was the tobacco factory of the firm Peletier & Philips and the ancillary coffee-roasting establishment. This, it appeared, was the only surviving industrial undertaking in the town which was worth recording for the purposes of the survey, and it was described as 'a good factory'. The employees numbered eight; the working day was of 11 hours in the summer and $9\frac{1}{2}$ hours in the winter; and there is a reference to 'frequent overtime'. The observation that workers were paid during sickness and that the proprietor, Frederik Philips, continued to employ workpeople when they became elderly, and supported them, cannot be allowed to pass unnoticed.

The modest scale of these activities in Zaltbommel is confirmation of the fact that Frederik Philips was mainly engaged in the *trade* in tobacco and

[22]  De Jonge, *De industrialisatie*, 56 ff; see this source also for further information.
[23]  Poll conducted by Struve and Bekaar, Nijverheidsstatistiek 1887–9; Government Archives, The Hague.

cigars, and that commerce lay at the root of his prosperity.[24] When, in 1876, Gerard Philips enrolled as a student at the Polytechnic in Delft, he gave as his father's profession 'tobacco merchant'.

This fact, however, did not prevent Frederik Philips operating in various other fields, notably banking and, for a brief period, as the proprietor of the gasworks at Bommel (an abbreviation of Zaltbommel). The origin of his diversification into banking was a decision in 1864 by De Nederlandsche Bank, the central bank, to establish a network of agents and correspondents across the country with the aim of greatly expanding its activities. The first phase of the plan was realized by the appointment in that year of twelve agents and fifty-six correspondents.[25] The bank exercised 'the greatest care' in making these appointments. Frederik Philips was approached on the subject of becoming the bank's correspondent in Zaltbommel, and on 15 December 1864 he reported to the Board of the bank, in Amsterdam, that he was willing to accept the post. Earlier, on 3 October 1864, the banker A. J. van Lanschot, of 's-Hertogenbosch, had put forward the names of J. M. van Hulsteijn, a well-to-do retired chemist, and L. Peerbolte, who for some time had been the local banker in Zaltbommel, for the post.[26] Because the latter, although 'industrious and honest', had no immovable assets which could serve as collateral for loans, preference was given to Van Hulsteijn. On further consideration, however, this choice appeared somewhat unfortunate to those in Amsterdam, and on 3 December of the same year the bank again approached Van Lanschot for information, this time concerning 'the merchant and manufacturer Benjamin Philips, also known as Frederik Philips'. Was this person known to Van Lanschot? The prompt reply of the agent for 's-Hertogenbosch re-emphasizes the established reputation of the merchant with whom we have concerned ourselves in the preceding pages:

I receive the most favourable reports concerning Mr Benjamin Philips, also known as Frederik Philips, of Bommel. He is the youngest partner in the firm of Peletier & Philips, which deals in tobacco and cigars.

As far as his means are concerned, he is to be preferred above Mr L. Peerbolte. He is highly praised for his drive in matters of commerce. I doubt whether he is at

---

24  The deed of partition of the estate of Lion Philips, dated 15.2.1867, shows that Frederik Philips inherited ƒ 28,265.70; The 'House, Shop premises, warehouses and land' in Zaltbommel, which he inherited, were valued at ƒ 8,000; Philips Archives, Eindhoven.

25  Annual Report of De Nederlandsche Bank, 1864–5.

26  Dossier of the correspondent at Zaltbommel; Archives of De Nederlandsche Bank; also for the other letters referred to here.

—

present as much involved in collection as Mr L. Peerbolte. Nor do I know whether he wishes to be considered for the post of correspondent of De Nederlandsche Bank.[27]

Van Lanschot's hesitancy as to whether or not Frederik Philips would be disposed to accept the post of correspondent was well founded. But this only emerged a few years later when Frederik advised the bank of his desire to be relieved of the duties. His letter of 26 July 1871 to the Board in Amsterdam reveals that however greatly he was honoured by his relationship with the central bank, he considered the post in so small a place as Zaltbommel to be insufficiently important 'to suit his convenience'. Hence his proposal that the local banker, Peerbolte, whom he thoroughly recommended, should still be appointed to the post. The bank, however, declined to accept Frederik's suggestion and threatened to delete Zaltbommel from its list of correspondentships. Faced with this situation, Frederik felt obliged to continue with the discounting, the exchanging of money and other minor banking operations[28] in order to protect the esteem which Zaltbommel enjoyed, however small the transactions might be.

Here lies the germ of Frederik's later banking business, the firm of Fred. Philips of Zaltbommel, which at that moment was embedded in the social obligations of a still young but prominent local magnate. Nor did he fail to assume local responsibilities in committees and branches of bodies such as the Reformed Church and the Maatschappij tot Nut van 't Algemeen (Society for the Common Weal). The facilities provided by the latter included a free library in Bommel, a kindergarten and, at a later stage, a bank to assist small traders.[29] The existence of the last-named was in keeping with the aim on the part of A. C. Wertheim, an Amsterdam banker, to establish local loan banks as a means of breathing new life into rural communities. When, in the early 1880s, a new fever gripped the Society – which had meanwhile lost much of its drive – it was Wertheim, for many years also the leader of the Liberals in Amsterdam, who was elected to the central committee.[30] That his election met with the approval of Frederik Philips (who since 1886 had been chairman of the Zaltbommel branch of the Society) is evidenced by the support given by this branch to Wertheim's candidature and that of B. Mees, a Rotterdam banker. Two years earlier, Wertheim and Frederik's brother, August Philips, together with a number

---

[27] A. J. van Lanschot to De Nederlandsche Bank, 8.12.1864.
[28] Frederik Philips in a letter to De Nederlandsche Bank, 30.9.1871.
[29] Archives Dept, Zaltbommel, Mij. tot Nut van 't Algemeen, 1886–7; Municipal Archives, Amsterdam.
[30] H. P. G. Quack, 'A. C. Wertheim 1832–1897', *De Gids*, Vol. 16, 1898, 64.

of leading figures from the Amsterdam money market, had saved the Nederlandsch-Indische Handelsbank from almost certain ruin. For, as the economist and historian H. P. G. Quack described the operation, Amsterdam at that time possessed a lawyer, August Philips, who 'with the most resilient, indefatigable, flexible, subtle and seemingly simple talent, succeeded in overcoming practically all the legal difficulties'.[31] August Philips was the legal adviser to several large undertakings, including the central bank.[32] Frederik Philips will certainly have enjoyed expert advice in this area, and within the family circle. In the course of the 1880s, partly as a result of an improvement in the economy and the general trend within the banking industry, his banking business in Bommel assumed greater significance. The same was true of E. Philips & Co., a banking house established by his uncle, Eduard, in Maastricht in 1871.

In this period, the small town of Zaltbommel was the hub of a prosperous area, the Bommelerwaard, and, according to Van Lanschot, the situation in agriculture there could not have been more favourable. In the nearby city of Den Bosch, this agent of De Nederlandsche Bank stated in his report for the year 1888/9, there was a very lively trade in coffee, especially with Denmark, France, Germany and Switzerland. The cigar industry had a less successful year, but a new margarine factory was established, bringing the number there to three. In 1890, while visiting N. G. Pierson, the president of the central bank, Frederik Philips learned that the correspondentship which he had once disdained was to be upgraded from Class III to Class I. In the view of Van Lanschot, Frederik Philips, with his skill, his solidity and his extensive mercantile connections, was better suited than any other person to expand the sphere of activities of the central bank.[33] In 1890, at the age of sixty, Frederik Philips, merchant, banker and manufacturer, was at the peak of his entrepreneurial career. A few years later, by which time the incandescent lamp works established at Eindhoven in 1891 was in production, a bulletin issued by the Schimmelpfeng information service to its German clients contained the following:

Early in 1891, Fred. Philips, treasurer and correspondent of De Nederlandsche Bank in Zaltbommel and of other important financial institutions in the country, became the sole owner of the long-established firm of Peletier & Philips, acquired the Schröder Brothers' factory building in Eindhoven, formed a partnership with his son, G. L. F. Philips, a mechanical and electrical engineer, and established Philips & Co., manufacturers of incandescent lamps.

31　Ibid., 40.
32　A. M. de Jong, *Geschiedenis van de Nederlandsche Bank*, Vol. 2, 427.
33　Van Lanschot in a letter to De Nederlandsche Bank, 8.12.1890.

The son, who had studied at Delft and was later employed by various electrical companies in Holland and abroad, is the active partner. The father is highly respected and owns a great deal of property in the area.[34]

The banking house was to prove to be of inestimable value in the establishment and subsistence of Philips & Co.'s incandescent lamp works – not as an impressive visiting card, but rather in practical terms.

It goes without saying that Frederik Philips encountered setbacks as well as successes in his business dealings. Perhaps the most striking example is his serious miscalculation when buying the Bommel gasworks, which was then situated in the thoroughfare known as Molenwal, near the harbour. This was sold by public tender and he acquired it for 24,106 guilders, which was considered to be a low price.[35] The works had been established by H. Willemstijn, of Gorkum, who in 1857 entered into a contract with the local council to provide street lighting for an annual sum of 1,499 guilders. The works had a capacity of four hundred cubic metres, divided between two gasholders, and was operated by two men.[36] In 1862 it was bought by J. J. van Tienhoven van den Bogaard & Co., and the new owners carried out major improvements which included laying a new network of cast iron pipes. With the small amount of gas consumed by the 150 or so private customers, revenue was limited. Moreover, continual complaints by the Town Architect concerning faulty operation of the street lamps were a permanent source of friction in relations with the Council. The new owners were ultimately obliged to turn to the Minister of Home Affairs in order to obtain the monies owed to them by the Council. A seemingly insignificant incident involving a fine of $f$9.50 was the last straw, and Van Tienhoven, in turn, decided to rid himself of this burden.

The terms on which Frederik Philips acquired the works included fulfilling the contract for street lighting, which was due to expire on 1 September 1877. The new owner appointed C. F. van Anrooy, a relative, as manager. Also, he reduced the price of gas from eighteen cents to fifteen cents per cubic metre, a step which was accompanied by the termination of the standing charge and the installation of gas meters in public places.[37] By 1872 there were already signs that Frederik Philips would share the fate of his predecessors; these came when Mayor Ketjen remarked at a meeting of

34  Report by Schimmelpfeng, 14.11.1896; archives of the Vitrite Works, Middelburg.
35  H. Roodhuijzen, *Mijn ontslag als curator van de Latijnsche School te Zaltbommel*, 1879, 76.
36  Reports of the General Meetings of the Association of Dutch Gas Manufacturers, 1874 and 1875.
37  Minute Book of the Zaltbommel Council, 20.2.1871; Municipal Archives, Zaltbommel.

the Council that the street lamps cast less light than they had previously.[38] The Town Architect was instructed to investigate the complaints, and subsequently, on 18 October 1875, a committee was set up to study the problems associated with the gasworks and the question of extending the contract. In 1876, the parties having failed to agree either on the terms for extending the contract or on an offer by the Council to purchase the works for a sum of 20,238 guilders, the Council voted to build and operate a gasworks to be situated outside the Oensel Gate. Frederik, who had not only improved the ancillary equipment but also increased the number of retorts from five to sixteen, said that he was willing to sell his 'well-maintained' works to the Council for 30,000 guilders, or to accept a valuation price fixed by three experts to be appointed by the Court of Justice in Tiel.[39] In spite of strong criticism of its policy throughout the area, the Council had set its mind upon building a gasworks, even if this cost twice as much as Frederik was asking. This was described by the opposition as an unwise decision which would cost the community thousands of guilders, while at the level of parish-pump politics the Rev. H. Roodhuijzen saw it as the satisfaction of 'personal feuds' and 'venting their hatred on one person'.[40] The affair produced a split between the thin upper crust of Bommel and the middle class, whose influence in local government was growing. In the Council, the representatives of the middle class had set their next objective, namely control of the 'rich' hospital, and also the orphanage and the almshouses for men and women, which were administered by governors.

In the area of gas supplies, a brief competitive struggle ensued when the Council reduced its price to thirteen cents and Frederik responded with twelve cents. Early in 1880, a few months after the introduction of the incandescent lamp, which caused gas shares to plummet, Frederik Philips suffered his first loss in the lighting business when he finally accepted 5,000 guilders from the Council as compensation for waiving his rights.[41] He wrote off his gasworks; a position was found for the manager, Van Anrooy, in the firm of Peletier & Philips.

In the absence of documentary evidence such as a family archive, or even an illustrative fragment of one, it is well-nigh impossible to plumb the depths

[38] Ibid., 25.11.1872.
[39] B. F. D. Philips in a letter to the Zaltbommel Council, 24.8.1876; Municipal Archives, Zaltbommel.
[40] Roodhuijzen, *Mijn ontslag*, 82.
[41] Minute Book of the Zaltbommel Council, 12.1.1880, and the dossier 'Gasvoorziening Zaltbommel', Nos. 25.06 and 107/1; Government Archives, Arnhem.

of Frederik Philips' personality.[42] What was his attitude to life? Did he, for example, as a nineteenth-century entrepreneur, ever feel himself drawn towards Saint-Simonism?[43] Or did his leaning towards Liberalism lead him to adopt a more independent stance? Any attempt to answer these questions would be speculative. With the exception of the Society for the Common Weal, he does not appear in the socially committed circles of his day or among the notables in the local branches of the Maatschappij van Nijverheid (Society for the Promotion of Industry), or the more socially inspired Vereeniging tot Bevordering van Fabrieks- en Handwerks-nijverheid in Nederland (Association for the Promotion of Manufacturing and Craft Industries in the Netherlands).[44] Professionally, as a merchant, as the sole proprietor of the firm of Peletier & Philips and as the founder of the banking house which bore his name, he projects himself as an individualist, albeit one with excellent relationships. A man with a sound insight into the commercial opportunities, who, in a none too favourable climate for enterprise, had created his own, sizeable, sphere of operations and was completely in his element maintaining and expanding this. It is in the composition of his entrepreneurial activities, which commenced in 1850 or thereabouts in the firm founded by his father and Gerlachus Ribbius Peletier, and reached their climax in the establishment of an incandescent lamp works in partnership with his son, that Frederik's modern and many-sided approach, based on the solid foundations of the family firm, is most clearly recognizable. As a result of his business contacts, including those with the Philipses in Germany, who likewise added banking to their other activities, his outlook and sphere of interest extended beyond the confines of his native land. To his large family[45] he was without doubt a devoted father who, although quite often obliged to be away from home, provided his children with the means and the opportunity to study or, like himself, to deploy their talents in the family business. His son Jacques (1870–98) studied chemistry, and the latter's younger brother Eduard (1872–1967) law. Henri Louis (1863–1935) who, like Anton Frederik (1874–1951), attended the public School of Commerce in Amsterdam, was offered a partnership in the firm of Peletier & Philips by his father in 1889.

Questioned many years later about his father's personal qualities, Anton

---

[42] Bouman, *Growth of an Enterprise*, 14.

[43] J. Meijer, *Zij lieten hun sporen achter, Joodse bijdragen tot de Nederlandse beschaving*, 134 ff; S. Brouwer, *De Amsterdamsche Bank 1871–1946*, 25 ff.

[44] Cf. Chapter 6, page 241 ff.

[45] Five sons, two daughters and three children who died at an early age.

Philips – himself an exceptionally competent merchant who had risen to become a captain of industry – described him as 'a very enterprising man of extraordinary intelligence'.[46] He went on to say that he had inherited his 'feeling for industry', his entrepreneurial spirit, from his father. In particular, the two men – although the times and circumstances in which they lived differed to the point of being incomparable – shared a common urge from within to press ahead with business deals, large or small, and to attempt to shift existing boundaries, even when all personal goals had been achieved. In character, they differed markedly from Gerard Philips, who was ambivalent, more reserved in his approach to the outside world and tended more towards reality than to what lay beyond the horizon. Gerard was accordingly drawn towards the axiom of first making sure of his ground; and he was just as independent and strongly motivated where those matters were concerned in which, as an engineer and co-director of an enterprise, he was primarily interested. In contrast to his father and his brother Anton, Gerard described himself as a *manufacturer*,[47] never as a merchant. In that respect, too, he and Anton, the youngest, were poles apart. Their ages differed by sixteen years, and for this reason alone Anton became an exponent of, and a link with, the succeeding generation. All this was naturally conducive to tension between the brothers, but whether and how this manifested itself is not relevant here. We shall revert to this in the next volume.

A fact which, although it stands alone, can be placed in an historical framework concerns the Jewish origins of the Philips family. It is a circumstance of which Philip Philips and his son Benjamin (1767–1854), in particular, must have been aware and of which the significance was lost to later generations by reason of assimilation. It raises questions concerning, *inter alia*, cultural and economic relationships in the period concerned, which, in the absence of a clear insight, we are unable to outline here. Nor shall we attempt to do so, if only to protect this subject, with its many facets, from narrow apriorism, for which there is no lack of opportunity.

Other prominent figures also were descended from Jewish stock – for example, the renowned margarine manufacturer Simon van den Bergh, of Oss (1819–1907), whose forbears moved from Germany to the tiny village of Geffen, in Brabant, in the eighteenth century. On the urban scene in the period concerned we find bankers like Julius Königswärter, L. R. Bisschoff-

---

[46] Extract from the text of an interview with A. F. Philips, first published in the *Nieuwe Rotterdamsche Courant* and reproduced in the *Meierijsche Courant* on 19.12.1927.
[47] According to various official deeds in which his profession was given.

sheim and S. Raphael & Co., international houses which had thriving offices in Amsterdam and led their competitors in the introduction of new inventions such as telegraphy.[48] They formed lively circles[49] in which the social and artistic problems of the day were discussed at a high intellectual level. After them came bankers like Fuld, Lippmann, Mendel, Rosenthal and many others: 'Their multifarious activities were to prove of the greatest importance to the development of the Netherlands during the transition to modern capitalism.'[50]

In Eindhoven, as in other industrial centres in the country, Jewish businessmen, employing modern methods, were to be found in almost every branch of manufacturing industry. Joseph Elias (1811–91), who hailed from the Hanover area, gave a fresh impulse to the development of linen weaving in Eindhoven when he introduced steam on a large scale for driving looms. He must therefore 'have possessed a different mentality from the rest of the manufacturers'.[51] Other names can be added to the list, including, in the present century, Henri van Abbe (1880–1940), the founder of the Karel I cigar works and of the municipal museum in Eindhoven which bears his name. We now arrive at the point at which the name of this city came to the notice of the world through the manufacture of an incandescent lamp. A century earlier, the Philipses who gave their name to this lamp had become part of the Protestant sector of the population. It was not so much the origin of the family which mattered as its ultimate choice of church in a predominantly Roman Catholic part of the country – a predominance which persisted in the factories, in the Chamber of Commerce in Eindhoven and in other institutions.

In principle, this development can be said to have culminated on 1 February 1826, on which date Benjamin and Lion Philips and their families, together with the Van Leeuwen family of Bommel, became members of the Reformed Church. This noteworthy event in the history of the Bommel congregation (at which twenty-one persons were baptized at the same time) and the entire pastoral preparation, which was conducted at the Philips' home by the Rev. R. Macalester Loup, minister of the Reformed Church in Zaltbommel, is described in 'minute detail' in letters from him to his erstwhile colleague, S. Crommelin.[52] It was a symbol of change in more than

---

[48] Joh. de Vries, *Een eeuw vol effecten – Historische schets van de Vereniging voor de Effectenhandel en de Amsterdamse Effectenbeurs 1876–1976*, 39.
[49] Quack, 'A. C. Wertheim', 27 ff.
[50] J. Meijer, *Zij lieten*, 134.
[51] W. Brand, *Eindhoven, Sociografie van de Lichtstad*, 1937, 61.
[52] R. Macalester Loup, *Omstandig Verhaal betreffende den overgang van Drie Israëlitische huisgezin-*

## Table 5. The descendants of Philip Philips, down to Anton Frederik, and their business activities

Philip Philips (dates unknown)
Tobacco merchant of Veenendaal →

Benjamin (1767–1854)
Tobacco and textile merchant. Moved to Zaltbommel round about 1790 →

**Column 2 (children of Benjamin):**

Lion (1794–1886)
Tobacco and coffee merchant and manufacturer of Zaltbommel →

Philip (1796–1883)
Tobacco merchant and manufacturer of Maastricht and Liège

Joseph (1799–1886)
Tobacco merchant and manufacturer of Maastricht

Frederik (1803–92)
Tobacco merchant and manufacturer of Maastricht and Liège

Isaac (1806–50)
Tobacco merchant and manufacturer of Aachen

Abraham (1810–90)
Tobacco merchant and manufacturer of Offenbach

Alexander (1813–91)
Tobacco merchant and manufacturer of Maastricht

Eduard (1816–1907)
Tobacco merchant and manufacturer of Budapest and later a partner in E. Philips & Co.'s Bank in Maastricht

**Column 3 (children of Lion):**

Karel Samuel (1821–96)
Cigar manufacturer of Aachen

August (1823–91)
Lawyer of Amsterdam

Johannes (1828–91)
Cigar manufacturer of Aachen

Benjamin Frederik David (1830–1900)
Tobacco and coffee merchant, manufacturer and banker of Zaltbommel, and founder partner of Philips & Co. of Eindhoven →

Leonard Isaac Hendrik (1833–1902)
President of the County Court at Tiel

**Column 4 (children of Benjamin Frederik David):**

Gerard Leonard Frederik (1858–1942)
Mechanical engineer, founder partner of Philips & Co. of Eindhoven and director of N.V. Philips Gloeilampenfabrieken

Henri Louis (1863–1935)
Tobacco manufacturer and banker of Zaltbommel

Jacques (1870–98)
Chemist

Eduard Jozef (1872–1967)
Lawyer

Anton Frederik (1874–1951)
Merchant, founder partner of Philips & Co. of Eindhoven, director and later president of N.V. Philips Gloeilampenfabrieken

one sense; and it had been foreseen four years earlier by the Jewish community in Zaltbommel, which had then expressed fears that a number of tax-paying members of the 'highest rank' would be lost to 'another religion'.[53] In the economic sense, the change coincided with the prelude to, or the existence of, the careers of Benjamin's eight sons in the tobacco industry in the Netherlands, Belgium and Germany, to which reference was made at the beginning of this chapter.

In the eighteenth century, for reasons which are unknown to us, Philip Philips moved to the Netherlands, probably from Prussia. He settled in Veenendaal, where in 1767 his son, Benjamin, was born. In 1790 or thereabouts, Benjamin settled in Zaltbommel, where he married Lea Hartog and built a career. In 1807 he bought the imposing house known as Markt 9, where in due course Frederik, Gerard and Anton Philips were born. This house marks the town of Zaltbommel as the home of the Philips family.

In the neighbouring Holy Roman Empire of Germany, which finally disintegrated in 1806, giving way to separate Lands, various reforms were introduced, including greater freedom in the exercise of professions, partial liberation of farmers and the right of ordinary citizens to acquire property from the nobility. But Germans living in the Netherlands – 'and the poorest Dutchman had more civil rights than the richest German' – were ashamed of the 'German situation'. This criticism was voiced in 1843 by an economist from Trier, Karl Marx, who occasionally visited his relatives in Nijmegen and Bommel.[54] Could that be the reason why Philip Philips, and like him Josef Elias and others, were attracted to this small country, with its heritage?

In addition to being the residence and place of business of the family, the house known as Markt 9, in Zaltbommel, played a beneficial role in the lives of visitors. It certainly afforded the most welcoming and hospitable atmosphere for the exiled nephew Karl Heinrich Marx (1818–83), the scientific founder of socialism. He was the son of the Jewish-born lawyer Heinrich Marx, who had been converted to the Protestant faith and who

nen te Zalt-Bommel woonachtig, tot den Hervormden Christelijken Godsdienst, 1826; Government Archives, The Hague.

53 M. Heiman Gans, Memorboek, 1972, 341.

54 W. Blumenberg, 'Ein unbekanntes Kapitel aus Marx' Leben, Briefe an die holländischen Verwandten', International Review of Social History, Vol. 1, 1956, 58.

House and business premises, Markt 9, Zaltbommel

practised in the bishopric of Trier, and Henriëtte Presburg, daughter of Isaac Presburg, a merchant residing in Nijmegen. Lion Philips married Sophie Presburg, a sister of Henriëtte, and thus became Karl Marx's uncle. During their youth the Marx children spent a number of holidays in Nijmegen, and even more with their Aunt Sophie in Zaltbommel.[55]

But we digress, and since we are engaged in the writing of history, we must guard against being carried too far. Questions such as how often the adult Marx revisited Zaltbommel and whether, while there, he spent much time working on his great *oeuvre* are thus not of primary importance in this context. Similarly incidental is the knowledge that Lion Philips acted as executor of the estate of Marx's parents, which was valued at 49,130 guilders, and that in 1863 Marx owed his uncle 5,250 guilders.[56] The surviving correspondence between the Marxes and their relatives in the Netherlands,[57] however, reflects the close-knit nature of the Philips family of Zaltbommel, who were considerably more enlightened than many people in the province. In his letters, Marx characterizes his Uncle Lion as a man who, through his rich experience of life, took a humane, unprejudiced and original view of world events and who, in spite of his years, had kept his youthful enthusiasm. 'I have never forgotten', he said in a letter to his cousin Nannette Philips, 'your father's remark concerning Thorbecke, that "the mules always hate the muleteer".'[58] This was a reference to the complications within the International, as a result of which his power base was threatened. If we look at the 1850s and 1860s, we observe that Marx also maintained close ties with his cousin Jacques (Leonard Isaac Hendrik), then a lawyer practising in Rotterdam, with whom he evidently corresponded on political subjects. He was on a similar footing with the lawyer August Philips, of Amsterdam, in whose company it was 'an intellectual delight'[59] to be, and with whom he stayed on a number of occasions. Frederik Philips, who in the mid-1850s had taken over the reins from his father, and instead of going to university carried on the family business, does not play a prominent role in Marx's letters. A number of them, however, end with cordial greetings to 'Fritz & Co.', a fact which imparts a specific emphasis to this relationship. Marx was charming towards Nannette Philips, who

---

[55] Ibid., 58, 60.      [56] Ibid., 66.

[57] Written between 1853 and 1872, and including seven letters from Marx to Lion (see also Appendix 3), five to Nannette and three from August to Marx. The originals are in the library of the International Institute for Social History, Amsterdam.

[58] Letter from Marx to Nannette, 18.3.1866; Johan Rudolf Thorbecke (1798–1872), Dutch statesman and liberal.

[59] Walrave Boissevain, *Mijn Leven, 1876–1944*, 1950, 44.

took upon herself the task of looking after her father, Lion. We can only guess whether this sympathy alone, or a deeper principle, led to her becoming the holder of the membership card bearing the number 1 which was issued by the Dutch branch of the First International, the international working men's association, which was founded in London in 1864.

After being expelled from his own country, and later from France, Marx had settled in London in 1849. There he tried to earn a living as correspondent of the *New York Tribune* and other newspapers. It was in London that he wrote *Zur Kritik der politischen Oekonomie* (1859), of which he sent a signed copy to August Philips.[60] In a letter dated 12 August 1864 to his Uncle Lion concerning the situation on the stock exchange, Marx mentioned the anxiety caused in commercial circles by the rise in the base lending rate in England, which then stood at 9%. He was convinced that if the rate were to be maintained for a few weeks, there would inevitably be a crash among the myriad of 'swindling joint stock companies'. Marx was referring to the severe international monetary crisis which had commenced in London and which did indeed make 1864 an 'uncommonly disastrous year' in financial and commercial circles.[61] Moreover, the continuation of the American Civil War and the outbreak of hostilities between Prussia and Austria on the one side, and Denmark on the other, left their mark. But besides reports such as these, there was a quite different facet of the correspondence between nephew and uncle. This is revealed in a letter in which Marx reports having obtained a copy of Grove's *Correlation of Physical Forces*. Grove, he informed Lion, had demonstrated that mechanical motive power, heat, light, electricity, magnetism and chemical affinity were in essence merely variants of one and the same force, thereby, according to Marx, disposing of 'repugnant metaphysical illusions' such as 'latent heat, invisible light and electrical effluvium'. This observation must be viewed in the context of an era in which Wilde, in a practical demonstration in Manchester, had shown that electromagnets could be better magnetized by a small dynamo-machine than by galvanic batteries.[62] The development of the dynamo, as a modern aid to production, was nearing the decisive phase. At least there would appear to be grounds for the assumption that the advance of physics was not a distant phenomenon which escaped the notice of Lion and Marx.

Marx stayed in Zaltbommel from 21 December 1863 until 19 February

---

[60] J. Stellingwerf, *Inleiding tot de Universiteit*, 205.
[61] *De Nederlandsche Financier*, 7.4.1865 and 28.4.1865: 'Terugblik op het jaar 1864'.
[62] P. v. Cappelle, *De Electriciteit, hare voortbrenging enz.*, 1893, 60.

Lion Philips (1794–1866)

1864 in order to settle his mother's estate. He was plagued by carbuncles, for which he was treated by the town doctor, A. J. W. van Anrooy, a son-in-law of Lion. 'My uncle even applies plasters and poultices',[63] he said in a letter to Friedrich Engels, who was then staying in Manchester. While in Bommel, Marx went for walks with Lion and Nannette, and he requested Engels to send her a photograph for the album. Without it, how could she believe in 'our Orestes–Pylades relationship'?

It appears that Marx paid another visit to Bommel in 1865.[64] When, in the following year, he was desperately short of money, he may again have looked to Zaltbommel, but presumably in vain. His approachable uncle Lion, who, partly as a result of the element of free thinking in his character, had been more to Marx than a tutorial relative, died on 28 December 1866. 'I have today received the sad news of the death of my uncle, a fine man', Marx said in a letter written to Engels on New Year's Eve. 'He passed away neatly, quickly, surrounded by all his children, fully conscious to the end and showering the vicar with subtle Voltairean irony.'[65] He had learned of Lion's death from Nannette.

Of the letters which passed between the Philipses and Marx in the ensuing years, only one has survived. In 1868 Marx reported to his fellow ideologist Engels that his cousins, of whom, as he put it, August was the only one whom he could 'use', were all travelling.[66] It may be assumed that the growing significance of the International – which by then was no longer merely a matter of working men's associations, but had become a disturbing factor in major European politics – was observed with increasing anxiety in Zaltbommel also. It is possible that Nannette Philips, who was described in one of Marx's letters as 'our Dutch secretary', for some time acted as correspondent, and that it was she who kept him informed about the situation in the Netherlands, where by the late 1860s a noteworthy advance was made in the organization of labour.[67] Be that as it may, the post of Dutch secretary of the International was officially given to Jacques van Rijen[68] on 18 October 1866, although a Dutch branch was not established until 1869. A year after the Paris Commune, the repercussions of which were clearly felt by the Dutch workers' organization, Nannette married H. Roodhuijzen (1833–1910), the minister of the Reformed

[63]  Blumenberg, 'Ein unbekanntes Kapitel', 66.
[64]  Ibid., 107.
[65]  Ibid., 69.        [66]  Ibid., 70.
[67]  I. J. Brugmans, *De Arbeidende klasse in Nederland in de 19e eeuw (1813–1870)*, 1958, Chapter 8.
[68]  Blumenberg, 'Ein unbekanntes Kapitel', 110–11.

Church in Zaltbommel and author of *Mijn ontslag als curator van de Latijnsche School te Zaltbommel* (My dismissal from the post of Governor of the Latin School at Zaltbommel), which was published in 1879 and shed some light on *la vie Bommelienne*. Nannette died in 1885 at the age of fifty.

The last known letter from the Philipses to Marx was written by August. In it he advised Marx not to accept a contract with the Paris publisher Lachâtre, the draft of which he had been asked to scrutinize and which concerned a French-language edition of *Das Kapital*. August Philips also made it clear that, 'even if the speculation were a better one', he was not prepared to advance the 2,000 francs for which Marx had asked. His argument was that he did not desire to encourage publicity for the International; moreover, he felt that the publication was not in Marx's best interests. 'If needs be, I am prepared to provide you, my friend and relative, with financial assistance; but I will not do so for your political or revolutionary aims.'[69]

Blumenberg, by whom the letters referred to here were published in 1957, with observations, took the view that the 'old uncle' would have adopted a similar attitude. His final conclusion, as a summing up of the realistic Lion, seems more than plausible.

In a letter of 31 October 1893 to Henri Polak, the founder of the Algemeene Nederlandsche Diamantbewerkersbond (General Union of Dutch Diamond Workers), Marx's daughter, Eleanor, referred to one of her father's uncles, a fairly well-to-do merchant – 'a very charming old man' – whom her father quite frequently visited. He had a large family, 'my father's cousins', and with them, too, her father was on 'familial terms' until about the time of the Commune. The uncle had died and the cousins 'became too respectable and too frightened', so that she had lost track of them.[70] Hers was an incomplete picture, viewed from a radicalized standpoint in which the co-existence of solidarity and divergent principles appears not to have been fully recognized.

One thing which endured on both sides was the heritage of social engagement. And also, perhaps, a furtive pride, revealed when one of the later cousins observed that 'Marxism has been an immense driving force for socialism and one which in this century has raised the standard of living of millions of workers and their families.'[71] These words were written by Eduard Philips, a brother of Gerard and Anton.

[69] Ibid., 111.      [70] Ibid., 56.
[71] Ed. Philips, *Gedachten en Herinneringen*, 1957, 48.

## Gerard Philips

Gerard Leonard Frederik Philips, co-founder of Philips & Co., Eindhoven – which in 1912 became N.V. Philips' Gloeilampenfabrieken, a public company – was born in Zaltbommel on 9 October 1858. After attending secondary schools in his birthplace and in Arnhem, he enrolled at the Delft Polytechnic in 1876 as a student of civil engineering and construction. In his fifth year there he moved on to mechanical engineering, and in 1883 sat the examinations in this subject. His report read as follows:

Theoretical and practical mechanics, adequate; knowledge of machine tools, more than adequate; mechanical technology, more than adequate; mechanical engineering, adequate; civil engineering, adequate; freehand drawing, adequate; machine tool drawing, good; administrative law, good.[72]

No authentic documents concerning Gerard Philips' youth and his years in Delft are available. To the best of our knowledge, no authorized biography of him exists, nor did he leave any detailed biographical notes. A reconstruction of his career, particularly in the period preceding the establishment of the incandescent lamp works, can therefore be only fragmentary and the product of a great deal of research. Much of what has been handed down, such as his contact with the physicist H. A. Lorentz during his years at the secondary school in Arnhem, or the supervision by him of the installation of electrical equipment on board the S.S. *Willem, Prins van Oranje* in Glasgow in 1883, is based on fantasy and dealt with accordingly.[73] The only personal source which is at our disposal – and this applies also to Gerard Philips' later years as a lamp manufacturer – comprises the surviving portion of his correspondence book for the period 1889–92,[74] a notebook for the period January–March 1893, and some valuable entries in Frederik Philips' current account book for the years 1884 to 1901.

Gerard Philips' closest friends and acquaintances included F. G. Waller, who was later to become the managing director of the Gist- en Spiritusfabriek in Delft, the Amsterdam technologist J. J. Reesse, who was engaged in sugar refining and the manufacture of Portland cement, and the

---

[72] According to information supplied by the Delft University of Technology, 28.2.1974; Philips Archives, Eindhoven.

[73] Leonard de Vries, *Het electron omspande de wereld*, 1951, 207.

[74] The original was lost in 1942. About 100 of the 500 pages which this had originally contained had previously been copied. Hereafter this is referred to as the 'copy-book of Gerard Philips'; Philips Archives, Eindhoven.

Gerard Philips (1858–1942)

engineers N. M. Gratama, J. J. s'Jacob and L. N. H. Dufour,[75] all of whom
were to enter the service of the railways; the last-named achieved fame as an
engineer-electrician with the Nederlandsche Rhijn Spoorweg Maatschappij. Another of his contemporaries, who like himself was destined for a
career in electrical engineering, was H. Doyer, a consulting engineer and the
founder of the Rotterdam-based N.V. Electriciteitsmaatschappij Electrostoom. He had worked at the electrical institute at Hanover which was
headed by Prof. W. Kohlrausch, later at Faraday House in London, and had
rounded off his electrical training with a period of practical experience in
the United States.[76] Two of Gerard's fellow students, J. Stroink and C. D.
Nagtglas Versteeg – both of whom were to become electrical consultants –
also went abroad owing to the absence of suitable training facilities in the
Netherlands. They chose Belgium, where since 1883 the Montefiore
Institute, a department of the University of Liège, had offered graduates of
higher technical colleges a one-year course leading to the diploma of
'ingénieur électricien'.[77] During the first eight years of its existence, this
institute, founded with funds provided by the well-known engineer and
philanthropist G. Montefiore-Lévy, trained more than two hundred electrical engineers, of whom ninety were from other countries. These included at
least fourteen Dutchmen,[78] among them Nagtglas Versteeg, who, after a
period in the employ of the Boudewijnse incandescent lamp works in
Middelburg, completed his studies there. Gerard Philips and he remained in
contact for many years.

   Was Gerard's decision, that his future lay in electrical engineering, taken
while he was at the Delft Polytechnic or shortly after he completed his
studies there? One would not deduce this from his early move to acquire
experience in the shipbuilding industry. In the autumn of 1883 he joined the
young Maatschappij 'De Schelde' in Flushing, which was then building the
S.S. *Batavia* and *Soerabaja*, the first passenger vessels commissioned by the
Rotterdam Lloyd Line. This order, incidentally, was extremely unprofit-
able for the company. The financial year 1883 showed a loss of 150,000
guilders, and by October 1884 the position had become critical. In the face
of this, and with no major orders in sight, 150 people out of a work force of
nearly 350 were made redundant. The directors announced that: 'Of the
office staff, two draughtsmen and two young clerks will leave; Engineer

[75] Copy-book of Gerard Philips, 26.8.1889.
[76] H. van Eeden, *Zestig Jaar Electrostoom 1892–1952*, 9.
[77] *The Electrician*, 18.8.1883: 'Diploma of electrical engineer at Liege University'; cf. *De Ingenieur*, 16.4.1887: 'Het Instituut Montefiore te Luik'.
[78] J. A. Snijders, *De vorderingen der Electrotechniek*, 226.

Plate has been informed that, due to a shortage of work, there is no longer a position for him; the master blacksmith, Van Coevorden, is dismissed, the casting shop contracted as far as possible.'[79] In this depressed situation, the yard must have lost its attraction for Gerard Philips; it is possible that he was one of the two draughtsmen who lost their jobs. At any rate, he left Flushing in November 1884 and moved to Glasgow, which was then the centre of world shipbuilding and the place where the most advanced techniques were employed. Such was its lead, and such the state of the shipbuilding industry in the Netherlands, that for many years the majority of steamships destined for Dutch owners had been built at yards on the Clyde.[80]

As Gerard Philips was later to record, it was in Scotland, after several years as a mechanical engineer at a shipyard in Glasgow, that the sight of a series of articles on the 'electric incandescent lamp' caused him 'to devote more than normal professional interest to this practical result of the application of electrical engineering'.[81] In the twenty-three articles concerned, which were written by James Swinburne and published in the weekly journal *The Electrician* between 26 November 1886 and 26 August 1887, all the stages in the manufacture of the incandescent lamp were explained in detail. But even if his most profound interest had not been thus aroused, he could not have failed to notice in the course of his daily work that installations employing incandescent lamps were widely used for lighting on board ship. They were also being employed on a growing scale for lighting factories and other buildings. Furthermore, it is conceivable that the city of Glasgow, with its electrically illuminated Buchanan Street and waterfront, and the imposing electric lighting in the Caledonian Railway Station, the Gaiety Theatre and the shopping arcades, made more than a passing impression on him. The same may be assumed to apply to the fact that electric lighting, as a teaching aid, had been installed at Glasgow University to illuminate experiments.[82] It accordingly transpired that it was not shipbuilding or mechanical engineering, but electric lighting, with its immense and virtually unexplored fields of knowledge and application, which most strongly attracted Gerard. Although this implied a change of direction, it did not of course yet signify his first, well-considered step as a

[79] G. A. de Kok, *De Koninklijke Weg, Gedenkboek t.g.v. Honderd Jaar 'De Schelde'*, 1977, 64, 72.
[80] Report prepared by the Maatschappij van Nijverheid and discussed at the General Meeting on 11.7.1882: 'The majority of Dutch steamships are being built in Scotland'.
[81] J. Feith, *N.V. Philips' Gloeilampenfabrieken 1891–1916*; the name of the yard at which Gerard worked is not stated.
[82] *The Electrician*, 29.4.1882: 'Electric lighting in Glasgow University'.

James Swinburne
(1858–1958)

Emile Garcke
(1856–1930)

'future incandescent lamp manufacturer'. It did, however, mark the start of
his orientation towards the electrical industry, whose activities at that time
were mainly concerned with electric lighting and telegraphy.

The opportunities then open to the electrical engineer were limited to a
position with a company in this field or with an installation contractor, or
becoming a manufacturer of one or more electrical articles. For those who
aspired to the last of these, the incandescent lamp – for which a large future
demand was anticipated – was the most suitable item for a company
starting on a small scale. Swinburne,[83] whose articles on the manufacture of
incandescent lamps had made such a deep impression on Gerard Philips,
had the following words for those who were interested in becoming
manufacturers – words which embodied both an instruction and a caution:

the success of a lamp maker must soon depend, not on secret processes but on good
business management, not only in making but in selling his lamps. The present high
price of lamps is not due to labour in making but to superintendence, to waste

[83] Sir James Swinburne (1858–1958), superintendent of the Swan factories in Paris and Boston, later
manager of Crompton's Dynamo Works Ltd, president of Bakelite Ltd and president of the
Institution of Electrical Engineers.

To be filled up for Matriculation.                                    SESSION 1886-87.

# UNIVERSITY OF GLASGOW.

№. *14*                              (UNIVERSITY ALBUM.)

Name in Full, *Gerard Leonard Frederik Philips.*

Age at last Birthday, *28*

Birthplace—(Town or Parish, and County; if not in Scotland, write the Country also), *Holland*

Father's Christian Name and Occupation, *Frederik*, *Merchant*

Branch of Study (i.e., Arts, Medicine, Law, or Theology), *Physics*

Classes for this Session, viz.— *Physical Laboratory*

Previous attendance at this University, viz. Sessions 18___

___ on Classes in the Faculty of___.

Present Address,___

Home Address, *Zalt Bommel Holland.*

Record of Gerard Philips' enrolment at the University of Glasgow

through manufacture of bad lamps, which are or are not sold, and to bad business management and waste of money generally. In addition, large sums have often been paid for patents of doubtful value…

Electric lighting, as a new business, needed men who had technical knowledge as well as business capacity. To begin with, electrical businesses had to be managed by men who were either scientific and unbusinesslike or businesslike and unscientific…

The industry is looking more promising now, as electricians are gradually acquiring business habits, and business men see that it is necessary to be technical also. Incandescent lamp making is the most purely scientific branch of electric lighting, and it has therefore suffered most from unbusinesslike management.[84]

In the autumn of 1886, Gerard became an evening student at the Glasgow College of Science and Arts where, under Prof. A. Jamieson, an expert in marine lighting and a man who was greatly in demand as a consultant, he took a course in 'Electric lighting and transmission of power'. At the same time, he enrolled at Glasgow University, where he became a member of the 1886–7 research group in the Natural Philosophy department, which was headed by the eminent physicist, Sir William Thomson (1824–1904), who

[84] *The Electrician*, 26.11.1886: 'Incandescent Lamp Manufacture'.

later became Lord Kelvin. Sir William was then described as the greatest living electrician[85] and, together with Faraday and Maxwell, was regarded as a founder of the science of electricity and magnetism. The copy-books and reports from his laboratory, which are preserved in Glasgow, contain at least twenty-six references to Gerard Philips in connection with research into, among other things, the standardization of electrical instruments, the measurement of the power of electric motors, the lamp counter (one of Thomson's many inventions), power loss in fuses, and the calibration of resistors.[86] His name is mentioned for the last time in a report dated 26 September 1887 to Sir William, in whose absence the details of the day's research were required to be submitted in writing. The report ends: 'Mr Philips has been testing the candlepower of some incandescent lamps and Mr Carver has been assisting him.' A few months earlier, in June 1887, he had passed the examination set by the City and Guilds of London Central Institution, South Kensington, to which the sub-university course 'Electric Lighting and transmission of power' led (see Appendix 4). His training in Delft entitled him to sit for an Honours Grade and he distinguished himself from thirty-three fellow examinees by winning the silver medal and a prize of £5 for the highest marks.[87]

Gerard Philips' 'schooldays' were now definitely over. An ambitious interest, and the acquisition of experience, in the practical aspects of electrical engineering commenced to play a greater role. His Scottish period, which had commenced in shipbuilding, was also over. The Anglo-American Brush Electric Light Corporation, Ltd, of London, which he joined as an engineer, was the new bridgehead of his now well-defined intention to build a future in the electrical engineering field. That this could lie in the manufacture of incandescent lamps did not emerge until later, and then only as one of several possibilities. The association between Gerard Philips and Brush, whose highly qualified staff were renowned for their *esprit de corps*,[88] commenced in the second half of 1887. The company's main works were situated at Belvedere Road in Lambeth, south London. There he was able to observe the multifarious activities of a full line producer in the electrical field and, moreover, one with international ramifications. Gerard was employed in the installation department, at the head of which stood J. S. Raworth, 'a man', as Gerard described him in a

---

85  *The Electrician*, 3.12.1881: 'The Age of Electricity'.
86  Report by J. T. Lloyd, 26.1.1977, Dept of Natural Philosophy, Glasgow University; Philips Archives, Eindhoven.
87  *De Ingenieur*, 1887, 398.
88  *The Electrician*, 10.8.1888, 433 ff.

letter of recommendation addressed to the Holland-America Line, 'whose constant aim is sound workmanship'.[89] Raworth had previously been employed by Siemens Bros., for whom he had installed an experimental arc lamp system for illuminating the saloons of the S.S. *City of Berlin*.[90] This, *The Times* reported on 30 December 1879, was the first successful interior lighting system on board a ship. Gerard Philips also came into contact with the chemical engineer A. Spiller, who was concerned with the manufacture of the 'Victoria' lamp, the Brush incandescent lamp, the assembly of which was mainly done by women and girls under conditions of extreme secrecy: 'our lips are sealed with regard to the contents of this building'.[91] Among the features which distinguished the 'Victoria' lamp from those of Edison and Swan was its squirted cellulose filament.

Of much wider significance than Gerard's engagement with Brush was his personal relationship with Emile Garcke (1856–1930), secretary and financial director of the company and the man upon whom rested the task of supervising its continental business.[92] In the last-named role, Garcke, who hailed from Germany, was responsible for Kremenezky, Mayer & Co., under which name the Brush lamp works in Vienna operated. At the instigation of Garcke, whose knowledge of Germany was of 'inestimable value' to Brush,[93] Gerard was transferred to the agency for the German Empire, in Berlin, at the end of 1887. There, working on his own initiative, he carried out a number of lighting projects, including the construction of a central station and the installation of 470 incandescent lamps and eleven arc lamps in a new building which housed small industries. The engineer in charge of Brush's Berlin branch, which had been set up in 1885, was J. Zacharias, a former German officer with a very keen interest in both the technical and the economic aspects of the incandescent lamp, and the author of a text-book entitled *Die Glühlampe, ihre Herstellung und Praxis*, which was published in 1890.

Brush also built central stations for electric lighting in Hamburg, Bremen and other German cities. The company submitted to the City Council of Berlin plans to illuminate the Wilhelmstrasse, the Askanischer Platz and the adjoining streets.[94] Garcke and Gerard Philips were closely involved in the promotion and planning of these projects and also in the introduction of

[89] Letter from Gerard Philips to the HAL, 14.1.1888; Philips Archives, Eindhoven.
[90] C. J. Basch, *Die Entwicklung der elektrischen Beleuchtung*, 1910, 10.
[91] *The Electrician*, 10.8.1888, 433 ff.
[92] *The Electrician, Electrical Trades' Directory and Handbook*, 1898: a biography of Garcke.
[93] *The Electrician*, 9.3.1888, 491 ff.
[94] *Elektrotechnische Zeitschrift*, May 1888: 'Neuer Plan für Beleuchtung Berliner Strassen'.

Table 6. *Electric lighting in Berlin in the period 1886–8*[a]

| | 1806* | | 1887 | | 1888 | | Increase during 1887–8 |
|---|---|---|---|---|---|---|---|
| Number of installations | 152 | | 333 | | 489 | | 156 |
| Number of arc lamps | 736 | | 1,554 | | 2,249 | | 695 |
| Number of incandescent lamps | 12,705 | | 22,363 | | 45,552 | | 23,189 |
| These installations were served by: | | | | | | | |
| Central stations | 43 | | 163 | | 300 | | 137 |
| Steam engines | 79 | 152 | 124 | 333 | 136 | 489 | 12 |
| Gas engines | 30 | | 46 | | 53 | | 7 |

*Notes:*
* Situation as at 1 April of this and succeeding years
[a] Annual Reports of the Berliner Städtischen Elektrizitätswerke A.G.; Siemens Archives, Munich

electric traction. That in the conversations between these two the notion of Brush setting up an incandescent lamp factory in Holland cropped up was no mere coincidence, as would become clear in 1889.

Brush's chances of gaining a foothold in Berlin, the stronghold of Siemens & Halske and Allgemeine Elektricitäts-Gesellschaft, can be gauged from the text of a convention concluded between these two companies in 1887/8. This provided for equal rights for the parties in their common territory and was aimed at curbing competition between them. It came at the end of protracted negotiations.[95] AEG was reorganized in the wake of this agreement, and its authorized capital was raised from five million marks to twelve million. The company would henceforth concentrate on the building and operation of central stations, although its incandescent lamp department would continue to play an important role. In 1888, AEG achieved an output of about 450,000 lamps and commenced to export this article.

As AEG, with its new corporate structure, also sought to acquire a dominant interest in, and with this control of, the Berliner Städtischen Elektrizitätswerke – a move which 'perhaps signified not an overt, but a secret reorganization'[96] – the company went out of its way to strengthen its ties with the City of Berlin. The effect of this was to bring to an end Gerard's assignment and with this his engagement with Brush, but not his sojourn in

[95]  *50 Jahre AEG*, 1956, 74 ff.
[96]  Felix Pinner, *Emil Rathenau und das elektrische Zeitalter*, 1918, 140.

Berlin. The fact that Brush were driven back is symptomatic of the forceful expansion of Siemens & Halske and AEG in the late 1880s, which led to the German electrical industry assuming the leadership on the Continent. It may be taken for granted that, apart from the confrontation between Brush and its German rivals, Gerard Philips was in a position to make more than a passing acquaintance with Emil Rathenau (1838–1915), the founder of AEG. This explains why, in the autumn of 1889, Rathenau offered him a temporary agency for AEG in Amsterdam.

During his period in Berlin, Gerard also learned a great deal, both technical and economic, about the German incandescent lamp industry, especially as a result of his contact with the Aktiengesellschaft für elektrische Glühlampen, Patent Seel, which had been established in 1886. It is impossible to discover whether Gerard was employed by Seel, and if so in what capacity. The company was headed by Hans Roeder, who, according to commercial intelligence,[97] took a rather optimistic view of life and was not well-versed in financial matters; nevertheless, he was said to be the 'soul' of the enterprise. The lamps which the company manufactured were based on patents granted to Carl Seel of Charlottenburg,[98] which embodied a method of making a homogeneous filament without resort to the flashing process developed by Sawyer and Man, which was also patented in Germany. Seel's filaments were made from silk or wool, impregnated with a mixture of sodium silicate and gum arabic.[99] This seemed to be a valuable discovery, the more so as Siemens and AEG had meanwhile acquired the German rights to Sawyer and Man's patents.

The Seel lamp, which was notable for its low current consumption and differed in appearance from other types by reason of its multiple filament,[100] was soon in great demand in Germany. In 1888, Roeder's company made a net profit of 128,000 marks, and this smoothed the way for a decision to increase the daily output of lamps from 800 to 2,300. In addition, a second works – S.A. Belge pour la Fabrication des Lampes à Incandescence – was opened in Brussels, and a new company – A.G. für elektrische Glühlampen Budapest – established in Austria-Hungary. The latter, which had an authorized capital of 400,000 kronen, was a joint venture with an existing lamp manufacturer, Egger & Co. Documents concerning its financial basis

[97] Report Auskunftei W. Schimmelpfeng, Berlin, 19.2.1895; archives of the Vitrite Works, Middelburg.
[98] Kaiserliches Patentamt, Patent No. 39 464, Class 21, 11.5.1886.
[99] Bright, *Electric-Lamp Industry*, 119.
[100] *The Electrician*, 8.6.1888: 'The Seel incandescent lamp filament'.

# THE SEEL LAMP COMPANY,
### MANUFACTURERS OF
# INCANDESCENT LAMPS
#### Of all voltages, and from 2 to 200 candle-power.

The new Multiple Filament Lamp supplied by this Company (as per drawing) gives DOUBLE LIGHT, and is the MOST ECONOMICAL LAMP yet introduced for Electric Lighting.

The Seel System is protected by patents in all countries, and is the ONLY ONE which does NOT IN-FRINGE on those of other makers.

☞ *A Sample Dozen of any voltage up to 20 candle-power (fitted with either brass collar, screw, spiral or vitrite caps) carriage paid on receipt of remittance of 45s.*

TRADE DISCOUNTS ALLOWED.

AGENTS WANTED
FOR
SPECIAL DISTRICTS.

#### TERMS AND PARTICULARS ON APPLICATION TO
# THE SEEL LAMP COMPANY,
### 13, KING STREET, CHEAPSIDE, LONDON, E.C.

Advertisement for the Seel lamp

reveal that Seel & Co. of Berlin received 130,000 kronen for their patents, and Egger & Co. 150,000 kronen for their assets, while the remaining shares were largely subscribed by Roeder.[101] By the following year (1889), the Hungarian company was obliged to write down the nominal value of its shares by 30%. Meanwhile, in 1888, following exaggerated reports to shareholders and with the co-operation of the banking house of L. & S. Wolff, the parent company had increased its capital from 300,000 marks to 1,800,000 marks, 'of which shares to a value of 1,000,000 marks were foisted on the public at one and a half times their nominal value in the same year, and the remaining 500,000 marks soon afterwards at up to 180% above the nominal value'.[102] Another view of the company's rapid decline was provided by J. Zacharias, to whom reference has already been made

---

[101] Report Auskunftei W. Schimmelpfeng, Vienna, 15.9.1896; archives of the Vitrite Works, Middelburg.
[102] *Elektrotechnische Zeitschrift*, 31.10.1890, 588.

and who, like Gerard Philips, resigned from Brush while still in Berlin. He subsequently spent a brief period as a director of Seel:

Here I took charge of the technical aspect of the incandescent lamp works and, as a result of my numerous journeys in England, Belgium, Switzerland, Italy, Austria and Hungary, the lamp is well known. As the trusted representative of the company, I was sent to Brussels, Vienna and Budapest in connection with the establishment of two factories.

The factory subsequently dismissed all its staff and now operates solely with master craftsmen. Since the beginning of last year I have worked on my own account as an author and patent agent.[103]

By 1889/90 the future of the firm was in doubt. The principal cause lay in dubious aspects of its financial management, such as manipulations with the shares of the Brussels subsidiary and the revaluation of patent rights which had been sold, and in a patent lawsuit brought by Siemens and AEG (did any newcomer at this stage escape?). These events foreshadowed the liquidation of Seel & Co. in 1893. Little concerning the affairs of this company – in the organizational sense, at least – remained hidden from Gerard Philips, as may be gauged from his critical remarks to E. Woschke, an ex-employee of Seel whom he engaged in 1890 for his projected lamp works and to whom he declared that he intended to work: 'quite differently from those Seel people, if possible economically, with no nonsense and with the smallest possible initial losses'.[104]

In view of the time element involved, it may be assumed that Gerard Philips, who moved back to London in January 1889 and joined Zacharias in laying the foundations for the establishment there of a sales outlet to be known as the Seel Lamp Company,[105] could then have had no inkling of the problems which lay ahead. They awarded the Seel agency to Shippey Brothers, Ltd, of Cheapside, London, electrical contractors and suppliers of the Zanni-Shippey lamp,[106] who were renowned for their efforts to break the Edison & Swan monopoly of incandescent lamps.[107] The prospects for the success of negotiations for the sale of the Seel patent in Great Britain seemed bright when, in July 1888, in the case of Edison & Swan against Brush, the lower court ruled that Edison's basic patent was invalid, but upheld the patent on the flashing process. This meant that in Britain there

[103] J. Zacharias to Wilhelm von Siemens, letter of application for position, 15.4.1890; Siemens Archives, No. 21 Lg 315, Munich.
[104] Copy-book of Gerard Philips, 30.12.1890.
[105] Zeitschrift für angewandte Elektricitätslehre, 1889, 124.
[106] British Patent No. 5955, granted to Deodati Zanni and Arthur Shippey in 1883.
[107] The Electrician, 24.8.1888: 'Edison & Swan versus Shippey Brothers'; The Electrician, 7.8.1888, 21.9.1888, and, earlier, 27.8.1886: 'Belling the cat'.

was no longer any legal obstacle to the manufacture of the unflashed Seel lamp. But, as we shall see, this would not be the case for very long.

Whatever may have been the nature of Gerard Philips' association with Seel, he must have had a close personal relationship with Hans Roeder. German firms to whom he wrote on 27 April 1869[108] were told that: 'Information about me can be obtained from Herr Direktor H. Roeder, Aktiengesellschaft für elektrische Glühlampen, Berlin.' He went on to say that he had established himself in London as agent for a number of German electrical manufacturers, chiefly in the areas of arc lamps, switchgear, electric gas regulators, etc., and that he sought other agencies. He had thus bidden farewell to Seel and the German capital. He looked for a new livelihood to England, where a recent piece of legislation, the Electric Amendment Act, 1888, had opened the prospect of substantial urban lighting projects. These, it was widely anticipated, would mark the end of the long recession, particularly in the electrical engineering industry. As stated earlier,[109] this had been brought about by the Electric Lighting Act of 1882, the aims of which included protecting British citizens against abuses at the hands of long-established monopolies, as had earlier resulted from gas concessions. The measure, however, had been too restrictive and had unintentionally slowed down the laying of cables and the construction of central stations. Gerard's desire to establish himself at that precise time provides a further indication of his determination to pursue an *independent* career in the electrical industry. To this end, he kept himself up to date with developments, especially in Britain and Germany. This he did partly by reading and partly by maintaining contact with many people in his field, among them Garcke, Rathenau and Zacharias, but also Grünwald, an engineer employed by Seel, from whom he learned that the situation in that company was no longer *couleur de rose*.[110]

Gerard Philips was now thirty-one. Since leaving Delft, the tide of events had taken him to Flushing, Glasgow, London and Berlin and back to London. It will be abundantly clear that, in the course of his travels, he had learned a great deal about life, built up valuable connections and accumulated a wide-ranging knowledge of electrical engineering. These attributes had enabled him to earn a living,[111] but what the next step would

108  Copy-book of Gerard Philips, 27.4.1889.
109  Cf. Chapter 1, page 26.
110  Copy-book of Gerard Philips, November 1890 (date illegible).
111  At times the impression was created that Gerard Philips was largely dependent upon financial support from his father; this was not so.

be, what deeper interest lay buried, could not be predicted at that juncture. In June 1889, while staying at his London address – 7 Western Road, Brixton – he applied for a position with Messrs Van Rietschoten & Houwens, installation contractors of Rotterdam, who had received an order for the electrical equipment on board the S.S. *Amsterdam*.[112] In his letter he suggested that he might be given a partnership with responsibility for the company's electrical department. This, however, came to nought. The final decision was made dependent upon the company receiving the contract for electric lighting on board twenty new vessels of the Koninklijke Paketvaart-Maatschappij (founded in 1888), and in the event this was awarded to a rival firm. Gerard Philips' next, now more definitive, step was soon to be determined by a totally unexpected development, namely a change in the patent situation in the British incandescent lamp industry. As a result, his position as the London agent for German manufacturers, on which he had but recently embarked, came to be of secondary importance. Before the year was out, he transferred his agencies to Georg Victor Braulik, a German national, in order to leave himself free. Braulik had settled in London, where he took up the British agency for Körting & Mathiesen, an arc lamp manufacturer established at Leipzig in 1889. The two men evidently got on well together, for within a few years Braulik was to become the British agent for Philips & Co. The story that 'Georg Victor claimed to have been first in importing incandescent lamps into the UK'[113] continues to circulate in his family up to the present day.

The City of London was taken by surprise, and the last hopes of those with an interest in the British incandescent lamp industry were dashed, when on 18 July 1889 the Anglo-American Brush Electric Light Corporation announced that it had ceased the production of lamps in the United Kingdom. The company had reluctantly agreed henceforth to purchase lamps from Edison & Swan on the most favourable terms which the latter granted to their dealers.[114] As a *quid pro quo*, Edison & Swan had accepted a licence from Brush on the Lane-Fox patents, for which they would pay a royalty of a farthing per lamp,[115] but in fact they made little or no use of these patents. The protracted legal battle on the subject of patents – which became known in Britain as 'The Great Incandescent Lamp Case', and in

[112] Copy-book of Gerard Philips, 26.6.1889.
[113] Report by P. I. Nicholson, Mullard, Ltd, London, 13.10.1978; Philips Archives, Eindhoven.
[114] Report to Shareholders, reproduced in full, with comments, in *The Electrician*, 19.7.1889 and 26.7.1889.
[115] *The Electrician*, 2.8.1889, 315.

Table 7. *Sales and gross profits of the Brush lamp works in London*[a]

|                      | 1885   | 1886   | 1887   | 1888   |
|----------------------|--------|--------|--------|--------|
| Total lamp sales     | 22,806 | 27,601 | 36,735 | 53,654 |
| Sales in U.K.        | 12,348 | 18,510 | 23,040 | 31,531 |
| Cost price (£)       | 2,690  | 2,898  | 4,311  | 4,993  |
| Value of sales (£)   | 4,585  | 4,815  | 6,809  | 9,501  |
| Gross profit (£)     | 1,895  | 1,917  | 2,498  | 4,508  |

*Note:*
[a] Garcke File, Brush Archives, Loughborough

which Brush's 'Litigation Suspense Account' rose to more than £15,000 by the end of 1888 – ended after three years in a compromise. We shall deal with this matter in due course. Lane-Fox, who was closely involved and who suffered as a result of the sharp fall in the value of his patents, vehemently rejected the agreement reached with Edison & Swan. The incandescent lamp, he argued at the extraordinary general meeting of shareholders, was of great significance for the progress and prosperity of the electrical industry, and it would be a serious setback if 'the manufacture of the lamp were to be in the hands of any one company'.[116] A few months later Lane-Fox terminated his eight-year-old association with Brush and regained control of the rights pertaining to his patents.

Commencing in 1886 – that is, from the time of the lawsuit between Edison & Swan and Woodhouse & Rawson[117] – Brush were obliged to indemnify their agents and clients against the consequences of legal action threatened by Edison & Swan.[118] By instituting proceedings against the Jablochkoff Electric Company and the General Electric Company, both Brush agents, and also against their client, William Holland, manager of the Albert Palace, Edison & Swan, of course, were indirectly attacking Brush's position. Pending the outcome of an appeal in the case against Woodhouse & Rawson, and in anticipation of the admission of Brush as a third party, the court ruled that the defendants could retain their stock of lamps, but might not add to this. Brush therefore had no choice but to attempt to undermine Edison & Swan's position in the area of patents. Referring to the impending dispute, Lord Thurlow, the chairman of Brush, said: 'We have not only a good case, but an overwhelmingly strong case.' He went on to express his distaste for the affair in the following words:

---

[116] *The Electrician*, 26.7.1889, 309.      [117] Cf. Chapter 1, page 28.
[118] *The Electrician*, 13.8.1886: 'Incandescent Lamp Patents' by E. Garcke.

This litigation, while exceedingly to be regretted, from its serious character to your interests, is however, of far graver importance to the Edison & Swan Co., involving as it does the validity of the most important of their incandescent lamp patents, which, as would appear from their Balance Sheet, stand at about £300,000, and upon which they rest their claims for an absolute monopoly of lamp making.

The Board takes this opportunity of placing on record their regret that their efforts to bring about an amicable settlement, consistent with your interests, have failed, and that everything points at present to the necessity of the case being submitted to the final decisions of the Courts of Law.[119]

The case against Edison & Swan came before the court in April 1888 and lasted twenty-three days.[120] Practically all the experts involved, including Swan himself, appeared as witnesses, but their testimonies were completely contradictory.[121] Mr Justice Kay, finding himself in a labyrinth of technical details and statements, could only conclude that it was pointless to try to reach a judgement on this basis, and he therefore decided to concern himself solely with facts. He proposed that each of the parties, in the presence of the other and of an independent expert, should have a number of *saleable* lamps manufactured by an 'intelligent workman' and in accordance with the specifications set out in Edison's basic patent.[122] The result of the test would determine whether, on the basis of Edison's description, a successful and thus saleable lamp could have been manufactured other than by a person such as Lane-Fox, who already possessed comparable or greater knowledge. Professor G. G. Stokes, the president of the Royal Society, who was invited to act as the independent expert, agreed to report the results to the court. It was decided that the tests should be conducted at the Edison & Swan works at Ponders End and at William Crookes' laboratory in Kensington Park Gardens, and they took place in June 1888. Crookes and Prof. Silvanus P. Thompson acted as observers representing Brush, while Prof. James Dewar and Dr John Hopkinson acted on behalf of Edison & Swan. The willingness of these prominent scientists to assist in the manner proposed implied that the technical criterion established was acceptable; it also illustrates the distinction between the technical and scientific disputability of exclusive rights to the use of the discovery and the purely legal claim to such rights.

On 28 June 1888, Professor Stokes submitted his report to the court.[123]

[119] Report to the Shareholders of the Anglo-American Brush Electric Light Corporation, Ltd, 1887.
[120] *The Electrician*, 20.4.1888: a full report. See also succeeding issues.
[121] *Elektrotechnische Zeitschrift*, August 1888, 400 ff.
[122] *The Electrician*, 1.6.1888, 115.
[123] *The Electrician*, 6.7.1888, 269 ff: 'Text of Prof. Stokes' report'.

The works of the Woodhouse and Rawson manufacturing company – one of the last infringers

During the tests at the Edison & Swan factory, two lamps failed immediately, seventeen others after an average burning time of thirteen hours, and twelve continued to burn after thirty-two hours. The results at Crookes' laboratory were even worse. Of the hundred lamps tested, Mr Justice Kay was informed, only four burned for more than sixty hours. The specifications of 1879, therefore, could not be said to produce a commercial success, i.e. a lamp which could be made in large quantities cheaply and, above all, possessed a long life. Such lamps had neither been used nor sold either in the United States or in Britain. One witness, Alexander Bernstein, an electrical engineer and incandescent lamp manufacturer, who travelled to the United States in December 1880, said, among other things: 'I was exceedingly anxious to see the incandescent lamps in the market, and made repeated inquiries as to the Edison lamp, of which I had seen so much in the papers, but could not find any in the market or elsewhere.'[124] In this context, it is interesting to note that a representative of Siemens Bros., who had earlier made a fruitless search in New York, reported on the activities of the Edison Electric Light Company as follows: 'It supplies an incandescent light, it makes a good deal of stir in the papers and amongst the more speculative portion of the public, but so far I have not discovered any evidence of its doing any business with the electric light.'[125] The conclusion was thus that the earliest incandescent lamp manufactured commercially by Edison – the one with the bamboo filament, which was patented in September 1880 – was not introduced until the Paris Electricity Exhibition of 1881. Mr Justice Kay had ruled in advance that the claim that the basic patent must in principle be held to apply to all types of carbon filament, including bamboo, was too far-reaching. What weighed most heavily, however, was the evidence based on the tests, which showed that, on the basis of the information published in 1879, no researcher could have produced a successful incandescent lamp unless, like Edison, Lane-Fox, Swan and others, he had earlier acquired special knowledge. Mr Justice Kay's verdict, delivered on 16 July 1888, therefore destroyed the validity in Great Britain of Edison's basic patent on the following grounds:

the claim for a monopoly of incandescent lamps containing a filament of
    carbon for a burner must be regarded as far too wide considering how
    little Edison had actually invented;

[124] *The Electrician*, 11.5.1888, 19.
[125] G. von Chauvin, New York, in a letter to Siemens Bros. & Co., London, 17.5.1881; Siemens Archives, No. 36 Lh 816, Munich.

the specification did not describe a lamp which ever became, or could
  have become, commercially successful;
the directions contained therein were so insufficient that no one could
  have made the carbons described without considerable previous
  experiment;
one of the processes described, namely mixing the carbons with volatile
  powder, was practically injurious if done as Edison directed;
coating with a non-conducting, non-carbonizing substance, if not
  injurious, was of no practical utility;
the same could be said of coiling the filaments, on which the patentee laid
  great stress.[126]

In the earlier case involving Woodhouse & Rawson, the Court of Appeal
had upheld Edison's basic patent, though only after evident hesitation.
Now, however, quite different, mainly technical, arguments proved
decisive. The other issue in dispute (the 'minor issue') concerned the patent
on the use of the flashing process,[127] which was known in Britain as the
Cheeseborough Patent, the British rights to which had been bought by
Edison & Swan. This patent, the judge ruled, was valid. He rejected Brush's
plea that this was an invention by the French chemist Despretz for
homogenizing the carbon rods used in arc lamps, a description of which,
identical to that in the Cheeseborough Patent, had appeared in the *Comptes
Rendus* of 1849.[128] He based his judgement on the fact that the use of the
process in the manufacture of an incandescent lamp filament constituted a
new application.

The outcome of the case, which was welcomed by many electrical engineers
in both Britain and Germany,[129] implied, among other things, that there was
no obstacle to the sale of the unflashed Seel lamp in Great Britain. As
mentioned earlier, Gerard Philips assisted in bringing this about. Woodhouse & Rawson reopened their lamp works in London and announced, in
addition to an order for 200,000 lamps, a new type which did not require to
be flashed.[130] After losing their case in January 1887, they had transferred
their lamp manufacturing activities to St Nicolas d'Airlemont, near
Dieppe,[131] where components – which were still made in England – were

---

[126] *The Electrician*, 20.7.1888, 344 ff: 'Judgement of Mr. Justice Kay'.
[127] Cf. Chapter 1, page 16.
[128] This description was republished in Britain round about 1877/8.
[129] *The Electrician*, 20.7.1888 and 27.7.1888.
[130] *The Electrician*, 24.8.1888 and 21.12.1888.        [131] *The Electrician*, 23.1.1887.

assembled, the bulbs exhausted and the finished lamps sold on the French market. In the Netherlands, too, the new freedom of trade in incandescent lamps was discernible. Two days after Mr Justice Kay's verdict, the Dutch manufacturer Johan Boudewijnse of Middelburg was approached by the General Electric Company in London on the subject of a contract for the supply of unflashed lamps. Boudewijnse, however, replied that no satisfactory result could be expected from such a lamp, 'so that I find it unnecessary to spend several hundred pounds to try it'.[132]

The Anglo-American Brush Electric Light Corporation, which felt that it had emerged from the court as the victor, was at pains to point out that its 'Victoria' lamp in no way infringed any patent and was superior to all other lamps, both British and foreign, in terms of price, useful life and efficiency. The company congratulated its shareholders on Mr Justice Kay's ruling on the main issue, and embarked on the building of a new factory at Brook Green, London, for the manufacture of this lamp on a large scale.[133] Edison & Swan engaged new legal advisers and entered an appeal against the judgement. The case was reopened in December 1888.

As before, Edison & Swan's target was not Brush, as the producer, but William Holland and other Brush clients. Paradoxically, the writs were issued by the very lawyers whom Brush had already retained for their defence, should the need arise:

Some time before the present action was commenced the Brush Company thought it would be wise on their part to secure the services of the three eminent counsel – Sir Richard Webster, Mr Aston and Mr Moulton, and accordingly retainers were duly offered and accepted. Shortly afterwards the Edison & Swan Company – who were evidently alive to this transaction – entered their action against Holland, and the same three above-named eminent counsel, knowing nothing of Holland, accepted retainers on behalf of Edison & Swan. The Brush Company was by no means willing to relinquish its claim upon their services, neither were the opponents. However, an understanding was eventually arrived at on this point of etiquette, and in the action against Holland the three eminent Q.C.s appeared on behalf of the plaintiffs. But now comes the rub: if Edison & Swan enter an action against the Brush Company to prove infringement and obtain damages, then the three eminent counsel will be found on the side of the alleged infringer![134]

The verdict of the Court of Appeal, which was delivered on 17 February 1889[135] and, primarily on legal grounds, revalidated Edison's basic patent,

132 Copy-book of Boudewijnse, 7.8.1888; archives of the Vitrite Works, Middelburg.
133 *The Electrician*, 12.10.1888, 742; 'Circular to shareholders by E. Garcke'.
134 *The Electrician*, 22.2.1889, 447.
135 *The Electrician*, 22.2.1889, 461 ff. *The Electrician* carried verbatim reports of this and the other cases referred to.

did not, however, signify the end of the conflict, which had dragged on for three years. It would require a fresh trial to determine whether or not the Brush lamp infringed the now restored Edison patent. In the short term – and this was a factor of great importance – neither party had any prospect of succeeding. The situation could be paraphrased in the sometimes heard lament that the patent regime in Britain was 'akin to the State lottery in France or Italy'.[136] The situation was made more intractable when Brush announced its intention to lay the most recent verdict – and, by implication, the question of sound patent legislation – before the highest court in the land, the House of Lords.

Almost inevitably, the tenets of the two parties governed their acquiescence in, and the terms of, the convention of 18 July 1889 referred to earlier. This could have been predicted when Brush, in an interim statement to shareholders, disclosed that the manufacture of incandescent lamps represented at most ten per cent of its total business, adding: 'We can get on without making lamps.'[137] Edison & Swan, in a statement issued in May, had in turn announced their intention of terminating their installation activities in order to concentrate on the manufacture of lamps and fittings.[138]

The Board of Brush, which spoke of 'a new point of departure', and changed the sonorous title of the company from Anglo-American Brush Electric Light Corporation, Ltd, to Brush Electrical Engineering Company, Ltd, heartened its shareholders with the announcement that it had acquired Falcon Works, a locomotive and carriage works in Loughborough.[139] With this, Brush entered upon the new and as yet unexplored area of electric traction. The simultaneous merger with the Australasian Electric Light, Power and Storage Company, Ltd, was but a first step towards the wide field of activity which lay in the British dominions and colonies. This was to become increasingly important, indeed indispensable, in the 1890s, when, in the face of German competition, the British steadily lost ground on the European continent. In 1896, after unsuccessful negotiations with AEG, Brush's substantial interests in Austria-Hungary were taken over by Schuckert & Co. of Nuremberg.[140] The companies concerned, which at that time employed about eight hundred people, formed the basis for Oester-

136  *The Electrician*, 20.7.1888, 329.
137  'Proceedings at the Eighth General Meeting, March 13th, 1889'; Brush Archives, Loughborough.
138  *The Electrician*, 31.5.1889, 82.
139  *The Electrician*, 19.7.1889, 285: 'Report to shareholders to be presented to the extraordinary general meeting, July 22nd, 1889'.
140  Meinhardt, *Entwicklung und Aufban*, 54; cf. minutes of the Board, 1895.

Table 8. *The Brush 'Victoria' lamp – manufacturing costs in the first six months of 1888 (London)*[a]

Number of lamps produced in the first six months of 1888: 42,313
Of these:

|  |  |
|---|---|
| 65¼% were sold | 27,620 |
| 6¼% failed while on test | 2,604 |
| 2 % were supplied as replacements | 879 |
| 26½% were put into stock | 11,210 |
| 100 % | 42,313 |

|  | Total (£) | Per lamp (d.) |
|---|---|---|
| Material costs | 1,382 | 7.8 |
| Wages | 625 | 3.5 |
| Salaries | 139 | 0.78 |
| Factory maintenance | 215 | 1.21 |
|  | 2,361 | 13.29 = 1s.1.29d. |

If allowance is made for rejects and the replacement of faulty lamps, the average cost per unit rises to 1s.2.59d. If the stock of lamps has to be viewed as unsaleable (in pursuance of a possible legal ban on their sale), the cost becomes 1s.8.51d. per unit. The average price received for the lamps was 3s.6½d.[b]

Notes:
[a] Extract from the Garcke File; Brush Archives, Loughborough
[b] Woodhouse & Rawson reported an average profit of between 1s.6d. when 2s.od. per lamp in 1889; cf. *The Electrician*, 6.7.1894, 278

reichische Schuckertwerke A.G. A few years later, the Brush lamp works in Vienna, which had been a success from the outset, was bought by Johann Kremenezky, who continued to operate it on his own account. The new and unused Brush factory at Brook Green, in London, was sold to the General Electric Company in 1893 for £1,500.[141] Henceforth, Lord Thurlow emphasized, the company's principal aim must be not the 'small jobs', but major industrial projects such as the application of electricity in the mining industry, electric traction and, most important of all, the construction of central stations. Whatever the future might bring, the manufacture of incandescent lamps in Britain – 'a troublesome business' – had not been a rich source of income for the Corporation.

The Electric Amendment Act of 1888 gave rise to an upsurge of

[141] Minutes of the Board, 1893.

electrification in Great Britain. On 19 September 1889, the *Financial News* reported plans for the construction of 474 central stations in England and Scotland, with an average capacity of 10,000 lamps. Edison & Swan's lamp sales in the United Kingdom were assured until 10 November 1893, the day on which the basic patent expired; but in the years which followed, the company would be exposed to severe competition from abroad. The erstwhile competitor, Brush, which had shed one activity and was now devoting most of its energies to heavy electrical engineering, benefited from the enforced specialization. The company never resumed the manufacture of lamps in Great Britain.

Under the terms of the compromise reached with Edison & Swan, Brush undertook not to produce lamps in Britain while Edison's basic patent remained in force. This imposed decision, which the company at first found difficult to swallow – 'I know that the majority of this Board was of the opinion that if we had gone to the House of Lords, we should have won our case'[142] – naturally created internal difficulties. Above all, it meant that years of work on the part of Emile Garcke, who bore responsibility for Brush's interests in this sector, had been wasted. It also led to renewed contact between Garcke and Gerard Philips, who in 1889, as we have seen, was living in London, where he had closely followed the progress of the court case. The burning question in the two men's minds was whether, and if so how, the production of the Brush lamp could be restarted in the Netherlands. The idea developed into a proposition,[143] and at that stage, not surprisingly, Gerard Philips, as an interested party, was permitted to study the details of the process.[144] In October 1889, firm proposals were submitted to the Board of Brush, and after considering these the Board decided that the negotiations with 'Messrs. Philips' – that is, Gerard and his father, Frederik Philips – should be continued.[145] It appears most probable to us that Brush sought an arrangement whereby its valuable processes, and with these the now surplus manufacturing plant in London, could be vested in a Dutch company in which the Messrs Philips could have an interest and undertake the role of local management. It would thus be analogous to the system – known as 'long-arm management' – which Brush had successfully employed at its lamp factory in Vienna, Kremenezky, Mayer & Co., since

---

[142] Lord Thurlow, addressing the Extraordinary Meeting of shareholders; cf. *The Electrician*, 26.7.1889, 308.

[143] The documents which could provide more detailed information to support this cannot be traced.

[144] Cf. Chapter 6, page 259 ff.          [145] Cf. Chapter 1, page 1.

1884. There, the day-to-day affairs were controlled by Johann Kremenezky and Ignatz Mayer.[146]

At the end of October 1889, pending further developments in the negotiations with Brush, Gerard Philips transferred his headquarters from London to Berlin. There he called on Hans Roeder, the managing director of A.G. für elektrische Glühlampen, Patent Seel, from whom he learned that the company was not doing at all well and that the price of lamps had fallen sharply to between 1.50 and 2 marks. Gerard also visited Emil Rathenau, from whom he received an offer to look after AEG's interests for the duration of the negotiations which were then in progress with the Municipality of Amsterdam. This offer was to assume unexpected significance. The temporary engagement, of itself a piquant interlude in the uncertain situation in regard to Brush, assumed unwelcome ramifications when it transpired that news of it had reached Garcke prematurely through J. Hannema, a partner in the electrical contractors Mijnssen & Co., and, moreover, that he had been given only part of the story. Garcke had been informed that Gerard Philips, who was then living in a guesthouse at 332 Nieuwe Zijds Voorburgwal in Amsterdam, had accepted the *full* agency for AEG. This led to a thorny situation which, Gerard decided, demanded not only an early meeting between them, but also an explanation on his part. 'Under these circumstances', he said in a letter to Garcke on 16 December 1889, 'you will probably not be inclined to give me any information concerning the prospects for the continental lamp industry, or the cost price of your lamps, which I requested in my earlier letters – questions which are of paramount importance if we are to start a factory over here.'[147] Alas, the further details are obscure, for there ends the last surviving letter from Gerard to Garcke. There too – and more importantly – ended the prospects for the establishment by Brush, in association with the Messrs Philips, of a lamp works in the Netherlands.

The later sources in London mention only that Garcke needed a long rest and a change of scene.[148] His health had suffered as a result of the years of wrangling over patents and of his immense efforts on behalf of Brush's interests in Austria-Hungary. A few months later, in April 1890, the Board of Brush voted a sum of £10,000 for the expansion of Kremenezky, Mayer & Co.'s works in Vienna, increasing its annual capacity to half a million

[146] Report Auskunftei W. Schimmelpfeng, Vienna, 17.10.1896; archives of the Vitrite Works, Middelburg.
[147] Copy-book of Gerard Philips, 16.12.1889.
[148] Minutes of the Board, 8.1.1890 and 22.1.1890.

lamps.[149] No further reference was made to the establishment of a lamp works in Holland.

Many years later, on the occasion of the twenty-fifth anniversary of Philips & Co. (in 1916), Gerard recalled how he had sought, and found, contact with the then 'pretty powerful' Anglo-American Brush Electric Light Corporation, Ltd. 'There was even talk of their setting up a factory in association with our people in Holland, but nothing came of this. They went somewhat too far in their demands.'[150] Be that as it may, it is certain that Gerard and Frederik Philips displayed keen interest in the plan in order, like other Dutch entrepreneurs, to play a real part in the manufacture of incandescent lamps. Before we proceed to reveal the progress of their plans in this direction and the manner in which this was achieved, we must examine the circumstances in which the Dutch lamp industry came into being, and, as a prelude to its existence, the development of electric lighting between 1880 and 1890. The latter is of importance in visualizing the consumer aspect of electric lighting, which in the first instance owed more to central stations and the work of the installation branch than to individual users.

149  Ibid., 23.4.1890.
150  *Nieuwe Rotterdamsche Courant*, 28.3.1916.

The Edison & Swan lamp works at Ponders End, Middlesex

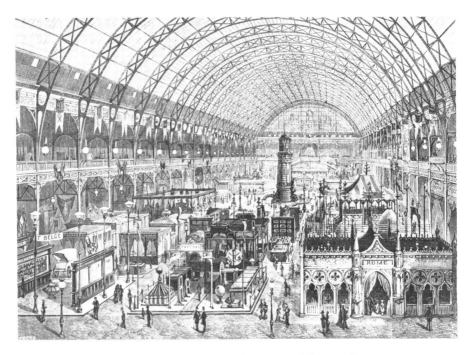

The main hall of the Paris Electricity Exhibition of 1881

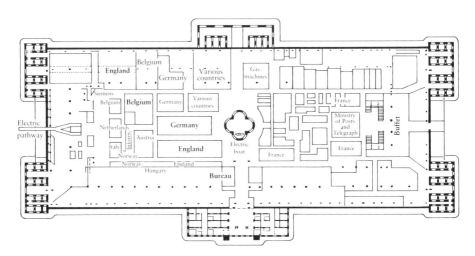

Plan of the exhibition area

# Chapter 3

# ELECTRIC LIGHTING 1880–90

A *tableau vivant* of the state of the art at the beginning of the 1880s was provided by the first international electricity exhibition, which took place at the Palais de l'Industrie on the Champs-Elysées in Paris from 1 August to 15 November 1881.

With its unusual variety of products of the application of electrical engineering, the exhibition was first and foremost a manifestation of the latest developments, such as mechanical power generation, telephony and, above all, electric lighting. The exhibits of electric telegraphy, which had been in use for forty years and constituted the oldest application, covered both the governmental and private sectors. The multiple telegraph system and signalling apparatus for railways and fire brigades occupied a prominent position. The initiative for the exhibition, in which sixteen countries participated, was taken by the French Minister for Posts and Telegraphs, A. Cochery.[1] A better time and place to observe the latest advances in electrical engineering, and the direction in which it was advancing, would be hard to imagine. With the exception of telegraphy and electrochemistry, both low-tension applications, the practical uses for electricity were then limited; ten years later, electrical engineering, as an independent branch of industry, was to prove to be a driving force in the United States and Europe, and especially in Germany. Amid the contemporary experiences of learned men and technicians, the Paris exhibition served to accentuate the transition to a direct relationship with, and the purposeful involvement of, research in the area of natural science for the benefit of commerce, industry and art.[2] Electric lighting and the dynamo made their debut as demonstrable examples of this development. The scientific interest aroused by the incandescent

---

[1] A. Cochery, Rapport au Président de la République, reproduced in *Catalogue Général Officiel*; Industry Department Archive, Government Archives, The Hague.
[2] *The Electrician*, 17.12.1881: 'Electric lighting at the Paris exhibition'; cf. various contributions in *La Lumière Electrique*, 1881.

87

The Edison Room at the International Electricity Exhibition in Paris, 1881

lamp, more than any other article on display, was ultimately to lead to a chain of products. In the shorter term, the lamp as demonstrated at the exhibition provided the main impulse for the construction of central stations and, with these, the spread of the system for the efficient generation and distribution of electricity. Once established, these stations encouraged the use of electric current for driving motors and for a whole range of other industrial and domestic purposes.[3] This vision was most convincingly evoked by the wide range of products displayed by Edison, who was represented in all sections of the exhibition.

With the Edison system and those of Swan, Lane-Fox and Maxim, the Paris exhibition was the commercial launching pad for a new and remarkable consumer article, the incandescent lamp. After 1881 it was available wherever demand arose.

Virtually every electric lighting system was on display in Paris. Night after night the public gathered to marvel at the spectacle of five hundred arc

[3] Bright, *Electric-Lamp Industry*, 10.

lamps and two thousand incandescent lamps. Mounted on the roof of the Palais de l'Industrie were two 40,000-candlepower Maxim arc lamps, one of which lit up the Place de la Concorde.

If one examines the various types of arc lamp shown on the basis of their origin, the superior ingenuity of the French, in both qualitative and quantitative terms, is immediately apparent. There were no less than ninety-three exhibits from France, bearing such names as Berjot, Cance, Carré, Chertemps, Debrun, Dubosq, Gérard, Gravier, Jamin, Méritens, Mersanne, Reynier, Sautter & Lemonnier and Serrin. It was again the French who took the initiative in employing arc lighting in industry, e.g. for illuminating factories, in which the steam engine was the source of power. The Ducommun foundry at Mulhouse and the Gramme dynamo factory in Paris had been lit in this manner, with Serrin lamps, since 1875. Within the space of a few years their example was copied at scores of manufacturing plants in France.[4] In a report prepared for the Société Industrielle in Lyons in 1878, Marchegay, an engineer, expressed the view that factory owners chose electric lighting not so much on grounds of lower cost, but because it enabled them 'to oversee everything, as in daylight'. For piecework, in particular, a more uniform work pattern had the advantage of preventing errors and loss of time.[5] In 1876, Gramme supplied thirty-five dynamo machines for the lighting of factories in Britain, Russia, Austria-Hungary and other countries.

In the area of arc lighting, which had reached the commercial stage by about 1875, the *regulateur* was the most widely used lamp.[6] In this self-adjusting lamp, in which the carbon rods were placed in line, a sequence of operations occurred automatically:

when the current was switched on, the tips of the rods were brought into contact with one another;

after the initial contact, the tips moved the desired distance apart so that the current and voltage passing between them corresponded to the correct values;

as the rods were consumed, the gap between them was adjusted, keeping current and voltage as constant as possible.

Until 1880 or thereabouts, electrical engineers took the view that only

---

[4]  *Revue Industrielle*, 1875 and successive years; *Tijdschrift Mij. van Nijverheid*, 1877, 179 ff: 'Over elektrieke verlichting'.

[5]  *Tijdschrift Mij. van Nijverheid*, 1879, 408 ff: 'Het tegenwoordig standpunt der elektrieke verlichting'.

[6]  Th. Dumoncel, *L'Eclairage Electrique*, 1879.

Table 9. *Cost estimate for a Jaspar arc lamp (guilders) (1881)*

| | |
|---|---:|
| *Initial cost* | |
| Jaspar-type *regulateur* | 125 |
| Fitting | 100 |
| Gramme dynamo for one lamp | 675 |
| Steam engine, 3 hp with enclosed boiler | 1,800 |
| Miscellaneous items | 70 |
| Freight, packing and duties | 80 |
| Total | 2,850 |
| | |
| *Hourly running costs* | |
| Carbon rods | 0.13 |
| Fuels | 0.12 |
| Engineer | 0.18 |
| Depreciation at 10% per annum, based on 6 hours' burning per day | 0.13 |
| Total | 0.56 |

direct current could be used for lighting purposes. In arc lamps, this resulted in the positive rod burning away more rapidly than the negative. In an effort to overcome this particular problem, the diameter of the positive rod was doubled; and with this and other difficulties in mind, improvements were made to the regulating mechanism. The refined differential *regulateurs* developed by Siemens, Brush, Crompton and a number of other manufacturers – which were also suitable for multiple current distribution systems – could also be used for street lighting. In the *lampe soleil* developed by Clerc and Bureau, which was conspicuous by its reddish light, the vertical carbon rods were separated by refractory material. The *regulateur monophote*, which was invented by Jaspar of Liège, was one of the simplest and most efficient lamps, and was principally used for illuminating public rooms and workshops. It gave a pleasing light and for this reason attracted attention to the relatively large Belgian stand at the Paris exhibition. A. J. van Eyndhoven, the supervisor of the municipal gasworks in Haarlem, who visited the stand,[7] received from Jaspar the cost estimate for a 2,500-candlepower arc lamp shown in Table 9.

Also among the products on display in Paris was Jablochkoff's 'electric candle', and this was considered to be a major advance in arc lighting. In an

[7] A. J. van Eyndhoven, *Verslag dd. 22.11.1881 aan B & W van Haarlem van den opzichter over de gasverlichting betr. zijn reis naar Parijs, ingevolge Raadsbesluit van 6.9.1881*, Municipal Archives, Haarlem; cf. *Tijdschrift Mij. van Nijverheid*, 1882, 1 ff.

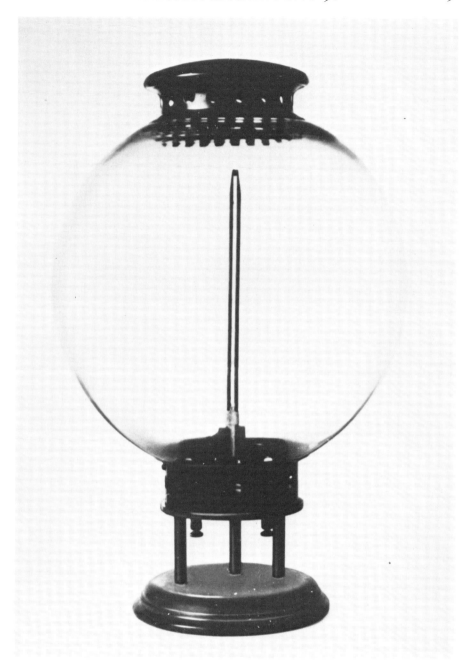

The Jablochkoff Candle, 1878

experiment conducted in the Avenue de l'Opéra in May 1878, thirty-two of these lamps in a single circuit had been energized simultaneously. Not only was this the first demonstration of the distribution of electric light,[8] but also a more or less successful example of electric street lighting.[9] Because of its simplicity, namely the absence of any mechanism for controlling the gap between the carbon rods, the electric candle, or *bougie*, seemed to have an assured future. It consisted of two parallel, vertically mounted carbon rods which were separated by an insulator made from plaster of paris and barium sulphate. The tips of the rods were coated with a thin layer of fine carbon which ignited as soon as the circuit was completed, whereupon the substance between the tips – which evaporated at the high temperature produced by the arc – assumed the role of conductor. Uniform consumption of the rods was achieved by feeding the lamp from an alternating current dynamo designed for the purpose by Gramme. Later models had five or six rods and incorporated a commutator which ensured that when one rod was burned away a new one would be ignited. A standard rod 25 cm long and 4 mm in diameter burned for two hours and thus it was necessary to replace the rods in these lamps after every ten to twelve hours of use.

The inventor of this electric candle, Paul Jablochkoff, was born in Serdobsk, in Russia, in 1847. It was in the workshop of the renowned French instrument maker Breguet, in Paris, that he realized his idea. In 1876, while on his way to the World Exhibition in Philadelphia, Jablochkoff stopped in the French capital and, finding much more to see there in the electrical field than could have been expected in the United States at that time, he decided to stay. Up to 1877, America had contributed little to the development of arc lighting or the dynamo.[10] Jablochkoff had received general technical training at the College of Military Engineering and the Military Galvano-Technical School in St Petersburg, where electrical engineering was among the subjects taught. Since 1872, five years before the outbreak of the Russo-Turkish War, the Russian navy had been equipped with electric searchlights[11] and, according to Figuier,[12] it was thanks to these that the ports of Odessa, Sebastopol and Orchakow had been spared from night bombardment by the Turkish fleet, which could be observed at a range of four to five kilometres. After a brief career as an army

---

[8]  Van Cappelle, *De Electriciteit*, 194; cf. *Tijdschrift Mij. van Nijverheid*, 1877, 223.
[9]  *Tijdschrift Mij. van Nijverheid*, 1878, 460 ff: 'Iets naders omtrent elektrieke verlichting'.
[10]  Bright, *Electric-Lamp Industry*, 30.
[11]  Cf. Chapter 4, page 140.
[12]  Figuier, *Het Elektrische Licht*, Chapters 4 and 17.

Table 10. *Prices of Jablochkoff standard candles in Paris (1878–81)*[a]

| Year | Price per unit[b] | Burning time[c] | Price per hour[b] |
| --- | --- | --- | --- |
| 1878 | 75 | $1\frac{1}{4}$ | 60 |
| 1879 | 60 | $1\frac{1}{2}$ | 40 |
| 1880 | 50 | 2 | 25 |
| 1881 first half | 40 | 2 | 20 |
| 1881 second half | 30 | 2 | 15 |

Notes:
[a] Van Eyndhoven, *Verslag dd. 22.11.1881*
[b] in centimes
[c] in hours

officer, Jablochkoff was appointed director of the telegraph link between Moscow and Kursk. In this position it fell to him to ensure that the railway line was illuminated when the Czar travelled at night – a measure which proved indispensable when the Nihilists resorted to violence in pursuit of their political aims.[13] Their actions were the grim counterpart of the violence witnessed in the New York slums during the 1880s, which was to contribute in the same measure to the spread of electric lighting.[14] Jablochkoff was moved by these events to concentrate on developing the arc lamp. Several years were to pass before he could apply the results of his work fully and profitably in western Europe.

With the ample funds provided by financiers, Jablochkoff's invention was actively promoted in France and elsewhere. This was done by the Compagnie Générale d'Electricité, which was established in 1877. Four years later the company increased its capital from Fr. 7.5 million to Fr. 20 million. By then, four thousand lamps had been sold all over the world and the demand for 'candles' was running at more than two million annually. Between 1878 and 1881, the price of standard candles, which had a power of 40–50 Carcels,[15] declined, as shown in Table 10.

The Jablochkoff lamp was the first type of electric light to be used on this scale.[16] In Paris, as well as in other French cities, it was widely employed in

[13] *The Electrician, Electrical Trades' Directory and Handbook*, 1893: 'In the year 1872 the Nihilist propaganda first began to inspire terror, and when the Emperor travelled by rail it was decided to light up the track in front of the engine by means of arc light. Jablochkoff was responsible…'
[14] *The Electrician*, 5.10.1888, 693: 'in the US police officers testify to its utility in the prevention of crime and protection of life and property'.
[15] A unit of luminous intensity in use until about 1885.
[16] *The Electrician*, 7.1.1882, 120 ff.

Table 11. *Cost of installing Jablochkoff lighting systems*[a]

|  | 4 lamps | 6 lamps | 8 lamps | 16 lamps |
|---|---|---|---|---|
| *Dynamo for* | | | | |
| 4 lamps | 3,000.00 | | | |
| 6 lamps | | 3,500.00 | | |
| 8 lamps | | | 4,000.00 | |
| 16 lamps | | | | 6,000.00 |
| *Conductor wire* | | | | |
| 150 metres | 225.00 | | | |
| 200 metres | | 300.00 | | |
| 300 metres | | | 450.00 | |
| 600 metres | | | | 900.00 |
| *Clamps* | | | | |
| 10 | 7.50 | | | |
| 10 | | 7.50 | | |
| 15 | | | 11.25 | |
| 20 | | | | 15.00 |
| *Connectors, excl. supports, approx. Fr. 100 per lamp* | 400.00 | 600.00 | 800.00 | 1,600.00 |
| *2-way switches* | | | | |
| 3 | 36.00 | | | |
| 3 | | 36.00 | | |
| 3 | | | 36.00 | |
| 5 | | | | 60.00 |
| | 3,668.50 | 4,443.50 | 5,297.25 | 8,575.00 |
| *Installation charge and 5% contingency allowance* | 183.40 | 222.15 | 264.85 | 428.75 |
| Total | 3,851.90 | 4,665.65 | 5,562.10 | 9,003.75 |

*Note:*
[a] According to a French price list dated July 1879; Siemens Archives, No. 36 Lh 815/817, Munich (Prices in Fr. francs)

theatres, department stores and public buildings, and for street lighting. In London, where the Jablochkoff Electric Light and Power Company, Ltd, had been established – and had acquired the relevant patent rights – an experiment in street lighting was carried out. This commenced on 1 April 1881 and took the form of a 'contest'[17] between Brush, Jablochkoff and Siemens, each of whom was allocated an area of the City which corresponded to a cable run of about 1,500 metres. Such was the rivalry that

[17] *Tijdschrift Mij. van Nijverheid*, 1881, 130.

Brush offered to illuminate the whole of the metropolis by electricity at the price charged by the gas manufacturers, but at a far greater intensity. The Brush, Jablochkoff and Siemens systems were the main contenders for the honour of electrically illuminating the cities of Europe. At that juncture, the desire for more and better light, but also the element of luxury, outweighed considerations of cost.

The public reaction to the incandescent lamp, as a new form of interior lighting, was no less favourable, according to G. Oyens, an official Dutch observer at the Paris exhibition.[18] He predicted that lamps of this type would soon be in general use in homes, particularly if the 'secondary batteries' attained the anticipated degree of perfection.[19] He was strengthened in this view by the fact that engineers were joining forces in order to turn what they had seen and learned at the exhibition to good account.

Van Eyndhoven, the Haarlem gas expert, was more reserved, particularly towards the incandescent lamp. The useful life of lamps of this type varied within very wide limits, some lasting for weeks or even months, while others failed after a few hours. 'And when you consider that they originally cost 15 guilders, now perhaps a little less,' he argued,[20] 'it is obvious that this system is still far too expensive for domestic use.' He was assured that lamps could be made for between one and two guilders, but this he seriously doubted, observing the difficulty which had been experienced in achieving a complete vacuum in these 'masterpieces of the glassblower's art'. It is clear from this that to him the notion of manual assembly giving way to mass production was beyond belief. His views on, and comparison of, the Edison, Swan, Lane-Fox and Maxim lamps[21] are also worthy of mention. The most powerful Edison lamp was rated at sixteen candlepower, and one horsepower was required to excite ten of these simultaneously. On this basis, Van Eyndhoven postulated, fear of competition with gas lighting was premature, unless one based one's calculations on the price of gas in New York, which was then equivalent to twenty guilder cents per cubic metre. In Paris the cost was fifteen cents, in Haarlem only nine cents, and in many parts of Holland it was even less. The spherical lamp produced by Swan, which Van Eyndhoven described as 'the best', was rated at 20–25 candlepower; ten of these lamps absorbed one horsepower, but as Swan did not

18  'Verslag en Algemeen Overzicht der Internationale Electriciteits-Tentoonstelling, 1881, aan Z.E. de Minister van Waterstaat, Handel en Nijverheid', January 1882; Government Archives, The Hague.
19  This is a reference to Faure's promising improvement of the accumulator in 1881.
20  Van Eyndhoven, *Verslag dd. 22.11.1881.*
21  See Table 12, page 98.

manufacture a dynamo, they were fed with Brush or Siemens units. With its looped filament, the Swan lamp gave the impression of being 'a glowing mass', whereas with the others the shape of the filament could be distinguished. A further insight is provided by his description of the method employed by Lane-Fox to make filaments, which then already included immersing the fibres in a zinc chloride solution. The Lane-Fox lamp, which was exhibited on the Brush stand, gave a good if somewhat yellowish light. Lastly there was the Maxim system, marketed by the United States Electric Lighting Company,[22] which like Edison's differed from the others in that it incorporated its own dynamo and other elements necessary for a complete lighting system. It performed less than satisfactorily at the exhibition, however. In Van Eyndhoven's description of the manufacturing process for the Maxim lamp, the flashing process is discernible. This lamp, it was said, had an average life of between six hundred and nine hundred hours and would sell for only ƒ3.50.

The overall conclusion reached by Van Eyndhoven was that with the appearance of the incandescent lamp, gas faced a strong competitor in the lighting field, certainly in areas where an abundance of light was required and cost was of secondary importance. He admitted that the two differed in a fundamental respect, namely that the additional light which could be provided by gas was limited owing to the effects on the atmosphere and temperature in an enclosed space. Two years later he was to explain this in detail with the aid of figures, and go on to show that whereas with gas lighting the products of combustion and the surplus heat had to be exhausted, an electrically lighted room required considerably less ventilation.[23] For these reasons, and in the light of the reduced fire risk, he concurred in the desirability of lighting theatres, coffee houses and similar establishments by electricity. From his numerous observations at the Paris exhibition, Van Eyndhoven drew the following conclusions:

> that in the space of a few years, major advances had been made in arc lighting and that a number of efficient lamps had been developed;
> that the distribution of electric light, which a short time beforehand was impossible, had become a fact thanks to the invention of electric candles, differential *regulateurs* and incandescent lamps;
> that electric lighting, particularly by means of incandescent lamps, nevertheless could not possibly compete with gas in terms of cost.

[22] Cf. Chapter 1, page 16.
[23] *Tijdschrift Mij. van Nijverheid*, 1884, 234 ff: 'Vergelijking uit een hygiënisch oogpunt tussen gas- en electrische verlichting'.

In his report to the Mayor and Aldermen of Haarlem, in which he expressed the opinion that the time for a pilot scheme to light part of the city by electricity was not ripe, Van Eyndhoven went so far as to predict that the incandescent lamp was not 'the light of the future'. This role, he believed, was preserved for the arc lamp, even though it had not yet been perfected to the point where it was suitable for domestic lighting. Like so many of his colleagues and contemporaries, Van Eyndhoven shared the view then held by Werner Siemens (1816–92), namely that if he, Siemens, could overcome this last hurdle, the arc lamp might still triumph over the incandescent lamp. The Board of Brush also continued to cling to this idea. Even allowing for Siemens' pride in being regarded as the proverbial authority in the world of electrical engineering – pride which had so far prevented him from employing foreign patents[24] – the idea of perfecting the arc lamp was an acceptable reason for declining Edison's offer of the continental rights to his lighting system.[25] Edison thereupon established the Compagnie Continentale Edison in Paris, from whom a consortium which included Emil Rathenau, the Berlin machinery manufacturer, bought the German patent rights which Siemens had spurned. For these the consortium paid 350,000 marks, which was considered to be a bargain. The engineer and merchant, Rathenau, who had visited the Paris exhibition, recognized the potential which the incandescent lamp offered for mass production.[26] As was stated earlier, this transaction – which covered the manufacturing rights for all the components of the 'complete lighting system' – gave rise to the Deutsche Edison Gesellschaft and later to AEG. In 1882, after the failure of Siemens' efforts to develop his own incandescent lamp, his company was obliged to opt for the Swan process.[27] But in the following year he came to terms with the Deutsche Edison Gesellschaft; the reconciliation stemmed partly from a desire to prevent the patent dispute between Edison and Swan being imported into Germany via the two companies.

During the 1880s, incandescent and arc lighting continued to be a focus of attention for electrical engineers – not, however, as competitors but as complementary systems. After that decade, in which the electric lighting

---

[24] Basch, *Entwicklung der elektrischen Beleuchtung*, 55 ff.

[25] Siemens initially described Edison as 'an American go-ahead inventor who had had neither time nor opportunity to educate himself, and who was out to make money quickly'; cf. *Zeitschrift für angewandte Elektricitätslehre*, Vol. 2, 1880, 83: 'Dr. Werner Siemens über die neue Edison'sche Lampe'.

[26] *50 Jahre AEG*, 27.

[27] G. Siemens, *History of the House of Siemens*, Vol. 1, 1847–1914, 1957, 93.

Table 12. *Incandescent and arc lighting, Paris Electricity Exhibition 1881*[a]

| Type of lighting | System | Make of dynamo | Intensity in standard candlepower per foyer | Horsepower required per foyer |
|---|---|---|---|---|
| *Incandescent lamp* | Lane-Fox | Brush | 10–25 | 1/10th |
| | Maxim | Maxim | 25–40 | 1/6th or 1/12th |
| | Swan | Various | 12–25 | 1/10th |
| | Edison | Edison | 8–16 | 1/19th and 1/10th |
| *Arc lamp* | Brush | Brush | 2,000 | 32/40ths or 13/16ths |
| | Gülcher | Gülcher | 500–1,000 | 10/12ths or 10/6ths |
| | Piette & Krizik | Schuckert | 1,000 | 10/12ths |
| | Gravier | Gramme | 4,000 | 1/2 |
| | Gérard | Siemens | 760–950 | 2/3rds and 1 |
| | Gramme | Gramme | 1,425 | $1\frac{1}{2}$ |
| | Jaspar | Gramme | 2,500 | $2\frac{1}{2}$ |
| | Sautter, Lemonnier & Co. | Gramme | 4,250 | 2 |

*Note:*
[a] Report by A. J. van Eyndhoven, superintendent of gas lighting in Haarlem, concerning h
visit to Paris pursuant to a decision taken by the Council on 6 September 1881 (Haarlem, 2
November 1881)

Remarks

ood light, but slightly yellow.

or light. Far less white than Swan's. Decidedly pinkish.

ear light, very pleasant to read by. Certainly the best of the incandescent lamps.

nsteady light. Not as good as Swan's. Yellowish in colour.

ood light, but an extremely dangerous system.

ne of the best systems, I feel. The lamp is very simple. The *regulateur* gives a constant,
od, white light.

ce white light. Excellent for distinguishing colours. A pity it is so unsteady.

ry fine, clear white light. The lamps are among the best to be found at the exhibition. Very
ady. The shape of the bulbs also makes this lighting very neat.

ood light, but not steady at all times. Makes quite a lot of noise, but the simplicity of the
ulateur makes it highly suitable for industrial purposes.

fferential lamps. Clear, white, soft light. Fairly steady. However, the lamps emit an
essant ticking noise. Certainly more suitable for industrial purposes.

ne of the best lamps at the exhibition. As installed there, the light was very pleasing to the
es and also very steady.

ghly suitable for lighting large squares. The lamp, however, is quite complicated and
uld, in my opinion, easily break down.

industry became firmly established, particularly in Germany and the United States, the emphasis moved to electric traction and long-distance power transmission.

After 1881, the Netherlands, which had been represented in Paris by a modest display of industrial products, but more importantly by its past scientific achievements, was to become a focal point of interest and, although a small nation, to play a part in the practical application of electrical engineering which was then taking place in the surrounding countries. In an article which appeared in the *Tijdschrift van de Nederlandsche Maatschappij van Nijverheid* in 1882, F. A. T. Delprat said: 'Anyone who has seen the magnificent lighting on the Champs-Elysées and the Place de la Concorde will be forced to concede that the public could no longer be satisfied with gas lighting, even if it were cheaper.'[28] Two years later this society, at Delprat's instigation, submitted proposals to the governors of the Delft Polytechnic for the training of 'electrical engineers' in order to meet the great need 'for suitable persons to control and carry out installations for electric lighting and other applications of electricity'.[29]

From the Dutch point of view, at least, the Paris exhibition had thus fulfilled its immediate purpose. This fact warrants a brief review of the modest nature and content of the Dutch exhibits in 1881 in comparison with the expansion which, as we shall see, ensued.

In spite of the view, expressed by both Chambers of the States-General, that the Netherlands should provisionally refrain from participating in international exhibitions, following the pathetic and widely criticized showing at the World Exhibition of 1878,[30] the government accepted the invitation extended by the President of France. It appointed three official representatives, men who could also represent the country at the International Congress for the Promotion of the Science of Electricity, which was to take place in Paris concurrently with the exhibition. The three were Prof. J. Bosscha, the director of the Delft Polytechnic; J. M. Collette, the inspector of the Government Telegraph Service; and J. J. van Kerkwijk, a former engineer with the Telegraph Service and at the time a member of the Lower

---

[28] *Tijdschrift Mij. van Nijverheid*, 1882, 102 ff: 'Toenemend verbruik van Elektrisch Licht; voordeelen, voorzorgen, enz.'.

[29] *Tijdschrift Mij. van Nijverheid*, 1884, 69: cf. Handelingen van het Congres van de Mij. te Assen, 8–10 July 1884, 22.

[30] H. Baudet, 'De dadels van Hassan en de start der Nederlandse industrialiteit', in the volume *Bedrijf en Samenleving*, presented to Prof. I. J. Brugmans, 1967.

Chamber. Gerard Oyens,[31] a member of the Board of Compagnie Générale d'Eclairage Electrique, in Paris, the company which marketed the Jamin arc lighting system, offered to represent the interests of the Dutch exhibitors. To generate interest in the exhibition, the Nederlandsche Maatschappij van Nijverheid circularized its members, pointing out the opportunity for private participation. This drew enquiries from forty-five individuals and bodies, including fifteen mechanical engineers, seven scientific instrument makers, five professors,[32] six scientific societies and a similar number of daily newspapers. The profession of 'electrician', which came into being a few years later, does not appear on the list.

The exhibits ultimately numbered 1,781, from sixteen countries (see Table 13 on page 102). These included eighteen from Holland, comprising:

1 M. A. Mills, Amsterdam: various inks for telegraphic apparatus (Bronze Medal).

2 Chr. Mirandolle, Rotterdam: wood preservatives and partially creosoted telegraph poles (Bronze Medal).

3 A. Marijt, mechanical engineer employed at the artillery workshops in Delft: an arc lamp which could operate on direct or alternating current and which was particularly suitable for lighthouses or for factory lighting.

4 Electrische Verlichting-Maatschappij Wisse, Piccaluga & Co., The Hague: electrochemically nickel-plated castings (Bronze Medal).

5 Croon & Co., Fabrikanten van Electrische Instrumenten, Amsterdam: electric clocks and indicators for use in auction rooms (Bronze Medal).

6 Dr P. J. Kaiser, instrument inspector of the Royal Netherlands Navy, Leiden: a collection of ships' compasses, a pair of magnetic scales, a torpedo with an electric indicator which reacted on approaching an armoured vessel, and reports on the tests carried out on these inventions (Gold Medal).

7 H. Olland, Utrecht: an intensity compass based on the ideas put forward by Prof. J. J. Stamkart, and an instrument for determining terrestrial magnetism (Silver Medal).

8 N. van Wetteren, Haarlem: magnetic rods for use in telephones, magnets for producing a rotary motion, magnets to counter the effect of

---

[31] Dossier Internationale Electriciteits-tentoonstelling 1881; Government Archives, The Hague; cf. archives of the Mij. van Nijverheid 1880/1; Municipal Archives, Haarlem.

[32] Professors J. Bosscha, Delft; C. H. D. Buys Ballot, Utrecht; P. L. Rijk, Leiden; J. D. van der Waals, Amsterdam; and W. A. Enschedé, Groningen.

Table 13. Exhibits at the International Electricity Exhibition held in Paris in 1881[a]

| | France | Belgium | Germany | Great Britain | Italy | U.S.A. | Russia | Austria | Sweden | Spain | Switzerland | Norway | Netherlands | Hungary | Denmark | Japan | Total |
|---|---|---|---|---|---|---|---|---|---|---|---|---|---|---|---|---|---|
| **Section I** | | | | | | | | | | | | | | | | | |
| Power generation, dynamos, accumulators | 121 | 14 | 19 | 17 | 15 | 14 | 9 | 8 | 1 | — | 2 | — | — | 2 | 1 | 1 | 224 |
| **Section II** | | | | | | | | | | | | | | | | | |
| Cables, conductor wires and lightning conductors | 56 | 20 | 3 | 14 | 7 | 6 | 1 | 2 | 4 | — | 1 | 1 | — | — | — | 1 | 116 |
| **Section III** | | | | | | | | | | | | | | | | | |
| Measuring instruments for use in electrical engineering | 24 | 5 | 10 | 10 | 3 | 1 | 4 | 1 | 3 | — | — | — | — | 2 | — | — | 63 |
| **Section IV** | | | | | | | | | | | | | | | | | |
| Applications of electricity | | | | | | | | | | | | | | | | | |
| Telegraphy, signalling | 112 | 27 | 14 | 16 | 8 | 11 | 2 | 8 | 5 | 8 | 1 | 1 | 2 | 1 | 2 | — | |
| Telephony, microphony, photophony | 30 | 18 | 5 | 10 | 8 | 5 | 3 | 4 | 2 | 3 | 3 | 2 | — | 1 | — | — | |
| Electric lighting | 93 | 5 | 10 | 14 | 2 | 10 | 4 | 3 | — | 2 | 1 | — | 1 | 2 | — | — | |
| Motive power, electric motors | 52 | 7 | 2 | 2 | — | 5 | 1 | — | — | — | 1 | — | — | 1 | — | — | |
| Medicine | 29 | 1 | 9 | 3 | 8 | — | — | 1 | — | — | — | 1 | — | 1 | — | — | |
| Electrochemistry | 43 | 9 | 4 | 2 | 5 | 3 | 3 | — | — | — | 1 | 2 | 1 | — | — | — | |
| Precision equipment, electric clocks, electromagnets, compasses | 107 | 15 | 2 | 6 | 7 | 3 | — | 6 | 3 | 1 | 3 | 4 | 4 | 1 | 1 | — | |
| Miscellaneous | 123 | 14 | 21 | 7 | 5 | 6 | 3 | 6 | 2 | 3 | 3 | 1 | 1 | — | 1 | — | |
| Total, Section IV | 589 | 96 | 67 | 60 | 43 | 43 | 16 | 28 | 12 | 17 | 13 | 11 | 9 | 6 | 3 | — | 1,013 |
| **Section V** | | | | | | | | | | | | | | | | | |
| Machinery, steam and gas engines, hydraulic motors | 73 | 10 | 3 | 9 | — | 3 | — | — | 1 | — | — | — | 1 | — | — | — | 100 |
| **Section VI** | | | | | | | | | | | | | | | | | |
| History of natural sciences, and electrical engineering, bibliographical collections, drawings, etc. | 80 | 67 | 48 | 11 | 13 | 5 | 10 | 11 | 3 | 6 | 5 | 7 | 8 | — | 1 | — | 265 |
| Total number of exhibits | 943 | 212 | 150 | 121 | 81 | 72 | 40 | 40 | 24 | 23 | 21 | 19 | 18 | 10 | 5 | 2 | 1,781 |

Note:

... of the 'Catalogue Général Officiel' of the exhibition

102

iron on ships' compasses, and magnetic needles of the type used by the Royal Netherlands Navy (Silver Medal).

9  Maurice de Léon & Co., Rotterdam: magnetic toys.

10  W. H. Jacobs, engineer and constructor, Haarlem: a steam engine designed to power dynamos (Bronze Medal).

11  Government Telegraph Service, The Hague: a report on the situation in regard to telegraphy in Holland in the period 1877–9, a description of the equipment and establishments, a manual and a map of the telegraph network in 1880 (Diploma of Honour).

12  V. C. Dijckmeulen, Chief Officer of the Amsterdam Fire Brigade: a map showing the telegraphic links with the various fire stations and alarm bells (Certificate of Recognition).

13  Prof. J. Bosscha, Director of the Delft Polytechnic: collection of papers by Martinus van Marum, including the description of his large frictionally excited disc machine at the Teylers Museum and reports of tests carried out on this between 1785 and 1795, and the description by J. R. Deiman and A. Paets van Troostwijk of the disc machine, with the aid of which they discovered that water could be broken down into its constituent elements by means of electricity (Certificate of Recognition).

14  Nederlandsche Bell Telefoon Maatschappij, Amsterdam: a map of the Amsterdam telephone area.

15  J. J. van Kerkwijk, member of the Lower Chamber and government-appointed adviser to the Telegraph Service, The Hague: his history of electromagnetic telegraphy in Holland, for which he had received an award at the congress of the Bataafsch Genootschap der Proefondervindelijke Wijsbegeerte in Rotterdam in 1870.

16  J. J. F. Steenbergen, bookseller and physicist, Amsterdam: Cuthbertson's book 'Electrische Toestellen', published in Amsterdam in 1784; three volumes of Cavallo's 'Geschriften inzake Electriciteit', Utrecht, 1780; and Deiman's 'Beschrijving van een Electriseermachine', Amsterdam, 1789.

17  Physisch Kabinet der Teylers Stichting, Haarlem: documents including a description by J. Enschedé and J. van Walree of the frictionally excited disc machine of Martinus van Marum, 1785, and accounts of their tests with this machine in 1787 and those carried out by J. J. Beets of Haarlem in 1795.

18  Teylers Stichting (second exhibit): Van Marum's large disc machine, built in 1784 and improved by Cuthbertson in the years which fol-

lowed; electrometers by Adam, Brook, Henley and Lane, used by Van Marum to measure the charge in his Leyden jars; a discharge apparatus used by Van Marum to study the effect of electric sparks on certain materials; a large natural magnet from Siberia with a pulling force of 85 kg; several other heavy magnets of natural and artificial origin, the latter made by Gebr. Van Wetteren of Haarlem (Certificate of Recognition).[33]

The Dutch exhibit was not competitive, nor does this appear to have been the intention. Its merits lies in its very existence, which was due to a small group of individuals and bodies having made up their minds to participate. Admittedly, they carried off twelve of the 607 awards,[34] Dr P. J. Kaiser receiving a gold medal, and H. Olland and N. van Wetteren each a silver medal; more importantly, however, they had demonstrated a desire to be part of a development which had only just commenced. The conclusion to be drawn is that they were moved not by the urge to display their own products, but rather by a wish to be present at this live electrical event. The reports that the electric indicator on Kaiser's torpedo 'drew general admiration from experts', and that the Van Wetteren Brothers' magnets, like Croon's and Olland's electric clocks, could compete with the best from other countries,[35] are therefore of secondary importance in this context.

After the exhibition, the Netherlands were offered a seat on the international committee which had just been formed for the purpose of determining electrical units. Prof. J. Bosscha (1831–1911), Professor of Applied Physics in Delft, was the man chosen to represent his country.[36] Had not the Teylers Stichting, with its display, provided the most convincing proof that the Dutch were still interested in 'everything connected with the dissemination and application of science'?[37]

The Maatschappij van Nijverheid, whose objects included keeping members informed about developments which were of importance to industry and commerce, was quick to declare its awareness of the economic aspects of electric lighting. As early as 1877 its director general, Delprat, taking France as an example, had voiced the expectation that electric lighting would in all probability soon displace all other forms, at least in

[33]  Descriptions derived from *Catalogue Général Officiel*.
[34]  The breakdown of the awards was as follows: France 304, Belgium 60, Great Britain 46, Germany 46, Italy 34, U.S.A. 29, Russia 21, Austria 18, Switzerland 14, Sweden 13, Holland 12, Spain 5, Denmark 2, Hungary 2, Japan 1.
[35]  Report and General Summary of the exhibition by G. Oyens.
[36]  P. N. Haaxman, 'De electrische eenheden', in *Tijdschrift Mij. van Nijverheid*, 1883, 83 ff.
[37]  According to G. Oyens, on page 7 of his report.

'larger establishments'.[38] This was admittedly his personal view, and he attempted to substantiate it with the limited technical and cost data which were then available; but at least it served to bring about a discussion on the subject of electricity versus gas, which in Holland, as elsewhere, was a prerequisite for the introduction of the new source of light. Although he favoured one above the other, Delprat was free of the extremism sometimes manifested in the rising controversy over 'Gas or electric light?' and put forward arguments in support of both. More light in the streets and in public rooms, he maintained, would result in a greater need for more light in the home – which implied electric light – but this would not jeopardize the future of the gas industry, provided, of course, that the gas industry gradually sought other markets and reduced the price of its product so as to make this attractive for heating and for the economic use of the gas engine. To him, therefore, the right path lay in the amalgamation of 'electrical companies' and gasworks – not only to assist in bringing about the anticipated 'revolution'[39] in both the lighting and heating sectors, but equally to protect the two sides from an unnecessary conflict. Between 1877 and 1887, the journal published by the Maatschappij contained at least thirty-five articles on electrical subjects from the pen of Delprat.[40] In particular, these dealt with electric lighting, a field in which he and J. J. Van Kerkwijk (later to become an engineer with the Government Telegraph Service)[41] had long before played an active role.

The earliest practical application of electric lighting in Holland dates from 1854. In November and December of that year it was used during the construction of an iron railway bridge over the River Mark at a point near

[38] *Tijdschrift Mij. van Nijverheid*, 1877, 179 ff: 'Over elektrieke verlichting'; cf. Verslag Algemeene Vergadering van de Vereeniging tot Bevordering van Fabrieks- en Handwerksnijverheid, 1882, 88.
[39] *Tijdschrift Mij. van Nijverheid*, 1882, 275 ff: 'Gas en electriciteit'.
[40] F. A. T. Delprat (1812–88) received his training at the School of Artillery and Engineering in Delft, and the Royal Military Academy in Breda. In 1871 he was promoted to the rank of major general. He became Minister of War in 1872, and was commanding officer of the fortifications of Amsterdam from 1873 to 1875. He then retired from the army. Between 1875 and 1885 he occupied various administrative posts, including the chairmanship of the Nederlandsche Maatschappij van Nijverheid and membership of the Amsterdam City Council. Cf. biography in *De Ingenieur*, 1888, 130.
[41] J. J. van Kerkwijk (1830–1901) received his training as a civil engineer at the Royal Academy in Delft. From 1852 to 1855 he was employed as an engineer by the Antwerpen-Rotterdamsche Spoorwegmaatschappij, and from then until 1875 as an engineer with the Government Telegraph Service. He was then appointed to the post of adviser to this service and to the Ministry of Finance. He became a member of the Lower Chamber of the States-General, the City Council of The Hague, and the central committee of the Vereeniging tot Bevordering van Fabrieks- en Handwerksnijverheid. He published papers on diverse subjects. Cf. biography in *De Ingenieur*, 1905, 355.

Zevenbergen. The time of year, adverse weather and other difficulties necessitated extraordinary measures if the work was to be completed before the onset of winter. To the engineer-in-charge, Van Kerkwijk, only one course was open: to double the labour force and work day and night. In this respect, the situation was identical to that which had faced French engineers a year previously during the rebuilding of the bridge which crossed the Seine near Notre Dame. The modern solution which they had devised led to a new method of working which had simultaneously gone down in history as the moment at which electric lighting was first used successfully to carry out major public works.[42] In Holland, this remarkable fact had been publicized in the 'Extracts from foreign journals'[43] published by the Koninklijk Instituut van Ingenieurs (Royal Institute of Engineers) and at the meeting of that body, and had thus come to Van Kerkwijk's notice. Looking back on the completion by this method of the bridge over the Mark, he observed:

The test to establish the suitability of electric lighting for works such as were carried out here can be said to have been a virtual success.

The electric lighting enabled more work to be done in the evening and at night than could be accomplished by sunlight during the day, for owing to the lateness of the season it was at times impossible to work more than seven hours in daylight; it was therefore mainly due to the use of electric light that the bridge, of which the final girders arrived on 5th December, could be crossed by the locomotive on the 21st. If one compares the time which it took to build this bridge with that required for other, much smaller bridges in this country, one will agree that a bridge of this size has never been built here in so short a space of time, and that this is largely, if not entirely, a result of the successful experiments with electric light.

That light may thus be recommended in many cases as a means of completing all manner of work in a shorter time, particularly if the number of workmen cannot be increased on account of lack of space or for other reasons.

It cannot be denied that the cost of the light is fairly high; nevertheless I believe that, in an age in which the value of the adage of our great neighbours – 'Time is Money' – is beginning to be really understood, it will be used on many future occasions.[44]

The artillery captain F. A. T. Delprat, to whom reference has already been made, and who was then lecturing at the Royal Military and Naval Academy in Breda, introduced students to the working of the electric arc lamp. He modified a Jaspar lamp which had been loaned to the academy, with the result that the carbon rods burned for nearly two hours and could

[42]  Figuier, *Het Elektrische Licht*, Chapter 15.
[43]  *Uittreksels uit vreemde tijdschriften*, KIVI, 1853–4, Nos. 2, 3 and 4.
[44]  J. J. van Kerkwijk, 'Over het gebruik van elektrisch licht enz. in den spoorweg van Antwerpen naar Rotterdam', in *Verhandelingen van het KIVI*, 1854–6, 200 ff.

be replaced in thirty seconds. Fed from a battery of forty Bunsen cells, the lamp emitted a glow by which 'the finest pencil writing' could be read within a radius of 14 ells (the Dutch ell was equivalent to about 27 inches), while at $2\frac{1}{2}$ hours' walking distance it conveyed the impression that 'something was on fire'. Van Kerkwijk estimated the running cost of this source of light at $f$ 1.14$\frac{1}{2}$ per hour, made up of $f$ 1.10$\frac{1}{2}$ for battery acid and four cents for carbon rods. The initial cost of the lamp (100 Fr. francs) and the Bunsen cells (four francs each) was not included in his figures.

Until the arrival of the dynamo in the mid-1870s, it was applications such as this which proved the incidental value, in practical terms, of electric lighting, e.g. for coastal illumination. This form of artificial light also served the cause of entertainment to some extent. An example is to be found in the appearances of the 'Ghost of Maju', which were part of the 'Spectres Impalpables', a pageant of light staged in the Butter Market in Amsterdam in 1864, with which L. K. Maju – in real life the optician Levie Kinsbergen (1823–86) – drew full houses for many years.[45] This electrical engineer *avant la lettre*, however, also understood the more serious applications, as is evidenced by a request in 1878 for a permit to illuminate the streets of The Hague with Jablochkoff candles,[46] and another, addressed to the Amsterdam City Council, for a permit to lay telephone links. The latter was made in 1879, which implies that he was a year ahead of the International Bell Telephone Company.[47]

The growth of all manner of activities in towns and factories increasingly influenced the latent demand for adequate means of lighting; but so, too, did the need on the part of individuals for comfort and for better education, from both reading and classroom lessons. This trend would not by-pass the Netherlands.

The deployment of arc lighting on a commercial scale, which commenced in France in 1875 and received a fillip with the invention of the Jablochkoff candle two years later, was soon emulated elsewhere. In Holland, an electric lighting company, Electrische Verlichting-Maatschappij Wisse, Piccaluga & Co., was established in The Hague on 24 November 1878.[48]

---

[45]  M. Keyser, *Lomt dat zien, de Amsterdamse Kermis in de 19e eeuw*, 1976, 27 ff.

[46]  L. K. Maju in a letter to the Mayor and Aldermen of The Hague, 28.11.1878; Municipal Archives, The Hague, inventory number 4845 (Maju described himself as a mechanical engineer).

[47]  J. H. van de Hoek Ostende, 'De Geest van Maju', in *Maandblad Amstelodamum*, October 1962.

[48]  W. J. Wisse in a letter to the Chamber of Commerce in The Hague, 10.2.1879; Municipal Archives, The Hague, inventory number 4845.

Willem Johannes Wisse (1846–1926)          Antoine Piccaluga (1811–84)

The partners were W. J. Wisse,[49] assistant director of the Government Telegraph Service in The Hague, A. Piccaluga, a mechanical engineer of Amsterdam, and A. C. van Rhijn, a clerk at the Ministry of Finance. Wisse, who had taken the initiative for the enterprise and been given leave of absence for the purpose by the minister concerned, had approached the City Council of The Hague on 11 October with a request that he be given a concession, subject to conditions to be agreed, for the installation and operation of electric lighting in the municipality for a period of twenty consecutive years.[50] Besides praising the quality of electric light, Wisse laid great emphasis on its 'inexpensiveness' in comparison with the existing lighting provided by municipal and private gasworks. As an example he quoted the development in France which we have already briefly described. Study and personal research, Wisse wrote, had convinced him that electric lighting would soon displace gas lighting in Holland, as elsewhere. Wisse had been studying the principles of electricity since 1867, when he was

[49] Willem Johannes Wisse (1846–1926); clerk at the Government Telegraph Service 1866; telegraphist 1868; assistant director of the Telegraph Service and the postal service in The Hague 1875.

[50] Inventory No. 4845, Municipal Archives, The Hague; cf. Ch. A. Cocheret, *Kamer van Koophandel en Fabrieken voor Den Haag, 1853–1953*, 56–7.

training to be a telegraphist. Antoine Piccaluga (1811–84), who was born in Geneva, also became involved in the science of electricity at a very early date, as is revealed by the fact that as early as 1845 he installed a telegraph line from Amsterdam to Haarlem for the Hollandsche IJzeren Spoorweg-Maatschappij. This was the first electromagnetic telegraph link to be built in the Netherlands.[51]

Wisse had sought the support of the Chamber of Commerce in The Hague for his plan, but before this could be formally discussed, the Council, at its meeting on 5 November 1878, rejected the application. The limited experience in the area concerned was considered to be sufficient reason for not entering into an obligation for so long a period; and, of course, there was the 'great harm' which the municipal gasworks would suffer.[52] The Chamber of Commerce was more receptive, certainly to the novelty as such, and although it was unwilling to voice suspicion concerning the Council's decision, it made clear its attitude, that:

the fact that the municipality operates its own gasworks may never be a reason for rejecting a new form of lighting if this, from whatever point of view, can be of general value; and that it is the duty of municipal authorities to avoid bias in approaching the improvements which science will undoubtedly provide in this area, as in others.[53]

The new company received active support from one of the committees of the Chamber, and to an even greater extent from the chairman, Dr J. Th. Mouton.[54] Moreover, the Chamber used its influence to counter bureaucratic interference on the part of local officials.[55]

In October 1879, the company was transformed into a limited partnership, with Leon Simon Enthoven, the vice-chairman of the Chamber of Commerce and co-proprietor of the engineering firm of L. J. Enthoven & Co. of The Hague, becoming the managing partner. Wisse assumed responsibility for the technical activities, especially electric lighting, while Piccaluga took over the mechanical engineering and chemical side of the business, Enthoven the commercial management and Van Rhijn the administration. The objects of the newly constituted enterprise were:

[51] W. Ringnalda, *De Rijkstelegraaf in Nederland, 1852–1902*, 20.
[52] Report of the council meeting held on 5.11.1878 and the recommendation of the advisory committee for local works, 18.10.1878; Municipal Archives, The Hague, inventory number 4845.
[53] Annual report of the Chamber of Commerce of The Hague, 1878.
[54] Cf. Chapter 6, pages 241–2.
[55] Wisse in a letter to the Chamber of Commerce dated 11.8.1879; archives of the Chamber of Commerce; Municipal Archives, The Hague.

to introduce, operate and supply electric lighting in the Netherlands and
   the Dutch possessions overseas;
to apply electrometallurgy in all its forms;
to act as a commission agent for Siemens & Halske, Berlin, and as agents
   for Fetu et Deliège, of Liège (manufacturers of gas engines), and to
   undertake such agencies as might subsequently be offered by other,
   solid business houses.[56]

After a brief period in another part of The Hague, the Electrische
Verlichting-Maatschappij moved into premises on the Buitensingel, The
Hague. In 1880, the year in which Wisse resigned from the Government
Telegraph Service, the activities were expanded by the addition of an
electrometallurgical works for the gold-, copper- and nickel-plating of
metals. The Chamber of Commerce, in its annual report for that year,
referred to the company's serious approach to business, adding that this
gave grounds for assuming that it had a sound future. The respect and
confidence which the firm enjoyed was enhanced by the acquisition in 1879
of the sole agency for Siemens & Halske in the Netherlands and the Dutch
colonies.[57] Expectations on both sides were high, as is strikingly illustrated
in the following extract from a letter written by Werner Siemens to his
brother, Carl, on 2 January 1882:

Our Dutch agent, Wisse, is here and has brought with him huge projects for lighting
and electric tramways in Holland. He is an industrious man and does good
business. It looks to me as if he is planning to illuminate the whole of Amsterdam,
for the old gasworks is to close next year.[58]

After 1881 there was a marked increase in the number of electric lighting
projects. Wisse, Piccaluga & Co. installed a system with 1,400 Swan
incandescent lamps and eight Siemens arc lamps in the Park Theatre in
Amsterdam. They also installed electric lighting in theatres in Haarlem and
The Hague, and in several railway stations. The firm scored a 'first' with the
electric tramway linking the seaside resort of Zandvoort with
Kostverloren,[59] which was completed in June 1882. In the following year,
large orders were received from principals in the Dutch East Indies, among
whom was the Sultan of Surakarta. On 24 April 1881, *The Electrician* had
carried the headline: 'The land of water has caught the fever', a reference to

[56] Supplement to the Government Gazette, 4.8.1882, No. 182.
[57] J. Wegner, *Siemens in den Niederlanden, Geschichte des Hauses Siemens im Ausland*, Vol. 10,
   1970, 21 ff.
[58] Rebske, *Lampen, Laternen, Leuchten*, 197.
[59] *The Electrician*, 1.7.1882, 146: 'Electric Railway in Holland'.

the lighting at the entrance to the *Passage* in Rotterdam. This and installations in the Arts and Sciences Building in The Hague (1879) and the head office of the Telegraph Service in Amsterdam (1880) were among the first lighting projects to be carried out by Wisse's company. At first it proved impossible to find suitable people in the Netherlands for this new type of work, in which components and materials supplied by Siemens & Halske in Berlin were installed and put into operation[60] by Wisse, Piccaluga & Co., and thus they had to be recruited abroad. This hurdle, however, was overcome within a few years, and by 1883, as the Chamber of Commerce noted in its report for that year, the work force consisted almost entirely of Dutchmen whom the company was continuing to train. By about 1885, Wisse, Piccaluga & Co. provided permanent employment for about fifty persons. Three years earlier, in 1882, the growth of business had led to a transformation from a limited partnership to a limited liability company with the title N.V. Nederlandsche Maatschappij voor Electriciteit en Metallurgie. The authorized capital of one million guilders was required to be fully paid up by 1 January 1888. The initial subscribers and their individual shareholdings were as follows:

L. S. Enthoven, merchant, 68 shares, *f* 34,000; A. C. van Rhijn, industrialist, 48 shares, *f* 24,000; W. J. Wisse, industrialist, 48 shares, *f* 24,000; A. Piccaluga, mechanical engineer, 48 shares, *f* 24,000; M. Giebert, banker, 40 shares, *f* 20,000; L. J. E. Hajenius, retired naval officer, 32 shares, *f* 16,000; G. F. C. Rose, retired naval officer, 36 shares, *f* 18,000; J. Stam, director of the State Lottery and a member of the City Council of The Hague, 32 shares, *f* 16,000; Jonkheer J. F. Schuurbeque Boeije, lawyer, 16 shares, *f* 8,000; H. Raat, retired army officer and a former mayor of Maastricht, 16 shares, *f* 8,000; W. A. Schroot, architect and a member of the City Council of The Hague, 8 shares, *f* 4,000; and M. L. Schroot, architect, 8 shares, *f* 4,000.[61]

The discussion by the City Council of The Hague in 1883 of a fresh application for a concession reflects the general change in attitudes towards electric lighting which had by then occurred. Although the Council at that juncture stopped short of revealing a willingness to grant such a concession to a private company, it clearly felt that, in view of the advances made in electric lighting, the development should not be opposed out of fear of competition with the municipal gasworks.[62] There was therefore no objec-

---

[60] Wegner, *Siemens in den Niederlanden*, 24.
[61] Supplement to the Government Gazette, 4.8.1882, No. 182.
[62] Report of the council meeting held on 2.10.1882; Municipal Archives, The Hague, inventory number 26, report of proceedings; cf. inventory number 28 for the discussion of the application in 1885.

tion to the issue of a mutually terminable permit for the construction of a
central station and the laying of cables within a radius of five hundred
metres of this. In 1885, after a time-consuming procedural phase, the
Nederlandsche Maatschappij voor Electriciteit en Metallurgie accepted the
conditions laid down by the Council, which were only provisional and
precluded a public lighting service. Wisse travelled to Berlin in October
1886 for the signing of the contract with Siemens & Halske for the central
station. Some difficulty was experienced in financing the project, and in the
end the Deutsche Bank and Delbrück, Leo & Co. of Berlin joined with the
Dutch company in providing the funds.[63] Thus was a central station, which
was modern by the standards of the day, built in the centre of The Hague. It
commenced to operate on 1 May 1889 and the Chamber of Commerce,
which had been among the advocates of the scheme, had this to say about it:

The central station on the Hofsingel was completed and made ready for operation.
The number of lamps connected to it was about 2,000. The machinery consists of
three boilers and 4 steam engines with 8 dynamos which can supply 12,000 lamps
of 16 candlepower. The street cables cover a significant portion of the old city. The
company also has a number of concessions abroad, namely in Luxembourg and
northern Italy. It has a branch in Amsterdam and has undertaken many contracts in
the electrical engineering field. Its permanent employees on average numbered 70.
If the municipality, like the Government, supports the company, this will assist its
efforts to provide many of our countrymen with a livelihood.[64]

Earlier, in 1886, the company had sought a concession to build four
central stations in Amsterdam; these would serve virtually the whole of the
old part of the city with the exception of the Jordaan and Eilanden
districts.[65] This application, which was refused, will be discussed in Chapter
5 in the context of Gerard Philips' efforts, on behalf of AEG, to secure the
concession for the supply of electricity in the capital in 1890.

In Amsterdam, too, the introduction of electric lighting coincided with the
arrival of the Jablochkoff candle. The records show that in 1879 the firm of
Gebr. Van Es, with offices in a building known as the Brakke Grond, which
had represented the Société Générale d'Electricité since the previous year,
carried out four successive installations in the city, the first for the
Hollandsche IJzeren Spoorweg-Maatschappij, the second and third at a
printing works and a diamond polishing works, and the fourth at the

63  *Tagebuch Wilhelm von Siemens 1886–1904*; Siemens Archives, No. 4 Lf 775, Munich.
64  Annual report of the Chamber of Commerce of The Hague, 1889; cf. *De Ingenieur*, 12.4.1890.
65  Cf. Chapter 5, page 186.

The main restaurant, or winter garden, at the Café Krasnapolsky

premises of Croon & Co.[66] Less than a year later, the prospective customers for electric lighting included the restaurant 'Die Port van Cleve',[67] Circus Carré, the Frascati Theatre and the Government Telegraph Service. In 1881, Mijnssen & Co., agents for the Compagnie Générale d'Eclairage Electrique of Paris, installed the famous electric lighting system in the Krasnapolsky restaurant and winter garden, the motive for which was said to be that the plants suffered greatly from the harmful effects of gas lighting.[68] Proof that this applies no less to the wellbeing of the human species was contained in the spontaneous reaction of a French guest: 'With all the hygienic advantages of the new lighting, a sojourn in the restaurant is truly a delight for the eyes and one which greatly predisposes to gastronomic enjoyment.'[69]

By that time (1884), the arc lighting installed at the Krasnapolsky had been replaced by a softer, more intimate system employing five hundred Edison incandescent lamps. The capacity of the existing generating plant, which comprised nine dynamos and had cost some $f$ 125,000, was far in excess of the requirements for the restaurant. Clearly, other factors were at work, and chief among these was the business relationship between A. W. Krasnapolsky and N.V. Nederlandsche Electriciteit-Maatschappij, which represented the Compagnie Continentale Edison of Paris.[70] This company had been established on 14 June 1882 with an authorized capital of one million guilders, of which 20% was initially subscribed by the following persons:

J. Dirks, member of the Lower Chamber of the States-General, 10 shares, $f$ 2,500; F. A. T. Delprat, member of the Amsterdam City Council, 4 shares, $f$ 1,000; L. B. Wertheim, stockbroker, 90 shares, $f$ 22,500; Leon Wertheim & Co., 200 shares, $f$ 50,000; I. A. Mesritz, stockbroker, 89 shares, $f$ 22,250; P. E. Tegelberg, a director of Stoomvaart-Maatschappij Nederland, 10 shares, $f$ 2,500; A. W. Krasnapolsky, 95 shares, $f$ 23,750; H. J. G. Mijnssen, a partner in the firm of Mijnssen & Co., 4 shares, $f$ 1,000; W. J. de Bordes, broker, 95 shares, $f$ 23,750; Jonkheer C. A. de Pesters, manufacturer, 94 shares, $f$ 23,500; C. van Notten, 95 shares, $f$ 23,750; Prof. T. M. C. Asser, 4 shares, $f$ 1,000; Jonkheer J. E. Huydecoper, lawyer, 10 shares, $f$ 2,500.

---

[66] Eclairage par la bougie électrique, Soc. Gén. d'Electricité, procédés Jablochkoff, catalogues 1879 and 1880; Siemens Archives, Munich.

[67] 'Die Port van Cleve', issue 68–9 of *Neerlands Welvaart*, 1920.

[68] G. Werkman, *Kras = 100/100 = Kras*, 1966, 84 ff; cf. *Volksalmanak 1885* published by Mij. tot Nut van 't Algemeen, 158.

[69] *La Lumière Electrique*, 1884, Vol. 13, 300 ff: 'Eclairage Electrique de la Brasserie-Restaurant Krasnapolsky à Amsterdam'; cf. *The Electrician*, 10.1.1885, 174: 'Electric light in the restaurant'.

[70] 'Second Bulletin Compagnie Continentale Edison', Paris, 10.10.1882, 22; Siemens Archives, Munich.

The Nederlandsche Electriciteit-Maatschappij sought a monopoly of electric lighting in the inner city area. On 10 July 1882, soon after its establishment, the company applied to the Amsterdam City Council for a permit to lay cables to supply electricity from the generating plant at the Krasnapolsky to the premises in the adjoining thoroughfares, Warmoes-straat, Nes and Kalverstraat, and to the Nieuwendijk, N.Z. Voorburgwal and Rokin.[71] However, the Council, pending a decision on the extension of the gas concession, was unable to deal with this application or the one which followed. Nor did subsequent requests, made in 1883 and 1886, succeed, in spite of support from interested individuals. The Council, which 'for years has maintained a stony silence on all issues',[72] delayed the granting of an electricity concession until 1890. This matter, one with political undertones, is dealt with at length in Chapter 5.

The Nederlandsche Electriciteit-Maatschappij was not alone in its efforts to obtain a concession. Similar applications were submitted to the All-gemeine Elektricitäts-Gesellschaft, Berlin, N.V. 'Electra', Maatschappij voor Electrische Stations, Amsterdam, and the Nederlandsche Maatschap-pij voor Electriciteit en Metallurgie, The Hague. The first-named ultimately failed in its principal objective, which was to obtain and operate conces-sions. The company did, however, achieve success, albeit short-lived, with its subsidiary activities in the field of installation. These commenced in 1882 with a lighting project at the steam-powered flour mill 'De Weichsel' in Amsterdam,[73] and in the same year similar installations were carried out at the Western Sugar Refinery in the city and at a spinning mill owned by C. W. Schönebaum in Groningen. *The Electrician* reported on 10 February 1883 that these orders had been successfully executed under the supervision of the company's chief engineer, H. C. van Mens.

The leading installation contractors, Mijnssen & Co., of Amsterdam, to whom several references have been made, stemmed from the company of the same name which had been established in 1868. The original Mijnssen & Co. started life as commission agents for machine tools and railway equipment, in addition to which they undertook the installation of gas and steam engines.[74] In 1882, when electrical installations commenced to play a

---

[71] Archives of the Public Works Department, inventory number 5001; Municipal Archives, Amsterdam.
[72] *Tijdschrift Mij. van Nijverheid*, 1887, 159: 'Op electrisch gebied'.
[73] *Tijdschrift Mij. van Nijverheid*, 1882, 365: 'Op electrisch gebied'.
[74] 'De Eerste 50 jaren', undated internal history of Mijnssen & Co.; archives of Landré-Mijnssen B.V., Diemen.

more significant role, H. L. A. van den Wall Bake, the Master of the Mint
and an engineer by profession, joined the company. Some years later a rift
occurred, and this led to the setting up of a new company, Electro-
Technisch-Installatie Bureau H. & J. van den Wall Bake, in Amsterdam. An
even more powerful offshoot appeared in 1887, when G. Groeneveld and
P. A. van der Poll, chief electrician and book-keeper respectively of Mijnssen & Co., announced the establishment of Groeneveld, Van der Poll & Co.
The objects of this company embraced 'all applications of electricity in
industry, especially the installation of electric lighting in factories, etc.,
coupled with an agency for and commission business in requisites, in both
the electrical and technical fields'.[75] Having worked for Mijnssen & Co. for
many years, the partners ventured to hope for 'a degree of success'. The
enterprise, which had a capital of 10,000 guilders and was soon employing
twenty people, was dependent to a large extent on Deutsche Elektrizitäts-
Werke, Garbe, Lahmeyer & Co. of Aachen, which was then producing
about 1,000 dynamos and electric motors annually.[76] Schuckert & Co. of
Nuremberg, the second largest dynamo manufacturer in Germany, after
Siemens,[77] had been represented in the Netherlands since 1885 by the
Amsterdam installation contractors, P. H. ter Meulen. Finally, there was
Technisch-Bureau Geveke & Co., founded in 1874, which, like others,
entered the electrical field in the 1880s. Mijnssen & Co., which had the best
reputation among the firms in Amsterdam, and for this reason has been
chosen as an example, represented several British, German and French
houses. In 1886, Mijnssen obtained the agency for Felten & Guilleaume of
Mühlheim an der Ruhr, a leading wire and cable manufacturer, thereby
significantly strengthening their position. Between 1887 and 1892, the
company carried out at least 150 electrical installations which were
'certainly not insignificant for that time'.[78]

In Rotterdam, the leading contractors were Van Rietschoten &
Houwens. In 1879, at which time they already represented the Silvertown
Telegraph Works of London for the supply of batteries and cables in the
Netherlands, they secured an agency, chiefly for arc lighting installations,
from Siemens Bros. & Co., also of London.[79] This brought them into direct

[75] Notice of Incorporation, August 1887, in Private Archive No. 156/1946 D 334; Municipal
Archives, Amsterdam; cf. commemorative book: *N.V. Groeneveld, Van der Poll & Co., 1887–
1927* (author unnamed).
[76] Snijders, *De vorderingen der Electrotechniek*, 8 ff.
[77] Ibid., 27 ff.          [78] 'De Eerste 50 jaren'.
[79] 'Korrespondenz mit London im Betreff der Vertretung in Holland', 9.1.1883; Siemens Archives,
No. 68 Li 159, Munich.

competition with Wisse, Piccaluga & Co. of The Hague, who represented
Siemens & Halske, Berlin. Despite arrangements made between London
and Berlin, the parties could not reach agreement, and the ultimate result
was a cessation of deliveries from Britain.[80] In 1885, Jan Jacob van
Rietschoten (1860–1938) succeeded his father as the head of the firm and
proceeded to create an independent electrical department.[81] He had knowledge and experience in this area, the product of two years spent with
Siemens Bros. & Co., where he had worked on electrical installations on
board naval and merchant vessels. At the time, this was a greatly coveted
opportunity, and it was there that the German electrical engineer, and later
industrialist, Robert Bosch (1861–1942) obtained part of his training.[82]
The firm of Van Rietschoten & Houwens was established in 1860 and, like
its Amsterdam rival, Mijnssen & Co., began by installing steam engines and
other machinery, in addition to which it represented foreign manufacturers.

Turning to the area of manufacture, Rotterdam already possessed an
incandescent lamp works in 1883, while in nearby Slikkerveer there was a
dynamo factory of even earlier date. These two basically industrial enterprises merit individual study.

When the applications for electricity developed in the Netherlands, there
naturally arose a need for people with theoretical and practical knowledge
to carry out the installations. At first, foreign workers were engaged, in
most cases only in order to obtain the benefit of their skills. But at the same
time the craft had its own attractions, notably for the younger generation,
who sought fresh opportunities. It appears that, in addition to individuals
who spent a period of time with a British or German firm in order to acquire
the necessary skills, and afterwards set up in business, it was the small
mechanical engineering companies which were attracted to electrical installation. Sometimes, as in the case of Mijnssen & Co. and Van Rietschoten &
Houwens, electrical work rapidly developed into the principal activity. This
was especially true where an agency for a leading foreign producer was
obtained, something which occurred regularly in the emerging electrical
industry. Agencies brought know-how to, and provided a basis for, the
installation branch, and in due course it was these which separated the
industrial undertakings in the field from the small-scale contractors. Both,
however, had their origins in the 1880s and the introduction of electric

[80] Wegner, *Siemens in den Niederlanden*, 23.
[81] Commemorative book: *Van Rietschoten & Houwens 1860–1960* (author unnamed).
[82] Theodor Heuss, *Robert Bosch – Leben und Leistung*, 1948, 69 ff.

lighting. Many started with a chief electrician who had been sent to Siemens or Schuckert in Germany for training, and later carried out installations with one or two apprentices. Others, as indicated, took the plunge with only the experience which they had gained while employed in the Telegraph Service. The electrical instrument maker and later installation contractor B. H. Croon (1848–1914),[83] like Wisse, is a classic example. Both were civil servants, yet this did not prevent them continuing their official duties for several years alongside their developing installation businesses. 'The industrialist, the manufacturer; it is they as producers who, first and foremost, strive to improve and perfect electric lighting, which must subsequently be installed.' This statement appears in the Electrician's Handbook written by Etienne de Fodor, which was published in 1885; it was subsequently translated into Dutch and edited by H. J. G. Mijnssen (1840–98), a partner in the contracting firm of the same name.[84] The work provided an insight into the practicalities. Not written for 'scholars', nor for those who were 'merely theoreticians', it contained guidelines for installers in calculating and executing their work. For it was they who in fact introduced electric lighting. In the early days, when neither standardization nor even official regulations existed, progress depended on a combination of ingenuity and skills proven by experiment, rather than on a profound understanding of the subject.

A clear example of this evolutionary process is to be found in the industrial approach on the part of Willem Smit & Co., who manufactured dynamos at their works in Slikkerveer. This company, too, owed its existence to electric light.

Willem Benjamin Smit (1860–1950) was the son of Johannes Smit, who owned a rivet factory at Slikkerveer. At the age of seventeen, Willem Benjamin was confronted with the premature termination of his education when the school which he attended in Rotterdam was closed following the death of the headmaster, a Mr Gorter.[85] It was a foregone conclusion that the young Smit would enter the shipbuilding industry, in which the family had been engaged for more than a century and to which it owed its prosperity. The Smits were not only expert shipbuilders, but also business-men who were not averse to speculation. In the nineteenth century,

[83]  F. N. van Es, *De eeuw van Croon & Co., 1876–1976, 100 jaar electrotechnische installaties*, 1976.
[84]  H. J. G. Mijnssen, *Het gloeilicht, zijn wezen en vorming; berekeningen en uitvoering van instal-laties*, etc., 1886; and *Practische Vraagstukken over Electrische verlichting*, 1883.
[85]  H. H. Emck, H. J. Hardeman *et al.*, *Ridderkerk, herdenking 500 jaar*, 1946.

Willem Benjamin Smit (1860–1950)               Adriaan Pot (1857–1932)

successful dealings in Portuguese securities boosted the family fortune to more than 700,000 guilders.[86] It was Arie Smit, Willem's uncle, who in 1875 founded Maatschappij 'De Schelde', shipbuilders, at Flushing. But it was to the J. & K. Smit yard at Kinderdijk, which had been established by his grandfather, that the young Willem, fresh from school, went to learn the rudiments of the family business. Soon the phenomenon of electricity and its applications claimed part of his attention. The first practical result of his interest was a dynamo which, however, when connected to the steam engine at the yard, promptly failed amid a shower of sparks.

In the mind of the young Smit, experimentation and fabrication were indivisible. This is evidenced by his application to the Maatschappij van Nijverheid for the 'Fabriek van Materiëel voor Electrische Verlichting' (Electric Lighting Equipment Works),[87] which he had founded, to be included among the exhibitors at the first electricity exhibition in Paris. By then he had for some time (several years, it is said)[88] been engaged in the

[86] J. H. Bolland, *Slepende Rijk – Het ontstaan van de Nederlandse zeesleepvaart*, 1968, 219.
[87] W. Smit in a letter to the Mij. van Nijverheid, 19.12.1880; Municipal Archives, Haarlem.
[88] Murk Lels, 'Electric Light in Holland', in *The Electrician*, 30.4.1881.

manufacture and installation of efficient dynamos for lighting the factories of local firms such as Diepeveen, Lels and Smit. But the time was not ripe for an appearance at the Paris exhibition, alongside the dynamos of Gramme, Siemens and others. Nevertheless, Willem Smit's machine received mention in a foreign column thanks to the attractive arc lighting installation at the agricultural exhibition at Bergen op Zoom, the dynamos for which, *The Electrician* reported on 17 September 1881, 'were manufactured by Mr Willem Smit of Slikkerveer near Rotterdam'. In Holland, the Smit dynamo gradually became an established component of lighting systems, especially in factories and on board ship.

It is already clear from the developments which took place in Britain that the shipbuilding industry there recognized the modern applications for electricity at an early date. Incandescent lighting installations by Swan and Edison soon became an integral part of the technical equipment on board ocean liners. Arc light, which at first was employed mainly in searchlights – enabling the Royal Navy to carry out the night bombardment of Alexandria in 1882 – increasingly came to be used for more peaceful forms of navigation in rivers and straits.[89] The decision by the Smit family to set up an electrical engineering company alongside the existing shipyards reflected this trend.[90] The practical consequence of the decision was the establishment on 1 November 1882 of Willem Smit & Co., with registered offices at Slikkerveer. The objects of the new company were stated to be the manufacture of equipment for electric lighting and the operation of electrical equipment and allied products. Willem's brother-in-law, Adriaan Pot (1857–1932), who had trained as a marine engineer at the Royal Naval College in Greenwich, entered the firm as a partner. Fop Smit, Willem's great-uncle, provided the company with a loan of 30,000 guilders, practically the whole of the working capital.[91]

During the years of experimenting and technical preparation, the firm canvassed for business, giving demonstrations with the aid of a dynamo mounted on a mobile steam engine. A steady stream of orders ensued: the incandescent lighting system on board the S.S. *Merwede I*; interior and exterior lighting at the Grand Hotel Coomans in Rotterdam, the installation including four hundred incandescent lamps and a 3,500-candlepower

[89] Figuier, *Het Elektrische Licht*, ch. 17.
[90] In 1888, W. Smit & Co. installed searchlights on board the Dutch Navy's ramming vessels *Luipaard* and *Panter*.
[91] G. H. Knap, *Mens en Bedrijf, 75 jaar Smit–Slikkerveer*, 1958, 31.

arc lamp;[92] electric lighting at a number of exhibitions; incandescent lighting in the prisons at Arnhem, Breda and Scheveningen; and the lighting of the main railway station in Amsterdam by means of twenty-five arc lamps. Willem Smit & Co., a pioneer of the Dutch electrical industry, used dynamos and, in appropriate cases, arc lamps of its own manufacture in these installations. In 1888 the company supplied 135 dynamos.

April 1886 saw the commissioning of a central station supplying current to private consumers and for street lighting. This was operated by N.V. Electrische Verlichting 'Kinderdijk'. The total cost of the building, the eighty-horsepower steam engine, two direct current dynamos and the remaining equipment was ƒ26,000, and this was raised among interested citizens in Kinderdijk and clients of Willem Smit & Co.[93] The initial load consisted of fifteen streetlamps and about 130 private installations totalling three hundred incandescent lamps; the price per lamp varied between ƒ15 and ƒ11 per year, depending upon the number. The wiring, fittings, etc. in the houses were provided free of charge, as were replacement bulbs. *The Electrician* reported on 26 November 1886 that villagers who earned no more than four shillings a day were among the subscribers, and it quoted a price of 10s.6d. per 16-candlepower lamp per year. Whatever the figure may have been, one thing is certain: the inhabitants of Kinderdijk were among the earliest users of incandescent lamps in Holland, the system being installed there only a few years after its introduction. Willem Smit was once presented with a number of lamps of the first type produced by Swan, and he recalled the occasion in the following words:

My mind goes back to the first incandescent lamps which I received from Swan of Newcastle in 1880, which had a cardboard holder and made contact with two copper springs ... then the eyelets with the coil-spring socket, then the bayonet fitting. I carried out a test with the first type, laboratory lamps from Swan, in a joinery loft at Kinderdijk, in which I had already installed arc lighting: two arc lamps with two Gramme dynamos.

I connected the lamps, of which there were about twelve, to the arc lamp circuit, which meant that they were affected by the fluctuations of the arc lamp; moreover, the steam engine was running very unevenly under the influence of the woodworking machines. As a result, the lamps, which were burning at too high an intensity, failed the same evening, burning out like Bengal fire. I had been given the lamps by my uncle, P. Smit Jzn. I was told that they had cost ƒ16 each.

---

[92]  W. Smit in a letter to the Rotterdam City Council, 29.10.1883; Municipal Archives, Rotterdam; cf. *Eigen Haard*, 1888, No. 16 and *Electro-Nieuws*, 1975, Nos. 10 and 12.

[93]  Knap, *Mens en Bedrijf*, 47.

My first incandescent lighting installation,[94] in February 1883, was for my Uncle Fop's paddle-driven saloon steamer. That had the Swan lamps with the eyelets. For the central station at Kinderdijk, I used, for the first time, screw-type Edison lamps of 16 and 32 candlepower. If I remember correctly, they consumed three watts per candlepower.[95]

An important test for W. Smit & Co. came with the commissioning of a street lighting system in Nijmegen. The desire for more light, particularly for the benefit of the busy pedestrian and goods traffic along the Embankment of the River Waal, together with the unsuitability of the soil there for the laying of gas pipes, led the gasworks committee to decide in 1885 that the solution lay in electric lighting. From the proposal for the Embankment came a plan which also embraced a number of public squares and parks, and demanded a 4.3-kilometre ring main. With ten 2,000-candlepower arc lamps connected in series to a six hundred-volt, twenty-ampere Smit Dynamo, the installation was the first in Holland to be operated by a municipal electricity undertaking. The total investment amounted to some 10,000 guilders, and in addition to generating costs the Council expended about nine man-hours daily on lamp maintenance and the replacement of carbon rods.[96] 'It was extremely difficult to make the lamps burn as evenly as the Mayor and Aldermen and the teacher of physics at the secondary school desired. They drove around in a landau, stopping for a few minutes at each lamp to see how steady the light was. At last I received the testimonial, which was dated 3 December 1891.'[97] It took something like five years for the local officials to become convinced that the installation had been properly carried out.

With this and other systems, in which the emphasis lay on the lighting of factories and ships, the company – which was the sole producer of dynamos in the Netherlands and a well-known contractor – proceeded to prove its viability; it went on to attain a level of development which put it on a par with electrical engineering concerns abroad. Its founders – the entrepreneur Willem Smit, who obtained his elementary knowledge from English, French and German literature on the subject, and, with his empirical bent, allowed himself to be led, and Adriaan Pot, the theoretician and draughtsman – ensured that Holland had a place, albeit modest, in the realm of heavy

[94]  *Rotterdamsch Nieuwsblad*, 17.2.1883: a report of the commissioning of the installation.
[95]  W. Smit in letters to N. A. Halbertsma, 22.11.1939 and 4.7.1941; Philips Archives, Eindhoven.
[96]  *Tijdschrift Mij. van Nijverheid*, 1887, 45 ff; *De Ingenieur*, 1887, 51; *De ontwikkeling van onze electriciteitsvoorziening 1880–1938*, Vol. 1, 22; *Veertig jaar electriciteit*, commemorative book published by the Gemeente Electriciteitsbedrijf Nijmegen, 1948.
[97]  W. Smit in a letter to N. A. Halbertsma, 27.8.1941; Philips Archives, Eindhoven.

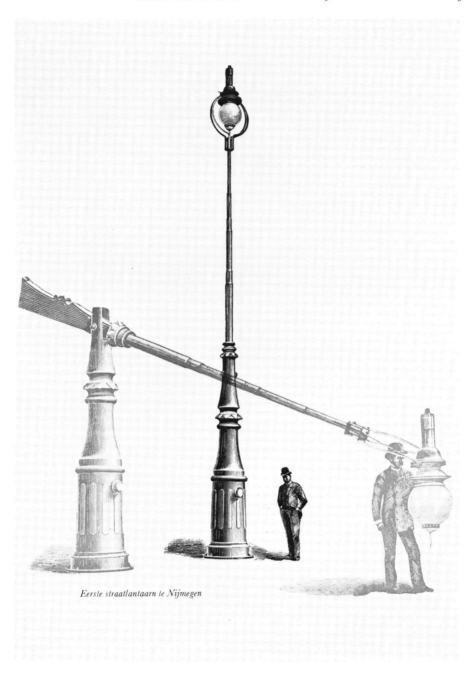

*Eerste straatlantaarn te Nijmegen*

Street lighting in Nijmegen, c. 1890

electrical engineering. By the mid-1880s the company was employing twenty-five people, and at the end of the century the workforce numbered more than a hundred.

In 1891, ten years after the great exposition in Paris, another international electricity exhibition took place. This was at Frankfurt am Main[98] and lasted from 16 May until 19 October. The emphasis was no longer on electric lighting, but on heavy electrical engineering, which was then growing in importance. Above the new central stations which were then being planned or built, in nearly all cases for lighting purposes, hung the prospect of expansion into power stations. The problems associated with the transmission of energy over long distances appeared to have been virtually solved. The development of the generator – which in 1881 had mostly been the outcome of successful experiments – had been put on a sound theoretical basis by the work of scientists and technicians. In making their calculations, electrical engineers could now choose not only between direct and alternating current, but between these two systems and a newly developed three-phase alternating current system. All these systems were now in use, although differences of opinion or a preference for one or other principle still existed. Whereas with direct current the technical problems associated with high-voltage generation followed by transformating to lower operating voltages were such as to make it impractical, with alternating current there was no difficulty. The economic advantage of this method lay in the possibility of working at high voltage with minimal losses, with the result that the current – and consequently the weight of copper in the transmission lines – could be limited. Alternating current was thus the answer to the dream of supplying a large area with electricity from a single source and at a cost, in terms of transmission lines and sub-stations, which did not jeopardize the profitability of the whole operation. If a central station served only for lighting purposes, alternating current was the obvious system. But if current was also required for motive power, consideration was also given to three-phase current. Round about 1890, however, in spite of the advances made in the generation of electricity by the electromagnetic method, many electrical engineers still regarded the accumulator – whose efficiency had meanwhile been greatly increased – as the best means of expanding interior lighting.

Dynamos and electric motors were the principal attraction at the Frank-

---

[98] *Elektrizität, Offizielle Zeitung der Intern. Elektrotechnischen Ausstellung, Frankfurt a/M., 1891;* AEG Archives, Brunswick.

The Smit dynamo

furt exhibition. The reason lay in their wide range of applications, especially in central stations and railway and tramway vehicles, but also in
cranes and other lifting gear, for powering pumps and fans, and driving
machinery in factories and workshops:

In the area of electric power transmission, however, the workshops have the largest
share. It seemed to me that efforts should be made to show artisans and small
manufacturers, in particular, how simple and easy it is to use an electric motor, how
little operation it requires, how easily it can be regulated, started and stopped, and
how little space it occupies.[99]

By now, Germany had become the leading producer of electrical goods in
Europe. The output of its electrical industry in 1891 was valued at
£1,360,000, of which arc lamps accounted for £100,000 and incandescent
lamps for £128,000.[100] The ensuing decade was to bring a sevenfold
increase in sales of virtually all types of electrical goods. In 1891 the
industry in Germany employed about 15,000 people, compared with just
over 1,000 in 1881.[101] In the course of the 1880s, Siemens & Halske,
traditionally a major manufacturer of low-voltage apparatus, was joined by
large independent firms such as AEG, Schuckert and 'Helios' A.G., which
specialized in heavy electrical equipment. The large sums of capital required
in the industry were obtained through the formation of share-based
companies and participation by the banks.

In France, where in 1880 l'Electricien had already predicted that: 'La
prusse va prendre l'avance en matière électrique', the situation was very
different. Electrical engineering was not a separate branch of industry, but
merely an offshoot of engineering in its entirety.[102] Moreover, in spite of the
fact that French manufacturers had been among the first in the field of arc
lamps and had spent large sums on patent rights, no national incandescent
lamp industry had developed. After the boom years of l'électromanie,
between 1878 and 1882, the confidence of financiers was sapped by failures
among the arc lighting companies, whose viability fell short of the original
expectations. In 1913 the capital invested in the electrical industry in France
was still only one-third of that invested in Germany.[103]

[99] Address to the meeting of the Electrical Association in Berlin on 24 March 1891, given by O. von
Miller, technical director of the Frankfurt Electricity Exhibition, in De Ingenieur, 1891, 181 ff.
[100] The Electrician, 28.10.1892, 686: 'The electrical industry in Germany'.
[101] K. Borchardt gives figures of 1,690 and 26,000 employees for the years 1882 and 1895, respectively;
cf. 'The industrial revolution in Germany 1700–1914', in C. M. Cipolla, The Fontana Economic
History of Europe, Vol. 4, Part 1, 1973, 135.
[102] W. Koch, Die Konzentrationsbewegung in der deutschen Elektroindustrie, 1907, 4, 18.
[103] J. H. Clapham, The Economic Development of France and Germany 1815–1914, 1923, 257.

In Great Britain, where American and German manufacturers had important interests, the electrical industry similarly lagged behind in relative terms, in spite of the high degree of industrialization and the presence of electrical engineers and leading theoreticians. This situation can be attributed partly to legislation which seriously held back electrification in Britain between 1882 and 1888, and partly to the rapid demise of the many speculative enterprises founded in the early 1880s, whose losses ran into tens of millions of pounds. The parlous state of the industry had been described by electrical circles in Germany in 1884, and had been blamed largely on unsound share transactions and the patent laws.[104] Besides phenomena such as the self-satisfaction on the part of Victorian entrepreneurs as a whole,[105] Swinburne had earlier cited errors in company management as a factor which inhibited growth.[106] In particular, the directors concerned lacked commercial skill and therefore failed to develop fully the market-oriented product strategy which was essential for growth in this new field. Much concerning the British attitude in this context can be gauged from the fact that Emile Garcke – whose relationship with Gerard Philips has already been referred to – and Hugo Hirst were counted among the most successful 'British' businessmen.[107] Both had left their native Germany in the 1880s and settled in England. The head start gained by British incandescent lamp manufacturers, which was of vital importance for the development of the electrical industry as a whole, was lost by the war of attrition in the area of patents and the monopoly held by Edison & Swan.[108] The entire electrical industry continued to stagnate throughout the 1890s. 'Some have attributed our backwardness entirely to the inadequacy of or want of organisation in our technical educational facilities', *The Electrician* wrote on 9 August 1901. The journal went on to give other reasons, including problems in the area of finance and the absence of standardization.[109] The British, unlike their continental counterparts, made no technical contribution to the metal-filament lamp, which was developed in the late 1890s and opened the way for the mass use of electric lighting.[110] In the battle for orders for central stations on the Continent, it was already clear by 1890 or thereabouts that British electrical manufacturers could no longer compete with their German rivals.

[104] *Zeitschrift für angewandte Elektricitätslehre*, Vol. 6, 1884, 572.
[105] E. J. Hobsbawm, *Industry and Empire. An Economic History of Britain since 1750*, 1968, 154.
[106] Cf. Chapter 2, page 64.
[107] Byatt, *British Electrical Industry*, 189.
[108] *Elektrotechnische Zeitschrift*, 6.2.1896, 77; 20.2.1896, 122 ff.
[109] *The Electrician*, 9.8.1901: 'The outlook in the electrical industry'.
[110] Bright, *Electric-Lamp Industry*, 161.

If, finally, we compare the situation in the Netherlands with that in the above-mentioned countries in the period 1880–90, we find that here, too, German manufacturers dominated all sectors except the manufacture of incandescent lamps. Indeed, as the following citation shows, they regarded Holland not merely as a competitive area, but as 'coming within a sphere of influence':

From the outset, the Netherlands had been a favourable market for the activities of Siemens & Halske; and it improved as the years went by. From time to time, the parent company was obliged to defend its long-established and just rights against British industry, which sought to add the Netherlands to the countries which formed its sphere of influence.
   When lighting assumed greater importance, the Netherlands proved to be an attractive market in this respect also. Between 1847 and 1896, sales to the Dutch market totalled 6,326,000 marks, quite a large sum for so small a country. The figure does not include the cost of the central station built in The Hague in 1888.[111]

Electric lighting was chiefly employed in factories, shops and establishments used by the public. To shopkeepers and restaurant owners, publicity, luxury and comfort outweighed the higher cost in comparison with gas. As the concept of district generating stations had scarcely been adopted in Holland, each installation was initially fed from a separate dynamo. The cost of generating current was by far the greatest single item. In factories which had a steam engine, the figure could be reduced somewhat by utilizing the spare capacity (see Table 14, page 130 and graph on page 129), and this explains why factories and workshops were the first to replace gas lighting by electricity for both economic and ergonomic reasons. For an independently powered incandescent lamp installation with between fifty and one thousand lamps, for example, the lamp costs in 1890 represented between ten and thirty per cent of the total, depending upon the method of producing current. By 1893 the downward trend in lamp prices had reduced the figure to between four and ten per cent. This information was given in a report entitled 'Which is preferable for lighting factories and workshops: gas or electricity?', which was drawn up under the chairmanship of Prof. J. A. Snijders and published by the Association for the Promotion of Manufacturing and Craft Industries in the Netherlands on 31 August 1893. So rapidly did the situation in this area change that the

---

[111] L. von Winterfeld, *Entwicklung und Tätigkeit der Firma Siemens & Halske in den Jahren 1847–1897*, 1913, 119.

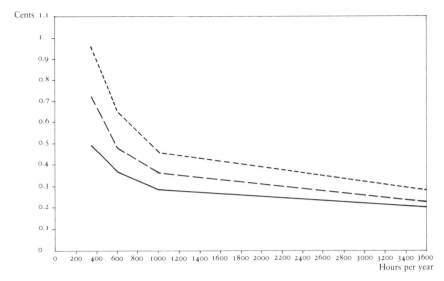

Hourly costs, in cents, of a lighting system with 1,000 incandescent lamps of 15 candlepower and 8 arc lamps (1893)[a]
———— Dynamo powered by an existing steam engine
——— Dynamo powered by a separate steam engine fed from boiler supplying existing steam engine
————— Dynamo powered by separate steam engine with its own boiler

[a] Cf. note 111 on page 128.

completion of the report was repeatedly postponed: the cost analysis had been based on the 1891 lamp price of $f$ 1.10, but this fell to 70 cents in 1892 and to 40–5 cents in 1893.

The introduction of electricity in the Netherlands, as in the neighbouring countries, was accompanied by the emergence of lighting companies which were of a comparatively speculative nature and soon lagged behind in technical terms. Most of them were situated in the three major cities (Amsterdam, Rotterdam and The Hague), where they hoped to obtain a concession from the local authority, notably for districts where the demand for lighting and the density of the installations might be presumed to be high. In the smaller towns, the introduction of electric lighting, which in some cases was preceded by privately owned district generating stations, would on average be delayed by ten years; there, the spectre of competition with the gasworks, most of which were operated by municipalities, was a powerful deterrent. This was the experience of the incandescent lamp manufacturer C. Boudewijnse of Middelburg, when in 1889 he applied to

Table 14. Cost of electric lighting from a dynamo powered by an existing steam engine and based on 1,000 running hours per year (guilders) (1893)[a]

| For installations with: | 50 incandescent lamps of 15 candlepower and 2 arc lamps | 100 incandescent lamps of 15 candlepower and 4 arc lamps | 300 incandescent lamps of 15 candlepower and 6 arc lamps | 1,000 incandescent lamps of 15 candlepower and 8 arc lamps[b] |
|---|---|---|---|---|
| Interest charges and depreciation | 180 | 300 | 660 | 1,800 |
| Incandescent lamps | 23 | 45 | 120 | 400 |
| Coal | 192 | 320 | 560 | 1,200 |
| Carbon rods | 20 | 40 | 60 | 80 |
| Sundry materials and maintenance | 120 | 190 | 285 | 430 |
| Total | 535 | 895 | 1,685 | 3,910 |
| Hourly running cost | 0.54 | 0.90 | 1.69 | 3.91 |
| Hourly cost per lamp, in cents | 0.8 | 0.6 | 0.5 | 0.4 |
| Cost of incandescent lamps as a proportion of total cost | 4% | 5% | 7% | 10% |

Notes:
[a] *Rapport van de Vereeniging tot Bevordering van Fabrieks- en Handwerksnijverheid in Nederland,* 31.8.1: 'Is gas of electriciteit voor verlichting van fabrieken en werkplaatsen het meest aan te bevelen?'
[b] One arc lamp is assumed to be the equivalent of 10 incandescent lamps of 15 candlepower

the local council for a permit to operate one or more central stations for the purpose of illuminating the town. In the ensuing battle with the erudite director of the gasworks, P. Polet, which was waged with pamphlets, Boudewijnse and his bold plan were defeated.[112] Local authorities had sound reasons for being hesitant to grant concessions, and even where the plans of the lighting companies did come to fruition in the years round about 1890, e.g. in The Hague and Amsterdam, the contracts were for a limited period, or were hedged about with conditions and restrictions. With only their own resources, these companies could never have grown into the full-scale electricity undertakings which later emerged; nor, indeed, was this envisaged at the outset. They were a transient phenomenon, part of a larger development, and this was due both to technological progress and to a public opinion which in the period round about 1890 and thereafter was highly critical of the monopolistic nature of concessionaires.[113] There is also the obvious question of the huge amounts of capital and the infrastructural facilities which the public interest demanded when the generating capacity was increased from that of a central station to that of a power station.

It is, however, to the credit of those companies – and not solely in economic terms – that, as private enterprises which reflected the spirit of the times, they were the first to introduce electric lighting in appropriate places. They thereby met a need on the part of what were then select consumer groups; most important of all – as will emerge in due course – they initiated a demand among a broader cross-section of society.

The international electricity exhibition in Frankfurt am Main attracted over 1,200,000 visitors. The Dutch contingent was proportionally the largest. Curiosity or ambition?[114] Prof. J. A. Snijders and his colleague, H. A. Ravenek, both of whom lectured in Delft, devoted part of their summer vacation to the event in order to bring themselves up to date with the latest developments in the electrical field. They later submitted a very comprehensive report to the Minister of Home Affairs, in which particular emphasis was placed on the quality of courses in advanced electrical engineering.[115] The Dutch exhibitors in Frankfurt included the young

---

[112] P. Polet, *Middelburg Electrisch Verlicht*, 1889; C. Boudewijnse, *Eenige beschouwingen over Electrische Verlichting n.a.v. de brochure van Polet*, 1889; also *Memorie van beantwoording aan B. en Repliek op de Memorie van beantwoording van P.*; cf. *De Ingenieur*, 1889, 199 ff and 1890, 97 ff.

[113] Cf. Chapter 5, pages 201 ff.

[114] F. C. Dufour, 'De Internationale Electro-technische Tentoonstelling te Frankfurt a/M.', Part 12 in *De Ingenieur*, 1891, 491 ff.

[115] Snijders, *De vorderingen der Electrotechniek*.

Amsterdam firm, Groeneveld, Van der Poll & Co., which displayed a complete electric lighting installation 'as an aid to the creation of a healthy atmosphere in factories and workshops, for the benefit of the workers'.[116] J. W. Giltay, the proprietor of P. J. Kipp en Zonen of Delft, exhibited a fully equipped laboratory for the development and testing of precision instruments. The Dutch representative of the Thomson-Houston Company of New York, and later founder of the Heemaf group, R. W. H. Hofstede Crull, attracted attention by the 'truly American manner' in which he set out to convince visitors of the advantages of the electric traction system which he marketed in Europe.[117]

The Dutch incandescent lamp industry was represented by three manufacturers: Goossens, Pope & Co. of Venlo, Messrs Roothaan & Alewijnse of Nijmegen, and Electriciteits-Maatschappij, Systeem 'De Khotinsky' of Rotterdam. The last-named company exhibited an accumulator of its own design, in addition to incandescent lamps. An unusual attraction on this stand was a demonstration of an incandescent lamp factory in operation, in which all the stages of manufacture were shown. A historically interesting aspect of this display is that it was a replica of the factory equipped for the Jablochkoff company in Paris in 1881, which employed the Maxim process; this was the very first incandescent lamp factory on the European continent.[118] It was situated at 17 Rue des Martyres, and the plant had been installed and put into operation by the electrical engineer A. de Khotinsky, who was a friend of Hiram Maxim.[119] He thereby scored a 'first', which he was to repeat a few years later in the Netherlands when he established an incandescent lamp works in Rotterdam.

For the manufacture of incandescent lamps, virtually the only industrial activity in the electrical engineering sector which did not demand resources in excess of the amount which Dutch capitalists were willing to invest, there was no lack of initiative in the years between 1880 and 1890.

---

[116] Ibid., 45.      [117] Ibid., 104.

[118] *Electrizität, Offizielle Zeitung der Internationalen Elektrotechnischen Ausstellung, Frankfurt am Main 1891*, AEG Archives, Brunswick: a detailed description of the method of manufacture at that time.

[119] A. de Khotinsky, *Der de Khotinsky-Accumulator und der Weg seiner Entstehung*, 1891, 11.

Electric motor on display at the exhibition in Frankfurt am Main, 1891

Incandescent lamp factory owned by Electriciteits-Maatschappij, Systeem 'De Khotinsky',
situated at 35 Prins Hendrikkade, Rotterdam

# Chapter 4

# THE FOUNDATIONS OF THE DUTCH INCANDESCENT LAMP INDUSTRY

In the previous chapter we saw how limited liability companies were established in Amsterdam and The Hague in 1882 with the object of installing and operating electric street lighting systems. In both cases the authorized capital was *f* 1,000,000, of which twenty per cent was initially paid up by the founders. A similar enterprise, again with substantial capital, was set up in Rotterdam on 24 December 1883. This was N.V. Electriciteits-Maatschappij, Systeem 'De Khotinsky' which, in addition to urban lighting, proposed to engage in the manufacture of incandescent lamps. Thus, the *Maasstad*, as Rotterdam is popularly known, likewise played a part in the growth of electric lighting, albeit from a somewhat different point of departure than the other two large cities.

The object of the new company was stated to be the exploitation of electricity in all its forms and of all related inventions, machinery and establishments, both in the Netherlands and elsewhere. In accordance with the concept of the 'complete electric lighting system', as this existed and was applied in the 1880s, the company envisaged supplying and installing lamps and other equipment as well as providing current. Its authorized capital amounted to *f* 600,000, of which *f* 120,000 was issued, at the time of establishment. The records show that the initial subscribers and their shareholdings were as follows:

L. W. Schöffer, merchant, 80 shares, *f* 20,000; J. W. Tabingh Suermondt, merchant, 80 shares, *f* 20,000; Henry La Grange, commercial agent, 60 shares, *f* 15,000; Jos. W. Anthony, commodity broker, 40 shares, *f* 10,000; E. F. H. Boden, merchant, 40 shares, *f* 10,000; G. Sauerbier, commodity broker, 20 shares, *f* 5,000; H. Elink Schuurman, commodity broker, 20 shares, *f* 5,000; M. M. de Monchy, merchant, 20 shares, *f* 5,000; F. Koch, commission agent, 20 shares, *f* 5,000; Willem Ruys, shipowner and shipbroker, 20 shares, *f* 5,000; Otto Horstmann, merchant, 20 shares, *f* 5,000; Moritz Markx, stockbroker, 20 shares, *f* 5,000; W.

Stok, architect, 20 shares, *f* 5,000; A. de Khotinsky, electrical engineer, 20 shares, *f* 5,000.[1]

With the aid of a consortium, again consisting of Rotterdam business-men, the second and third tranches, issued on 2 October 1884, were successfully placed. The funds which these afforded, the Board calculated, were sufficient to finance the construction of a central station with a capacity of between five and six thousand lamps, the cost of which was estimated to be *f* 200,000. To enlarge the capacity to 10,000–12,000 lamps would require a fourth share issue. At the stated capacity, the return on the capital invested in the 'light factory' was expected to be between 11% and 18%. This was based on an electricity tariff of 1.4 cents per hour for a 15-candlepower lamp. The estimates included a sum of *f* 35,000 for a factory for the production of accumulators, incandescent lamps and accessories. In a detailed report to shareholders on 15 September 1884,[2] the Board and the supervisory directors promised that the manufacture of incandescent lamps, in particular, 'will immediately show a profit'. The average selling price of an incandescent lamp was then *f* 3. The salient feature of the plan for the construction of this lamp factory – the first in the Netherlands – is that the greater part of the output was destined for the consumers served by the central station. There was already a trade in incandescent lamps, but the market had scarcely begun to take shape.

The promoter of N.V. Electriciteits-Maatschappij, Systeem 'De Khotinsky', and later president of its Supervisory Board, was Ludwig Wilhelm Schöffer (1831–1904), a partner in W. Schöffer & Co., coffee traders, of Rotterdam. He was the youngest son of a merchant in the small town of Gelnhausen, near Frankfurt am Main, and had family ties with the house of J. H. Hofmann Jr of Frankfurt, which traded in colonial produce. Hofmann had affiliates in Amsterdam, Antwerp, Le Havre and London, and it was through them that Schöffer had been enabled to settle in Rotterdam in 1855.[3] His brother Heinrich was a partner in Hofmann Schöffer & Co. of Amsterdam, which traded in coffee on a commission basis.[4] The temperamental Ludwig Wilhelm, who became a Dutch citizen, was the first to import Santos coffee into the Netherlands. He was also

[1] Articles of Association, approved by an Order in Council dated 9.12.1883; Municipal Archives, Rotterdam; see also *Tweede bijvoegsel tot de Nederlandsche Staatscourant* of 13 and 14 January 1884, No. 11.
[2] Report by the Board and Supervisory Directors of Electriciteits-Maatschappij, Systeem 'De Khotinsky' to shareholders, 15.9.1884; Municipal Archives, Rotterdam.
[3] Cf. G. Maier, *Erinnerungen aus dem Leben von Wilhelm Schöffer*, 1901, 20.
[4] C. Schöffer, *Het Huis Hofmann Schöffer & Co.*, 1888.

Ludwig Wilhelm Schöffer (1831–1904)        Achilles de Khotinsky (1850–1933)

instrumental in putting an end to the outdated twice-yearly coffee auc-
tions.[5] His insight into the market, together with a number of notable
transactions, earned him high regard in commercial circles in Rotterdam.
As a successful merchant, he returned to his birthplace round about 1870,
visiting the Rotterdam office only when important business made his
presence there desirable.

But in 1872, following the establishment of the Deutsche Handelsgesellschaft, a body which co-ordinated the activities of the banks and merchant
houses in Frankfurt, Schöffer returned to Rotterdam.[6] The Deutsche
Handelsgesellschaft, whose roots lay in the urge for economic expansion
following the Franco-German War, set out to create a worldwide network
of import and export trade. It established consortia in the produce
exchange, financed industrial initiatives and acquired interests in many
sectors, including American oilfields. Schöffer & Co., a limited partner in
the Deutsche Handelsgesellschaft, set up a large-scale consortium in coffee
and proceeded to make record profits. The boom reached its height in 1874,
by which time Schöffer had become an extremely wealthy man. But in the

---

[5] *Ein Beitrag zur Geschichte des Kaffee-Handels, den Freunden der Firma W. Schöffer & Co.,
Rotterdam gewidmet*, etc., 1905, 5, 14.
[6] Maier, *Erinnerungen*, 35 ff.

same year, hastened by an economic crisis, the tide turned. Trading losses and others arising from the speculative deals which its nature encouraged, together running into many millions, heralded the disintegration of the Deutsche Handelsgesellschaft.

In the area of Schöffer's personal involvements – which were marked by a preference for innovation – a similar situation existed, high expectations alternating with disappointment. His first venture was to finance the manufacture of an improved burner for gas lamps, which had been invented by his fellow townsman Julius Brönner, a chemist.[7] Soon, however, this was being copied abroad and so the anticipated commercial success failed to materialize. But the consequences of his participation in Brönner's chemical works, set up to manufacture alizarin,[8] a synthetic dye which became popular in the textile industry as a substitute for madder, were far more serious. The company was established in 1874 and Schöffer initially invested 150,000 marks. The market subsequently declined, with the result that no profits were forthcoming. In 1881, when it appeared virtually certain that a dye cartel would be formed, the capital was increased to two million marks, Schöffer substantially enlarging his holding. In 1883 the shares stood well above par, but in the following year the plan for the cartel fell through and alizarin became a staple product of which there was a surplus. The capital was lost, and with it the greater part of Schöffer's fortune.

Earlier, in 1880, the Deutsche Handelsgesellschaft had run into a crisis which occasioned serious losses, and even liquidations. Aided by its limited partners, Willem Ruys and Marinus de Monchy, however, Schöffer & Co. escaped.[9] In spite of his errors of judgement, notably in industrial ventures, Schöffer's personal reputation was unscathed. It was assured by his position as the senior partner in the firm, and strengthened by the authority with which in 1879, together with De Monchy, he rescued Pincoffs' Rotterdamsche Handelsvereeniging from the brink of bankruptcy.[10] For the house of Schöffer & Co., the coffee trade, with which it was so familiar, again became the principal source of revenue. But in Schöffer himself, an exponent of the doctrine of pantheism,[11] adversity did not finally quench a passion for turning technological progress to the advantage of society.

This explains why Schöffer was at pains to visit the Paris electricity exhibition of 1881, with its technical innovations.[12] Impressed by what he had seen there, he addressed a gathering of his friends in Rotterdam, to

[7] Ibid., 96 ff.    [8] Ibid., 98 ff.    [9] Ibid., 106.
[10] Ibid., 78 ff.    [11] Ibid., 34, 70, 97, 122.    [12] Ibid., 110.

whom he explained his vision of dramatic changes in industry and throughout society as a result of the application of electricity. He must have done more than simply amaze his audience, for one of their number, Henry La Grange,[13] drew his attention to A. de Khotinsky, the Russian electrical engineer and inventor of an accumulator and an incandescent lamp, whom he met while visiting London on business in June 1883. But the matter did not end there. De Khotinsky was invited to give a demonstration in Rotterdam, though this apparently involved overcoming some reserve on Schöffer's part:

He was all the more agreeably surprised when a smart, intelligent man, well-mannered and reserved rather than obtrusive, approached him. The conversation was conducted in French, and Khotinsky commenced with a resumé of his life. (...) After this he proceeded to describe his accumulator, concerning which he was already able to show excellent testimonials from the Director-General of Telegraphs in England, Mr W. Preece. When, around midnight, the company moved to the dining room, they found to their surprise that it was splendidly illuminated by incandescent lamps.

Khotinsky, using the only dynamo in Rotterdam which at that time could be driven, had charged a small battery of his accumulators in order to demonstrate his invention.[14]

After more elaborate experiments and the calculation of the return, based on the gas price, on the investment in a central station, the prospects exceeded the expectations. La Grange, Schöffer and his partner, Ernst Boden, thereupon took the initiative in forming a syndicate to issue shares of an electricity supply and lighting company in Rotterdam. De Khotinsky was appointed to the post of technical director, with an annual salary of ƒ10,000. Like La Grange, he received twenty shares in recognition of his contribution to the setting up of the company. Years later De Khotinsky admitted that he had been obliged to accept the post in order to support himself.[15]

Achilles de Khotinsky (1850–1933) was commissioned at the Imperial Naval Academy in St Petersburg in 1869. He went on to study mechanical engineering and natural sciences at the city's university.[16] His inventive talent was soon apparent. While serving as Flag Officer with the Baltic

---

13  Heinrich La Grange (1848–99), who called himself Henry, was an agent for foreign business houses.
14  Maier, *Erinnerungen*, 110.
15  De Khotinsky, *Der De Khotinsky-Accumulator*, 13.
16  *The National Cyclopaedia of American Biography*, New York, 1936, Vol. 25, 63 ff; a comprehensive biography.

Fleet, he was charged with the development of electrical detonation systems for mines and torpedoes, and was also responsible for supervising electric lighting. In 1872 he designed and installed a searchlight, the first to be used on board a warship. In the same year he made experimental incandescent lamps with platinum and carbon filaments, both being placed in a glass bulb from which air had been exhausted. De Khotinsky's researches in the area of incandescent lighting commenced in 1871 and brought him into contact with others who were then similarly engaged, including Konn, Kosloff and Bouliguine.[17] They were members of the circle surrounding the prominent physicist Lodyguine, who at about that time, as already mentioned,[18] made a fresh attempt to solve the problem of electric lighting by the incandescent method, but whose lamp did not progress beyond the experimental stage.

In 1878, while the Russo-Turkish War was in progress, De Khotinsky was sent to the United States to supervise the construction of three cruisers for the Russian Navy. There he became friendly with the American inventor Hiram S. Maxim (1840–1916), for whom he later equipped an incandescent lamp factory in Paris. He also visited Edison, who in the summer of that very year proceeded to devote all his energies to the development of the incandescent lamp, and to whom he presented samples of the Lodyguine lamp:

At the same time as Lodyguine was continuing to work in the face of great difficulties on perfecting the incandescent lamp, lamps constructed by him were taken to America. The naval officer A. De Khotinsky, a trained electrical engineer and inventor, was sent to the U.S.A. to supervise the construction of some ships which had been ordered there for the Russian Naval Ministry. He took with him a few of Lodyguine's lamps and showed them to Edison.[19]

Upon his return to Russia, De Khotinsky was appointed chief engineer of the Jablochkoff Works in St Petersburg.[20] A year later, in 1881, he visited Paris, where, in accordance with instructions from Maxim, he installed an incandescent lighting system at the Opera House. During his sojourn in the French capital, H. Fontaine, the president of the Société Electrique Gramme, challenged him to produce a high-voltage (250-volt) lamp of 200 candlepower and consuming no more than 600 watts, to replace the Jablochkoff candles which illuminated the Avenue de l'Opéra.[21] Although

---

[17] Frank L. Dyer and Thomas Commerford Martin, *Edison, his Life and Inventions*, 1910, Vol. 1, 240.
[18] Cf. Chapter 1, page 7.
[19] L. D. Belkind, *Aleksandr Nikolaevich Lodygin*, Moscow, 1948, 45 ff.
[20] M. A. Satelen, *Russkie elektrotechniki vtoroj poloviny, XIX Veka*, Moscow, 1950, 319.
[21] *The Electrician*, 2.9.1892, 480: 'High voltage lamps by A. de Khotinsky'.

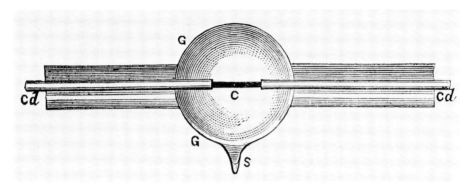

Experimental De Khotinsky lamp of 1872

he succeeded in making such a lamp, from which the factory in Rotterdam in due course became the first to benefit – 'So far as we know these are the only lamps at present attainable to work at so high a potential'[22] – it was ahead of its time from a technical point of view.

In 1882, De Khotinsky moved to London, where for a time he was employed by the incandescent lamp manufacturer Alexander Bernstein, and simultaneously completed the development of the accumulator on which he had worked for ten years.[23] He then moved to the laboratory of L. Warnerke in London, where he continued his researches in the area of filament-making. These led in 1883 to: 'a homogeneous material for manufacturing filaments which, after carbonising, gave a carbon of specific gravity equal to 1.45'.[24] It says much for De Khotinsky's long experience, and even more for the advances made in electric lighting, that the exhibits at the international electricity exhibition in Vienna in 1883 included 'the archaeological apparatus of Lodyguine and others', which included an experimental incandescent lamp made by De Khotinsky in 1872.[25]

By this time De Khotinsky had become known in England as 'a man of scientific mark'; but a new and quite different facet was added to his character when, as a former officer of the Russian Navy, his name was linked with plots laid in 1881 to assassinate Czar Alexander II, the novel aspect of which was the use of electrically detonated mines.[26] Suspicion fell

---

[22] *The Electrician*, 9.3.1888, 466: 'The de Khotinsky incandescent lamp'.
[23] De Khotinsky, *Der De Khotinsky-Accumulator*, 13.
[24] *The Electrician*, 2.9.1892, 481.
[25] *The Electrician*, 15.9.1883, 421 ff: 'The electrical exhibition at Vienna'.
[26] *The Electrician*, 26.3.1881, 230 ff: 'Electricity and crime'; idem, 25.6.1881 and 23.7.1881: 'Electricity among the Nihilists'.

upon the Nihilists, and the trail led to the Navy's electrical institute at St Petersburg.[27] De Khotinsky denied any personal involvement in the conspiracy; nevertheless he chose a new career in Rotterdam in preference to returning to his native land.

The site chosen by the Electriciteits-Maatschappij, Systeem 'De Khotinsky' for its accumulator and incandescent lamp factory was situated on the Noordereiland, a small island in the River Meuse, and was known as 35 Prins Hendrikkade. The building was completed in August 1884.[28] In the boilerhouse stood a 150-horsepower steam engine which powered an Edison dynamo. The current was divided between two circuits, one feeding a bank of accumulators supplying electricity to the factory and the other terminating at a riverside berth to which exhausted accumulators were brought daily and, after recharging, returned to the northern bank of the river. With this temporary solution to the problem of illuminating the offices of the Rotterdam Bank and Schöffer & Co., which caused a sensation, the company deliberately anticipated the construction of one or more central stations, for which it sought a concession.

The application was duly discussed by the City Council, and it is clear from the deliberations that the desirability of a *municipal* electricity undertaking was already recognized – 'so that all such (private) companies will know what they are in for'.[29] On 2 April 1885, the company was given permission – by way of an experiment and until further notice – to lay supply cables in the Boompjes district of Rotterdam. A provisional installation with a capacity of about 300 incandescent lamps came into operation in June 1885. This led to a demand for something like 6,000 lighting points.[30] Schöffer, looking to the future, said that when the station had been enlarged, the company hoped to convince not only the local council but all interested parties, both at home and abroad, that with application of the De Khotinsky system – of which the special accumulator with horizontal plates was the *pièce de résistance*[31] – the objections to, and distrust of, electric lighting had been overcome. In the short term, at least, this statement was certainly not without foundation, as is shown by the foreign orders, which the company received in 1886:

---

[27] R. Seth, *The Russian Terrorists*, 1966, 81.
[28] *Nieuwe Rotterdamsche Courant*, 23.8.1884: 'Nijverheid en Technische Kunsten'.
[29] *Nieuwe Rotterdamsche Courant*, 3.4.1885: report of the council meeting on 2.4.1885.
[30] Maier, *Erinnerungen*, 112.
[31] Van Cappelle, *De Electriciteit*, 148 ff; cf. A. C. Zoethout, *Handboek voor den electriciën*, 1908, 85.

Germany, seventeen large and small installations; Austria, four large installations; Denmark, three installations; Great Britain, three installations; France, one installation; U.S.A., one installation.[32]

The De Khotinsky system was based on the principle that the accumulators could be charged during the period when the dynamo produced more current than was required by the consumers, while in the evening, when demand was at its maximum, additional current could be obtained from the accumulators. This had the twin advantages of simpler operation of the station and optimum economy in the use of the dynamo.

The company attached great importance to the construction, in 1887, of a central station of this type in the Neue Friedrichstrasse in Berlin, the city which was then the principal *champs de bataille* of the electrical companies.[33] This station had an initial capacity of 1,200 lamps rated at 150 volts and 16 candlepower, and remained in operation until after the turn of the century. With it, the company sought to publicize its lighting system, earlier attempts to do so from its base in Rotterdam having failed. Admittedly, the company had been offered a concession by the Council; but on such onerous terms that it had been obliged to decline. For, according to Schöffer, the Council had decided shortly beforehand to assume control of gas supplies, and this naturally gave rise to hostility towards his company, which was manifested in official opposition to its plans.[34] This was in strong contrast to the situation in Germany, where there was growing interest in the De Khotinsky system, albeit patent disputes and competition from the Tudor accumulator adversely affected the results. Teething troubles and other factors combined to make the early years more difficult and costly than had been anticipated.

The year 1884 merits special mention, for it was then that the first incandescent lamp was manufactured in the Netherlands; this was made by the Electriciteits-Maatschappij, Systeem 'De Khotinsky' at its works in Rotterdam. A historic moment, which can have been appreciated only by those most closely concerned. On 22 August of that year, representatives of the Press and other guests were given an opportunity to inspect the factory.[35] The manufacture of lamps on a significant scale was not, however, achieved without setbacks and disappointments; indeed, these

32  *Rotterdamsch Nieuwsblad*, 26.6.1886: report of the Annual General Meeting.
33  *Nieuwe Rotterdamsche Courant*, 16.7.1887: 'in spite of opposition from Siemens'.
34  Maier, *Erinnerungen*, 112.
35  *Nieuwe Rotterdamsche Courant*, 23.8.1884.

were such that the initial efforts had to be seen as a failure.[36] Moreover, it took a considerable time to attract skilled foremen and 'to find and train suitable persons for this new, delicate work'.[37] Not until De Khotinsky himself found time to 'personally overhaul the manufacturing procedure', and experienced men, including the German engineer Hans Urban, were recruited, did the factory succeed in producing saleable incandescent lamps. It was by then mid-1885.[38]

The glassblowing department, in which compressed air was used, was manned by skilled workers from England and Germany (until 1888 or thereabouts, many lamp manufacturers produced their own bulbs). The accumulators were tested for charge in the laboratory, and the lamps were tested for intensity in the photometry department. There was a department in which the filaments were carbonized (at 2000°C), and others for the exhaustion and assembly of the lamps. The pattern room and the stores completed the factory, which covered an area of 544 square metres. The manufacturing capacity was three hundred lamps per day. The German electrical engineer J. Zacharias, who at this time was working at the Seel lamp works in Berlin, paid a formal visit to the Rotterdam factory in 1887, which he afterwards described thus:

Mr De Khotinsky charmingly explained the various stages of manufacture and the equipment used in these. In the interests of the factory, however, I was requested not to give any detailed explanation of the process, because the method of manufacturing the filament, in particular, was considered to be a trade secret.

The carbon filament is made from a special substance[39] and has a very high resistance. The wire, which is coiled into a loop, can, like a steel wire, be uncoiled by hand and resumes its original shape when it is released. These properties of the material make it possible to manufacture incandescent lamps for a potential of up to 150 volts and with an intensity of 300 candlepower. The carbon filament does not easily overheat, and the life can be varied within certain limits.

As a result of a very simple but ingenious improvement to the mercury pumps, one man can supervise and operate a large number of pumps, whereas up to now one man has been required for each pump, handling at most ten lamps. This invention has not only simplified the operation of the pumps, but has also reduced the time required to exhaust a bulb from seven hours to three.

We saw an attractive collection of coloured and matt-finish lamps, and white

36  *Rotterdamsch Nieuwsblad*, 26.6.1886.
37  *Nieuwe Rotterdamsche Courant*, 5.6.1885.
38  *Rotterdamsch Nieuwsblad*, 26.6.1886.
39  Describing the De Khotinsky filament, the *Elektrotechnische Zeitschrift*, 1887, 86, said: 'Der Kohlenfaden besteht aus einem amorphen, homogenen, structurlosen Material'; the *Zeitschrift für angewandte Elektricitätslehre*, 1889, 102, referred to: 'Gelatine oder nitrierte Zellulose'.

ones with coloured stripes. The colours and the matt finish are not achieved with lacquer, as in German lamps, but by staining the glass.[40]

The Rotterdam factory justly claimed that its lamps were among the best in terms of quality, and this was confirmed by the remarkably widespread and favourable reviews of the De Khotinsky lamp which appeared in English and German trade journals. The range covered voltages from 5 to 200 and light intensities from 2 to 300 candlepower. The life of the lamps varied from 300 hours at a consumption of 2.25 watts per candlepower to 2,000 hours at 5 watts per candlepower.[41]

Demand increased rapidly, especially in Germany and France, where local representatives were appointed. But there was also a market in Belgium, Spain and Russia. Even in Britain, where Shippey Bros.[42] were the agents, things were moving ahead, Schöffer informed his shareholders in July 1887. Output was running at three hundred lamps per day while at least one thousand could be sold, and therefore substantial expansion was required. And because 'land is too costly in Rotterdam, and building costs too high', Schöffer told the annual meeting of shareholders, 'added to which the product is unduly burdened by freight charges and duties when imported into Germany', it had been decided to establish a second lamp factory in his birthplace, Gelnhausen.[43] One might well suspect that this decision stemmed not only from personal considerations on the part of Schöffer and commercial advantages of siting the works in Germany, but also from the rigid attitude experienced by the company, especially from 'technical officials of the municipality'.[44] The increasing demands which the manufacture of lamps, in particular, made on the management's time, and the above-mentioned savings on freight and import duty (12%), made it attractive to transfer the production of accumulators to Germany as well, and with a view to this a factory was built adjacent to the lead rolling mill in Cologne owned by Gottfried Hagen, with whom the company entered into a licence agreement. The rapid growth of electric lighting in Germany after 1885, as a factor in itself, was also among the motives for the move.

From 1887, at which time the initial problems had scarcely been overcome, the greater part of the production was centred in Germany,

[40] *Zeitschrift für angewandte Elektricitätslehre*, 1887, 352.
[41] *Elektrotechnische Zeitschrift*, 1887, 86.
[42] Cf. Chapter 2, page 71.
[43] *Nieuwe Rotterdamsche Courant*, 16.7.1887.
[44] *Nieuwe Rotterdamsche Courant*, 5.6.1885.

although the factory in Rotterdam continued to operate until 1891. The company also continued to be domiciled there. Thus in the space of four years, chiefly as a result of economic factors, the company moved to transfer the emphasis of its operations abroad.

It was an unfortunate circumstance that in 1886 the Deutsche Edison Gesellschaft had embarked on litigation with the aim of forcing the De Khotinsky lamp off the German market.[45] The company, however, believed that its patent position in Germany afforded adequate security. In France, too, it was confronted with a lawsuit, this time from the Société des Lampes Incandescentes Edison-Swan.[46] In this dispute, the Paris Court ultimately ruled that the De Khotinsky filament, which was made from an amorphous, colloidal cellulose paste, had nothing in common with the Edison filament, which was made from bamboo fibre.[47] It is clear from this, as from similar suits against other manufacturers, that in Germany and France, in contrast to Britain, Edison's basic patent was not interpreted as conferring an absolute monopoly of the manufacture of incandescent lamps. But these often protracted lawsuits harmed the commercial interests of the defendants and involved them in a great deal of additional expense. The legal costs faced by the Rotterdam company in France alone amounted to more than Fr. francs 100,000.[48]

The first quarter of the financial year 1887/8 produced the first operating profit by the Electriciteits-Maatschappij, Systeem 'De Khotinsky'. Addressing the shareholders at their annual meeting, Schöffer expressed the view that, as a result of strenuous efforts – and until such time as others discovered something better – the company had brilliant prospects.[49] These words are characteristic of the merchant who *en passant* betrays a realization of his vulnerability in an industrial role. With the commissioning of the factory in Gelnhausen, it seemed that a 'new era of prosperity'[50] had dawned. In March 1889, output from the works reached 1,000 lamps per day, whereupon the Board voted to increase this to 2,500. In spite of keener competition, which caused the average lamp price to fall to *f*1.75, and a sharp rise in raw material costs, the company ended the year 1889/90 with a profit of *f*125,000. To cover earlier losses, but also in view of the urgent

45  *Electrical Review*, 1887, 509; cf. *La Lumière Electrique*, 1887, 398, and *50 Jahre AEG*, 114.
46  *The Electrician*, 10.4.1891, 687: 'Incandescent lamp litigation in France'.
47  *The Electrician*, 19.5.1893, 58: 'The Edison lamp patent in France'.
48  Maier, *Erinnerungen*, 119.
49  *Nieuwe Rotterdamsche Courant*, 16.7.1887.
50  Maier, *Erinnerungen*, 117.

need to strengthen the working capital to meet the increase in business, the whole of the profit was retained. The company, the report stated, 'may now be regarded as resting on very sound foundations'.[51] Previous losses no longer appeared in the balance sheet; the prospect was one of sound profits based almost entirely on the manufacture of incandescent lamps. The product which had originally held pride of place – the electric lighting system with banks of accumulators – had meanwhile been overtaken in importance by the incandescent lamp, the market for which had developed independently and on a scale which exceeded expectations. In the Netherlands, too, the demand for lamps increased, as may be gauged from the fact that in 1890 Groeneveld, Van der Poll & Co. alone entered into a contract for the supply of 10,000 De Khotinsky lamps annually.[52]

It is worthy of note that the prosperity which the company enjoyed in the area of lamp manufacture – so convincingly voiced – coincided with the decision, taken in 1889, by Messrs Goossens, bankers and coffee traders of Venlo, to commence making lamps. Little information is available concerning the setting up of this factory, but one detail stands out, namely that the director and co-founder, Emile Goossens, carried on the business of merchant in Rotterdam from 1883 to 1889. Coming in the autumn of 1889, the event also coincided with the negotiations between the Messrs Philips and Brush, the breakdown of which led the former to decide to establish a lamp factory. The records of Peletier & Philips reveal that Frederik Philips, through his coffee-roasting establishment, had connections with Schöffer & Co. of Rotterdam.[53] Moreover, it is reasonable to assume that Frederik Philips and Ludwig Wilhelm Schöffer, as prominent merchants of similar age and with interests in the business world in Rotterdam, knew each other.

These circumstances highlight the remarkable concatenation of coffee and incandescent lamps which then suddenly occurred, and which strengthens our belief that Schöffer's industrial adventure served as an example to at least two of his colleagues in the coffee trade. It facilitated the realization of a latent ambition on the part of these wealthy merchants to expand into a new area of entrepreneurial skill – the more so since, as we shall see, both Philips and Goossens had access to the necessary technical knowledge.

In describing the later fortunes of the Electriciteits-Maatschappij, Systeem 'De Khotinsky', whose prosperity was short-lived, we must perforce be

---

[51] *Nieuwe Rotterdamsche Courant*, 4.6.1890.
[52] Copy-book of Gerard Philips, 28.1.1890 and 21.2.1890: two letters to AEG.
[53] Current account book of Frederik Philips; Philips Archives, Eindhoven.

brief. Differences of opinion concerning the organization of the company and the reduction of costs, and others of a personal nature, led in 1891 to a rift between De Khotinsky and Schöffer.[54] This occurred at the very moment when the growth potential of the company was at a peak and when a further step towards large-scale industrial activity, particularly in the production of lamps, had to be taken. It came as a hard blow to Schöffer that the chemist, Dr M. Fremery, and the chief engineer, H. Urban, simultaneously tendered their resignations. Obviously, there had been a lack of mutual understanding and cohesion at the top. Put more bluntly, the incidental ties between the inventor De Khotinsky and the *Kommerzienrat* Schöffer, however fruitful they may have been, afforded no guarantee for the stable development of the enterprise. Certainly not when prices fell and it became necessary to adapt the production methods to the new situation. On 2 December 1891, De Khotinsky embarked in a ship bound for the United States; that night the factory in Gelnhausen was burned to the ground.[55] 'One after another the old technicians went to work for competitors and ultimately only Schöffer and his still young son were left.'[56]

Faced with this brain drain, Schöffer engaged Dr Rud. Weber, who held a professorship in Berlin, as his adviser in order to ensure the continuity of the company in technical terms.[57] His youngest son, Willy, whom De Khotinsky had trained as an electrical engineer, was made a director. In 1892, by which time the factory in Rotterdam had closed, the registered office was transferred to Germany and the name changed to Electricitäts-Gesellschaft Gelnhausen m.b.H. After a financial reorganization, the shareholders raised the authorized capital to 650,000 marks. The rebuilt factory at Gelnhausen provided work for about two hundred men and women.

Aided by the profits of the accumulator factory and those from the manufacture of tin oxide and other chemical products, upon which it had meanwhile embarked, the company survived the fierce competition of the 1890s with its lamp-making activities intact. In 1894 the price of an incandescent lamp reached a low of twenty-five (Dutch) cents, and when, in the same year, the European manufacturers formed a cartel, the Verein europäischer Glühlampenfabrikanten, Schöffer was chosen as its chairman.[58] Upon the establishment in 1903 of the European incandescent lamp syndicate – the Verkaufstelle Vereinigter Glühlampenfabriken G.m.b.H. of

[54]  Maier, *Erinnerungen*, 118 ff.
[55]  *Elektrotechnische Zeitschrift*, 1891, 682.
[56]  Maier, *Erinnerungen*, 121.
[57]  *Elektrotechnische Zeitschrift*, 1893, 280.
[58]  Maier, *Erinnerungen*, 122; cf. *De Ingenieur*, 1894, 226.

Berlin – the factory in Gelnhausen was allotted a quota of 1.9% compared with, for example, the 10.8% of Philips & Co. In terms of annual output, this meant 525,000 lamps compared with 3,000,000. It is clear from this that after 1891 the company was unable to increase its market share to any appreciable extent. In 1903, practically all the shares of Electricitäts-Gesellschaft Gelnhausen m.b.H. were held by Schöffer & Co. of Rotterdam.[59] As a minor producer, the Gelnhausen factory remained a member of the Verkaufstelle until the latter was dissolved in 1913.

Ludwig Wilhelm Schöffer was a successful merchant, but the same fortune did not attend him in the industrial sphere. Owing to too much diversity on too small a scale, his lamp factory, despite the product quality for which it was famed,[60] did not choose the path of highly specialized mass production, probably because the necessity for such a course was not recognized. In spite of his abilities and his zeal for progress, Schöffer was destined to be no more than a pioneer among lamp manufacturers. On the other hand, for this very reason he had the lasting merit of having served as a springboard for others. According to the *Elektrotechnische Zeitschrift* of 2 September 1892, his ex-associates Fremery and Urban established the Rheinische Glühlampenfabrik at Oberbruch, near Aachen in that year. With their long experience and technical knowledge, the journal wrote, one might anticipate a sound product; and this expectation was indeed borne out. Tests carried out by these engineers during their research into the incandescent lamp led to discoveries and patents which were of value to the synthetic fibres industry and in 1899 led directly to the founding of Vereinigte Glanzstoff-Fabriken AG.[61]

Although Achilles de Khotinsky's sojourn in Holland was brief, the preparatory work which he undertook also served to stimulate and educate others. Jos Roothaan, co-founder in 1889 of an incandescent lamp works and later a director of N.V. Electrostoom, learned the science of electricity from De Khotinsky, commencing with the tracing of 'those wretched cable faults' in the Boompjes district of Rotterdam.[62] Others who, as apprentices, acquired knowledge and experience of electrical engineering in the factories in Rotterdam and Gelnhausen included F. Hazemeyer, who later became an

[59] Report Auskunftei W. Schimmelpfeng, Frankfurt am Main, 14.5.1903; archives of the Vitrite Works, Middelburg.
[60] *The Electrician*, 25.11.1892: 'Life and efficiency tests of incandescent lamps'.
[61] L. J. van der Valk, 'Vijf en twintig jaar Nederlandse kunstzijde', in *Economisch-Statistische Berichten*, 8.6.1938, 424 ff.
[62] J. Roothaan to C. Alewijnse, 12.10.1929; family archive of C. B. Alewijnse, Ubbergen.

electrical manufacturer in Hengelo ('I can still remember celebrating the 1,000th lamp')[63] and C. Alewijnse, the lamp manufacturer and installation contractor of Nijmegen. They described their 'Rotterdam tutor', to whom they dedicated an essay, in the following words:

He was a pioneer in the true sense of the word, an organizer of great stature from whom much originated and who inspired those who worked with him. He taught us how things should be done, and also how they should not be done; but his technical imagination and the energy with which he brought his plans to fruition were an example to many.

We were concerned, not with experiments but with manufacture, which filled a need and thereby contributed to the development of electrical engineering at that time.[64]

At the end of 1891, De Khotinsky arrived in the New World, where he joined the Board of the Germania Electric Company in Boston, Massachusetts. There he set up a lamp works, but this was forced to close a year later following the final verdict of the American courts in the long-running legal battle over Edison's basic patent. As a result of this litigation, virtually all Edison's rivals in the United States had been eliminated by 1892.[65] In America, through his association with various firms and institutes, his membership of the development staff of the Central Scientific Company during the First World War and his long engagements with the universities of Chicago and Michigan, De Khotinsky's scientific and technical talents were, for the first time, fully deployed.[66] His eventful life came to an end in 1933. Schöffer, in his biography, written in 1901, was quoted as saying that much of the fruit of De Khotinsky's labours 'will be of lasting value'.[67]

Holland's second incandescent lamp factory was established by the firm of Johan Boudewijnse, of Middelburg, in July 1887. The management was in the hands of Johan Boudewijnse (1866–88), the son of a merchant, Cornelis Boudewijnse, who had died in 1882. Immediately after leaving secondary school, Johan embarked on the installation of telephones and electrical bells, the first step towards his goal of an independent career. In 1887 he became the Dutch agent for electrical apparatus and materials manufactured by the General Electric Company of London. His interest in electrical

[63] F. Hazemeyer, 'Een terugblik', in *Electro-Technische Opstellen, aangeboden aan prof. C. Feldmann op 8 juni 1937*, 200.
[64] Ibid.
[65] Bright, *Electric-Lamp Industry*, 88 ff.
[66] *The National Cyclopaedia of American Biography*.
[67] Maier, *Erinnerungen*, 121.

engineering, which he shared with his younger brother Cornelis, was aroused while he was attending the secondary school in Middelburg. There, both boys acquired basic knowledge, which they expanded by studying at home. As was the case with Willem Smit, these future businessmen resorted to English and French sources, and authoritative journals such as *The Electrician* and *La Lumière Electrique* played a significant part in their theoretical and practical training.

Financial assistance for the formation of the company, which was described as 'a factory for the manufacture of incandescent lamps and electrical apparatus, and the installation thereof',[68] was provided by their uncles and guardians J. P. and P. Boudewijnse, installation contractors and ironmongers. Their trading company – de Gebroeders Boudewijnse – whose activities included installing gas lighting, represented the Wenham Company of London, a manufacturer of gas lamps, and Arden Hill & Co. of Birmingham, who produced gas fires and gas stoves. That they were willing to adapt to the changing circumstances is shown by their efforts in 1887 to have electrical engineers admitted to membership of the Vereeniging van Gasfabriekanten in Nederland, the association of gas manufacturers, to which they belonged.[69] But their proposal was rejected by thirty-five votes to fifteen. The arrangement was that if the lamp manufacturing company, Johan Boudewijnse, received an order for the installation of electric lighting in private houses or factories, the work would be carried out by the installation department of Gebroeders Boudewijnse. This characterizes the nature and structure of this active family business, in which gas and electric lighting, trading, manufacture and installation were seen as complementary activities.

Among those who provided the initial capital of ƒ20,000 was Ph. Boudewijnse, a tobacco merchant and cigar manufacturer of Middelburg. In 1890, by which time the capital had risen to about ƒ40,000, Marinus Adriaan van der Leijé (1868–1941), the son of a local banker, became co-director of the lamp factory.

With the fairly strong orientation of these Middelburg businessmen towards Britain – and in particular their connections with British suppliers, including Gustav Binswanger, the founder of the General Electric Company, then a small electrical engineering firm in London[70] – the decision to

[68] Council Report, 1887; Municipal Archives, Middelburg.
[69] *Het Gas*, journal of the Vereeniging van Gasfabriekanten in Nederland, August/September 1887; minutes of the General Meeting of 26 and 27 June 1887.
[70] R. Jones and O. Marriott, *Anatomy of a Merger*, 1970, 70.

I hereby declare to take Mr. C. J. Robertson,
electrician of Invergarry. Crouch End, London N.
in my employ for a period of not less than
six months, to begin on the first day of June
eighteen hundred & eighty seven And to pay
him at the rate of Six pounds Sterling
per week.

Middelburg. April 9th 1887.

Johan Boudewijnse

(Witness) H. J. de Nooijnck.

I hereby declare to come in the employ
of Mr. Johan Boudewijnse, electrician of
Middelburg on the first day of June
eighteen hundred & eighty seven to remain
so for a period of not less than six months,
to fulfill my duties as foreman of his
incandescent lamp factory & to do everything
in my power to bring out a good, lasting
& reliable lamp.

London, April 4th 1887.

C. J. Robertson.

(Witness) Charles Marshall.

Contract of employment between C. J. Robertson and Johan Boudewijnse

set up a lamp works was not entirely coincidental. The immediate reason, however, lay in the patent legislation in Britain, the implications of which have already been briefly referred to and were closely watched by electrical engineers in other countries including the Netherlands. When, in January 1887, following the outcome of the case brought by Edison & Swan against Woodhouse & Rawson, virtually every British incandescent lamp manufacturer decided to cease production,[71] the unfettered transfer of knowledge and experience became a fact. Among the experts who fled abroad in order to turn their know-how into money (and many had no alternative) was C. J. Robertson, manager of the Bernstein Electric Light Company, Ltd, of London.[72] Robertson's circumstances obliged him to accept a position in Johan Boudewijnse's incandescent lamp factory where, for a salary of £6 per week, he was to do his best to produce a sound lamp. Both parties, therefore, benefited from the situation. In the course of 1887, Robertson equipped the factory, learned the Dutch language and trained the 'raw native hands'[73] for the delicate work which lay ahead. At the Boudewijnse factory, work of this nature was performed only by men. Robertson was to earn fame as an expert on carbon-filament lamps (the significance of his work will be dealt with later) and thus certain details of his career — which, moreover, reveal just how limited was the circle of experts who were involved in the development of the incandescent lamp at that time — merit reference here.

Charles John Robertson (1860–1909), the son of a bullion maker, attended the Merchant Taylors' School in London, where he obtained a well-endowed scholarship to St John's College, Oxford; this, however, he was unable to take up for personal reasons. Instead he attended the Finsbury Technical College in London, where he studied electrical engineering under Professors Ayrton and Perry, and took a three-year course in analytical chemistry under Professor Armstrong. In 1881 he joined the Anglo-American Brush Electric Light Corporation as assistant to Lane-Fox, but after two years he accepted the post of manager of the incandescent lamp department of Pilsen-Joel. Later he moved to a similar position with the General Electric Company in London. He was principally engaged in the development of colloidal materials and methods of manufacturing filaments from these. In 1885 we find him in the employ of Alexander

[71] Cf. Chapter 1, page 28.

[72] The General Electric Company Ltd, *The Story of the Lamp*, 1924, 3.

[73] *The Electrician, Electrical Trades' Directory and Handbook*, 1899: a biography of C. J. Robertson.

Charles John Robertson (1860–1909)      Cornelis Dirk Nagtglas Versteeg
                                                (1861–1924)

Bernstein, for whom he equipped a new lamp factory in London, where he pursued his research. In 1887, however, he was forced to abandon his work when the factory, like others, closed under the threat of legal action over patents. Robertson, through his own experience, was familiar with both the technical and economic aspects of the British incandescent lamp industry from its inception.

The Boudewijnse lamp factory, which flanked the harbour in Middelburg, commenced production in January 1888.[74]

The factory exuded a peculiar and mysterious fascination. A number of metal chimneys rose up from the buildings. When we passed it on the way home from school, we occasionally saw that one of the chimneys was red-hot and flames were escaping from it, creating a reddish glow.[75]

In the course of 1888 the work force increased to thirty, including Englishmen and Germans who were employed as 'flashers' and glass-

---

[74] The company's first invoice for incandescent lamps was despatched on 18 January 1888. These were supplied to the Stearine-kaarsenfabriek, a candle factory, in Gouda. Cf. copy-book of the Boudewijnse family.
[75] Farewell speech by Ir. H. C. Ghijsen, managing director of the Vitrite Works, 26.9.1953; archives of the Vitrite Works, Middelburg.

Cornelis Boudewijnse (1869–1936)

blowers. At the end of the first year's operations it was decided that in future the glass bulbs should be obtained from an outside supplier, whereupon the number of glassblowers was reduced to two or three.[76] Tenders were invited from Dutch and foreign glassworks for the supply of 125,000–150,000 bulbs per year, and the most favourable bid, which averaged 5.8 guilder cents per bulb, was submitted by Rheinsche Glashütten A.G. of Cologne. This company had specialized in this new article, for which airtight glass was used, and was a regular supplier to several lamp factories.[77]

The Boudewijnse company suffered a severe blow with the death, after a brief illness, of Johan on 14 February 1888.[78] The day-to-day management passed into the hands of his brother, Cornelis (1869–1936). On 1 July of the same year, he obtained the assistance of the civil engineer Cornelis Dirk Nagtglas Versteeg (1861–1924), who lived in Middelburg.[79] It is remarkable that the responsibility for the company should have been placed in such young hands. The arrival of Nagtglas Versteeg, who had studied in Delft,

[76] Boudewijnse in a letter to J. J. B. J. Bouvy, Dordrecht, dated 7.12.1888.
[77] Basch, *Die Entwicklung*, 61.
[78] *Middelburgsche Courant*, 18.2.1888: an obituary.
[79] A. Heerding, 'C. D. Nagtglas Versteeg', in *Biografisch Woordenboek van Nederland*, Vol. 1, 1979, 422 ff.

did more than simply fill the void left by the death of Johan Boudewijnse, even though his formal authority was limited. The service contract shows that Nagtglas Versteeg agreed 'to recognize Mr Cornelis Boudewijnse as managing director' and to carry out industriously the installation works assigned to him by Messrs J. P. and P. Boudewijnse.[80] Furthermore, he undertook, upon a bond of $f$ 5,000, not to establish a rival lamp factory within eight years. Other conditions of his employment included a working week of at least sixty hours, in return for which, as deputy managing director, he was to receive a salary of $f$ 1,250 per annum. It is interesting to note that his introduction to electrical engineering inspired him to enrol at the University of Liège a few years later, where he obtained a degree in this subject. As an expert on electric lighting, but more importantly as the founder of Technisch Inspectie- en Adviesbureau Nagtglas Versteeg, a firm of consulting engineers with headquarters in Amsterdam, he was to play a prominent part in the drawing up of electrical safety regulations in the Netherlands.[81] In 1912, when Philips & Co. became a limited company, it was Nagtglas Versteeg whom the banks appointed to value the technical installations at Eindhoven.

Robertson, however, was the one who possessed the vital necessary technical knowledge; his contract of employment embodied a clause permitting him to sell lamps privately to former Bernstein clients in Germany and France. He received the wholesale discount of thirty per cent and was required to observe the customary retail discounts of twenty per cent on quantities of 100 lamps or more and twenty-five per cent on orders for more than 1,000. This privilege lasted until 1889, when his remuneration was changed to a fixed salary of $f$ 400 a month plus one per cent of the total turnover.[82] This made him the highest-paid employee in the company. From 1890 onwards, the founding partners, C. Boudewijnse and M. A. van der Leijé, as managing directors each received a salary of $f$ 3,600 a year. Skilled workers from other countries were paid between $f$ 27 and $f$ 36 per week, Dutch workers from six to twelve cents per hour, and boys under the age of fifteen – of whom there were two – three cents an hour. The working conditions were laid down in a *Fabrieksreglement*. The company had privately insured its employees against disability and industrial accidents,

80   Agreement dated 21.8.1888; archives of the Vitrite Works, Middelburg.
81   C. D. Nagtglas Versteeg, *De wenschelijkheid eener betere controle van Electrische Installatiën*, 1900; cf. S. de Jonge Mulock Houwer, *Het ontstaan en de eerste jaren van het Bureau C. D. Nagtglas Versteeg*, 1956.
82   Contracts of employment dated 20.2.1888, 1.12.1888 and 1.1.1891; archives of the Vitrite Works, Middelburg.

Table 15. *Johan Boudewijnse & Co. Sales, cost and operating account,*
*1888–93 (guilders)*

| Year | Number of lamps sold | Number of employees | Wages | Salaries | Materials | General expenses | Revenue | Profit/ (loss) |
|------|------|------|------|------|------|------|------|------|
| 1888 | 40,000 | 30 | 15,500 | 9,000 | 14,500 | 2,000 | 60,000 | 19,000 |
| 1889 | 80,000 | 40 | 18,000 | 9,500 | 29,500 | 3,500 | 108,000 | 47,500 |
| 1890 | 90,000 | 35 | 16,500 | 13,500 | 34,000 | 4,000 | 90,000 | 22,000 |
| 1891 | 130,000 | 35 | 17,000 | 11,000 | 49,500 | 3,500 | 104,000 | 23,000 |
| 1892 | 100,000 | 30 | 15,000 | 9,500 | 38,000 | 3,000 | 65,000 | (500) |
| 1893 | 90,000 | 25 | 12,000 | 7,500 | 32,500 | 3,000 | 41,000 | (14,000) |

paying the premiums amounting to 0.7% of the annual salary or wage.[83] In doing so, Cornelis Boudewijnse followed the policy advocated by the Vereeniging tot Bevordering van Fabrieks- en Handwerksnijverheid in Nederland, of which he was a member.[84]

The surviving portion of the archives of the firm of Johan Boudewijnse, which includes the correspondence books for the period 1888–97, enables us to achieve a breakdown of the trading result and a number of cost elements. The cost price of lamps produced in Middelburg, computed on the basis of sales,[85] averaged *f* 1.02 in 1888. In 1889 and 1890 the figure was approximately 75 cents, and in the next three years 62, 66 and 61 cents respectively. In 1890, the German engineer J. Zacharias put the cost of lamps produced in a factory with a daily output of 1,000 units – three times the capacity of the Boudewijnse works – at 63 cents with a possible deviation of twenty-five to thirty per cent.[86] This figure, it appears, was made up of (a) labour, 24 cents; (b) direct and indirect material costs, including the customary margin of ten per cent for wastage, 27 cents; (c) wages, salaries and overheads, 12 cents.

In addition to the striking similarity between the types of cost shown in this estimate and those faced by Boudewijnse, Zacharias' figures closely approximate to the manufacturing cost at the Brush factory in London, which in 1888 corresponded to 67 cents per lamp (see Table 8 on page 81).

[83] Policy No. 2924 issued by Eerste Nederlandsche Verzekerings-Mij., The Hague, 5.2.1890; archives of the Vitrite Works, Middelburg.
[84] Cf. Chapter 6, page 242.
[85] As it was not feasible to reconstruct the annual production figures, we took the sales figures as our starting point. The high level of sales in 1891 was in part made possible by stocks formed in 1890. In arriving at the losses sustained in 1892 and 1893, account was taken of 30,000 unsold lamps valued at *f* 12,000; see Table 15 above.
[86] Zacharias, *Die Glühlampe*, 56 ff, 159.

In Paris, the Compagnie Générale des Lampes Incandescentes arrived at a cost price of 92 cents in 1890, based on an output of 1,000 lamps a day. This comprised (a) labour, 38 cents; (b) materials, 32 cents; (c) general costs, 22 cents. The company, a subsidiary of Edison & Swan, published these figures with the aim of impressing on the government that the French lamp industry was threatened by the substantially lower level of wages in other countries, notably Germany.[87]

Labour costs in the French incandescent lamp industry may have been comparatively high; raw material costs, on the other hand, were virtually the same in all countries. By far the most important single material was platinum, which was used for the wires which carried the current to the filament. The keen demand for this metal caused the price to rise from $f$ 500 per kg in 1888 to $f$ 1,350 in 1890.[88] For a standard 16-candlepower lamp, this implied a cost of 18–20 cents for platinum alone, rendering it economic to buy back used lamps in order to recover the precious metal.[89] This explains why the Boudewijnse Company also traded in platinum. In 1890, for example, it paid 5 cents for a burned-out 100-volt, 16-candlepower lamp, and 20 cents for one of 50 volts and 50 candlepower.[90]

A contemporary description of the manufacturing process employed at the Middelburg factory is contained in a report sent by Boudewijnse to Professor J. A. Snijders of the Delft Polytechnic in February 1889:

In the first place, my factory makes the filaments, of which I am sending you a few. As you will understand, I cannot give you details of how these are made. The filaments normally undergo another process, the so-called 'flashing', before they are inserted in the platinum.

The platinum wire is cut to the right length, and one of the ends is flattened on one side. The flattened ends are drawn through a narrow orifice (the so-called drawing trough), causing the flat part to become curved into a small tube, into which the filament fits exactly.

Two of these platinum tubes are fused into a small piece of glass to produce the so-called platinum bridge. The filament, which has been cut to length, is now inserted in the bridge and secured with carbon. In the Edison lamps, this is achieved by electrolysis, using copper. The filaments are then flashed again; that is to say, the resistance of the filament is regulated. After this process, the filament is ready to be placed inside the bulb.

The bulbs are made from glass tube in the following manner: [...] to which, of

[87]  M. G. Sciama, 'Rapport présenté au nom de la commission des douanes de la chambre syndicale des industries électriques', in *La Lumière Electrique*, Vol. 38, 1890, 433 ff.
[88]  A. Rigaut, 'La platine dans l'industrie électrique', in *La Lumière Electrique*, Vol. 38, 1890, 295 ff.
[89]  Van Cappelle, *De Electriciteit*, 225.
[90]  Correspondence between the Boudewijnse Company and its representatives in Berlin and Copenhagen, 1890 and succeeding years.

course, a small tube must be attached for connection to the pump. The end of the bulb is now removed and the tube opened to permit the filament to be introduced, after which the bulb is ready to be sealed on the pumps in order to obtain a vacuum.

When this process has been carried out, the lamps are ready; all that remains is to measure them, for all the lamps for one order must be completely identical in voltage, current and light intensity.[91]

The lamp in question had quite a large bulb. It was believed at the time that the improved thermal conductivity had a beneficial effect on the life of the lamp. In a letter to Bouckaert & Co. of Brussels, a trading company, Boudewijnse said: 'My lamps are completely identical to those produced by Bernstein, with which, I believe, you are familiar.' The frankness of this statement illustrates the extent to which the use by one manufacturer of the various processes developed by another was accepted. In the area of lamp manufacture, this situation had existed since before Edison's day, and it is amazing to observe how freely rival producers often disclosed details of their processes 'in confidence' to their competitors.[92] It is important to bear in mind that the essence of the secret lay not in the process itself, but in the ability to combine this with an efficient method of production and thus apply it economically. This was certainly true in 1888 and the years which followed.

In accordance with the prevailing view that 'a factory takes about two years to get into swing, but after that lamps can be made very cheaply',[93] the Boudewijnse Company proceeded to solve the manufacturing problem and that of the cost price. The factory produced lamps of between 5 and 50 candlepower, for voltages of 10 to 125, and with an average life of 800–1,000 hours. To publicize its products, the company, in addition to despatching samples, advertised in markets as far away as Italy, Spain, the Scandinavian countries, Russia and Switzerland. The initial response was such that agents had to be appointed in France, Belgium and Germany. By May 1888, there was talk of increasing the capacity of the factory from 300 to 2,000 lamps per week.[94] In June of that year, the E. H. Cadiot Company of Paris which had previously represented Woodhouse & Rawson, entered into a contract for the supply of 50,000 lamps (see Appendix 5). The factory proved incapable of executing this order, and a number from other markets, within the stipulated period.

[91] Copy-book of Boudewijnse, 14.2.1889.
[92] Jones and Marriott, *Anatomy of a Merger*, 73.
[93] *Electrical Review*, Vol. 19, No. 454, 6.8.1886.
[94] Copy-book of Boudewijnse, 17.5.1888 and 16.1.1889.

Incidental orders were received from large-scale users in Germany. In Prussia, Poznan, Silesia and Rhineland–Westphalia, in particular, installation contractors also traded in electrical goods. Sales in Berlin, a city which could consume the entire output of a lamp factory,[95] were of special importance. These Boudewijnse rightly interpreted as proof that their lamps, despite import duty of 12%, could compete with the products of domestic factories. In this context, we would mention that the price of lamps in this market, which in 1890 still averaged 2 marks, was kept artificially high by the German lamp industry. This was pointed out by the French in their efforts to resist German competition in their home market.

France was Boudewijnse's best export market, and in the early period nearly two-thirds of the output was sold there. The decision by the French government in 1891 to levy a duty of twenty per cent on imported lamps was a serious setback. France's entire electrical industry was protected by tariffs, and although these were primarily directed against imports from Germany, Boudewijnse's sales, like those of a number of other Dutch producers, suffered greatly. The Compagnie Générale des Lampes Incandescentes, pointing to the high level of wages in France and the fall in lamp prices from six francs to two francs, had gone so far as to demand a tariff of twenty-five per cent.[96] The imposition of duty on lamps led Cadiot to terminate the agency for Boudewijnse, although they continued to place occasional orders.

In 1890, in an effort to strengthen their sales organization, Boudewijnse entered into an agreement with Fred. Stieltjes & Co.,[97] an Amsterdam-based firm which traded in technical articles. The immediate aim was to obtain a firmer foothold in the Belgian, Russian and Scandinavian markets, in which Stieltjes had branches. In 1892, this firm accepted the agency for France also, but it regained little of the ground which had been lost there. In Britain, where hopes of being able to supply the General Electric Company had existed at the outset, the market was firmly closed as a result of the monopoly held by Edison & Swan. Nor had Boudewijnse any hope of business in the United States: 'The American licence acts forbid me to import.'[98]

---

[95] Zacharias, *Die Glühlampe*, 137.

[96] *The Electrician*, 5.12.1890, 144 ff: 'The protection of the electrical industry in France'; cf. *The Electrician*, 31.7.1891, 366 ff.

[97] F. Stieltjes, A.S.M.E. (1857–1902), a former employee of Mijnssen & Co., who was described as 'the best American in Amsterdam'; obituary in *De Ingenieur*, 1902, 21 ff.

[98] Boudewijnse in a letter to J. C. Perkins, Ithaca, N.Y., dated 9.5.1891; Bright, *Electric-Lamp Industry*, 77, refers to a prohibitive tariff of thirty per cent or more on lamps entering the United States.

Table 16. *Joh. Boudewijnse & Co. Geographical distribution of lamp sales (expressed as percentage), 1888–93*[a]

|  | 1888 | 1889 | 1890 | 1891 | 1892 | 1893 |
|---|---|---|---|---|---|---|
| The Netherlands | 6 | 10 | 13 | 13 | 23 | 38 |
| France | 63 | 66 | 54 | 28 | 15 | 12 |
| Germany | 8 | 10 | 24 | 7 | 10 | 12 |
| Belgium | 10 | 6 | 4 | 10 | 4 | 4 |
| Spain | 8 | 5 | 2 | 26 | 14 | 10 |
| Great Britain[b] | — | — | — | — | — | 12 |
| Japan | — | — | — | — | — | 11 |
| Miscellaneous: Scandinavia, Russia, Dutch East Indies and South America | 5 | 3 | 3 | 16 | 34 | 1 |

*Notes:*

[a] Figures derived from the annual returns to the Chamber of Commerce and from correspondence between Boudewijnse and the Commissie voor Handelspolitiek (Trade Policy) in The Hague

[b] Commencing November 1893, following expiry of Edison & Swan monopoly

In the Netherlands, lamps were usually sold direct to major users, such as factories and installation contractors. In Amsterdam, the lamps produced in Middelburg were sold by Mijnssen & Co., whose clients included the Maatschappij voor Electrische Stations 'Electra', which owned the central station commissioned in the city in 1889. This company tested the lamps for intensity and current consumption, for which it charged five cents per lamp, and resold them, with its seal of approval, to its customers, who consisted principally of shops and places of entertainment in the inner city area. A steady rise in domestic sales of Boudewijnse lamps, from 2,500 in 1888 to 34,000 in 1893, is a pointer to the growth of electric lighting in the Netherlands. In an effort to increase sales in the central districts of Amsterdam and Rotterdam, the company engaged two salesmen in 1892, but they were unable to make a living.

Upon closer examination, the sales activities of the Boudewijnse Company are seen to have been dominated by the search for regular outlets. Apart from a limited number of private individuals, the users of incandescent lamps were chiefly found in the industrial sector. After the boom in the lamp trade, which continued until about 1890, it was difficult to secure large, long-term contracts. The situation was exacerbated by the steady decline in lamp prices, added to which neither a stable trade in lamps nor a clear preference on the part of consumers had yet developed. After

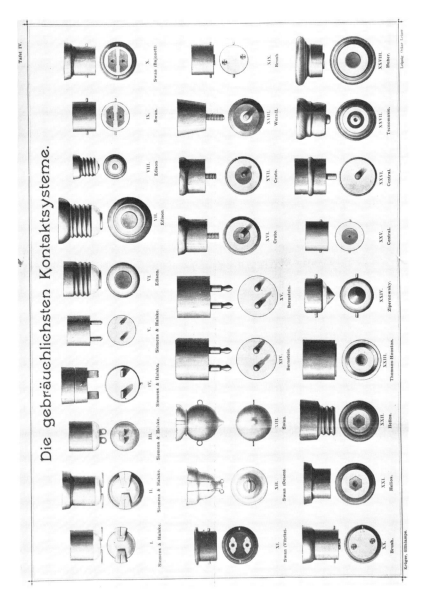

Die gebräuchlichsten Kontaktsysteme.

Types of lamp base in use around 1890

1890, the producers' greatest problem lay not in the manufacture of lamps (most makes were reasonably satisfactory), but in selling them.

The first decade in the history of the European incandescent lamp industry, which ran roughly from 1882 to 1892 and produced a series of battles for monopoly positions based on patents, was to be followed by a similar period of commercial competition which few survived. Against the background of tempestuous growth in the lamp market in the 1890s, accompanied by a dramatic fall in prices and a no less dramatic enlargement of scale, we shall examine this commercial problem and its relationship to Philips & Co. and other Dutch lamp manufacturers in the next volume.

The establishment of the Vitrite Works in Middelburg in 1889 merits a separate description. Like the founding of the Boudewijnse Company, the unexpected arrival in the Netherlands of this company, which specialized in the manufacture of lamp bases, was a product of the rules of play imposed on manufacturers by British court decisions in patent lawsuits. The company, established at Gateshead on the Tyne in 1884, supplied independent lamp manufacturers, such as Boudewijnse, who had no lamp base of their own design, but freely used the types developed by Edison, Siemens and Swan, and numerous variants of these. The Vitrite Works met their requirements with its own speciality, a base which employed a glass-like insulating and filling material known as vitrite, instead of the more common plaster of paris. The secret of this product, therefore, lay not in the brass cap itself, but in the composition of the vitrite.[99]

The Vitrite Works was owned by the American inventor Theodore Mace. He was also the proprietor of the Aluminous Incandescent Lamp Company, in Harrison, N.J., and had business links with Alfred Swan, a brother of Joseph Wilson Swan, and with the White-Vitrite and Luminoid Company of New York.[100] Once a year, Mace, who was on friendly terms with De Khotinsky, visited his clients on the European continent, with a number of whom he had allied himself in the inevitable patent conflicts. When his factory at Gateshead was threatened with seizure as a result of litigation, he opted to transfer the production to the Netherlands, where several of his customers were able to operate in complete freedom. The entire inventory –

[99] *The Electrician*, 28.2.1885, 333: 'Vitrite lamp holders, a new invention, both with regard to material and design'.
[100] *The Electrician, Electrical Trades' Directory and Handbook*, 1889 and 1890; cf. *75 jaar Vitrite*, published to mark the Jubilee 1893–1968.

including the stock of sheet brass, the steam engine and the presses – and the archive having been shipped to Holland,[101] the Vitrite Works commenced production of lamp bases in Middelburg in 1889. The mayor and aldermen co-operated fully – to the extent, indeed, of making the buildings vacated by the former Commercie Compagnie available to the company without delay – and without previously informing the City Council. They felt that their action was justified not only by Mr Mace's 'hurried departure', but also by their desire to see 'so important a factory' (which then employed about thirty people) in the municipality rather than in Rotterdam.[102]

In 1893, Cornelis Boudewijnse purchased the factory from Mace and proceeded to develop it most successfully, becoming in the process the principal industrialist in Middelburg. As the youthful representative of the town's industry, he was given a seat on the national committee of the Vereeniging tot Bevordering van Fabrieks- en Handwerksnijverheid in Nederland in the following year. In the national debate on the reintroduction of a Patents Act in Holland, the Middelburg branch of the association, not surprisingly, sided with the opponents.[103] Similarly, the Chamber of Commerce in Middelburg, replying to a 'Memorandum concerning a Patents Act' circulated by the Minister for Waterways, Trade and Industry on 31 August 1893, expressed the view that such legislation would be against the public interest.[104]

The operation of the patent laws which then existed in Britain gave Middelburg first an incandescent lamp factory and later an industrial undertaking which is still the largest in the town – the Vitrite Works.[105]

The establishment in 1889 of two more Dutch lamp-making companies – Roothaan & Alewijnse, in Nijmegen, and Emile Goossens, Pope & Van der Kaa, in Venlo – reflects the view which then prevailed, namely that a profitable enterprise could be built up in this sector, provided that the requisite technical knowledge and skill were available. The two partners in the Nijmegen venture, who had learned the secrets of lamp manufacture while working at the De Khotinsky factories in Rotterdam and Gelnhausen, chose 1889 as the most opportune moment to set up in business.

---

[101] Correspondence and wages books from 1884 onwards.
[102] Proceedings of the Council, 9.8.1889, 300–6, Municipal Archives, Middelburg.
[103] Report of the 43rd Annual General Meeting held in Utrecht on 6 and 7 July 1894, 131.
[104] Letter from the Chamber of Commerce to the Minister, dated 8.1.1894; this formed an appendix to the Report of the Middelburg City Council, 1894.
[105] In 1977, the Vitrite Works in Middelburg had an average work force of 750 and a turnover of ƒ85 million.

Frederic Roberts Pope (1865–1934)        Antoine Emile Hubert Goossens
(1860–1926)

From the technical point of view, the establishment of the lamp works in
Venlo was made possible by the skill of the British engineer Frederic
Roberts Pope (1865–1934),[106] who had left his native country under
circumstances similar to those which overtook Robertson. After working in
factories in France and Germany, he entered into an arrangement with the
Goossens, a wealthy family of merchants and bankers in Venlo.

It appears more than plausible that the Goossens' decision was motivated
by the satisfactory and widely publicized results then achieved by the lamp
factory owned by the Rotterdam coffee trader, L. W. Schöffer. They must
also have been aware that the absence of a patent law in the Netherlands
and the abundance of labour, especially in the south-eastern region,
favoured the setting up of such a factory. As will be clear from the
negotiations which Frederik and Gerard Philips conducted with Brush,[107]
the Goossens were not the only family of merchants whose thoughts in
1889 turned to the manufacture of incandescent lamps. To Roothaan and
Alewijnse, it appealed chiefly as a path to the status of entrepreneur. Prior to
entering De Khotinsky's employ in 1884, they had worked as improvers in

---

[106] *The Electrician*, 17.5.1895, 100: 'Mr. Pope, who was one of the first to engage in the incandescent
lamp industry in this country'.
[107] Cf. Chapter 1, pages 33 and 35.

Josephus Ph. Roothaan (1864–1933)        Cornelis Alewijnse (1861–1936)

the electric lighting company Wisse, Piccaluga & Co., which had given them an opportunity to obtain basic training in electrical engineering at the Berlin works of Siemens & Halske.

The objects of the Roothaan & Alewijnse Company were to operate a factory for the manufacture of electric lamps and all related apparatus, and to apply the same.[108] The wording implies an intention to engage in installation as well as the manufacture of lamps. The partners were Carel Marie Victor Roothaan (1865–1930), of independent means, who was responsible for administration and for the management of the company's finances and assets; his brother, Josephus Philippus Roothaan (1864–1933), electrician, who assumed the technical and commercial management; and Cornelis Alewijnse (1861–1936), electrician, who was in charge of the lamp factory.

The authorized capital at the time of establishment amounted to ƒ39,000, subscribed in equal shares by the partners, with the proviso that Alewijnse should meet his obligation from his share of the profit. The

---

[108]  Deed of establishment dated 24.12.1888; the partnership commenced on 1.1.1889; archive of the Alewijnse family, Ubbergen.

available funds were adequate for the purchase of a site, buildings and factory equipment. The necessary working capital was obtained privately.

The factory, which was situated at 398 Berg en Dalscheweg in Nijmegen, went into production in July 1889 or thereabouts. Two years later the work force numbered fifty-one, comprising seventeen men, nineteen women, five boys and ten girls.[109] The output at that time is assumed to have been of the order of 100,000 lamps annually.[110] These were sold in widely separated markets, including Germany, Italy, Spain and Russia, but the focus of the sales activities was Belgium, whose incandescent lamp industry at that time was limited to a branch factory of the Seel Company near Brussels, which, however, never really got into its stride. The opportunity thus presented led the enterprising Nijmegen manufacturers to decide in 1891 to set up a factory in Belgium. This implied entering a limited market in which Boudewijnse also operated. The impending competition did not escape the attention of the latter, for on 22 January 1892 he informed Fred. Stieltjes & Co. of Brussels that: 'Messrs. Roothaan & Alewijnse, whose incandescent lamps are already well known in Belgium, are planning to establish a factory in Belgium.'[111] Boudewijnse lost no time in spurring his Belgian agent to greater efforts.

With the activities being divided between two countries, Jos Roothaan took over as director of the Brussels works, while Alewijnse headed the operation in Nijmegen. The third partner, C. M. V. Roothaan, left the company in the course of 1892 in order to succeed his late father, Ph. J. Roothaan, as municipal treasurer; however, he remained a sleeping partner. Thereafter, according to a report sent by W. Schimmelpfeng to the Vitrite Works, the business was carried on by the other two partners and with sound expectations:

The company is doing good business and is continually expanding. The proprietors are competent, industrious and highly qualified young men: Alewijnse is not rich, but possesses sound technical knowledge; Roothaan has inherited a handsome fortune from his father.[112]

Quantitative data on production at the Nijmegen factory are scarce in comparison with those concerning the lamp works in Middelburg and Venlo. The weekly publication *De Nederlandsche Industrieel*, in its issue of

---

[109]  Municipal Archives, Nijmegen: report dated 9 July 1975, compiled from council reports and permits issued under the Nuisance Act; Philips Archives, Eindhoven.
[110]  Based on work force and comparison of business volume.
[111]  Copy-book of Boudewijnse, 22.1.1892.
[112]  Report by W. Schimmelpfeng, 2.11.1893; archives of the Vitrite Works, Middelburg.

Examples of the lamps produced by Roothaan & Alewijnse

26 April 1891, gave a clear description of the method of manufacturing the filament and of the remaining stages from processing to final product.[113] The company produced a wide range of lamps for voltages of 2 to 200 and with intensities of between 2 and 300 candlepower, and this corresponded to the De Khotinsky range.[114] Besides manufacturing incandescent lamps, it undertook installations and traded in accumulators, arc lamps, telephones, cables, switchgear and insulating materials.

In 1894, H. Schuurman, a member of the banking house of Schuurman & de Bas, The Hague, was admitted to partnership. Two years later the enterprise reached the point where it was necessary to transform it into a limited company. Thus was born N.V. Electriciteits-Maatschappij 'Phaëton', formerly Roothaan, Alewijnse & Co., whose authorized capital amounted to ƒ500,000.[115] The shares were issued by the Nijmeegsche Bankvereeniging, ƒ298,000 being placed. The accounts were audited by E. J. Korthals Altes, an Amsterdam lawyer, and a senior member of the Netherlands Institute of Accountants. In a statement contained in the prospectus, he expressed every confidence in the viability of the new enterprise – not so much on grounds of past profits, but rather in the light of the immense growth of sales which was anticipated in the future: 'The company operates in a partially virgin area (one has only to think of the East Indies, where there is still so much to be done in the field of electrical engineering), it employs cheap labour and it is well-managed.'[116]

The capacity of the Nijmegen works was subsequently increased to one million lamps a year. At the same time, a 'third department for lighting installations' and a department for wholesale and export business in all electrical articles were created.[117] The company was also interested in acquiring and operating concessions for lighting and power. In addition to the Brussels factory, a subsidiary, the Phaëton Electrical Company Limited, was established in London, and plans were made to set up a branch in the Dutch East Indies.

The later fortunes of this enterprising electrical company, which came to face severe competition, notably in the incandescent lamp sector, will be dealt with in a subsequent chapter.

---

[113] Reproduced from *Provinciale Geldersche en Nijmeegsche Courant* of 22.4.1891.

[114] E. A. Krüger, *Die Herstellung*, 93.

[115] Articles of Association, approved by an Order in Council dated 23.7.1896, *Government Gazette*, 29.9.1896.

[116] Share prospectus issued by the Nijmeegsche Bankvereeniging, Van Engelenburg & Schippers, May 1896; archive of the Alewijnse family, Ubbergen.

[117] *De Ingenieur*, 1896, 514.

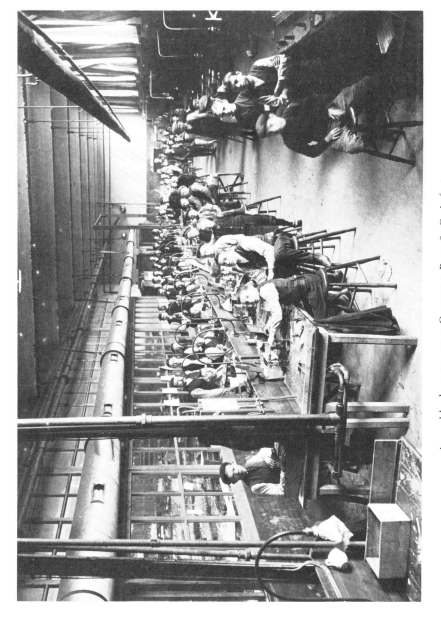

Assembly department at Goossens, Pope & Co.'s factory

The driving force behind the establishment of a lamp factory in Venlo was Antoine Emile Hubert Goossens (1860–1926), who preferred to be known as Emile Goossens. He enjoyed a reputation as a 'very sound and intelligent merchant',[118] and in the realization of his plan 'was assisted financially by his wealthy father and other relatives'.[119] The Goossens family, which ranked among the highest in Venlo in terms of licence taxes,[120] was not tied to a single business. Its entrepreneurial activities embraced a steam-powered grain and oilseed mill, a saltworks, a tileworks, a stonemason's yard and – like the Philipses of Zaltbommel – a tobacco and cigar factory, and interests in the coffee trade and banking.

As a prelude to the setting up of the incandescent lamp factory, a limited partnership was formed by private deed on 20 March 1889. The partners and their interests were: Emile Goossens, managing director, ƒ3,000; his father, Laurent Goossens, coffee trader, ƒ12,000; an uncle, August Goossens, coffee trader, ƒ12,000; and another uncle, Henri Goossens, proprietor of the Venloosche Handelsbank, ƒ6,000. Two outsiders, who were without private means, were also given partnerships. The first of these, Frederic Roberts Pope, was accepted on the grounds of his knowledge and expertise. The second, J. G. van der Kaa, was to have assumed responsibility for sales, but, having been the cause of 'financial unpleasantnesses', he was forced to resign after only a few months. As a result of this affair, the company was reorganized on 27 September 1889 and the name changed to E. Goossens, Pope & Co.[121]

It is important to note at this point that the objects of the company were limited to the establishment and operation of an incandescent lamp factory. In contrast to the Dutch producers already mentioned, Goossens, Pope & Co. were thus solely concerned with the manufacture of lamps. They were therefore exponents of the emerging trend towards *Spezialfabriken* which heralded a new phase in the evolution of lamp manufacture: far-reaching specialization in the production of a single article, independent of any particular lighting system or of installation works.

Following the investment of ƒ16,000 in land and buildings, and ƒ20,000 in manufacturing equipment, the incandescent lamp works at

[118] Report by W. Schimmelpfeng, Amsterdam, 6.10.1893; archives of the Vitrite Works, Middelburg.
[119] Ibid.
[120] G. C. P. Linssen, *Verandering en Verschuiving, industriële ontwikkeling naar bedrijfstak in midden- en noord-Limburg, 1839–1914*, 1969, 169 ff.
[121] *Venloosche Courant*, 28.9.1889.
[122] Ledger for 1889 and succeeding years; Philips Archives, Eindhoven.

Mercatorstraat in Venlo commenced production in August 1889.[122] It soon became necessary to invest a further *f*20,000 in the venture. By 1893, investment totalled well over *f*100,000.[123] Pope, with his considerable experience, succeeded in getting the plant into production in an exceptionally short period. The English foreman, O'Connell, and the German engineer, Christiany, trained the unskilled workers. The minimum age for employment was twelve years. Legend has it that Emile Goossens, 'in a musical Venlo dialect', asked applicants whether they could count up to one hundred; Pope inspected their hands.[124] Women and girls accounted for about two-thirds of the work force, men and boys making up the remainder. The working day was of ten to twelve hours and the factory operated six days a week. The starting wage for a young worker was $2\frac{1}{2}$ cents an hour, rising with experience to six cents. This differed substantially from the wages paid at, say, the Gebr. Stork engineering works in Hengelo, where in 1889 the rate for boys of fourteen to eighteen years of age ranged from four to twelve cents an hour, though this, of course, reflected the higher degree of skill involved.[125]

Comparison of the average labour costs at the Venlo and Middelburg lamp factories in the period 1889–93 reveals figures of seven and seventeen cents per hour respectively. This discrepancy was due not only to the significant variation in local wage rates, but also reflected the high wages which Boudewijnse paid to his skilled foreign employees. Pope's view – which he was not slow to put into practice – was that skilled operations could also be performed by local workpeople. Moreover, the Venlo works relied mainly on female labour, and as a rule engaged young girls. It is indicative of a contrast in commercial and social attitudes between the rationalized *Specialfabrik* in Venlo and the more craft-based factory in Middelburg, whose policy was soon to lead to a loss of competitive power.

When Zacharias worked out a cost price for a German lamp manufacturer in 1890, he arrived at a figure of twenty-four cents per lamp for labour.[126] Over the period 1890–3, during which the average selling price of the lamps made by Goossens, Pope & Co. fell from *f*1.00 to forty-six cents, this company succeeded in reducing its labour costs – which were already relatively low – from fourteen cents per lamp to nine cents.

---

[123] Report by W. Schimmelpfeng, Amsterdam, 26.4.1895; archives of the Vitrite Works, Middelburg.

[124] Jan Heyn Jr, *Mijlpaal 60, 1889–1949, jubileumuitgave t.g.v. het zestigjarig bestaan der N.V. Pope's Draad- en Lampenfabrieken te Venlo*, 16.

[125] *De Machinefabriek van Gebroeders Stork & Co. te Hengelo*, memoir marking the twenty-fifth anniversary on 4 September 1893, 28.

[126] Zacharias, *Die Glühlampe*, 57.

Table 17. *E. Goossens, Pope & Co. Sales, cost and operating account,*
*1889–93 (in guilders)*[a]

| Year | Number of lamps sold | Number of employees | Wages | Other costs and depreciation | Revenue | Average lamp price | Profit |
|---|---|---|---|---|---|---|---|
| 1889[b] | 10,000 | 25 | 2,900 | 7,500 | 11,000 | 1.10 | 600 |
| 1890 | 85,000 | 48 | 11,700 | 42,800 | 85,000 | 1.00 | 30,500 |
| 1891 | 158,000 | 60 | 16,900 | 52,300 | 146,000 | 0.92 | 76,800 |
| 1892 | 163,000 | 68 | 18,900 | 54,100 | 101,000 | 0.62 | 28,000 |
| 1893 | 245,000 | 86 | 22,500 | 65,900 | 112,000 | 0.46 | 25,600 |

*Notes:*
[a] Figures taken from the ledger and purchase and sale books, Philips Archives, Eindhoven
[b] Production commenced on 1.8.1889

In Venlo, they originally had two German glassblowers, but this is no longer the case. Everything is now done by girls. That makes a great difference. We must also try this in due course, in order to be thoroughly competitive. The factory in Venlo is in a healthy condition, quite different from Seel. They are doing good business and we must try to emulate those gentlemen.[127]

Clearly, the policy pursued in Venlo did not escape the attention of outsiders, for these remarks were made by Gerard Philips in a letter to Emile Woschke, who was then in Brussels and was assisting him in laying the foundations for his projected lamp factory. It seems probable that this example of a specialized lamp works attracted the notice of others also, for in addition to the one which Gerard founded in Eindhoven in 1891, a new works at Breda and a second works in Venlo were established in 1892.[128] The attraction lay not only in the technical concept, but also in the large profit achieved by Goossens, Pope & Co., who in the financial year 1890 recouped practically the whole of their initial capital (see Table 17, above). The experience gained by the Venlo factory and the lessons which it provided may be viewed as having, in fact, determined the location of the incandescent lamp industry in this country, which soon extended from Nijmegen and Venlo to Eindhoven and thence to Breda.

Pope lamps quickly achieved a high reputation. They were made in a voltage range from 10 to 150 and the current consumption was given as 4.5 watts per candlepower for lamps of 5 c.p., 4 watts per candlepower at 8 c.p., 3.5 watts per candlepower for lamps of 16, 25 and 32 c.p., and 3.3

127 Copy-book of Gerard Philips, 28.2.1891.
128 The factories of Rogier, Smagghe & Co. at Breda and 'Constantia' at Venlo.

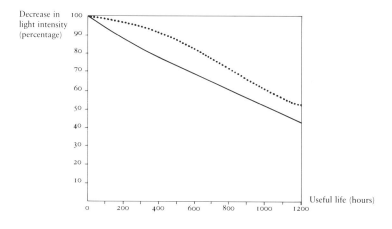

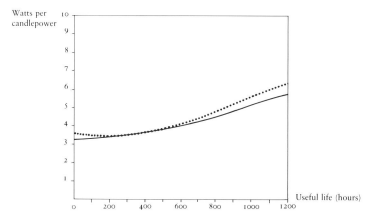

Comparison of lamp quality based on light intensity and current consumption
...... Pope lamp of 16 candlepower and 3.56 watts
——— De Khotinsky lamp of 16 candlepower and 3.32 watts

watts per candlepower for 50 and 100 c.p. lamps. The normal life was
1,000 hours. The filament used in these lamps was made from artificial silk
fibre, which was carbonized and then homogenized by means of flashing.
The lamps were tested by C. P. Feldmann, chief engineer of 'Helios' A.G.,
Cologne,[129] and the results were published in *The Electrician* of 25
November 1892. In terms of economy and useful life, Feldmann put the
Pope lamp virtually on a par with the high quality lamp produced by De
Khotinsky (see graphs above).

Germany was the principal market for Goossens, Pope & Co., but sales

[129]  Clarence P. Feldmann, Professor of Electricity at the Technical University of Delft.

Table 18. *E. Goossens, Pope & Co. Geographical distribution of lamp sales (expressed as percentage), 1890–3*[a]

|  | 1890 | 1891 | 1892 | 1893 |
|---|---|---|---|---|
| The Netherlands | 7 | 6 | 17 | 10 |
| Germany | 36 | 20 | 38 | 26 |
| France | 14 | 4 | — | — |
| Great Britain | — | — | — | 26 |
| Hungary | 14 | 43 | 12 | 2 |
| Russia | 17 | 22 | 21 | 18 |
| Miscellaneous: Austria, Belgium, Italy, Scandinavia, Spain and Switzerland | 12 | 5 | 12 | 18 |

*Note:*
[a] Figures are taken from the sale books, Philips Archives, Eindhoven

to Russia were substantial and showed steady growth. France ceased to be attractive after 1890 when, as already explained, lamps became subject to import duty.[130] As competition on the European continent intensified, the company looked increasingly to Britain. There the Edison & Swan monopoly was due to expire in November 1893 and the market would be open to others. For Pope, the sale in November and December 1893 of more than 63,000 lamps in Britain – 26% of the turnover for the year – was the fulfilment of a personal ambition. This commercial breakthrough afforded a lasting foothold on the British market, which was continuously strengthened by the efforts of Pope, Boddy & Co., the sales office in Liverpool,[131] and ultimately led to a production line being set up in London.

In the Netherlands, where the selling activities were limited to the granting of agencies to installation contractors in the three main cities, lamp sales amounted to 6,000 in 1890, 9,500 in 1891, 28,000 in 1892 and 24,500 in 1893. In the last of these years supplies to the local agents suffered as a result of deliveries to Britain. The importance of exports may be gauged from the fact that a full-time representative was engaged to cover foreign markets, in which Emile Goossens himself also took an active interest.

Despite keen competition and a steady fall in prices during the 1890s, the upward trend in sales by the Venlo works was to continue for a long time.

If, in conclusion, we move ahead to the company's position in the market in 1903 – the year in which, after protracted dislocation of the market, the

[130] See page 160.    [131] *The Electrician*, 10.8.1894, 436.

*Verkaufsstelle* (European lamp cartel) came into being[132] – we find that it had an annual quota of 3.05 per cent, equivalent to about 850,000 lamps. Adding this to the quota of the only other surviving Dutch producer, Philips & Co., we find that this country's share amounted to some 3.8 million lamps, or fourteen per cent of the total annual production in Europe, which was estimated by the members of the cartel to be of the order of 27.5 million lamps. If we aggregate the sales figures in Holland in 1890 – when four factories were in operation, plus a subsidiary works at Gelnhausen, in neighbouring Germany – we arrive at an annual output of about 700,000 lamps. Relating this figure to the total European production of 5,000,000 lamps in 1890[133] we see that the Dutch share at that time was similarly fourteen per cent.

This figure may be taken as a measure of the drive displayed by Dutch enterprise in the 1880s, mainly in the shape of family firms, in the manufacture of a modern product based on a completely new technology. A second conclusion – and one which anticipates our further research – is that Philips & Co., more than any other, succeeded in maintaining the Netherlands' early share of lamp manufacture in Europe and consolidating this in 1903, by which time the market had grown substantially.

It is equally clear that the incandescent lamp, while constituting the nucleus of the 'complete lighting system', could be manufactured and sold *separately*. Another specific factor is that the way in which patent legislation operated in Britain encouraged the export of the relevant technical knowledge, and in doing so contributed in no small measure to a situation in which, at that early stage, the Netherlands became Europe's second largest producer of incandescent lamps, after Germany. The absence of a heavy electrical sector, such as emerged in Germany, can be explained simply by a lack of finance and skilled middle management. In spite of this – or perhaps precisely because of it – the Dutch, with modest financial means and a combination of commercial spirit and practical ingenuity, successfully applied themselves to that part of the electrical industry which was accessible to them initially, i.e. the manufacture of incandescent lamps.

By the end of 1890, the lamp factories, the Vitrite Works and Willem Smit & Co. together employed about 250 people. We estimate that a further 350 found work in installation companies, central stations, electro-chemical plants and telephone companies. The national electrical industry therefore provided some six hundred jobs at that time. No statistics are

---

[132] W. Koch, *Die Konzentrationsbewegung in der deutschen Elektroindustrie*, 1907, 107.
[133] See Chapter 1, page 33.

available concerning employment or the number of electrical installations then in use. The consumption of lamps in the Netherlands can thus only be roughly estimated. On the basis of data which we have assembled, we would put the figure in 1890 at about 50,000, consisting of 32,000 domestically produced lamps and 18,000 of German manufacture. After 1890, the number rose annually by leaps and bounds.

The list of the 146 founder members of the Nederlandsche Vereeniging voor Electro-techniek, the national electrical engineering association, which was established on 25 October 1895, affords a cross-sectional view of the *cadre* in the electrical industry at that time. It contains the names of four electrical manufacturers, forty-one persons engaged in installation or consultancy, twenty-two employees of the Telegraph Service, nineteen lecturers (including five professors), ten employees of railway companies, eight military or naval men, six employees of municipal gasworks, five of electricity supply companies, four of telephone companies and twenty-seven of various professions including mechanical engineers in the employ of widely differing firms or in government service. Besides the collection of statistical data, the principal aims of the association, which was under the chairmanship of Prof. Snijders, were the training of electrical 'craftsmen' and the compilation of a manual for electricians.[134]

The decision of the Delft Polytechnic in 1888 to provide a separate course of electrical engineering was of significance for the future development of the industry in the Netherlands. The course was designed for third- and fourth-year students of mechanical engineering who had an interest in electricity, and initially occupied four hours a week. It provided Professor J. A. Snijders (1844–1922)[135] with an opportunity to teach the theory of electricity, in addition to his lectures on mathematics and physics.[136] From 1890 onwards, as the country's first professor of electrical engineering, he was enabled to devote himself entirely to this branch of science.

Although quick to criticize shortcomings, particularly in the area of practical training facilities, Snijders was to take a firm line in cases where the country lagged behind others in adopting certain applications of electricity, and where this could be attributed not to the specific Dutch situation but to slackness and lack of enterprise. To him, the general

[134] Minutes of the Board meeting, 13.5.1896, included in the Annual Report 1895/6 of the Ned. Vereeniging voor Electro-techniek.
[135] *De Ingenieur*, 1922, 349: an obituary.
[136] J. A. Snijders, *Electrotechnisch Onderwijs aan de Polytechnische School te Delft*, reprinted from the 'Delftschen Studenten-Almanak' for 1889.

Professor J. A. Snijders (1844–1922)

antipathy towards the introduction of electric trams was inexplicable – for it was quite impossible to prove that horse-drawn and steam-driven trams were cheaper to operate in the Netherlands than in other countries.

This type of dialogue characterizes the many-sided nature of the new ground which Snijders had to break. He was, however, gratified to observe that the three largest municipalities had possessed 'a central installation of substantial size for electric lighting' since the beginning of the 1890s, that the question of electric light was being discussed in numerous smaller parishes and, moreover, that the Netherlands were at that moment 'so comparatively rich in incandescent lamp factories'.[137]

This brings us to Amsterdam and to Gerard Philips, who was there in 1890 and whose mind was fully occupied with two issues: lighting the capital by electricity and setting up an incandescent lamp factory.

[137] *De Ingenieur*, 1895, 491.

The Delft Polytechnic

Sub-station installed by Maatschappij 'Electra' in Amsterdam

Chapter 5

# THE AMSTERDAM ELECTRICITY CONCESSION

After a five-year sojourn abroad, Gerard Philips returned to the Nether-lands in November 1889 in order to represent temporarily the Allgemeine Elektricitäts-Gesellschaft in its negotiations with the authorities in Amsterdam in the matter of an electricity concession for the city. He had been approached on the subject by Emil Rathenau, the managing director of AEG, during a brief visit to Berlin a few weeks earlier.[1] The negotiations were at an advanced stage and, in addition to keen competition from other would-be concessionaires, there was the problem of effectively presenting the extremely complex electrical information in the context of a long-term concession for lighting an urban area – and this to a council which had no experience whatsoever in this field, yet faced the task of stimulating the development of electricity while at the same time subjecting it to conditions which most benefited the municipality and its citizens.

At the outset, AEG did not seek a concession in its own name. Instead it entered into an agreement with the Nederlandsche Electriciteit-Maatschap-pij of Amsterdam (NEM),[2] the effect of which was to enable this Dutch company to compete strongly for a concession which exceeded its financial and technical resources. Earlier, on 5 December 1887, the City Council had suggested to the NEM that it should base its application for a concession on the spirit and the standards pertaining to the contract between the City Council in Berlin and the Deutsche Edison Gesellschaft – which earlier that year had changed its name to AEG. A call on Rathenau by the day-to-day management team of the NEM – W. J. de Bordes, A. W. Krasnapolsky and P. E. Tegelberg – laid the foundations for an agreement which on 30 January 1888 enabled the NEM to inform the Municipal Executive that, as a result of association with the Allgemeine Elektricitäts-Gesellschaft, it had

---

[1] Cf. Chapter 2, page 83.
[2] Cf. Chapter 3, pages 114 ff.

181

Emil Rathenau (1838–1915)

obtained the co-operation of a company 'which, by reason of the work which it has already carried out, affords a guarantee that any concession granted to us would lead to the provision and operation of a system of electric lighting which would satisfy all the parties'.[3]

In Berlin, the provision of electricity was the subject of a non-exclusive concession granted for thirty years to Berliner Elektrizitätswerke, a company which had close administrative and financial links with AEG. The latter supplied the materials necessary for the equipping and operation of central stations, with the exception of the large dynamos which, under the terms of a contract which still had several years to run, AEG was obliged to purchase from Siemens & Halske. Between 1885 and 1889, three stations were built and put into operation on this basis in Berlin, and work was started on a fourth. The completion of this brought the total capacity of the four (coupled) stations to about 92,000 ampères – sufficient to power 185,000 lamps of 16 candlepower. Initial demand was put at just over 50% of the available capacity. Including a number of independent stations, the total generating capacity in operation in Berlin in 1890 was sufficient to supply 140,000 lamps of 16 candlepower.

The draft document providing for a concession in Amsterdam, which the Municipal Executive laid before the full council on 21 May 1889 and which was largely based on the example of Berlin – 'the best-lit city on this continent'[4] – assumed an initial capacity of 15,000 incandescent lamps, rising gradually to 41,000. This draft, which was the product of lengthy negotiations between the municipality and the NEM, reveals an approach which was quite bold for that time. Two years of preliminary study had produced agreement on the duration of the concession – twenty-nine years – the consideration payable to the municipality – 5% of gross revenue and 40% of any profit in excess of an 8% return on the capital – and many other details. The NEM was forced to give way on numerous issues.[5] There would be no question of a monopoly such as had been given to the Imperial Continental Gas Association in 1883 for the provision of gas supplies in Amsterdam. On the contrary, prior to the Council's discussion of the draft, the Executive encouraged the NEM's principal competitor, the Maatschappij 'Electra', to submit an application for a concession on the terms already

---

[3] NEM in a letter to the Municipal Executive, 30.1.1888; PW archive, No. 705, Municipal Archives, Amsterdam.

[4] This view was expressed by Edison during a tour of Europe: cf. J. A. Snijders, *De vorderingen der Electrotechniek*, 1894, 42.

[5] Proposal submitted by the Municipal Executive, 21.5.1889; item No. 299, Municipal Archives, Amsterdam.

described; this would replace the temporary permit which had already been given to the company.[6] Competition from other quarters was soon forthcoming.

In the light of this development, the NEM, in a letter of 14 June 1889, expressed disappointment at the fact that the electricity concession had not been discussed at the Council's meeting on 12 June, in spite of having been on the agenda.[7] As the draft provided for the concession to take effect on 1 July 1889, the company requested that the matter be dealt with at the next meeting. But when the Council met on 27 June, by which time 'Electra' had expressed a willingness to accept a concession on the same terms as those offered to the NEM, it referred both proposals back to the departments concerned. With this, the battle for the supply of electric lighting in Amsterdam broke out in earnest. The NEM was obliged to report to AEG that the concession, which shortly beforehand had seemed certain, had been delayed pending further study.

On 21 August 1889, Rathenau, who was not lacking in self-assurance, despatched a personal letter to the Mayor of Amsterdam, G. van Tienhoven, inviting him and the members of the Council to inspect the central stations in operation in Berlin and to acquaint themselves with the latest advances in electrical engineering.[8] The Council, while formally noting the invitation, took no action, and only one of its members, R. W. J. C. van den Wall Bake, made the journey – at his own expense.[9] A few months later Rathenau stayed at the Krasnapolsky Hotel, where he further explored the situation with the NEM and with Gerard Philips, whose services he had meanwhile retained. The NEM played little if any part in the later phases of the negotiations, AEG now having a direct representative, in the person of Gerard Philips, to defend its interests in the matter of the concession.

Although the affair initially absorbed most of Gerard's time and attention, his stay in Amsterdam saw not only the maturing of his plan to establish an incandescent lamp factory, following the breakdown of the talks with Brush,[10] but also the completion of much of his preparatory research into incandescent lighting. His involvement in the negotiations

---

6   Letter from the Municipal Executive to 'Electra', 23.5.1889; PW archive, No. 3399, Municipal Archives, Amsterdam.
7   NEM in a letter to the Municipal Executive, 14.6.1889; PW archive, No. 4031, Municipal Archives, Amsterdam.
8   Rathenau in a letter to Van Tienhoven dated 21.8.1889; PW archive, No. 5579, Municipal Archives, Amsterdam.
9   Municipal Executive in a letter to Berliner Elektrizitätswerke dated 23.10.1889; PW archive, No. 6977, Municipal Archives, Amsterdam.
10  Cf. Chapter 2, page 83.

between the municipality and AEG in Berlin was at least to provide him with valuable experience of a future large-scale user of incandescent lamps – the central station. Some details of the previous history of the affair, notably the relationship of the NEM and the Maatschappij 'Electra' to the City Council, merit reference.

The first application for a concession for electric lighting in Amsterdam dates from September 1881.[11] By October of the following year the number of applications had risen to ten, including two submitted by the NEM and one by Wisse, Piccaluga & Co. All were referred to the Municipal Executive for consideration and report. The Executive, however, in a memorandum to the Council of 28 December 1882, expressed the view that it would be unwise to anticipate the impending decision concerning the renewal of the gas concession, which was soon to expire, by granting a concession for electricity, the more so because 'according to the scientists – assuming that electric light can be taken to be the principal form of public and special lighting – gas must continue to serve as a stand-by, if not as a replacement, for electric light'.[12] Similarly, applications for permits to carry out tests with electric lighting were provisionally refused, except where such tests would have no influence on the impending tenders for the gas concession.

Shortly after the future of the gas concession had been decided, at the meeting of the Council on 27 July 1883, the subject of electricity was again raised. This time the interested parties were content to seek a permit to lay and own cables beneath street level. The first application, dated 22 October 1883, was submitted by Mijnssen & Co., and this was followed on 30 October by one from the NEM which, by way of an experiment, wished to lay cables connecting the Café Krasnapolsky with a number of adjacent properties in the thoroughfares known as Warmoesstraat, Nes, Nieuwendijk, Kalverstraat and Rokin. A third aspiring concessionaire, Ribbink, Van Bork & Co., sought permission to illuminate electrically Rembrandt Square and its surroundings. On 17 June 1884, Mijnssen & Co. lodged a second application, this time for the laying of cables beneath the Kalverstraat for the purpose of illuminating the shops there.

The Municipal Executive produced its second report on 3 October 1885.[13] It pointed to the advances made in the intervening years and to the

---

11  Petition submitted by Dr S. Oudschans of Leeuwarden; cf. *Gemeenteblad*, 1882, Section 1, 1274.
12  Report of the City Council, 1889, 144: 'Vergunningen electrische verlichting Geschiedkundig overzicht'.
13  *Gemeenteblad*, 1885, Section 1, 1015–21.

experience with electric lighting in a number of major cities, especially Berlin. In the light of the report, the Council, at its meeting on 25 October, approved a procedure for the granting, under certain conditions, of 'permission for the laying and owning of cables beneath public land and water owned by the municipality, for the lighting by electricity of areas of the city and the transmission of power'.

The Council took the view that the time was not ripe for a long-term concession. The general conditions which had now been laid down paved the way, officially at least, for negotiations with interested parties on these and possibly other, special, conditions. Prior to the council meeting, the NEM – pointing to the fact that in other countries thirty years was the accepted period for concessions[14] – had criticized the procedure on the commercial ground that a contract for a short period, or an undefined period, would make it impossible for the electric lighting industry to attract the capital necessary to construct a central station. Moreover, it would not be able to compete adequately with the low price of gas, not to mention the additional demand by the Council for at least ten per cent of the gross revenue.

Persevering in its efforts to obtain a concession in Amsterdam, as opposed to a provisional permit, the NEM allied itself with the Nederlandsche Maatschappij voor Electriciteit en Metallurgie, which had already reached agreement with the council in The Hague.[15] In 1886 the Municipal Executive in Amsterdam received an elaborate quotation drawn up on behalf of both companies.[16] This covered the construction of no less than four central stations, to be sited in the Frederiksplein, Rembrandtsplein, Dam and Plantage districts of the city. The companies demanded an *exclusive* concession of at least fifteen years, and at most thirty, in return for which the municipality would have the right to take over the installations after five years at actual cost less depreciation at three per cent per annum. In spite of an assurance of approval and financial support for the project 'from powerful quarters' (Siemens & Halske of Berlin and Schuckert & Co. of Nuremberg), this plan also failed, because it ran counter to the earlier council decision which precluded concessions. Its rejection marked the end of this seemingly over-ambitious joint initiative as well as of the alliance between the two companies.

---

[14]  NEM in a letter to the City Council, 20.10.1885; *Gemeenteblad*, 1885, Section 1, 561, 596.
[15]  Cf. Chapter 3, page 112.
[16]  Joint letter from the companies to the Municipal Executive, 16.3.1886; PW archive, No. 1765, Municipal Archives, Amsterdam.

Later in 1886, the Nederlandsche Maatschappij voor Electriciteit en Metallurgie, on its own behalf and that of Siemens & Halske, again applied for an exclusive concession for four central stations in Amsterdam. The NEM opted for a more modest plan, reverting to its initial proposal of 1882, namely the laying and ownership of cables leading to the installation at the Café Krasnapolsky, or, to be more precise, in an area within a radius of eight hundred metres, subject to an exclusive concession for a minimum of twenty years, under which current would be supplied at a cost of not more than $2\frac{3}{4}$ cents per hour for a 16-candlepower lamp.[17] A third contender, 'Helios' A.G. für elektrisches Licht und Telegraphenbau, of Cologne, had meanwhile entered the field with detailed plans for illuminating the entire city.[18] Its representative, Ernst Boeing, a German, moved into the Palais Royal Hotel, from where he sought support among local investors. Like his competitors, he learned from Mayor Van Tienhoven that there was no monopoly to be obtained in Amsterdam, and also that the financial benefit accruing to the municipality must match that which the authorities in Berlin had succeeded in obtaining from the Deutsche Edison Gesellschaft.[19] In the face of this countermove by the authorities, the lighting companies were obliged to adopt a new strategy.

On 24 March 1887, under the continuing pressure of these quotations, and of public opinion, the Public Works Department advised the alderman concerned that, subject to the provisional exclusion of companies not domiciled in Amsterdam, the way was clear for negotiations with the NEM. This heralded a change in council policy, in the direction of a non-exclusive concession, and it led to fresh proposals from the NEM, culminating in the aforementioned association with AEG. The assistant chief engineer of the Gas and Water Department, F. J. Lugt – to whom further reference will be made – was instructed to prepare a draft concession document, a set of rules, an explanatory memorandum and a 'municipal plan'. He was to devote himself to a detailed and profound study of this novel issue.

In the meantime, other initiatives were deployed which at first sight appear to be of limited significance. An intriguing example is the establishment of N.V. 'Electra', Maatschappij voor Electrische Stations by a deed of

---

[17] NEM in a letter to the Municipal Executive, 21.1.1887; PW archive, No. 841, Municipal Archives, Amsterdam.

[18] 'Helios' in a letter to the Municipal Executive, 16.9.1886; PW archive, No. 6525, Municipal Archives, Amsterdam.

[19] Municipal Executive in a letter to E. Boeing, 'local', dated 5.12.1887; PW archive, No. 10203, Municipal Archives, Amsterdam.

incorporation enacted before the notary G. Verrijn Stuart in Amsterdam on 24 February 1888. This company, while at first seeking only a permit from the Council, did of course intend to supply electricity and, ultimately, to secure a concession. It had an authorized capital of f 600,000. The directors were Jonkheer Jacob Hartsen (1842–92), an engineer and the manager of the gasworks at Baarn,[20] and Ernst Boeing, an electrical engineer employed by 'Helios' of Cologne, to whom reference has already been made. The shareholders included Carl Coerper, a German citizen and a director of 'Helios', Th. Heemskerk, a member of the City Council, and H. F. R. Hubrecht, a director of the Nederlandsche Bell-Telephoon Maatschappij. The majority of the participants had links with Amsterdam financiers, and included B. L. Gompertz, Jonkheer H. M. Huydecoper, H. J. Jolles, A. D. and H. J. de Marez Oyens, G. M. Titsingh, J. E. Veltman, A. L. Wurfbain and G. L. Wijsman.

The participation of F. S. van Nierop, a director of the Amsterdamsche Bank, and the lawyer A. F. K. Hartogh[21] – both in their official capacity as directors of the Financieele Maatschappij voor Nijverheidsondernemingen, which provided finance for industry[22] – underlined the involvement of Amsterdam bankers. Soon this was intensified by the inclusion of B. W. Blijdenstein, a managing partner of Twentsche Bankvereeniging B. W. Blijdenstein & Co.

On 30 April 1888, and again on 5 July of that year, 'Electra' approached the City Council with a request for a permit to own cables from the generating station which it had installed in premises at 36 Kalverstraat. The applications, however, did not meet the conditions embodied in the Council's decision of 28 October 1885. But when the company consented to pay the municipality an annual sum equivalent to 60 cents for each 16-candlepower lamp installed, the Executive promptly agreed to further talks.[23] A novel aspect of these discussions was that they concerned the erection of cables above the public highway by affixing them to the facades of buildings; this did not require a permit to *lay* cables beneath land owned by the municipality. The Executive therefore took the line that the procedure laid down by the Council in the above-mentioned decision of 1885

---

[20]  A cousin of Jonkheer P. Hartsen (1833–1913), a director of the Ned. Handel-Mij., Amsterdam.
[21]  Also a director of a life insurance company and a Liberal Member of Parliament for Amsterdam. He was born in 1843 and died in 1901.
[22]  Established in 1883 at the instigation of the Amsterdamsche Bank; cf. S. Brouwer, *De Amsterdamsche Bank 1871–1946*.
[23]  Municipal Executive in a letter to 'Electra', 1.9.1888; PW archive, No. 4756, Municipal Archives, Amsterdam.

need not apply to the application, and indeed could not do so. The willingness on the part of the Executive to grant 'Electra' a permit, on a trial basis, was the greater by reason of the fact that the company did not demand a monopoly, but consented to a permit 'subject to termination by either party'. This was the spirit of the proposal which the Executive laid before the Council on 1 November 1888 for public discussion.[24] But before the meeting could take place, representatives of the NEM, in a state of alarm, visited the Town Hall and requested that, pending a further decision on their application for a twenty-year concession, they should be given a 'similar' permit to the one promised to 'Electra'. The Executive, with commendable speed and impartiality, promptly drew up a proposal in favour of the NEM.[25] At its meeting on 11 November 1888, the Council, after much squabbling among the members, decided to defer discussion of both proposals. The public clash of interests led to fresh proposals being made, this time directly to the Council. The primary aim of 'Electra' was that the NEM should be allotted a section of the city which lay outside the area which it had chosen. The latter, evidently surprised by the ingenuity of the local rival, and the response which it elicited, was moved to declare prematurely that: 'The refusal to grant a permit to the company, which has been established in this city for many years, and the accession to the request of the younger Maatschappij "Electra" would constitute an injustice.'[26] In spite of this, the two proposals were unanimously adopted, on practically identical terms, on 28 November 1888. The claim by the NEM to prior rights was a product of its conservative background in comparison with the youthful Maatschappij 'Electra', which had the support of the Liberals.

Thus did 'Electra' secure the bridgehead for which it had fought: a conditional permit to erect cables above the public highway and running from its central station in the Kalverstraat to premises in the blocks on the eastern side of this street, between the Dam and Watersteeg, the other boundaries being Beursstraat and Rokin; and, moreover, to premises in the block between the Jonge Roelensteeg, the Paleisstraat, the Kalverstraat and the Nieuwezijds Voorburgwal; and those in the block between the St Luciënsteeg and Nieuwezijds Voorburgwal. The area of the city allocated to the NEM comprised the Nieuwezijds Kolk, Kolksteeg, Oude Brugsteeg,

[24] Proposal submitted to the Council by the Municipal Executive, 1.11.1888; No. 508, Municipal Archives, Amsterdam.
[25] Proposal submitted to the Council by the Municipal Executive, 12.11.1888; No. 525, Municipal Archives, Amsterdam.
[26] Submission by NEM to the Council, 24.11.1888; PW archive, No. 8449, Municipal Archives, Amsterdam.

Lange-en Korte Niezel, Korte Stormsteeg, Zeedijk, Nieuwmarkt, Kloveniersburgwal, Binnen-Amstel, Sophiaplein, Singel, Spui and Nieuwezijds Voorburgwal.

The conditions imposed on 'Electra' and the NEM differed only in that the former was given a smaller but more lucrative area and that its mains supply was limited to seventy volts; the latter condition could not be imposed on the NEM because its central station, in the Café Krasnapolsky, operated at 110 volts. Cables, 'as a rule above the ground', had to be installed in accordance with the guidelines laid down by the municipality,[27] whose supervision extended to checking voltage and current and the accuracy of the volt–ampère marking on every incandescent lamp. The annual sum payable to the municipality was finally agreed at 60 cents per 65 volt–amp lamp.

Of the two companies, only the Maatschappij 'Electra' pressed ahead with the implementation of its permit. It commenced to supply electric light on 5 February 1889. During the ensuing spring, the company embarked on the erection of cables across the Dam to the Nieuwendijk, and before the year was out 1,000 or so lamps were burning in the Kalverstraat and the surrounding area. The initial consignment came from the Seel lamp works in Berlin, but soon these were replaced, on grounds of quality, by lamps manufactured by Goossens, Pope & Co.[28] The Council, at its meeting on 19 December 1888, had meanwhile summarily approved an amendment to the 'Electra' permit, increasing the area of the city in which the company might install cables. This now included part of the area originally allocated to the NEM. With the change, the delineation of territories ceased to exist.[29]

Contrary to the purpose of the permit, the NEM did not make immediate use of it, but viewed this merely as a means of securing a right which it had been refused on an earlier occasion. The company had no thought of entering the electric lighting field until such time as the negotiations on a concession had been completed. During discussion of the two proposals by the Council, the Municipal Executive had emphasized that the permits granted were, naturally, of a *temporary* nature and in no way prejudiced the conclusion of a concession, to which careful consideration was being given.[30]

27 A translation, edited by F. J. Lugt, of the regulations drawn up in Magdeburg, Germany; cf. Deliberatiën van B. & W., 26.2.1889.

28 Copy-book of the Mij. 'Electra', 1888–9; Municipal Archives, Amsterdam.

29 Municipal Executive in a letter to 'Electra', 4.1.1889; PW archive, No. 8709, Municipal Archives, Amsterdam.

30 Electriciteits-concessie, Toelichting van enkele Hoofdpunten, 1889, 5; published by the Municipality of Amsterdam.

Extent of the concession of Maatschappij 'Electra'

The NEM, therefore, had not suspended the negotiations because its partner, AEG, or Rathenau himself, had made a concession *per se* a condition for doing business with Amsterdam, even though there was no likelihood of an early proposal on this subject from the Council.

The possibility of obtaining a provisional permit encouraged a number of others. Groeneveld, Van der Poll & Co. and the firm of P. H. ter Meulen, which represented Schuckert, joined the ranks of would-be suppliers of electric lighting.[31] The relevant proposals by the Municipal Executive were adopted at the council meeting of 23 January 1889. But these companies, like the NEM, made no early move. Only the Maatschappij 'Electra' had the courage to invest in an enterprise carrying risks which could not then be predicted. In the mind of the public – and a sizeable body of local admirers – 'Electra' had won a clear advantage in the battle to illuminate Amsterdam by electricity, notwithstanding the fact that the company had provisionally left the matter of negotiating a concession entirely to the NEM.

Professor J. A. Snijders gave the following impression of the operation

---

[31] Applications by Groeneveld, Van der Poll & Co. and P. H. ter Meulen, 20.11.1888 and 28.11.1888 respectively, Municipal Archives, Amsterdam.

and technical arrangement of the 'Electra' lighting system in the Kalverstraat:

On the evening of Monday, 4 August 1890, we visited the installation of the Maatschappij 'Electra' at 36 Kalverstraat in Amsterdam. We were received by one of the managing directors, Mr Boeing, and two engineers, Messrs Beekman and Schöller, and taken round the cramped station. There was no indication that behind the narrow frontage of these ordinary shop premises stood an installation with three steam engines, one of 160 and the others of 120 horsepower, and three dynamos, one of which supplied alternating current at a potential of 2,000 volts.

One must admire the courage and determination of Messrs Hartsen and Boeing who, in such highly unfavourable conditions, in the heart of Amsterdam and virtually without any standby equipment – for which there was no room – ventured to place an installation which, merely by reason of the use of high-voltage alternating currents, was initially frightening to all who were unfamiliar with this system.

For my colleague and myself, the visit possessed special significance inasmuch as this was the first station in which we had seen the system of alternating current applied; and because we visited it in the evening, we were also able to see it working.

The entire equipment gave the impression that a great deal of ingenuity and forethought had been employed, and that the absence of serious breakdowns is due to the soundness of the system, the excellent construction of the machinery and the care exercised in its use.[32]

On 17 May 1888, the assistant chief engineer of the Gas and Water Department, F. J. Lugt, had put the finishing touches to the first draft of a concession in the name of the Nederlandsche Electriciteit-Maatschappij[33] and submitted this to the head of the department, D. A. Wittop Koning. The latter, who earlier in his career had helped to draw up the gas concession,[34] and had daily experience of the way in which it operated, added his critical comments to the draft before passing it on to the Director of Public Works. It was not Lugt's well-prepared draft which caused offence to Wittop Koning: this received the praise which it deserved. It was still unmistakably the charged issue of electric lighting versus gas – on which the Council now had to take a decision in principle – which upset the man who was known as 'our municipal oracle where gas is concerned'.[35] To him, the terms of the

[32] Snijders, *De vorderingen der Electrotechniek*, 46 ff; report of a tour by Prof. Snijders and Prof. H. A. Ravenek (abridged).
[33] Memorandum and appendices submitted by Lugt to Wittop Koning, 17.5.1888; PW archive, No. 3895, Municipal Archives, Amsterdam.
[34] S. Zadoks, *Geschiedenis der Amsterdamsche Concessies*, 1889, 43.
[35] G. P. Zahn Jr, *Geschiedenis der verlichting van Amsterdam*, 1911, 123.

D.C. dynamo in the Maatschappij 'Electra' district generating station at 36 Kalverstraat, Amsterdam

concession sounded too much like a monopoly which was about to be given away. A more immediate aspect of his objection lay in his view that, on economic grounds, it was wrong in principle – and especially for a local authority – to encourage a concession that was based on luxury and would lead to the citizenry being obliged to adopt the more costly electric light. It was wrong, Wittop Koning argued, to compare the capital of the German Empire – 'the metropolis where life is governed by the material wealth of the victors in major wars' – with 'the situation in Amsterdam, where, alas, the effects of a malaise are still far from being overcome'.[36] To encourage this notion, he argued, was tantamount to delivering the citizenry into the hands of a few electricity companies, to be exploited by those companies for their own gain, the sole object being 'to attract into the city's coffers an insignificant portion of the proceeds of that fleecing-operation'. Do we detect here an echo of the widespread criticism of the price of gas, which in Amsterdam had been fixed at nine cents per cubic metre in 1883? Be that as it may, and leaving aside the numerous other complaints about this concession, Wittop ended his highly emotive discourse with the unsolicited advice to avoid an 'extremely complicated concession' on this occasion and, by issuing an *unlimited* number of permits, to commence with several small installations. And then only in areas where this *de luxe* form of lighting was justified from the consumer's point of view.

The revision and elaboration of the draft conditions for a concession were to give rise to a great deal of controversy in the Gas and Water Department. Lugt, in particular, was involved in this, but not his superior, Wittop Koning, who had meanwhile bowed out of the fray. Wittop turned his back on electric lighting in order, as he informed the Director of Public Works, 'to avoid any suggestion that I should wish to pry into matters which have been dealt with without my knowledge'.[37] This clash between executive officers, as personal as it was acrimonious, ended with the observation that to take cognizance of something does not amount to concurring in it. The free application of the principle of competition, though not by the method advocated by Wittop Koning, would ultimately prove to be the only practical path open to the alderman and the Council, and would remain so until the issue of the concession was finally settled.

As already indicated,[38] the proposal by the Municipal Executive to grant

---

[36] Wittop Koning to J. A. Schuurman, Director of Public Works, 22.5.1888; PW archive, Nos. 1437/3895, Municipal Archives, Amsterdam.

[37] Wittop Koning to J. Coninck Westenberg, alderman for public works, 26.4.1889; PW archive, No. 2081, Municipal Archives, Amsterdam.

[38] Cf. page 183; also *Gemeenteblad*, 1889, Section 1, 271–307.

a concession to the NEM was submitted for public debate by the full Council on 21 May 1889. Having met the Council's final wishes,[39] the NEM took it for granted that, broadly speaking, the negotiations were at an end. The company anticipated being in a position to start implementing the agreement within a short time, and indeed this was vital in view of the agreed date of commencement, namely 1 July 1889.

The proposed concession, the expiry of which coincided with that of the gas concession, on 31 July 1918, embraced the whole of the municipality. At first the NEM had not envisaged covering such a large area all at once, but competition and the desire on the part of AEG to illuminate Amsterdam by electricity had later influenced its thinking. The municipality, for its part, felt that in fairness to its citizens, all districts should in principle have supplies of electricity. In the matters of technical regulations and guarantees for the municipality, the conditions of the Berlin concession had served as a model. The lengthy memorandum from the Executive dealt in detail with the possible consequences for the local gasworks. Experience in other countries, however, had shown that gas production had continued to increase in spite of the growth of electric lighting. The Executive expressed the view that no one was better qualified to testify to the certainty of the 'science of electric lighting' than those who were threatened by the 'rising sun', namely the gas technicians. And, it continued, it is indeed remarkable that 'the celebrated German gas expert, Dr Schilling, who in 1885 still predicted a poor future for the electrical industry,[40] largely withdrew his conclusions in a paper written scarcely two years later under the same title' – a citation which did not stand alone and must have been resented by Wittop Koning, and even more by the Imperial Continental Gas Association.[41]

The Executive had great difficulty in determining in advance a correct standard of remuneration for the municipality. In Berlin, where the concessionaire had failed to make a profit in the years 1884 to 1888, this amounted to ten per cent of gross revenue[42] plus twenty-five per cent of any surplus in excess of six per cent return on the capital invested. In the draft concession for Amsterdam, the charges were fixed at five per cent of gross revenue after 1 July 1891 and forty per cent of any surplus after the payment of a dividend of eight per cent, the latter to become effective on 1

---

[39]  Municipal Executive in a letter to the NEM, 4.4.1889; PW archive, No. 2081, Municipal Archives, Amsterdam.

[40]  R. H. Schilling, *Bemerkungen über den gegenwärtigen Stand der elektrischen Beleuchtung.*

[41]  *Algemeen Handelsblad*, 15.6.1889; concerning the 'unfairness' of the conditions of the concession.

[42]  Under the ten per cent clause, the Municipality of Berlin received 91,000 marks for the year 1888.

July 1896. In addition, the municipality demanded an annual sum of
$f$ 5,000 to cover the cost of supervision. When the negotiations opened, the
NEM had requested a three-year period of grace, after which it was
prepared to pay the municipality three per cent, or at most five per cent, of
gross revenue. According to the Executive, it could scarcely be said that
Amsterdam's demands were small in comparison with those of cities like
Bremen, Paris and Vienna. If one looked at Berlin, where the consumer
density was very high and current consumption much greater than was
anticipated in Amsterdam, it could not be argued that the NEM's costs
would be low. This they certainly would not be, bearing in mind that the
presence of canals often meant a doubling of the quantity of cable to be laid.

The Council was requested to approve not only the draft concession,
which ran to 29 articles, but also the accompanying 'Regulations' in which
the conditions for the supply of electricity to private individuals were set
out. Every connection to the main supply, every interior installation, the
supply of lamps and accessories – in short, the complete electric lighting
system[43] – was to be carried out exclusively by, or on behalf of, the
concessionaire and at the consumer's expense. The meter hire ranged from
$f$ 9 per year for ten lamps of 16 candlepower to $f$ 60 per year for six hundred
lamps. The charge for electricity was provisionally fixed at $2\frac{3}{4}$ cents an
hour[44] and was based on the current which one 16-candlepower Edison
lamp consumed at that time, expressed in volt–ampères. As the technology
advanced, it was reasoned, less current would be required to sustain a given
light intensity per hour, enabling the price, expressed in 16-candlepower
incandescent light per hour, to be reduced. The annual charge for each
lamp, of between 10 and 32 candlepower, was set at $f$ 3.50; while this
exceeded the market price, it was devised as a fixed charge upon which the
concessionaire could depend. In return, the company was required to
replace immediately any lamp which failed. A system of discounts on the
charge for electricity, which ranged from $5\frac{1}{2}$% after 800 hours to twenty-
five per cent after 3,000 hours, based on the consumption of a 16-
candlepower lamp, completed the proposed tariff.

Thus the supply of electricity and the provision of the installation up to
and including the incandescent lamp formed an integral part of the
complete lighting system. With the appearance of specialized incandescent

---

43  Cf. Chapter 1, page 25.
44  At that time, the normal charge for a 16-candlepower lamp in the Netherlands and elsewhere was $2\frac{1}{2}$
    cents per hour; cf. Annual Report of the Vereeniging tot Bevordering van Fabrieks- en Hand-
    werksnijverheid in Nederland, 1890, 97.

Table 19. *Relative costs of gas and electric lighting in a number of European cities round about 1888*

|  | Standard gas price per m³ | Gas price per 16 c.p. flame per hour | Electricity per 16 c.p. lamp per hour | Additional cost of electric light (as percentage) |
|---|---|---|---|---|
| Berlin | 9.6 cents | 1.54 cents | 2.40 cents | 56% |
| Bremen | 12.0 | 1.92 | 2.69 | 40 |
| Hamburg | 12.0 | 1.92 | 2.40 | 25 |
| Darmstadt | 13.2 | 2.11 | 2.40 | 14 |
| Paris | 15.0 | 2.40 | 3.75 | 56 |
| Rome | 14.5 | 2.32 | 3.00 | 29 |
| Vienna | 11.4 | 1.82 | 3.60 | 98 |
| The Hague | 7.0 | 1.12 | 2.50 | 123 |
| Amsterdam | 9.0 | 1.44 | 2.75[a] | 91 |

*Note:*
[a] Based on draft concession, 21.5.1889, to be granted to the NEM

lamp manufacturers in the late 1880s, however, the principle of supplying lamps was superseded.

According to the figures which Lugt drew up for the City Council, incandescent lighting was at that time considerably more costly than gas (see Table 19 above). Local differences, it was found, were largely a result of wide variations in the price of gas. In the Netherlands, gas averaged seven cents per cubic metre, a relatively low figure.[45] In the memorandum which accompanied the draft, the Executive emphasized that the Council, in considering the question of electric lighting, must bear in mind that at that stage it was significantly more costly than gas lighting. A 'substantial' price had to be paid for the advantages of low heat radiation, reduced pollution of the atmosphere and the practicability of high-powered light sources. On the other hand, according to the Executive, if the price were not controlled and sank to the point where it competed with gas, or if an over-eager concessionaire were to accept an imposed price which was uneconomic, the company concerned would fail.

Electric light, therefore, had its price; and the success of the company which provided it was certainly a factor of importance in the interests of the city as well as in other ways. Indeed its significance was increased by the

[45] *De Ingenieur*, 15.6.1889: 'Gas- of Electrisch Licht?'

Table 20. *Cost of building and commissioning central stations in a number of major European cities*[a]

| | Opening date | Machinery output, incl. stand-by equipment h.p. | Offtake at 31 July or 31 Dec. 1898 kW | Cost up to 31 Dec. 1898 guilders | Cost per installed horsepower guilders | Cost per connected kilowatt guilders |
|---|---|---|---|---|---|---|
| Vienna | Nov. 1890 | 11,500 | 11,545 | 7,500,000 | 652 | 650 |
| Frankfurt am Main | Oct. 1894 | 4,500 | 4,594 | 2,324,050 | 516 | 506 |
| Dresden | Dec. 1895 | 3,840 | 4,493 | 2,065,873 | 538 | 460 |
| Budapest | Oct. 1893 | 4,500 | 4,272 | 3,299,279 | 733 | 772 |
| Leipzig[b] | Sept. 1895 | 3,000 | 3,638 | 2,000,105 | 667 | 550 |
| Nuremberg | May 1896 | 4,000 | 3,405 | 1,838,400 | 460 | 540 |
| Cologne[b] | Oct. 1891 | 2,400 | 2,745 | 1,615,235 | 673 | 589 |
| Stuttgart[b] | Oct. 1891 | 2,200 | 2,764 | 1,810,600 | 823 | 669 |
| Hanover | Mar. 1891 | 2,800 | 2,596 | 1,867,880 | 667 | 720 |
| Oslo | Dec. 1892 | 1,900 | 1,906 | 1,087,270 | 572 | 570 |
| Darmstadt | Mar. 1889 | 1,575 | 1,334 | 857,706 | 545 | 643 |
| Elberfeld | Nov. 1887 | 1,650 | 1,269 | 1,026,506 | 622 | 809 |
| Chemnitz | July 1894 | 1,800 | 1,457 | 1,094,040 | 680 | 751 |
| Aachen | Jan. 1893 | 1,760 | 2,363 | 1,141,476 | 648 | 843 |
| Amsterdam[b] | July 1892 | 3,100 | 1,550 | 2,570,683 | 829 | 1,685 |

PHILIP10B   6/08/1985   [04]   L16

Notes:
[a] A. W. Ressing, *De levering van Electriciteit te Amsterdam*, 1900, 63.
[b] Cost of land not included.

much-regretted Article 3 in the gas concession, which, for the duration of the arrangement, precluded the municipality from entering the area of lighting. The draft concession drawn up by the NEM contained a clause which could be invoked after twelve years and provided for a transfer of ownership, enabling the lighting system to be operated by the local authority. In the meantime, granting the NEM a regular concession, instead of a series of temporary permits, would meet a need on the part of the city and also enable the electric lighting company to operate. Admittedly, this was first and foremost a question of luxury, but that was not out of place in a major city.

Whether or not Amsterdam regretted that it had thus far adopted a cautious attitude, the Executive's proposals concluded, the moment of decision 'appears to have come'.

Bearing in mind the state of electrical engineering at that time, one would be justified in concluding that, at the most suitable moment for a decision in the matter, the Executive assessed the introduction of electric lighting correctly in commercial terms. Whether the conditions on which this was to be realized could also bear examination remained to be seen. It was now up to the members of the Council not to think simply in terms of the pros and cons of a concession, but to immerse themselves much more deeply than before in the practicalities. In the course of doing so, they came to the conclusion that, with the exception of the alderman concerned, none knew anything about the subject.[46]

On 1 June 1889, having studied the conditions proposed by the Municipal Executive for the granting of a concession to the NEM, the Maatschappij 'Electra' declared its willingness to compete on the same terms.[47] As proof of its earnest and incisiveness, the company despatched the relevant documents to the Executive by return of post, marked 'Agreed' and bearing the signatures of Hartsen and Boeing. Five days later, a second proposal, this time in the name of the Maatschappij 'Electra', was laid before the Council. This complication meant that the granting of the concession, which was on the agenda for 12 June, could not be proceeded with in a single meeting – to the profound disappointment of the NEM. The company, pointing to the heavy commitments which it was scheduled to

[46] A. W. C. Berns in a letter to the City Council, 21.3.1890; PW archive, No. 69, Municipal Archives, Amsterdam.

[47] 'Electra' in a letter to the Municipal Executive, 1.6.1889; PW archive, No. 3620, Municipal Archives, Amsterdam.

undertake on 1 July, entreated the Executive to make every effort to ensure that the long-awaited decision was taken at the very next meeting of the Council.[48] The Executive, however, made it clear that the equivalent offer by 'Electra' could not be ignored. It was obvious that a new *modus operandi* would have to be found, the more so since, in the approach to the problem of concessions, the emphasis had shifted from the administrative and technical aspect to one of principles. Councillor L. Serrurier expressed the change in a memorandum to the Council on 28 June 1889.[49] His main objection was that the proposal did not contain adequate safeguards for consumers, so that they could quite easily find themselves powerless at the hands of a monopoly. Furthermore, Serrurier maintained, the concession, which gave the holder the sole right to carry out installations in private houses and other buildings, went much further than was really necessary. He also drew attention to a modification of the concession in Berlin, the effect of which had been to allow persons other than the concessionaire to undertake installations in private dwellings. That the Berlin concession had served as a model for Amsterdam made no impression whatsoever on him, for in his view malpractices arose only after a concessionaire had assured himself of a sufficiently large share of the market. The contention that the Amsterdam concession was not exclusive, and that there was thus no reason to fear a monopoly, was dismissed by Serrurier as a hallucination. He believed that once electricity became an article of general consumption, like gas, 'it would in fact always give rise to a monopoly, as the history of the gasworks in this city has so clearly shown'.

In a lengthy memorandum dated 23 July 1889, Serrurier, who had been a member of the Council since the previous January, reiterated his strong views.[50] Prompted by Lugt, he argued that neither in Paris nor in London did the electricity concession provide exclusive rights for installations in houses – 'a milch cow for a powerful concessionaire-monopolist'. Worst of all, in his opinion, the concession document did not contain a single reference to supervision by the municipality to ensure that the voltage and the supply of electricity were adequate. Looking ahead, he indicated that one or more central stations should be built on the outskirts of the city, since 'the black smoke produced by Electra does nothing to enhance the view of the area around the Rokin'.

---

[48]  NEM in a letter to the Municipal Executive, 14.5.1889; PW archive, No. 4031, Municipal Archives, Amsterdam.
[49]  *Gemeenteblad*, Section 1, 419 ff.
[50]  *Gemeenteblad*, Section 1, 439 ff.

During the summer of 1889, council elections in Amsterdam, followed by the replacement – manifestly for political reasons – of the alderman responsible for public works, brought the negotiations to a standstill. As far as the positions of political power in the city were concerned, the split which had occurred in the conservative–liberal electoral association 'Burgerplicht' (Civic Duty) in 1888 proved to have been more than a sensational incident. Most significantly, the so-called radicals who had broken away proceeded to form a democratic electoral association with the title 'Amsterdam'.[51] The alderman for public works, J. Coninck Westenberg (1830–1907), quite suddenly found himself replaced by a member of this powerful, radical opposition. The leader of the new movement and later statesman M. W. F. Treub (1858–1931) made it clear that, 'in addition to universal suffrage, we, the younger generation, favoured public sector monopolies'.[52] Aspirations such as these, which had met with objections based to a greater or lesser degree on principle in the Burgerplicht group, were unreservedly opposed by Coninck Westenberg, a conservative, who where this issue was concerned could be positively explosive.[53] He dismissed the concept of municipal undertakings as pernicious, a view which was very much in line with the efforts of the NEM to acquire a concession from the Council. But a number of events, chief among which was the 'drinking-water issue' and the severe criticism of the Duinwaterleiding Maatschappij[54] in the summer drought of 1889, cost him re-election. On 3 September of that year, L. Serrurier (1844–1916), a councillor to whom reference has already been made and who at best favoured a limited electricity concession, was placed in charge of public works.

As a major shareholder of N.V. Maatschappij voor Zwavelzuurbereiding, formerly G. Ketjen & Co., a leading chemical manufacturer, Serrurier (a chemical engineer by profession) was respected in financial circles in Amsterdam. With their assistance, Ketjen & Co. had been transformed into a limited liability company in 1888.[55] A. F. K. Hartogh, a radical liberal, and A. Roelvink, both of whom were among the financial backers of 'Electra', were members of the Supervisory Board of the new company. For

[51] Th. van Tijn, 'De sociale bewegingen van 1888 tot circa 1895', in *Algemene Geschiedenis der Nederlanden*, Vol. 13, 1978, 297.
[52] M. W. F. Treub, *Herinneringen en overpeinzingen*, 1931, 74.
[53] *Algemeen Handelsblad*, 9.12.1907: an obituary.
[54] The majority of the shares of this company were in the hands of British investors; cf. Treub, *Herinneringen*, 140.
[55] *Honderd Jaar Zwavelzuur-Fabricatie*, 1835–1935, 11 ff.

this reason alone, it will be clear that Serrurier's arrival was not welcomed by the directors of the NEM. Rathenau, who was evidently accustomed to exerting influence on the Berliner Städtischen Elektrizitätswerke, viewed the appointment as extremely inconvenient. Indeed, it was among the factors which led him to engage the services of Gerard Philips for the next phase of the negotiations. Gerard pointed out to Rathenau that the representatives of the NEM bore no blame for the resignation of Coninck Westenberg, an unexpected setback which had occurred 'last summer, just when the end was in sight'.[56] It was clear to all concerned that, with the arrival of the new alderman, a completely new and less binding draft concession would be laid before the Council.

On 23 October 1889, Serrurier informed the Maatschappij 'Electra' in strict confidence of the new conditions which he proposed to lay before the Municipal Executive.[57] He added that he would prefer to see fundamental issues such as the matter of recompense debated publicly, but that he was open to suggestions on technical matters. The documents which lay before the Council at that juncture comprised:

> Serrurier's memorandum of 28 June 1889, containing a number of comments regarding the proposed concession;
> a memorandum from the Municipal Executive, dealing with some of the main issues;
> the report of the departmental discussions on electricity concessions, held on Monday, 8 July 1889;
> a memorandum from Serrurier dated 23 July 1889 in response to the report of the departmental discussions.[58]

When the Municipal Executive met on 28 November 1889, the question of using Serrurier's memoranda as a guideline for the new draft conditions was discussed. At the end of the deliberations, the Executive voted in favour of the principle embodied in the draft, the effect of which was to limit the activities of the concessionaire to the supply of electric current, and therefore precluded a monopoly of installation and the supply of lamps. This was a fundamental change and one which in part resulted from

---

[56]  Copy-book of Gerard Philips, 5.12.1889; Philips Archives, Eindhoven.
[57]  Alderman L. Serrurier in a letter to the Maatschappij 'Electra' dated 23.10.1889; PW archive, No. 6994, Municipal Archives, Amsterdam.
[58]  *Gemeenteblad*, 1889, Section 1, 417–42.

objections lodged by G. Groeneveld and H. L. A. van den Wall Bake,[59] who saw the granting of such a privilege to the concessionaire as a threat to the freedom of action of their installation companies. The limitation implied a significant reduction of the anticipated and lasting market; its effect was less serious for the Maatschappij 'Electra', as a user of dynamos manufactured by 'Helios' A.G. of Cologne, than for AEG, which desired to install and maintain a 'complete electric lighting system'. As will emerge, Rathenau was at first unwilling to give up the idea of the sole right to carry out installation work, coupled with the establishment of a branch in Amsterdam, and the right to supply lamps. With some reservation, one may wonder whether Gerard Philips, who had several irons in the fire, was influenced in his choice by the possibility of settling in Amsterdam as installation contractor to AEG, or becoming manager of the station. There is no firm evidence of this; it is, however, known that in the summer of 1889 he had sought a partnership with Van Rietschoten & Houwens of Rotterdam. It is thus clear that he still entertained the idea of entering the installation field, even though the position in Rotterdam failed to materialize.[60]

The contest between the NEM and the Maatschappij 'Electra' had taken a new and intriguing turn on 4 November 1889 with the announcement by Wisse, who claimed to be the authorized agent of Siemens & Halske, that he wished to compete for the concession on behalf of the Berlin house.[61] Wisse invoked the earlier applications made by his company, the Nederlandsche Maatschappij voor Electriciteit en Metallurgie, and, basing himself on the Municipal Executive's memorandum of 21 May,[62] claimed that he could offer the municipality more favourable terms than his competitors. This offer, which Wisse submitted on his own initiative, cut across the agreement of 1887 providing for co-operation between Siemens & Halske and AEG, a fact which can probably be explained by unresolved differences of interpretation on the part of the officials charged with the implementation of the agreement. This was not a new phenomenon; indeed, it had on occasions led to considerable tension between Rathenau and Werner Siemens,[63] and

---

[59] A partner in Mijnssen & Co. and brother of R. W. J. C. van den Wall Bake, a member of the City Council.

[60] Cf. Chapter 2, page 73.

[61] Ned. Mij. voor Electriciteit en Metallurgie in a letter to the City Council, dated 4.11.1889; PW archive, No. 7285, Municipal Archives, Amsterdam.

[62] See page 187.

[63] Rathenau in a letter to W. Siemens dated 21.1.1888; Siemens Archives, No. 2 Li 553, Munich.

in 1888 caused Rathenau formally to tender his resignation to the Supervisory Board of AEG. The interest now displayed in the Amsterdam concession, through the Dutch representative of Siemens & Halske, at any rate shows that, as an instrument to limit competition between the two, the agreement was still not working smoothly.

On 13 December 1889, Serrurier sent the NEM a copy of the new draft which had been drawn up at the behest of the Municipal Executive. The directors of this company, W. J. de Bordes and P. E. Tegelberg, now assisted by Gerard Philips, indicated their wish to meet the Executive for an exchange of views.[64] The text of their reply, translated by Gerard, was sent to AEG in Berlin with a request for further instructions. Rathenau replied that he wished to attend the proposed meeting, but was unable to leave Berlin until the early part of January. In the meantime, Gerard devoted himself to consultancy, including the preparation of a plan to illuminate electrically the hospital and mental institution operated by the Netherlands-Israelite Poor Relief Board in Amsterdam. He also negotiated with Mijnssen & Co. for the supply of a dynamo and light fittings. In this period he was approached by the restaurateur A. W. Krasnapolsky on the subject of an illuminated fountain, and during their discussions the latter hit on the idea of having the name of his establishment engraved on future lamps installed there.[65]

Evidence of tension in the relations between the NEM and AEG following the departure of Coninck Westenberg and the postponement of the concession came with Rathenau's instruction to Gerard Philips to inform the directors of the company that he was no longer willing to bear alone the total cost of the project. In his reply, Gerard informed his principal that:

Mr De Bordes was very surprised to learn of your view that the directors are not doing enough in the matter, for they are continually making every effort to speed up the negotiations. Admittedly, they have of late not concerned themselves with influencing public opinion by means of printed matter, etc., which Mr De Bordes does not consider desirable in the present situation. Only if it appears that no agreement can be reached with the majority of the members of the Council will publicity be employed in an attempt to swing public opinion in our favour.[66]

Gerard went on to say that the directors of the NEM were not averse to shouldering their portion of the costs after January, 'that is, provided the

[64]  NEM in a letter to the Municipal Executive dated 28.12.1889; PW archive, No. 8396, Municipal Archives, Amsterdam.
[65]  Copy-book of Gerard Philips, 8.12.1889 and 27.1.1890.
[66]  Copy-book of Gerard Philips, 5.12.1889; a letter to the Board of AEG.

affair does not enter a new phase, as a result of which you feel obliged to withdraw'. The NEM, he explained, was counting on the matter being settled by the end of January at the latest. He himself was less optimistic, for he had learned from Serrurier that differences of opinion had arisen within the Executive. More encouraging from Rathenau's position was the assurance given by Serrurier that he wished to deal only with the Maatschappij 'Electra' and AEG, and that the Council would therefore not consider the application from Siemens & Halske. Most noticeable to Gerard Philips were the serious accusations which passed back and forth between Rathenau and the NEM, in which the NEM was held to have been insufficiently incisive. During a meeting with De Bordes, Gerard learned that: 'If, as had been agreed with Lugt, Rathenau had taken prompt and effective action in the face of the rejection of proposals by the Council, it would in all probability have speeded up the settlement of the affair.'[67] De Bordes added that if Rathenau wanted to back out of the agreement with the NEM, he should say so. It is clear beyond any doubt that Gerard Philips had unwittingly stirred up a hornets' nest in Amsterdam.

Unlike the NEM, the Maatschappij 'Electra' – in a letter of 6 January 1890 – had informed the Municipal Executive of its full acceptance of the draft conditions for a general concession, which it had received on 14 December. It made only two stipulations, namely that the price for electricity (which had not been prescribed by the Executive) should be at least fifty-one cents per unit, and that none of its competitors should be offered more favourable terms.[68] The company also sought to lease, from the same date, a piece of land owned by the municipality and situated on the Barendszkade, on which it desired to site a larger generating station. The NEM, which was suspicious of many aspects of the draft, opted to place its specific objections before the Executive and to defer adopting a definitive attitude until the meeting at which Rathenau would be present.[69] It is interesting to follow the progress of the NEM's written objection, which still contained practically every element of the 'complete lighting system' and which was composed in consultation with Gerard Philips.

The company's attitude was that the new draft prepared by the Executive – which it regarded more as a *cahier des charges*, and which under no circumstances allowed of an exclusive concession – ought certainly not to

---

[67] Ibid.

[68] 'Electra' in a letter to the Municipal Executive dated 6.1.1890; PW archive, No. 69, Municipal Archives, Amsterdam.

[69] NEM in a letter to the Municipal Executive dated 11.1.1890; PW archive, No. 849, Municipal Archives, Amsterdam.

offer scope for three or more candidates. If this were the case, said the company in a defensive opening paragraph, it would feel obliged to withdraw. It was even opposed to the concession being divided between two firms. Any further dilution by the admission of others would undoubtedly have fatal consequences for all. The municipality should therefore accept a situation in which the concession was limited to two companies for a number of years, long enough for them to show what they could do. Evidently the NEM, or AEG, although not yet reconciled to that idea, had already accepted the inevitability of reaching an accommodation with the Maatschappij 'Electra'.

The matter of the right to carry out domestic installations, supply lamps, etc., which Rathenau had initially been at great pains to retain, was now at issue; and it was one hedged about with restrictions. As it appeared likely that the Executive would reject this demand, Gerard had already suggested on 13 December that a compromise be found, for:

Firstly, there is every probability that, with or without a monopoly, 80%–90% of the domestic installations and the lamps will be provided by you; secondly, it may be possible to obtain instead a reduction of the amount to be paid to the city, so that, for example, the $f$ 3,000 may not have to be paid, or the 5% of gross revenue demanded may be reduced.[70]

The influence of liberal minds on the draft was perhaps most evident in the stipulation that public lighting should be subject to the same conditions as domestic installations. This demanded a mentality which was hard to reconcile with Rathenau's commercial approach (a product of the situation in Berlin) and totally incompatible with the lengthy process of decision-making which was common in Amsterdam, and which Gerard Philips described as 'rocking to and fro on the waves of council debate'.[71] On 17 December 1889, Gerard had advised Rathenau that a monopoly for the duration of the concession – which the latter had laid down as a prime condition during their discussions in Berlin in the previous October – was completely out of the question.[72] And Serrurier had already intimated that a monopoly of lamp supplies had evoked even greater objections than one of domestic installations. This process of give and take typifies Gerard Philips' laborious efforts to persuade Rathenau to change his mind on this issue. The outcome can be seen in the preamble to the talks between the Municipal Executive and Rathenau, which we shall now examine.[73]

[70]  Copy-book of Gerard Philips, 13.12.1889; a letter to the Board of AEG.
[71]  Ibid., 17.12.1889.        [72]  Ibid.
[73]  NEM in a letter to the Municipal Executive dated 11.1.1890; PW archive, No. 849, Municipal Archives, Amsterdam.

The opening assertion was that during the period in which the lighting company was becoming established, it was justified in 'keeping control of all related matters', and not having to be dependent upon others, which in most cases meant competitors. Reference was also made to the importance of the method of installation and the use of sound materials in relation to the quality of the electric lighting. In this context, it is interesting to note that a few months later Rathenau enquired of Gerard Philips which of the two installation contractors, Mijnssen & Co. or Groeneveld, Van der Poll & Co., would best serve AEG; and here lay a dilemma, for the choice of either would result in the loss of the other as a customer.[74]

The second motive for not relinquishing the right to carry out domestic installations was based on safety. Connection to a 'large central station', the company maintained, demanded insulation of a higher quality than was required with a self-contained installation. The 'outward and return paths for the current' had to be assured, for 'with poor installation' there was a possibility that the current would find its way back via the ground, or via the wiring in another house, which was not designed for so powerful a current. This could lead to 'overheating and possibly fire'. Admittedly, the letter continued, there were methods of increasing safety, even in poor installations, but these were in no case adequate. The remedy lay in conscientious installation and the use of the best materials, in the concessionaire's own interest. After all, as the supplier of electricity, he had both to maintain his reputation and protect himself against the risk of 'huge damages'. Hence the submission that a lasting and exclusive right to carry out domestic installations was the most desirable basis. It is clear, however, that the NEM and AEG eventually recognized that this point of view could not be sustained forever, as they foresaw that with the passing of time there would be less cause to fear poor-quality installation work by others, 'because by then there will be a corps of workmen familiar with the high standards involved in making connections to a generating station'. It was argued that such workmen were 'still rare exceptions' in Amsterdam, and this brought out once again the role of self-education in the training of electricians at that time. As we have already seen, the local installation contractors were unable to accept this helping hand from AEG; they did not appreciate what they saw as interference.

The third issue for negotiation concerned a financial contribution by the municipality during the early, difficult years; this, it was postulated, was a reasonable request. Reference was made to the share of surplus profits

[74] Copy-book of Gerard Philips, pages 113 and 114 (date illegible).

demanded by the municipality after the initial period. As a *quid pro quo*, the NEM and AEG again proposed that the entire concession and the rights of installation, lamp supply, etc. should be granted exclusively to the two initial concessionaires – now, however, only for a period of five years. The letter then dealt in detail with various technical and financial matters. It is surprising to observe that, in the approach to the proposal for maximum prices, no regard was paid to the intention on the part of the NEM and AEG to supply current on a twenty-four hour basis from the outset. During the day-time this would be motive power and be substantially cheaper than the current for lighting in the evening and night hours. From an economic point of view, it was argued, differentiation was highly desirable: 'on the one hand, the comparatively expensive light as a luxury article, and on the other hand the cheap motive power for large and small industries, as an article for which there is a general demand'. The NEM's proposals also contained the suggestion that, 'for the furtherance of Amsterdam's industries', no levy should be imposed on revenue from the supply of electricity used to power machinery.

An indication of the anticipated growth of consumption is provided by the difference of opinion between the Executive and the NEM regarding the proposed obligation to raise the output of the installation to 2,500 units per hour.[75] This the NEM regarded as far too high, the more so as the consumption per 16-candlepower lamp was expected to decline substantially in the course of time. The company therefore assumed that, 'in twenty years' time, 2,500 units per hour would represent 50,000–60,000 lamps, making a total of 100,000–120,000 lamps for the two concessionaires'. This level of consumption, it argued – and here the voice is that of Gerard Philips – was unlikely to be achieved even by 1918, when the concession was due to expire. The objection centred on a stipulation whereby the concessionaire could be obliged to go on enlarging the capacity up to the final day of the concession – with the risk of having then to hand over the entire installation to the Council without recompense. Here it should be mentioned that, in contrast to the above-mentioned estimates, the actual consumption in Amsterdam in 1918 was 28,000 units per hour, the equivalent of 560,000 lamps of 16 candlepower.[76] The earlier figure throws

---

[75] In the new draft, 1,000 volt–ampère-hours (1 kWh) was taken as the measure of the amount of current; this unit, which was used in Britain, was more objective than the derived measure employed in the earlier draft.

[76] 'De ontwikkeling van de electriciteitsvoorziening van de gemeente Amsterdam', in *Gedenkboek uitgegeven naar aanleiding van het 10-jarig bestaan van de Vereeniging van Directeuren van Electriciteitsbedrijven in Nederland*, 1926, Table 3.

some light on Gerard Philips' plan, on which he embarked in 1890, to set up an incandescent lamp factory with a capacity of 1,000 lamps per day – a high rate of production when viewed in the context of the contemporary situation.

The letter from the NEM and AEG to the Municipal Executive ended with the statement that the companies would reserve their judgement regarding the amount to be paid to the municipality until the proposed meeting, at which Rathenau would be present. Nor did they make any further reference to the cost of electricity. With this substantially reduced package of demands, particularly as regards the duration of the monopoly of installation and the supply of lamps, the NEM and AEG had provided much food for thought. Their approach was in strong contrast to that of the Maatschappij 'Electra', which had meanwhile commenced to operate on the basis of the temporary permit, and desired no major changes in the new draft.

On 22 January 1890, Gerard sent a telegram to Berlin, informing Rathenau that the meeting with the Municipal Executive had been arranged for 2 p.m. on Friday the twenty-fourth. This he confirmed by letter, adding that 'Mr Hartogh cordially invites you to stay with him'.[77] M. H. Hartogh, a civil engineer, was employed by AEG to look after the Dutch market. He had left Berlin ahead of Rathenau and, curiously enough, was staying at 455 Herengracht, the home of his brother, A. F. K. Hartogh, one of the founders of 'Electra'. Within AEG circles, M. H. Hartogh was recognized as a valuable man: as manager of Bernstein's Elektricitätswerke, which was taken over by AEG in 1891,[78] he was to look after the company's interests in Hamburg for many years. He regularly visited customers in the Netherlands. This time he was in Amsterdam to strengthen the AEG delegation, the other members of which were Rathenau, Philips, Krasnapolsky and De Bordes. The Municipal Executive was represented by Mayor Van Tienhoven and the aldermen Serrurier, Dyserinck and Van Lennep. At the meeting, AEG's objections, as set out above, were summarized by Rathenau. These, he stated, 'are for the greater part of secondary importance; the most important is directed against Article 15. The Company would wish it to be stipulated that the concessionaire is also charged with carrying out the installations in houses.'[79] The very brief report of the

---

[77] Copy-book of Gerard Philips, 22.1.1890.
[78] Report by Auskunftei W. Schimmelpfeng, Hamburg, 4.10.1893; archives of the Vitrite Works, Middelburg.
[79] Deliberations of the Municipal Executive, 24.1.1890; Municipal Archives, Amsterdam.

meeting gives no indication regarding the price of electricity or the amount to be paid to the municipality, and therefore it is probable that these issues were held in abeyance. Rathenau, however, did provide clarification by explaining the agreement under which Siemens & Halske had undertaken not to engage in direct competition with AEG.[80] At the end of the discussions, Mayor Van Tienhoven promised that the Executive would consider the objections and communicate its finding to the NEM. It would appear that no fresh points of view were put forward: rather, the talks give the impression that Rathenau was still hoping to obtain a monopoly of installation and supply by his personal efforts. A few days later, Gerard reported to him that Serrurier had amended the draft in a number of respects, as requested, but that the monopoly of domestic installations had not been conceded. Nor, it had been decided, could the concessionaire be compelled to carry out the work.[81] The Municipal Executive also reserved the right to examine critically the chosen site for the central station. Lugt had drawn Serrurier on this point and had learned that an adjacent property, such as had been chosen by the Maatschappij 'Electra' in the Kalverstraat, would not again be considered. A series of later letters illustrate Gerard's difficult position in between the municipality and his recalcitrant principal, Rathenau, to whom he indicated that further changes were on the way.[82]

Rathenau's continued unwillingness to accept the new conditions was reflected in the Municipal Executive's recommendations to the City Council of 11 February 1890, in which it was stated that the NEM, in contrast to the Maatschappij 'Electra', had still not adopted a definitive stance. It is abundantly clear that Rathenau's manner during the Amsterdam talks, if not actually producing the opposite of the desired effect, had scarcely been a diplomatic success against an executive which was averse to fresh monopolies, and which certainly did not appear to have been impressed by his arguments. Nor was the coincidence of this affair and a judgement by the Divisional Court on 26 February 1890, under which the municipality was ordered to pay several hundred thousand guilders to the Imperial Continental Gas Association, conducive to any binding arrangements in the area of electricity. The lawsuit, which concerned the intensity of the gas lighting – and in which August Philips, Gerard's uncle, acted as

[80] Copy-book of Gerard Philips, 5.3.1890.
[81] Ibid., page 50 (date illegible).
[82] Copy-book of Gerard Philips, various dates.

counsel for the I.C.G.A. – caused a sensation in Amsterdam. It was ultimately to end in victory for the municipality.[83]

Serrurier published the text of his draft at the beginning of February – in good time for the council meeting scheduled for 12 March.[84] In the introduction he stated that if the two companies, 'Electra' and the NEM, accepted the terms to be agreed, the application by the Nederlandsche Maatschappij voor Electriciteit en Metallurgie, submitted on behalf of Siemens & Halske, would be declined. For practical reasons, in particular, the Municipal Executive felt that it was undesirable to admit a third competitor at the outset. It also expressed doubt whether the existing system of terminable permits could ever lead to the general introduction of electric lighting. The erection of overhead wires, as had been done by the Maatschappij 'Electra', must be absolutely forbidden. The dangers arising from this method had also been studied by the Amsterdam branch of the Association for the Promotion of Manufacturing and Craft Industry, and its conclusion was that the use of other than 'underground main conductors' should be expressly prohibited.[85]

As regards the right to carry out domestic installations, the draft stated that the consumer should be free to choose the installer. The concessionaire was given no right of supervision of installations except, under arbitration by the Council, to refuse to connect the supply to a defective installation. The maximum price per unit of energy of 1,000 volt–ampère-hours was provisionally set at 51 cents, the figure suggested by 'Electra', with the proviso that a discount would operate after an average consumption of 800 units; the old and new schemes differed little in this respect. The obligation to supply lamps at ƒ3.50 per lighting point per year had been withdrawn; however, it was felt that the concessionaire should still receive the ƒ1 or thereabouts which had been included in the earlier lamp price as compensation for the obligation to supply electricity to large installations which consumed little or no current. The above-mentioned electricity price, which included the extra guilder, was equivalent to $2\frac{3}{4}$ cents per 16-candlepower lamp per hour, the figure which had appeared in the original draft.[86] No

[83]  Zahn, *Verlichting van Amsterdam*, 125, 130, 133.

[84]  Recommendations of the Municipal Executive to the City Council, 11.2.1890, No. 100; Municipal Archives, Amsterdam.

[85]  Annual Report of the Vereeniging tot Bevordering van Fabrieks- en Handwerksnijverheid in Nederland 1890, 81–110 and 175–81.

[86]  Cf. page 196.

essential changes had been made in regard to the amount payable to the municipality: five per cent of all revenue from the supply of electricity, including power, and forty per cent of net profits in excess of an eight per cent return on the paid-up capital. There was, however, one addition – a 'social' clause which obliged the concessionaire to pay regular employees sufficiently well to enable them to insure themselves against sickness and accident, and to meet pension premiums. Finally, the proposed concession, like that covered by the earlier draft, would not run beyond 31 July 1918.

'It will not now be easy to secure anything approaching fundamental changes', Gerard informed Rathenau on 20 February 1890, 'because "Electra" has signified agreement with the entire draft.'[87] In a conversation with a councillor who was well disposed towards 'Electra', he had again brought up the question of exemption from payment in respect of electricity supplied for power purposes, in the hope that the company would go along with the proposals. The provisions of the new draft on this important point, among others, were unacceptable to Rathenau. And time was short, for the draft was due to be debated publicly in March.

In addition to his involvement in the concession, Gerard acted as AEG's agent in obtaining business from the State Railways, Heineken's Brewery and other undertakings. In a letter to the AEG lamp factory in Berlin, he said: 'It has been my experience that custom can best be retained by supplying so-called "old economy" lamps [of 70 or 75 watts], because in this country long life is generally regarded as the most important factor.'[88] The cost of electricity, therefore, was not the primary consideration – a persistent phenomenon with which he was often to be confronted. He wrote a letter to the *Algemeen Handelsblad*, entitled 'Electric lighting; dangers for the individual' (see Appendix 6). This reflected his experience in the field of lighting, acquired both in London and Berlin, and was, of course, designed to influence the impending decision in Amsterdam. 'If only people would not look for an example to America, where human lives count for little, but to our eastern neighbours who, where the sound, lasting, rational lighting of cities is concerned, not only set the tone in Europe, but also outdo America, and in the area of safety are far ahead of that country.' The letter appeared in the 11 March edition of the Amsterdam daily under the pseudonym 'Ingenieur'. It left no doubt as to the writer's personal

---

[87] Copy-book of Gerard Philips, 20.2.1890.
[88] Ibid., 21.2.1890.

preference for optimum quality in the application of the technology, coupled with a 'sound concession'.[89]

The successive and varied developments in the course of the council debates between March and September, however worthy of examination, go beyond the scope of this study. In the words of the *Algemeen Handelsblad* on the eve of the debate: 'If ever there was a need for a sincere prayer for "wisdom and foresight", this is certainly the moment, now that the members of the Council are called upon to decide on such a difficult, technical matter.' The paper gave 'Electra' – the only candidate which had shown that it was in earnest – the credit for having introduced electric lighting in the capital. For the NEM – 'whom Fortune has kept waiting too long' – the affair seemed to have lost its attraction: 'at least, it is unwilling to come to an immediate decision'. The *Algemeen Handelsblad*, which was clearly well informed, went on to say that there was little point in throwing a monopoly out of the front door, only to let it in through three back doors.[90] It concluded by saying that it would not be surprised to see the Council facing the dilemma of either having to grant a monopoly to the candidate which offered the most, or opting for a municipal system.

The allusion to three 'back doors' concerned the surprise action on the part of Wisse, who, this time without informing Siemens & Halske, had submitted a tender on behalf of his own company, the Nederlandsche Maatschappij voor Electriciteit en Metallurgie. In an earlier communication to the Council, dated 5 March,[91] he had expressed surprise at the rejection, without explanation, of the tender of 4 November 1889. To show that he was competitive and could therefore not be ignored, he now offered a price of 45 cents per unit of electricity, compared with the 51 cents contained in Serrurier's proposals. Wisse also sought publicity – for example, by having published in 'De Amsterdammer' of 19 March *his* view of the reasons why Siemens & Halske had withdrawn. He made it clear that further co-operation with that company and, more importantly, the use of materials supplied by it, was still perfectly feasible; and he went on to claim that his own company had built the country's first and largest central station for electric lighting.[92] His high-handed action obliged Siemens &

---

[89]  Ibid., page 75 (date illegible); Gerard advises Rathenau that he is the author of this article and of a second which, also under the pseudonym 'Ingenieur', appeared on 26.3.1890.

[90]  *Algemeen Handelsblad*, 12.3.1890.

[91]  Ned. Mij. voor Electriciteit en Metallurgie in letters to the City Council, 5.3.1890 and 10.3.1890; PW archive, No. 4377, Municipal Archives, Amsterdam.

[92]  Cf. Chapter 3, page 112.

Halske to write to the Municipal Executive, expressly denying any involvement. At the same time, the company indicated a new shift: in view of its close ties with AEG, it intended to undertake the electric lighting project in Amsterdam in association with the latter. In a letter to the Municipal Executive dated 24 March 1890 (reproduced on page 215), Siemens & Halske stated that they were not associated with any other company in the matter of the concession – a standpoint which, incidentally, they had adopted only after Gerard Philips had laid the matter of Wisse's claim before Rathenau with an urgent request that he remind Siemens & Halske of their contractual obligations:

As I informed you on the 19th instant, the only thing which, under these circumstances, would create a really significant impression is a denial by S. & H. themselves, immediately and if possible in the form of a letter to the City Council.

You may not find this easy, but it is absolutely vital. S. & H. are in any case not dependent upon their representatives. They can obtain as many as they need here, and much more easily than the company in The Hague.[93]

But the seeds of confusion had already been sown, for at the general review of the subject on 12 March, Wisse proved already to have an ally in a councillor, A. Daniëls, who saw great advantages for the citizens and the Council in a situation in which, for example, each of three competing companies had its own area. He also seized upon the substantial difference in price in comparison with the original proposals. Other members of the Council, including C. J. M. Dijkmans, W. Heineken, C. N. J. Moltzer, M. J. Pijnappel and M. W. F. Treub, proceeded to table a series of amendments to the clauses dealing with monopoly, expropriation and remuneration, the effect of which was to kill any hopes of a business-like discussion of the draft, leading to a practical solution.[94] In the matter of a monopoly, Pijnappel,[95] a legal expert who favoured a 'natural development', urged that the Council should not bind itself to the concessionaire, but leave itself free to grant further concessions if it so desired. In his view, only the responsibility for safety and the levying of charges on the use of municipal land could be subject to regulation. Treub paraded his hobby-horse, participation in profits, in front of the supporters of remuneration. On the analogy of the gas concession, he calculated that with dues amounting to ƒ500,000, the total cost to the consumer would rise by ƒ800,000. For this

93  Copy-book of Gerard Philips, 22.3.1890.
94  Amendments in PW archive, No. 69, Municipal Archives, Amsterdam.
95  M. J. Pijnappel (1830–1906); Doyen of the Orde van Advocaten and a member of parliament for several periods.

**SIEMENS & HALSKE**
Berlin S.W.
Markgrafen-Strasse 04.

An
den Magistrat der Stadt Amsterdam

A m s t e r d a m.
●●●●●●●●●●●●●●●●●●●●●

Berlin, den 24.März 1890.

J.No. *10324*

Dem Verehrlichen Magistrat der Stadt
Amsterdam beehren wir uns ergebenst anzuzeigen,
dass wir die durch die Niederländische Maatschappij
voor Electriciteit en Metallurgie zu 's-Gravenhage
für uns eingereichte Offerte auf Ertheilung der
Konzession für eine Elektrische Beleuchtungs-An-
lage in der Stadt Amsterdam zurückgezogen haben,
weil die Allgemeine Electricitäts-Gesellschaft
hierselbst nach ihrer Mittheilung an uns bereits
eine Offerte eingereicht hat und wir mit dieser
Gesellschaft, im Hinblick auf unsere nahen Bezie-
hungen zu derselben, die Anlage der Stadt Amsterdam gemeinsam auszuführen beabsichtigen. Unsere
Firma steht daher in Bezug auf die in dortiger
Stadt nachzusuchende Konzession nur mit der Allge-
meinen Electricitäts-Gesellschaft hierselbst und
mit keinem anderen Konkurrenten in Verbindung.

In vorzüglicher Hochachtung

*Siemens Halske*

Letter of Siemens & Halske to the Amsterdam City Council, 24.3.1890 (translated as
Appendix 7)

reason, and in the light of the offer from Wisse, he requested that a decision on the matter be deferred. Treub, moreover, argued that the Municipal Executive, having earlier stated that it was opposed to a monopoly, was now proposing one; the draft would therefore have to be revised. The supporters of a system of remuneration countered this by saying that if Treub's view prevailed, the Council would be drawn too closely into the area of management and, if endless disputes were to arise, would be obliged to supervise every operation. Mayor Van Tienhoven's response to Treub was that 'where there are two, there is no monopoly', but this Serrurier complaisantly undermined with the comment that 'if the two companies reach agreement, a monopoly will be created'.[96] The meeting, which was for the purpose of discussing matters of principle, did not get round to dealing with technical questions such as the choice between alternating and direct current and the supply voltage. The notion of a lower tariff for electric power – 'Why?' – was rejected on the ground that the price charged for the competitive source of energy, gas, was the same for lighting as for powering gas engines.

'The exchange of views has not produced anything positive', the *Algemeen Handelsblad* reported on 15 March 1890, adding a warning that if the choice were to fall on a short-term concession the consumer would have to be prepared to pay dearly, as otherwise it would be impossible to find anyone to finance the investment. The man who had tabled the draft proposal, Serrurier – 'the technician with a golden character, who could be pushed in any direction', as he was described by his later colleague, Treub[97] – had shown remarkable weakness in presenting his creation. 'If a different conclusion is desired in this new, difficult issue', the Council had only to make known its views and he, Serrurier, would gladly work out the details. Thus ended the debut of this alderman, caught in a hail of crossfire.[98]

At a private meeting on 31 March, the Municipal Executive pondered the question of inviting the Council to choose between:

a system embodying complete freedom to lay electrical cables, as had been suggested by the Pijnappel faction; and

the monopoly system favoured by the group comprising Dijkmans, its spokesman, Korthals Altes, Vas Visser and Van den Wall Bake.[99]

[96] *Algemeen Handelsblad*, 13.3.1890: report of the council meeting.
[97] Treub, *Herinneringen*, 123, 139, 143.
[98] *Algemeen Handelsblad*, 13.3.1890.
[99] Deliberations of the Municipal Executive, 31.3.1890; Municipal Archives, Amsterdam.

These alternatives did not, of course, fully reflect the complex opinions put forward; but they served as guidance for the impending council meeting. A public discussion was scheduled for 2 April. In the week preceding this, Gerard Philips, in an article published in the *Algemeen Handelsblad* under the heading 'Electric Lighting', again intervened in the public debate.[100]

In the past, Gerard wrote, Amsterdam had often allowed concessionaires too great a measure of freedom; now, 'the natural reaction to this has reached its peak under the pressure of public opinion, or what is taken to be public opinion'. No one who compared the conditions for the supply of electricity with those for the supply of gas could fail to see the considerable differences. The new draft left the Council free to amend the price of electricity after, say, five years – 'a very severe condition' – and gave it a great deal of power in other areas also. It was surprising that there were still any concessionaires at all. To limit the concession to a period of twelve years, as had been mooted in the Council, would in his view raise prices to a level at which no serious company, able to perform, would ever become involved. 'Concessionaires, that is possible! Who knows, before the next meeting of the Council, another "bargain" offer may be forthcoming from one or other company.' With this remark, which was aimed at Wisse, Gerard also took a passing shot at Councillor Daniëls.

In an unemotional review of the gas concession and the demands for the expropriation of the gasworks, Gerard Philips went on to remind the readers of the newspaper that the Council, in granting the concession, had relinquished its right to provide lighting, heating and motive power for private individuals until 1918. Admittedly the concession could be withdrawn in 1897, but there would then be the protracted procedures for acquisition and compensation. The idea of taking control of both the gas and electricity supply sources within the space of twelve years appeared to him to be impossible in financial or practical terms. 'And the gas concession is a matter to be taken very seriously, as they were recently, and so painfully, reminded', Gerard warned in an allusion to the conflict between the municipality and the Imperial Continental Gas Association.[101] His approach to this sore subject was that the gas concession was the work of the older members of the Council and that the radicals were fully justified in their attitude towards it. He evidently sought to avoid a direct confron-

---

[100] *Algemeen Handelsblad*, 26.3.1890; the article is reproduced as Appendix 8.
[101] Cf. page 210.

Table 21. *Growth of central stations in Great Britain, 1885–95*[a]

|                                          | 1885   | 1887   | 1889    | 1891      | 1893      | 1895      |
|------------------------------------------|--------|--------|---------|-----------|-----------|-----------|
| Number of stations in operation          | 4      | 6      | 14      | 32        | 63        | 100       |
| Number of 16-c.p. lamps connected        | 7,000  | 13,000 | 50,000  | 225,000   | 570,000   | 1,225,000 |
| Capital investment (£)                   | 30,000 | 60,000 | 450,000 | 2,950,000 | 4,195,000 | 7,808,000 |

Note:
[a] *Electrical Review*, 12.11. 1897, page 683.

tation with Treub and his supporters. As for the duration of the concession, Gerard stressed in his article that thirty years was the rule in the majority of cities on the European continent. 'One might wish that, in this context, more advice was sought abroad where, unlike in Amsterdam, local authorities have not burned their fingers on earlier concessions, and where greater moderation is employed in this area.' As a close observer, he gave as an example the developments in England, whence he had returned the previous autumn:

In England, the concessions for the supply of electricity were limited by the law of 1882 to 21 years, and the result was complete stagnation in electric lighting of the towns and cities. This situation lasted until 1888, when the law was amended and the period extended to 42 years, and very soon afterwards there was a sharp increase in the supply of energy from central stations.

This comment affords a glimpse of Gerard's orientation towards technical progress. To press home the point, he concluded by saying that the days of Jan van der Heijden and the first fire engine were well and truly past.[102]

A striking aspect of the article is the difference of view, if not actual friction, between the administrators and the technician, Gerard Philips. But in the non-technical field, too, he considered that the 'attitudes of the lawyers were far from unimpeachable'. He therefore had greater respect for the technical staff of the municipality, who, by seeking information at lectures and the advice of others, 'have given evidence of serious preparation in regard to this matter'. First and foremost, Gerard praised the work of the assistant engineer, F. J. Lugt, with whom he had studied in Delft and whose knowledge of, and interest in, gas and electric lighting had already been manifested in his student days by, among other things, articles in the

---

[102] *Algemeen Handelsblad*, 26.3.1890. Jan van der Heijden (1637–1712), famous sevententh-century Dutch painter who *inter alia* installed the first streetlighting in Amsterdam.

journal *de Natuur*.[103] In later years Gerard and Lugt were often to collaborate in the lighting field.

On 2 April 1890, the Council met again to debate the electricity concession. The proceedings were complicated by a variety of motions and amendments, but to an even greater extent by a long letter sent from Freiburg by Dr A. W. C. Berns, a surgeon[104] and member of the Council, who urged that the whole issue be postponed.[105] Moreover, two new aspiring concessionaires presented themselves to the Council, Technisch Bureau Nierstrasz, of Amsterdam, and H. P. N. Halbertsma, an engineer residing in The Hague. The latter offered to establish a limited company, domiciled in Amsterdam, and to submit the articles of association to the Council for approval. He added that he could count upon the co-operation of 'one of the most powerful foreign electricity companies', whose name, however, he declined to reveal.[106]

Councillor Berns, an ally of Treub, had obtained his knowledge of electrical matters from the installation contractor G. Groeneveld. In the letter sent from Freiburg he said that during a train journey in Germany he had accidentally met the prominent German electrical engineer, Professor E. Kittler, and that during their conversation the latter had expressed the opinion that Amsterdam should go for a municipal electricity system from the outset, on the ground that the ratio between gas and electricity prices, then 3:4, would rise to 3:5 or more if the supply were in the hands of a concessionaire. Kittler, who acted as adviser to the authorities in Breslau, Düsseldorf and Frankfurt, had also stated that no concession had been, or would be, granted in any German town or city, with the exception of Berlin. This lay behind Berns' appeal to the Council, even at this late stage, to postpone a decision so that a reputable expert could be appointed to investigate the pros and cons of municipal control and give an unbiased opinion. 'In all conscience', Berns wrote, 'it is time to put an end to the creation of monopolies. Soon, not an inch of our streets will belong to us if the Duin and Vecht Water Company, the Imperial Continental Gas Association, the Omnibus Company and goodness knows how many electric lighting companies fight us, and each other, for title.'[107]

---

[103] Lugt family archive; archivist P. J. Lugt, The Hague.

[104] A. W. C. Berns (1837–1911); founder of the Burgerziekenhuis, an Amsterdam hospital.

[105] Berns to the City Council, 21.3.1890; PW archive, No. 69, Municipal Archives, Amsterdam.

[106] N. P. N. Halbertsma to the City Council, 1.4.1890; PW archive, No. 4377, Municipal Archives, Amsterdam.

[107] Minutes of the council meeting on 2.4.1890, page 143; for a full report of the proceedings, see the *Algemeen Handelsblad*, 3.4.1890.

Although various factors, including the terms of the gas concession, made it impossible for Berns' suggestions to be adopted, they did serve to increase support for the amendment tabled by Pijnappel, which played on the members' fear of tying themselves to another long-term monopoly. The adoption of this amendment implied that the Council accepted no responsibility except to do all in its power to ensure a 'natural development' in the matter of electricity supply. Treub, in a sub-amendment, proposed that in the relevant permits the right of termination by the municipality after five years should be balanced by a minimum period of ten years. This, too, was adopted by twenty-five votes to nine, the supporters including Serrurier and all the other aldermen – a surprising development since the proposal was diametrically opposed to their draft. This amendment, in principle, paved the way for the admission of an unlimited number of small electricity companies. It also gave the Council the right freely to review the electricity concession when the gas concession expired. The *Algemeen Handelsblad*, in an editorial criticizing this development, posed the question: 'What serious company will risk its capital and work force with the chance of being shown the door after ten years, with no compensation and simply a "thank you"?'[108] If the Council's aim had been to create an impossible situation under the guise of advancing the issue, it could probably not have done better. The paper, rightly, could not accept that this permit for 'no offers, or botching, or very expensive lighting' was the objective of Treub and his supporters. 'We cannot believe it, and we sincerely hope that the decision will be reversed', the editorial concluded.

The wrath of Gerard Philips, a front-row spectator, was almost unbounded. His opinion of Berns' letter (which had also appeared in the Press)[109] was that the councillor had been deluded by Kittler; and because Rathenau had been too late in reacting, he, Gerard, had been unable to take timely steps to refute Berns' suggestion. 'If you had asked me for my first reaction after the council meeting,' he informed Rathenau on 4 April, 'I should have advised you promptly to withdraw your offer.' Gerard considered it pointless, and too time-consuming, to send a detailed report of the meeting. 'There was a lot of discussion, to and fro, and a great deal of nonsense was talked.'[110] The inevitable reaction came when, on 22 April, the day prior to its next meeting, the Council received a formal submission from the Allgemeine Elektricitäts-Gesellschaft, bearing the signature of Gerard Philips (see reproduction on page 221) and urging it:

[108] *Algemeen Handelsblad*, 5.4.1890.     [109] *Algemeen Handelsblad*, 26.3.1890.
[110] Copy-book of Gerard Philips, 4.4.1890.

*Aan aen Raad der Gemeente Amsterdam.*

Geeft met verschuldigden eerbied te kennen,

de **Allgemeine Elektricitäts Gesellschaft,** gevestigd te Berlijn, welke Maatschappij ten name der **Nederlandsche Electriciteits-Maatschappij** alhier, met het College van Burgemeester en Wethouders in onderhandeling is getreden betreffende een concessie tot het leveren van electrischen stroom binnen deze Gemeente;

dat zij kennis genomen heeft van de laatst betreffende dit onderwerp bij den Raad ingediende voordracht van Burgemeester en Wethouders;

dat zij meent de aandacht van Uwen Raad op dit punt te moeten vestigen: dat de termijn, binnen welken het Bestuur volgens die voordracht de bevoegdheid heeft de concessie te doen eindigen, adressanten veel te kort voorkomt; dat toch een ernstig en eerlijk exploitant geen groot kapitaal, gelijk voor een dergelijke exploitatie uit den aard der zaak noodig is, in een onderneming zal vastleggen, waarvan het te vreezen staat dat hij, nadat de moeielijke jaren zullen zijn voorbij gegaan en het kapitaal nauwelijks rentegevend zal zijn geworden, de concessie zal zien intrekken; dat hij daarenboven, bij een zóó korten duur, niet in staat is, een gewettigde amortisatie als factor in de prijsberekening op te nemen;

dat adressante zich, mocht het voorstel van Burgemeester en Wethouders, zooals het daar ligt, onverhoopt door Uwen Raad worden aangenomen, zij het ook noode, in de verplichting zou zien gebracht, van verdere mededinging tot levering van electrischen stroom binnen deze gemeente af te zien;

dat zij, op grond van het bovenstaande, met den meesten nadruk er op aandringt, het voornoemde voorstel te verwerpen, of wel, de behandeling er van gedurende hoogstens een maand te verdagen, gedurende welke adressante zich voorstelt, zoodanige andere voorstellen te doen, waarbij rekening zal worden gehouden met de in de laatste zittingen over dit onderwerp bij Uwen Raad geopperde bezwaren.

Redenen waarom zij Uwen Raad eerbiedig doet verzoeken:

*a.* Het voorstel van Burgemeester en Wethouders te verwerpen.

*b.* Of wel, de behandeling der electriciteits-quaestie gedurende hoogstens een maand te verdagen, ten fine als boven nader omschreven.

Hetwelk doende enz.

Namens de Allgemeine Elektricitäts-Gesellschaft,

*G. L. F. Philips.*

**Vertegenwoordiger.**

AMSTERDAM, 22 April 1890.

Letter of Gerard Philips to the Amsterdam City Council, 22.4.1890 (translated as Appendix 9)

to reject the proposal tabled by the Mayor and Aldermen; or
to postpone discussion of the electricity issue for up to a month.

In a somewhat differently worded letter of the same date (see reproduction on page 223), the Maatschappij 'Electra' championed the same cause. It, too, stressed the impossibility of obtaining capital for an enterprise which could be forced to close down after ten years and without compensation.

Concerning the final, capricious, turn of events, we can be fairly brief. On 23 April the new proposal, embodying the amendments tabled by Pijnappel and Treub,[111] was declared unacceptable. The effect was to reinstate Serrurier's proposal of 11 February 1890. The reversal was brought about by a motion tabled by Councillors Luden[112] and Dijkmans, which was carried by eighteen votes to fourteen. The ayes were: H. L. M. Luden, C. J. M. Dijkmans, J. W. Alting Mees, C. ten Brummeler, A. Daniëls, P. van Eeghen, W. Hovy, S. W. Josephus Jitta, J. P. Korthals Altes, H. S. van Lennep, W. W. van Lennep, C. N. J. Moltzer, C. Muysken, A. Sassen, J. A. Sillem, G. Vas Visser, C. M. J. Willeumier and R. W. J. C. van den Wall Bake. The opponents were: J. Ankersmit, J. Becker, A. W. C. Berns, B. H. M. Driessen, C. Dyserinck, E. J. Everwijn Lange, J. N. van Hall, W. Heineken, M. J. Pijnappel, L. Serrurier, Jonkheer C. J. den Tex, M. W. F. Treub, J. C. de Vries and M. de Vries van Buuren.

The action of aldermen Driessen, Dyserinck and Serrurier in opposing the motion, thereby distancing themselves from the spirit of their own memoranda and their earlier proposals, came as a further surprise. At this stage, the contortions displayed in the political forum were wellnigh incomprehensible, and the *Algemeen Handelsblad* was alone in reducing the debate to plain language, albeit the paper treated the affair as a comedy.[113] The *Handelsblad* called on the councillors to maintain a stout defence of the original draft and to approve it, for 'in the prevailing circumstances' that was the only way to lead a new branch of industry, which so many desired, to a healthy development. The paper urged the anti-monopolists, headed by Treub, to show courage and confidence in order not to hold up progress any longer. 'Electricity is simply not a commodity to

---

[111] Recommendations submitted to the City Council by the Municipal Executive, 17.4.1890; No. 233, Municipal Archives, Amsterdam.

[112] H. L. M. Luden (1828–1903); President of the Amsterdam District Court and a member of the Supervisory Boards of the Nederlandsche Bank, the Nederlandsche Handel-Maatschappij and other financial institutions.

[113] *Algemeen Handelsblad*, 24.4.1890.

*Aan den Gemeenteraad van Amsterdam.*

*Edel Achtbare Heeren!*

Geven met gepasten eerbied te kennen Jhr. JACOB HARTSEN en ERNEST BOEING in hunne hoedanigheid van Directeuren der Vennootschap „Electra", Maatschappij voor Electrische Stations, gevestigd en kantoor houdende te Amsterdam, Kalverstraat No. 36;

dat zij met belangstelling kennis genomen hebben van de omgewerkte voordracht van Burgemeester en Wethouders d.d. 17 April 1890 (No. 233) tot het vaststellen der voorwaarden, waarop concessie zal worden verleend tot het gebruik maken van gemeentegrond en gemeentewater tot het leggen van Electrische stroomgeleidingen;

dat zij tegen concessie zonder monopolie geen bezwaar hebben, en evenmin tegen de in het ontwerp-besluit vervatte bepalingen, doch alleen tegen den termijn der opzegbaarheid;

dat toch volgens de voordracht de concessie na tien jaar zal kunnen zijn geëindigd door eene eenvoudige opzegging;

dat het onmogelijk is voor zoo korten tijd kapitaal voor eene groote onderneming, te verkrijgen en het wel zeer duidelijk is, dat indien men zich voorstelde bij eene exploitatie gedurende tien jaren het kapitaal gedekt te hebben, dit niet anders zou kunnen dan tegen buitensporig hooge winsten, zoodanige de Maatschappij niet bedoelt te maken en ook niet zou kunnen maken, daar tegen die stroomberekening geene afnemers te vinden zouden zijn;

dat een waarborg behoort te bestaan, dat, althans gedurende dertig of acht en twintig jaren, de ondernemers zullen kunnen werken; behoudens bevoegdheid der gemeente tot naasting, zij het ook voor het einde van dien tijd, op den voet als in art. 13 van het ontwerp-besluit omschreven;

dat toch het bezwaar van requestranten niet gericht is tegen de bevoegdheid der gemeente om na 10 jaren te naasten, maar tegen de mogelijkheid dat na 10 jaren de concessie zal zijn opgezegd *zonder naasting*, en het met het oog op deze eventualiteiten onmogelijk is eene soliede onderneming tot stand te brengen, doch daarvoor eene concessie van dertig of minstens acht en twintig jaren noodig is.

Redenen waarom requestranten zich in hunne qualiteit wenden tot U.Edelachtbaren met het eerbiedig verzoek, dat in Art. 2 en zoo noodig in daarmede in verband staande artikelen zoodanige wijzigingen worden gebracht, dat de concessie voor minstens 28 jaren wordt verleend.

Hetwelk doende:

*Amsterdam,* 22 April 1890.

Letter of Jacob Hartsen and Ernest Boeing to the Amsterdam City Council, 22.4.1890
(translated as Appendix 10)

which the laws of supply and demand can be expected to apply; and control by the municipality is ruled out by the gas concession.' The writer of the editorial was clearly repeating the argument put forward by Gerard Philips on 26 March, and, remarkably, he placed particular emphasis on the use of electricity for motive power. In conclusion, he pointed out that the success of the operation depended mainly on the quality of the concessionaire and the persons responsible for supervision.[114]

In addition to following the laborious progress of the council debate, Gerard Philips was becoming ever more deeply involved in the problems caused by the cooling of relations between the NEM and AEG. The former company, which had been established in 1882 with the aim of obtaining concessions,[115] had for some time existed almost entirely at AEG's expense but had so far not achieved its objective. This situation, which was especially disappointing as it had seemed that the matter of the concession was close to being decided in the summer of 1889, had dashed Rathenau's expectations and greatly angered him. It had even made him question whether AEG's interests in Amsterdam – which had been among the reasons for consulting Gerard – were still in capable hands. To make matters worse, the Maatschappij 'Electra', an energetic company which enjoyed the support of Amsterdam financiers, had meanwhile begun to overtake the NEM. The latter had undeniably lost favour in Amsterdam circles. What had led Rathenau to embark on the collaboration was not the company's expertise – for it possessed none – but its contacts and its claim to hold the 'oldest' rights to the concession. Illustrious names like Krasnapolsky and Tegelberg,[116] Amsterdam businessmen with whom Rathenau had negotiated in 1888, must have strengthened his conviction that he had chosen the best partner. Subsequent events were to indicate the reverse. Not only was the influence of the NEM directors upon the municipal authorities waning, to be further reduced after the resignation of Alderman Coninck Westenberg, but, far more serious, it steadily became clear – particularly to Gerard Philips – that the NEM no longer had the desired entrée in Amsterdam, nor was its standing such as to ensure that local finance would be forthcoming for the project. In view of this, Gerard had earlier advised Rathenau to compete for the concession, not in the name of the NEM but in the respected name of his own company, AEG, and

[114] *Algemeen Handelsblad*, 25.4.1890.
[115] Cf. Chapter 3, pages 114 ff.
[116] P. E. Tegelberg, a director of the Stoomvaart-Maatschappij 'Nederland' and delegate member of the Supervisory Board of the NEM.

with the support of local bankers. 'I regret to note that you do not share my opinion regarding the association with the financiers here',[117] he said in a letter sent shortly after Luden and Dijkmans had tabled their motion, 'the more so because I know that it is held by our best friends among the councillors'. He went on to say that he had discussed the issue with Vas Visser and Dijkmans – 'both outstanding councillors with a reputation for efficiency' – and that their firm advice was that Rathenau should get in touch with influential financiers. Dijkmans had said:

What is the use of visiting a strange town with an introduction from men whose names carry less weight than your own? You would do better to say to the people in the strange town: 'Make enquiries in my home town, there they will tell you what you want to know.' That applies in this case. You would have done better to submit an offer to the Council yourself. You would do even better to secure a first-class introduction here.[118]

Although Dijkmans, who was managing director of the Nederlandsche Hypotheekbank, did not consider it necessary for the financial arrangements to be finalized immediately, he felt that the foundations should at least be laid – not only in order to circumvent the NEM and its difficulties, Gerard informed Rathenau, but also to win additional support in the Council. The recipient of this advice, however, proved to have serious doubts whether, after all the failures, he still wanted to do business with Amsterdam. On 10 May, he informed Gerard that the affair was becoming too costly. In his reply, Gerard intimated a desire to be relieved of his obligations and free to act as he thought best. 'If you are still interested in the contract here', he told Rathenau, 'you will have to obtain the services of someone else after the summer holiday.' He thereby deliberately set a date for terminating his role as mediator, though in fact this continued until September.

The relationship between the NEM and AEG was not formally terminated at that stage, because in the absence of fresh proposals from the Municipal Executive it was not relevant. 'It remains to be seen what the Council intends to do,' Gerard wrote, 'invite tenders from all interested parties or appoint a committee to negotiate with selected companies. In either case, the relationship with the NEM will die a natural death.'[119] Pressed by Rathenau, he investigated the possibilities for a partnership with Mijnssen & Co., whose shares stood higher than those of any other

---

[117] Copy-book of Gerard Philips, page 91 (date illegible, but round about 13.5.1890).
[118] Ibid.
[119] Copy-book of Gerard Philips, page 98 (date illegible, but round about 20.5.1890).

installation contractor in Amsterdam; but here, too, there were drawbacks. While he considered the company, with its excellent reputation, capable of providing a portion of the capital, Gerard's advice to his principal was that an alliance with Siemens & Halske – which Gerard felt was by far the best course – would put AEG in a far stronger position than a partnership with Mijnssen.[120] There was also the point that R. W. J. C. van den Wall Bake, a councillor and brother of H. L. A. van den Wall Bake, was a partner in Mijnssen & Co. and would certainly abstain from voting in the council debate. This was a crucial argument, bearing in mind that he was the only member of the Council who had travelled to Berlin at Rathenau's invitation,[121] and that he had made no secret of his preference for AEG over 'Electra'.

Gerard's last and most important advice to Rathenau was thus that AEG and Siemens & Halske should form an overt partnership and submit a joint offer in time for the next round of the battle for the Amsterdam concession. No more powerful combination could be imagined at that time.

On 10 June 1890, the Council received the amended draft, in which the motions submitted by Luden et al. and the amendments to these were combined in a report.[122] This draft, the third, was based on the flexible principle that the terms of the concession – in which the emphasis had clearly shifted towards a call for tenders – should be seen as *provisional*. All that the aspirant concessionaire was asked to do was to state the maximum price per unit of electricity which he wished to see inserted in the contract. The Council, while not being bound to accept the lowest figure, would be able to choose a provisional tender from those submitted and, perhaps after further negotiation with the tenderer, lay down the definitive conditions. Under no circumstances would a monopoly be given, be it general or for house installations. On the contrary, the municipality retained the right to engage in the supply and distribution of electricity, or to grant concessions to third parties, at any time. The levying of a charge per linear metre was felt to be undesirable as it would discourage the expansion of the cable network, and thus the system of remuneration envisaged in the original draft – five per cent of gross revenue and forty per cent of the net profit in excess of eight per cent – was maintained.

120  Ibid., pages 113 and 114 (date illegible, but round about 13.6.1890).
121  See page 184.
122  Draft submitted to the City Council by the Municipal Executive, 10.6.1890; PW archive, No. 2628, Municipal Archives, Amsterdam.

Broadly speaking, the conditions permitted the concessionaire no more than a reasonable profit. If his net profit exceeded eight per cent, the Council would be empowered to reduce the maximum prices for electricity by up to three cents per unit. The date of expiry of the concession was fixed at 1 July 1918, with the proviso that the system could be taken over by the Council after twelve years subject to the payment of compensation and a severance bonus according to a sliding scale. The new draft, the Municipal Executive hoped, would obviate further complications arising from the numerous applications, notably the sham offer submitted by Wisse. Moreover, the system of public tender was expected to produce the most favourable price from the point of view of the city and its inhabitants.

From then on, Serrurier's second draft made relatively swift progress, being adopted by the Council in the course of meetings on 19, 20 and 25 June. The only amendment of significance concerned the much-discussed system of remuneration. It was ultimately agreed that the municipality should receive five per cent of all revenue from the supply of electricity, and the consumer fifty per cent of any net profit in excess of six per cent.[123]

After a long and often laborious exercise in virtually unknown territory, the alderman and the members of the Council, those who favoured a public utility above a monopoly, and vice versa, had made a virtue out of necessity – and with a not unsatisfactory result. Had its hands not been tied by the conditions applying to the gas concession, the Amsterdam City Council would almost certainly have opted for a public electricity supply system, as did its counterpart in Rotterdam at the same time. By recalling Amsterdam's well-known motto, 'Cent fois sur le métier remettez vous ouvrage', the *Algemeen Handelsblad* demonstrated its complete satisfaction with the outcome.[124]

The interval between the first and second Acts – the period for the submission of tenders, which expired on 31 August 1890 – was marked by silence almost until the final minute. In mid-August Gerard was still without instructions from Berlin. 'As you are aware,' he wrote to Rathenau, 'tenders must be in by the thirty-first, and I do not yet know whether you intend to compete.'[125] On 30 August, Rathenau's instructions reached him in the form of a joint tender by AEG and Siemens & Halske, which he delivered to the Town Hall (see Appendix 11). Gerard was not optimistic

---

123  'Extract from the Minutes of the meeting of the Council', 26.6.1890, No. 313, Municipal Archives, Amsterdam.

124  *Algemeen Handelsblad*, issues of 12, 13, 18, 20, 21, 22 and 26 June 1890.

125  Copy-book of Gerard Philips, 13.8.1890.

regarding the outcome. Sixty cents per unit (1,000 volt–ampère-hours, or 1 kWh) could certainly not be described as low, he informed Berlin by return of post. At that price, he complained bitterly, no market of any size could be created, certainly not if, as was anticipated, the price of gas in Amsterdam fell from nine to seven cents.[126] On 3 September, the *Algemeen Handelsblad* reported that the Maatschappij 'Electra' had quoted a price of forty-six cents per unit and was prepared to accept all the conditions laid down by the municipality. Gerard experienced a painful shock when, on recalculating the figures, he discovered that Berlin had used the wrong basis for computing the maximum consumption and the rebate based on this, with the inevitable result that the unit price was too high.

The Municipal Archives in Amsterdam contain the correspondence between Gerard and Serrurier in which the former, in the interest of his principals, attempted to put right the error.[127] But his efforts were to no avail, for the procedure did not admit postponement or the submission of a lower price after the closing date.[128] On 18 September, the Municipal Executive informed the Council that 'Electra' had meanwhile deposited 100,000 guilders with the treasurer by way of security and that the company, in addition to the co-operation of 'Helios' A.G. of Ehrenfeld, near Cologne, was assured of the necessary financial support. From various members of the Council and from the Public Works Support Committee, Gerard learned in confidence that the Council would certainly have accorded preference to AEG if its price had been only a few cents above that of its competitor; but the gap had been too wide.[129]

On 24 September 1890, the Council ratified the decision to grant the concession to the Maatschappij 'Electra'. Gerard Philips, who for several months had devoted a portion of his energies to a plan to establish an incandescent lamp factory in partnership with J. J. Reese of Amsterdam, learned much from this experience, which brought to an end his career as the agent of another.

The contrast between the opening of the battle for the Amsterdam concession, marked by fierce competition, and its anti-climactic *dénouement*

---

[126] Ibid., 31.8.1890.

[127] Letter from Gerard Philips to Serrurier dated 13.9.1890 and reply dated 18.9.1890; copies of the relevant correspondence between Gerard Philips and Rathenau are appended; PW archive, No. 5744, Municipal Archives, Amsterdam.

[128] Minutes of the meeting of the Support Committee on 15.9.1890, page 154; PW archive, Municipal Archives, Amsterdam.

[129] Copy-book of Gerard Philips, 24.9.1890; letter to Rathenau.

leaves ample scope for questions. In particular, Rathenau, who was keenly interested at the outset, appears at the end to have been a victim of indecision. Closer examination shows that in weighing the matter he was influenced by other lighting projects which he considered equally important. A clue is provided by a letter written by Arnold von Siemens on 21 August 1890 to his brother Wilhelm, who was then staying at the Deutschmann Hotel in Scheveningen, in which he said: 'Today I discussed the Amsterdam affair with Rathenau . . . and he made no secret of the fact that if we could be sure of Brussels he would abandon the project right away.'[130] Even at that stage, before the closing date for tenders, interest on the part of Siemens & Halske in collaborating with AEG in Amsterdam had reached rock bottom. There was little inclination to invest large sums, for it was clear that, in Amsterdam, hardly anyone could be found to take over Siemens & Halske's and AEG's share of the capital after the installation had been handed over. The capital needs of the electrical engineering industry were such that there was no margin for companies to tie up their own resources in central stations for long periods. Efforts were therefore made to find ways whereby, while retaining the commercial ties, the stations which were built were transformed into independent companies and their shares listed on the stock exchange 'in order to provide liquid funds'.[131] In this vital area, the Maatschappij 'Electra' had early secured a strong position by ensuring the support of prominent Amsterdam financiers. The financial risk involved was not simply a matter of estimation, as was shown by the painful experience which befell Siemens & Halske at that same moment, when the post-financing of the central station in The Hague, handed over in 1889, miscarried.[132] This error in calculation grew into a crisis of confidence between the company and Wisse, which, needless to say, did not escape Rathenau's notice. 'Rathenau, moreover, has little interest in Amsterdam unless we are still agreeable to participate', Arnold von Siemens reported to Wilhelm, whom he had meanwhile requested to make a final check on the situation in the capital:

He said that if we withdrew, he would consider the matter just once more, but he already thought that under those circumstances he would do the same. He felt that as you are in the vicinity, you could perhaps make one more attempt to ascertain the position. If you feel that it is worthwhile for him to meet you there, he is willing to do so. The matter is now one of urgency.[133]

---

[130] A. von Siemens to W. von Siemens, 21.8.1890; Siemens Archives, No. 4 Lk 62, Munich.
[131] Koch, *Die Konzentrationsbewegung*, 16.
[132] Cf. Chapter 3, page 112.
[133] Letter of 21.8.1890, referred to in note 130, above.

Of decisive importance also, in our view, is the advice against proceeding, given by Dr J. Rosenthal, the influential adviser to Siemens & Halske, and quoted in Arnold's letter. In 1887 he had played a major part in drawing up the agreement of association with AEG.[134] The letter ends: 'If you are in agreement with him, send me a telegram so that I can inform him immediately.' This sentence is the clearest evidence of the severing of the last link, the dissociation of Siemens & Halske from the Amsterdam concession; it also goes some way to explaining why Rathenau ultimately failed to submit a competitive tender.

AEG's former partner, the Nederlandsche Electriciteit-Maatschappij, which after eight years of competing for the Amsterdam concession had got the worst of the bargain, was soon obliged to go into liquidation. Its original aim, to light the inner city area by electricity, had evaporated, as had its financial reserves. The liquidation account, published in 1892, revealed only sufficient assets to permit a payment of $f6.70$ per $f250$ share.[135] Of the paid-up capital of $f200,000$, the greater part had been swallowed up by the renowned lighting system at the Café Krasnapolsky and by plans which did not come to fruition.

This story was repeated in The Hague, where, as mentioned earlier, the counterpart of the NEM, the Nederlandsche Maatschappij voor Electriciteit en Metallurgie – with which Siemens & Halske were also associated – ran into financial difficulties[136] which in part were caused by an over-expansive policy: shortcomings in the management skill of Wisse and his fellow directors became increasingly apparent as the business grew. The most obvious example was the foolhardy participation in the construction of central stations at Fano and Modena, in northern Italy, and in Luxembourg, the sequel to which was a failure to consolidate the financing of the central station in The Hague. This led to an accumulation of debts to Siemens & Halske and ultimately to the liquidation of the Nederlandsche Maatschappij voor Electriciteit en Metallurgie in 1891. As recently as 1886, Wisse had been among the foreign guests of Wilhelm von Siemens on the occasion of the trials of the first battery-powered vessel on the River Spree.[137] Four years later, Wisse was teetering on the brink of bankruptcy and had forfeited the confidence of his partner. An ultimatum delivered by Siemens & Halske on 18 August 1890 required that he should substantiate

134   *50 Jahre AEG*, 1956, 73 ff.
135   *De Ingenieur*, 1892, 132.
136   Wegner, *Siemens in den Niederlanden*, 27.
137   *Tagebuch Wilhelm von Siemens, 1886–1904*, Siemens Archives, No. 4 Lf 775, Munich.

his expectation of attracting half a million guilders of fresh capital and also pay his debts to them: 'Then we can talk about further business.'[138] Although H. Raat and G. Blaauw, chairman and secretary respectively of the Supervisory Board of the Nederlandsche Maatschappij voor Electriciteit en Metallurgie, confirmed their faith in the prospective capital increase in a letter to Siemens & Halske, Berlin, on 9 December 1890, the promise was obviously not fulfilled. For on 3 June 1891 the Hollandsche Bank, de Vos & Vreede, in The Hague, issued a circular announcing that the liquidation of the Nederlandsche Maatschappij voor Electriciteit en Metallurgie was imminent and that not less than seventy-five per cent of its capital had been lost.[139]

Wisse, who was mercilessly characterized as a bankrupt with the gift of the gab – 'The capital, one million guilders, has been gobbled up'[140] – thereupon accepted a seat on the Board of the General Ozone and Electrical Supply Company, of Amsterdam, which had been established in 1892 by Jonkheer H. P. Tindal[141] and similarly had an authorized capital of a million guilders. In a report to his principals, P. H. ter Meulen, the Amsterdam agent of Schuckert & Co. of Nuremberg and a man sensitive to competition, said: 'I am sorry that Wisse has gone, for his place has been taken by a very pleasant, energetic young man who, as the representative of Siemens & Halske, can become a dangerous competitor.'[142] Ter Meulen was referring to the mechanical engineer N. J. Singels, the technical director of the central station in The Hague, who had also taken over the running of the official branch of Siemens & Halske there.[143] This office took over the business of the Nederlandsche Maatschappij voor Electriciteit en Metallurgie on 9 October 1891, under its own name. It was the forerunner of the Nederlandsche Siemens Maatschappij N.V. of The Hague.

In Amsterdam, the Maatschappij 'Electra', having won the concession, proceeded to construct a new central station in the Haarlemmerweg, which in its day was the largest in the country. Discussions held in Cologne on 13 March 1891 between the Financieele Maatschappij voor Nijverheidsondernemingen and 'Helios' A.G. had produced agreement on the financ-

[138] File: Wisse, The Hague; Siemens Archives, No. 4 Lb 829/830, Munich.
[139] Ibid.
[140] Electrotechnisch Bureau P. H. ter Meulen, Amsterdam, in a letter to Schuckert & Co., Nuremberg, 29.6.1891; Siemens Archives, No. 4 Lb 829/830, Munich.
[141] H. J. Scheffer, *Henry Tindal – een ongewoon heer met ongewone besognes*, 1977, 223 ff; also *De Ingenieur*, 1894, 186.
[142] See note 140 above.
[143] *Nieuwe Rotterdamsche Courant*, 8.12.1891; deed enacted by J. D. Dietze, notary of The Hague.

Table 22. N.V. 'Electra', Maatschappij voor Electrische Stations,
Amsterdam (1889–99)[a]

| Year | No. of lamps connected[b] | No. of electric motors | No. of consumers | Length of cable network (km) | Revenue from the supply of current ($f$) | Dividend paid |
|------|------|------|------|------|------|------|
| 1889 | 950 | — | 29 | 2 | 9,500 | — |
| 1891 | 2,000 | — | 53 | 4 | 20,000 | — |
| 1893 | 13,000 | — | 328 | 20 | 172,000 | — |
| 1895 | 21,000 | 8 ( 36 hp) | 451 | 34 | 270,000 | $4\frac{1}{2}$% |
| 1897 | 26,000 | 15 ( 46 hp) | 526 | 42 | 310,000 | 6% |
| 1899 | 33,000 | 34 (115 hp) | 625 | 45 | 351,000 | 7% |

Notes:
[a] Annual Reports of the Maatschappij 'Electra', Municipal Archives, Amsterdam
[b] Based on the standard 16-candlepower lamp

ing of the new station. It was decided to raise the paid-up capital to
$f$1,200,000 and to issue debentures to a value of $f$900,000.[144] The cost of
the station, including buildings, machinery, cables and transformers,
amounted to approximately two million guilders. The commissioning,
which was accompanied by festivities, took place on 14 May 1892. From
then on, the small district station in the Kalverstraat was of no more than
historical significance.

Although it met its obligations promptly, and notwithstanding the steady
growth of its cable network, the continuing existence of the Maatschappij
'Electra' remained a matter of discussion.[145] On 12 November 1897,
following the takeover by the municipality of the Imperial Continental Gas
Association, J. P. Mijnssen, a councillor, addressed a letter to the Council in
which he proposed that either 'Electra' should be taken over or that a
municipal central station should be built in addition to the one operated by
the company. The latter proposal, in fact, was the first step towards the
establishment of the Gemeentelijke Electriciteitswerken (Municipal Electricity Works), upon which the Council was to decide on 21 November
1900. The contract for the first publicly owned generating station in
Amsterdam was placed on 1 April 1901, the electrical installation being
entrusted to the Allgemeine Elektricitäts-Gesellschaft of Berlin, which had

[144] 'Protokoll Conferenz im Lokal des Helios am 13 Maerz 1891' and 'Vertrag Helios/Electra',
21.3.1891; archive of Mij. 'Electra'; Municipal Archives, Amsterdam.
[145] A. W. Ressing, De levering van Electriciteit te Amsterdam, 1900; A. Roelvink, De gemeente
Amsterdam en de electriciteit, 1900; N. van Harpen, De gemeentelijke electrische centrale en
Electra, 1903.

been represented in the capital since 1896 by Mijnssen & Co.[146] The station was commissioned during the Christmas holiday in 1903 and almost immediately found itself locked in a fierce competitive struggle with its privately owned predecessor, 'Electra', which in the following year dramatically reduced its price to an average of seventeen cents per unit.

On 1 July 1913, five years prior to the expiry of the concession, the station owned by 'Electra' was purchased by the municipality for *f* 920,655 and its cable network connected to that of the municipal station.[147] The long battle against the so-called Concession Companies had been fought, and the proponents of a municipal service had emerged the victors.

[146] F. J. M. Bothe, *75 Jaar AEG-Telefunken Nederland N.V.*, 1977, 11.
[147] *De Koppeling*, June 1963, 136.

220 Herengracht, Amsterdam

# Chapter 6

# THE BIRTH OF THE EINDHOVEN LAMP WORKS

During the summer of 1890, the Palace of Industry in Amsterdam – 'that proud building destined to advance the prosperity of the country's industries'[1] – housed a national exhibition to promote safety and health in factories and workshops. In addition to presenting a comprehensive picture of ways of preventing accidents, the emphasis being on working conditions in modern branches of the manufacturing industry, the exhibition and an accompanying congress provided an excellent meeting place for entrepreneurs, engineers and other interested persons in the public service and the liberal professions.

The exhibits, which were divided into eighteen groups, comprised machinery, equipment and methods to protect workers against physical injury, harmful gases, dust, inadequate ventilation and other hazards which, although comparatively simple to eliminate, were all too prevalent. Two things had to be done: industrialists as a whole had to be shaken out of their complacency and induced to follow the praiseworthy example of a few pioneers, while the workers had to be persuaded to abandon their opposition to improvements, which, often through lack of education, led them to prefer the dubious advantages of sickness benefit and extra wages for long hours. 'These are the objectives of the exhibition', *De Ingenieur* reported on 2 August 1890, thereby touching upon the social dimension which was then being added to the role of the engineer.[2]

Several applications of electricity proved to have a place in the trend towards greater safety. The principal exhibit by Groeneveld, Van der Poll & Co. was a self-contained electric lighting installation which, it was claimed, ensured a healthy atmosphere in places of work. Experts were very

---

[1] Report of the 13th General Meeting of the Association for the Promotion of Manufacturing and Craft Industries (hereafter APMCI), 18.8.1864.

[2] H. Lintsen, *Ingenieurs in Nederland in de Negentiende Eeuw, een streven naar erkenning en macht*, 1980, para. 9d.

Safety Exhibition held at the Palace of Industry in Amsterdam, 1890

favourably impressed by its design, which, according to Professor J. A. Snijders, also served 'to show laymen who have not visited the principal exhibitions in this field *just how far incandescent lighting has progressed* and how well, in terms of shape and colour, the systems – in this case De Khotinsky – combine variety with elegance'.[3] Another Amsterdam firm, Technisch Bureau De Voogt, demonstrated its transportable arc lamp, known as the Y-lamp. According to the brochure, this lighting system was operating on land and sea to the full satisfaction of engineers, architects, shipowners, railway and tramway companies, manufacturers and countless festival committees. Other well-known manufacturers of electrical equipment and signalling systems, including Croon & Co., were also among the exhibitors.

The initiative for the exhibition, which attracted more than 112,000 visitors, was taken by the Association for the Promotion of Manufacturing and Craft Industries in the Netherlands (APMCI). The venture was supported financially by the government, the municipality of Amsterdam and a number of private institutions, and the date chosen coincided with the thirty-ninth annual general meeting of the Association. The organizing committee comprised twelve industrialists, fifteen representatives of central and local government, and twenty-six prominent figures from other groups in society, including fourteen Members of Parliament.[4] The exhibition, which attracted some 275 entries from the Netherlands and fifty from other countries, crowned the activities of the Association in one of many areas, all of which were concerned with promoting manufacturing industry and raising the standard of living of factory workers. The idea was first mooted within the Association in 1887. It was then studied by a committee headed by Dr W. P. Ruysch, Inspector of the State Medical Service and a member of the Association's branch in The Hague, which produced a preliminary report.[5] The success of the event, to which reference was made in the Queen's Speech, was perpetuated by the establishment of a Museum of Objects to prevent Accidents and Illness in Factories and Workshops. This was followed by the opening on 1 January 1893 of a permanent exhibition in one of the halls of the Palace of Industry. That exhibition, later to become the Safety Museum in Amsterdam, in part owed its existence to objects donated by many of the original exhibitors. Two years later the first Safety Act in the Netherlands came into force.

---

[3] Snijders, *Der Vorderingen der Electrotechniek*, 43 ff.
[4] Exhibition catalogue published by the Association, 1890.
[5] Report of the 37th General Meeting of the APMCI, 1888.

Jan Jacob Reesse (1853–1910)

The safety exhibition of 1890, like the diverse issues which found their way on to the agenda of the Association – and which included the constantly recurring question 'whether the reintroduction of a Patent Act is desirable, valuable and necessary' – expresses something of the atmosphere which surrounded Gerard Philips in Amsterdam while he was carrying out his mission for AEG. It provided him with a rendezvous and an opportunity to renew acquaintance with a number of former fellow students at Delft University with whom he had lost contact since going abroad to work in 1885. With one of them, Jan Jacob Reesse, a member of the executive committee of the exhibition, he went so far as to make plans for the future. At Reesse's house, flanking the Herengracht canal in Amsterdam, the two men – both of whom sought a new career in manufacturing – discussed the initial plans for an incandescent lamp works.

In May 1890 Gerard had moved into the Hotel Mille Colonnes in Rembrandt Square, a favourite haunt of journalists and artists. The hotel was lit by electricity,[6] and with his fee of 4,000 marks from AEG[7] he

---

[6] Zahn, *Verlichting van Amsterdam*, 179.
[7] Gerard's private account, in the Cash Book of Frederik Philips, 7.6.1890; Philips Archives, Eindhoven.

permitted himself the luxury of a room costing $f2$ per day including breakfast, service and the provision of an 'electric candle'. A year later, by which time he was engaged in setting up his lamp factory, he was obliged to exchange this accommodation and the attractions of the big city for lodgings in Eindhoven. Gerard spent his thirty-second birthday in Amsterdam. At the age of sixteen, while a pupil in the fourth form at the secondary school in Arnhem, he had severed his ties with his birthplace, Zaltbommel. Now, Fate was soon to decree that his permanent domicile and his destiny lay in Eindhoven.

Where Gerard Philips was concerned, the activities of the Association for the Promotion of Manufacturing and Craft Industries possessed remarkable facets. Under its auspices, the engineer P. H. ter Meulen, whom he knew well, and Dr N. P. Kapteyn[8] gave popular evening lectures on subjects such as electric lighting and the gramophone, the latter illustrated by experiments;[9] the interests of the Association, notably the Amsterdam branch,[10] however, covered a much wider field. Its involvement with the pressing problems associated with social, managerial and technical developments is reflected in the long agenda for the general meeting of members held at the Palace of Industry on 29 and 30 August 1890, which included the following items:

> Discussion of the report of the Amsterdam branch dated 24 May 1890, drawn up with the assistance of Professor N. G. Pierson, on maximum working hours in factories and workshops.
> Advice concerning the Bill proposing *ad valorem* import duty on goods and in the matter of import, export and transshipment statistics, provided by the Amsterdam branch.
> A petition to the Government, urging the establishment of a Central Statistical Office, prepared by the Amsterdam branch in consultation with the economist, C. A. Verrijn Stuart.
> An introductory address on the subject: 'Which is preferable on safety and economic grounds, gas or electric light?', a matter raised by the Wageningen branch and referred to the Snijders Committee for a preliminary report.
> A petition to the Government, signed by the Central Committee, urging

---

[8]  Copy-book of Gerard Philips, 15.4.1889.
[9]  Report of the 39th General Meeting of the APMCI, 1890, 166.
[10]  Report of the 25th General Meeting of the APMCI, 1885, 125–39: 'Terugblik op het 25-jarig bestaan der Afd. Amsterdam'.

the abolition of the duty levied on the laying of intercommunal telephone lines.

Discussion of the report on the dangers of electric cables above the ground, drawn up in May 1890 by P. H. ter Meulen, Dr N. P. Kapteyn, J. Hannema and P. J. P. Sluiter, members of the Amsterdam branch.

A debate on the subject: 'Is it desirable that a Patent Law should be introduced in the Netherlands?', proposed by the Amsterdam branch.

The Association, to which reference has already been made on a number of occasions[11] and which displayed a remarkable interest in electrical engineering matters round about 1890, merits more than simple mention. Its role in the political and economic sphere at that time has been little researched.[12] In this study, however, its voice may not be ignored, for it was to the Association and its members that Gerard Philips owed his vivid impression of the position of Dutch industry and the problems which it faced. Measured by the standards which he acquired in Britain and Germany, his impression was on the whole mixed, as he showed by citing other countries as an example in his letters to the *Algemeen Handelsblad*.[13] At the same time, given the interest in electric lighting at that moment, the prospects for an incandescent lamp works will not have been discouraging to him. Here lies the explanation for his view that the initially modest output of the works which he proposed to found – some ten thousand lamps a year – could largely be sold on the home market. For his appearances in public as AEG's representative had brought him into contact not only with aldermen and councillors, but also with various representatives of the electrical engineering industry. Moreover, he met fellow engineers who were employed by railway companies and other large-scale users of incandescent lamps. As a result of these contacts, Gerard, unlike other Dutch lamp manufacturers, placed great emphasis on the home market from the outset and assured himself in advance of the marketing channels which were nearest in geographical terms. This decision, as will emerge later, formed part of his well-considered policy as a budding manufacturer who needed several years to get into his stride and did not grudge himself the time. In a retrospective article published in the *Nieuwe Rotterdamsche Courant* of 28 March 1916, Gerard described his approach to the market in the following words: 'The home market was, of

---

[11] Cf. Chapters 3, 4 and 5, pages 156 ff, 164 and 211, respectively.

[12] The principal sections of the archive are housed in the Municipal Archives in The Hague; cf. Economisch-Historisch Jaarboek, 1942, 379 ff.

[13] Cf. Chapter 5, page 217.

course, our main concern. The installation contractors were our customers and they were getting to know us.'

The Philips customers in Amsterdam were the prosperous contractors like Mijnssen & Co., Groeneveld, Van der Poll & Co. and P. H. ter Meulen, who at that time were mainly engaged in electric lighting. Without exception, the partners in these companies were members of the Association for the Promotion of Manufacturing and Craft Industries. So, too, were Reesse and the engineer F. J. Lugt,[14] who was well known to Gerard and, as an employee of the municipality of Amsterdam, had drawn up the original terms for an electricity concession there. Other members included the leading banker A. C. Wertheim, who was then 'more or less the leader of a wide cross-section of the citizenry of Amsterdam'.[15] The broad social spectrum represented in the Association characterizes the diversity and scope of its interests and those of its patrons. The 327 members of the Amsterdam branch at the time included the president of the central bank, N. G. Pierson, Mayor Van Tienhoven, Aldermen Serrurier and his opponent, Treub, and, of course, manufacturers, craftsmen and large and small merchants.

In 1890 the Association had ten branches with a total membership of about 1,000. It inclined towards free trade, but from the outset, in 1851,[16] it had had a reputation for being more inclined towards social reforms – notably those aimed at improving the lot of the working class and the weakest in the society – than its sister organization, the Society for the Promotion of Industry, which was seventy-five years older and had twice as many members. Describing the two, the lamp manufacturer C. Boudewijnse, who accepted a seat on the Central Committee of the Association in 1894, said: 'Whereas in the latter the interests of the industrialists chiefly came to the fore, the former also devoted itself to social interests, insofar as these were related to industry.'[17] The Delft industrialist J. C. van Marken (1845–1903), who set a pattern among employers with his response to social issues, which included instituting employee representation at his yeast and spirit factory in 1878, was an associate member of the Association. Among the most remarkable members of the 1880s was Dr J. Th. Mouton (1840–1912), who owned margarine and pharmaceutical factories in The Hague.

[14] Cf. Chapter 5, pages 187 and 218.
[15] Quack, 'A. C. Wertheim', 52.
[16] J. H. W. Kemman, 'Historisch Overzicht 1851–1892'; Municipal Archives, The Hague.
[17] Supplement to *Middelburgsche Courant*, 23.9.1918.

Johannes Theodorus Mouton (1840–1912)

Besides being chairman of the Chamber of Commerce, he devoted many years to public service as a councillor and alderman for education.[18] Another prominent member was D. W. Stork (1855–1932), who in 1881 introduced a jointly managed pension and sickness benefit scheme at his engineering works in Hengelo. He gave Mouton and the APMCI the credit for having shown him the way by means of a report.[19] As chairman of the Association from 1877 to 1889, Mouton, in his annual reports, not only dealt with the interests of industry but also made a point of critically examining the position of the working class, thereby associating himself with those who urged that a start be made with social legislation in the Netherlands:

'Les idées marchent', but progress is slower in some countries than in others. While we have gone on year after year, perhaps for twenty years, trying to persuade our petrified Parliament that it is high time, indeed almost too late, to pay more attention to the interests of the working classes, while we continue to wait [...], we see that in other countries legislation in the area of labour is developing – here in accordance with a certain system, there as circumstances dictate, everywhere with thoughtfulness and circumspection. If we wish to follow the trend in this area, in

18  *De Wereldkroniek*, 17.8.1912: an obituary of Johannes Theodorus Mouton, a Doctor of Mathematics and Physics.
19  *Jubileum-uitgave van de Vereeniging tot behartiging van de belangen van het personeel, verbonden aan de Machinefabriek van Gebr. Stork & Co.*, Hengelo, 1881–1906, 53, 205.

order to educate ourselves and prepare ourselves for new obligations, in keeping with the new forms towards which society is already feeling its way, we must turn our eyes from the impotence and unwillingness which have hitherto been the rule in our economy, and see what is happening elsewhere.[20]

To Mouton, supporting and assisting the creation of workers' organizations, educating the masses and reforming the 'state of affairs of working men' by legal means, as advocated by the Algemeen Nederlandsch Werklieden Verbond (literally, General Union of Workers in the Netherlands), which had been established by B. H. Heldt, constituted a credo. He thus adhered to one of the earliest principles of the Association of which he was a prominent member. On the *Juristendag* (Lawyers' Day) in 1888, he defended these principles against critics who equated social legislation with tariff barriers, regarding both as a means of protecting the economically weak, and rejecting them for this reason.[21] Mouton rebutted this classic stance by exposing the manifest distinction between the socially weak individual and the economically weak manufacturing economy, and concluded his argument in a manner characteristic of the Association and its supporters: 'I therefore vindicate to our Association and to myself the right to continue to favour free trade in spite of our evident inclination to cooperate in the introduction of social legislation.'[22] With these words he echoed the Association's stance within the existing socio-economic constellation. To an even greater extent, of course, the APMCI was concerned with the material aspects of commerce and industry. An event which commands our attention is a discussion which took place in Amsterdam on 30 August 1890, at which the Association raised the question of the reintroduction of a Patent Act in the Netherlands.

That this question, which was crucial for the manufacture of incandescent lamps in the Netherlands, aroused interest on the part of Gerard and Reesse while they were elaborating their plan to set up a lamp works will be abundantly clear from the preceding chapters. The wording of the relevant item on the agenda of the Amsterdam meeting was:

Is the introduction of a Patent Act in the Netherlands desirable? If so, the Central Committee will be instructed to press vigorously for the introduction of a Patent Act.

Patent legislation had been suspended in 1869, but the voices of supporters and opponents had never been completely silenced. Sharp clashes of

[20] Report of the 35th General Meeting of the APMCI, 1886, 2 ff.
[21] *De Economist*, May 1888.
[22] Report of the 37th General Meeting of the APMCI, 1888, 27.

opinion alternated with periods of silent dissension, often within the ranks
on either side. But on one issue the parties were unanimous: the experience
with the old law had been unsatisfactory. Of the 140 patents which on
average had been granted annually in the period 1851–65, no less than 124
had concerned foreign inventions. Fees had been paid in respect of only
forty-three patents, and of these thirty-four related to foreign inventions.[23]
Moreover, the opportunity presented by the law to appropriate all manner
of inventions and monopolize these by means of import-patents had
encouraged abuse.[24] This phenomenon had been at least as prevalent in the
neighbouring countries and had brought criticism of the system of patent
protection there also. The growing opposition, in the shape of an international anti-patent movement – the Dutch supporters of which included the
author of legal works E. Star Busmann[25] and the economist J. L. de Bruyn
Kops – and, to an even greater extent, the spirit of free trade which
prevailed in industry in the 1860s, made it easy for the minister concerned,
C. Fock, to get his Bill through Parliament.[26] It was also felt that, by
abolishing the patent law, the Netherlands could set an example to the
world. Germany, too, was virtually without patent legislation from 1868 to
1877, and round about 1870 there were signs that a similar situation would
soon come about in Britain.

In the Netherlands, the APMCI in 1867 had described the Patent Act as
an obstacle to the growth of industry and prejudicial to the national
prosperity, and had urged its suspension. More than fifteen years later, at its
annual meeting in 1883, which was also devoted to this subject, it reiterated
its opposition to 'so reactionary a measure as a Patent Act'[27] on the ground
that, in comparison with the period prior to 1869, the situation in industry
could only be said to have improved. A study committee reported that the
majority of the existing companies had achieved greater prosperity and that
new enterprises had been established. Healthier tariff principles were said
to have contributed significantly to this development. The sister organization, the Society for the Promotion of Industry, which had petitioned the
King for the abolition of the Act as early as 1854, and did so again in 1860,
now performed a volte-face and in 1870 requested the Minister of Water-

[23]  Report of the 32nd General Meeting of the APMCI, 1883, 58.
[24]  Doorman, *Het Nederlandsch Octrooiwezen*, 46 ff.
[25]  E. Star Busmann, *Over octrooijen van uitvinding*, 1867.
[26]  Bill of 15.7.1869, Government Gazette No. 126, approved by the Lower House by 49 votes to 8,
      and by the Upper House by 29 votes to 1.
[27]  Report of the 32nd General Meeting of the APMCI, 1883, 79 ff.

ways, Trade and Industry to introduce a new Patent Act.[28] To enliven the debate, it organized an essay competition in 1883, the subject of which was 'The principles upon which a Patent Act for the Netherlands and an international guarantee for industrial property should be based, with a description of the provisions which such an Act should embody'. At this juncture, however, it was clear that not only had the trend towards a revival of patent legislation which had earlier been observed, and on which the patent agents[29] had played in their insinuative propaganda campaign in the 1870s, been reversed, but that public opinion in the Netherlands round about 1885 was so strongly opposed to a new patent law that the Government would have faced certain defeat if it had attempted to introduce one.[30] The advocates were therefore obliged to seek another forum. Their quest ended with the establishment in 1887 of the 'Vereeniging van Voorstanders eener Nederlandsche Octrooiwet' (Association of Supporters of a Dutch Patent Law), of which A. Huët, a teacher at the Delft Polytechnic, became chairman. New elements, more international than national, were added to the controversy.

The right of an inventor to a patent or a temporary monopoly had been expressly rejected at the time of the suspension of the Patent Act in 1869. Amid the various arguments, the conviction prevailed that a *sound* law governing patents was impracticable. And any other sort of law would simply encourage legalized injustice. In 1873, the first international congress on the protection of industrial property took place in Vienna in the wake of an American refusal to take part in the World Exhibition owing to inadequate patent protection.[31] At the second such meeting, which coincided with the World Exhibition of 1878 in Paris, the idea of an international union in the area of patents was mooted. In 1883, l'Union pour la protection de la propriété industrielle was formally established in the French capital. The Netherlands, although it had no patent law, became a member of this body. The treaty was ratified by the majority of the member governments in the following year. Using moral pressure – 'Vous êtes un peuple de brigands',[32] the Dutch delegate was informed – the other

[28] Proceedings of the Society, 1854, 282, 315; ibid., 1860, 34; also the Journal of the Society, 1879, 337, and 1880, 165.
[29] F. Machlup and E. Penrose, 'The patent controversy in the nineteenth century', in *The Journal of Economic History*, Vol. X, No. 1, May 1950, 5 ff.
[30] According to Snijders van Wissekerke, Ministry of Justice; cf. Report of the Vereeniging, 1890, 112.
[31] A. Heggen, *Erfindungsschutz und Industrialisierung in Preussen 1793–1877*, 1975, 111 ff.
[32] W. J. van Overbeek de Meijer, *Eenige opmerkingen over Octrooien en Octrooiwetten*, 1891, 19.

members repeatedly urged the Netherlands to introduce patent legislation in order to impart more practical significance to its membership.[33] The issue caused a great deal of anxiety at the Foreign Office in The Hague. But the country as a whole, and certainly the APMCI – as the minutes of the meetings of its members plainly show – judged the issue by totally different standards. Its chairman, Mouton, in an attempt to circumvent the problem, observed that 'It is one thing to say that we do not want a new patent law, and another to say that we will not join in an international system. The Netherlands need have no qualms about taking part in the deliberations and having a representative there; if no satisfactory system emerges', as he expected to be the case, 'we can stand on the sidelines'.[34] In the mind of Mouton – and here we quote his own words – there was no doubt whatsoever that:

patents will disappear when industry frees itself from the dominant influence of those who govern it and who control the labour of hundreds and thousands; when labour attains greater freedom and the development of industry is no longer virtually dependent upon the owners of the large factories.

It appears to me that, in the urge to reintroduce a patent law in this country, there is a failure to take account of the history of this industrial institution, of the demands of the times, of the logic of facts, of the experience of nations in this area, and that we should do our country a disservice were we to add our voice to those of the advocates of patents, for while this would benefit some of those who hold positions of power in industry, it would be at the expense of the nation as a whole.[35]

In January 1884, the Bill to ratify the international agreement on the protection of industrial property was published. The principal benefit to Dutch manufacturers lay in the safeguarding of trademarks, but as far as the introduction of patent legislation was concerned, the Netherlands – like Switzerland – accepted no obligations. The need felt by the Association to reject this Bill, like the one before it, was not made public, since the Dutch delegate to the conference, H. C. Verniers van der Loeff, had assured the Central Committee that the country was in no way bound in the matter of patent legislation, a fact which the government confirmed.[36]

The absence of a patent law made little or no difference to everyday life. A report by the Dordrecht branch of the Association states that the major

[33] 'Uit de Geschiedenis der Vereeniging', compiled by De Internationale Vereeniging voor de bescherming van den Industrieelen Eigendom on the occasion of its General Meeting in Amsterdam, September 1903.

[34] Report of the 27th General Meeting of the APMCI, 1878, 144.

[35] Report of the 28th General Meeting of the APMCI, 1879, 25.

[36] Report of the 33rd General Meeting of the APMCI, 1884, 17.

inventions of the day were successfully introduced, 'as is evidenced by the various sorts of electric lighting and the Bell telephone'.[37] To the compilers of the report, following their visits to the various world exhibitions, it was clear beyond any doubt that many of the inventions were made simultaneously and independently of each other; and they mention the names of Edison, Swan and Maxim, among others, in this context. The undisguised allegation of poaching, levelled against the Netherlands in Paris, drew the retort that in 'patent-loving' countries, the revenues from an invention were more likely to accrue to shareholders or to the monopolist who had acquired the rights than to the deserving inventor. In the opinion of the Dutch, therefore, simple reality took precedence over a new order which might or might not be desirable and in any case had still to be created. Most manufacturers almost certainly regarded this as an inevitable development; but their personal aversion to it remained predominant. Mouton had this to say on the subject: 'Berlin is crawling with patent agents who exist to help the industrialist, but whose help would not be necessary if the law had not created artificial obstacles.'[38] No one better than he could sustain for years this reticence on the part of Dutch manufacturers to tread an erroneous, protectionist path.

Beside philosophical and legal interpretations of the right of ownership of the inventor, opposing interests naturally determined the viewpoints of supporters and opponents and these varied from one sector of industry and product category to another. The opponents, moreover, had an almost irrefutable argument in the shortcomings of the existing patents laws in the various countries, which were evident from the countless lawsuits, short-comings which the supporters admittedly did not deny and which stimulated them to make improvements, nationally and internationally, in this area. These they not only regarded as a condition for industrial growth and the release of knowledge, but also necessary on the ground of 'the sense of justice existing in all civilized nations'. Neither side was able to produce a conclusive theory regarding the role played by patent protection in the development of industry in the past though each party asserted that it had historical evidence to support its stance.[39]

Objective proof that Dutch industry would have progressed further in the

---

[37] Report of the APMCI for 1883, 56 ff; this was compiled by F. N. Sickinga, banker, J. J. B. J. Bouvy, glass manufacturer, and Ph. J. Waller, engineer.

[38] J. Th. Mouton, in *Vragen des Tijds*, Vol. 2, 1890, 93–116.

[39] Reports of the APMCI, 1879, 6–26; 1883, 56–63; and 1888, 85–100. The latest of these contains an extensive bibliography.

1880s if patent legislation had existed is lacking. Indeed, the opposite can more easily be demonstrated, particularly as far as the electrical industry is concerned and with specific reference to the birth of incandescent lamp manufacture. The scope of this statement is of course limited, for we are mainly concerned with one article, the incandescent lamp – a product which, although representative of the then still young science-based industries, had an extremely turbulent history in terms of patents. If Edison's basic patent had been valid in the Netherlands, and had been interpreted there as it was in the United Kingdom and the United States, the 1880s would certainly not have seen the birth of a Dutch incandescent lamp industry. Not only because De Khotinsky, Robertson and Pope would assuredly not have gone there, but equally because burgeoning lamp manufacturers would immediately have become embroiled in patent lawsuits, as, for example, were Lane-Fox and Swan in England in 1882.[40] This threat would have stifled the spirit of enterprise of the Dutch manufacturers, who were obliged by circumstances to start on a modest scale. Their policies would have been determined not by the laws of competition, but by the 'juristic' method of running a business which had become commonplace among Edison's American competitors but was still viewed with scepticism in Europe, even by as large a concern as Siemens:

I had a conversation with Mr Flint about the prospects of his Company, the United States Electric Lighting Company, and he informed me that in a couple of months the new Works would be ready to start manufacturing.

He incidentally told me that the fees paid by the Company to experts and lawyers amounted to a sum of from $40,000 to $50,000 per annum. I expect the Company will have to sell a good many lamps and machines if it desires to see anything of these 50,000 dollars again.[41]

In general terms, too, the Netherlands' relative backwardness in the economic and technical fields, and the absence of major electrical companies, should be taken into account. For at the higher levels of industrialization, companies are seen to achieve significant expansion by exploiting their patents. At that time the country was in an unequal position, in which, in the absence of patent legislation and appropriately for the Dutch situation, small companies or those which were just starting up were unintentionally given protection, and with this the best chance of survival. It was this class of manufacturer which the APMCI primarily

[40]  Cf. Chapter 1, page 26.
[41]  G. von Chauvin (a director) in a letter sent from New York to Siemens Bros. & Co., London, 17.5.1881; Siemens Archives, No. 36 Lh 816, Munich.

sought to serve. As early as 1879, Baron J. d'Aulnis de Bourouill (1850–1930), Professor of Economics at Utrecht University and a leading publicist and adviser to the Association, elaborated his theory that patent protection as a rule hampered the industrial application of inventions.[42] Referring to the recent establishment of Wisse, Piccaluga & Co., he pointed out that in the Netherlands, where no royalties had to be paid, electrical articles equal in quality to their foreign counterparts could be produced for two-thirds of the cost. Had it not all too often been argued that economists of repute, such as Michel Chevalier and Arthur Legrand in France[43] – the patent land *par excellence*[44] – not to mention virtually all the German economists,[45] in contrast to most engineers, were against the principle of patents? In the Netherlands, a similar opinion was voiced in the columns of *De Economist* and, as we have already seen, tested by both doctrinal and pragmatic standards.

Direct protests from interested parties abroad continued to be heard spasmodically. These came chiefly from Paris, the seat of the Compagnie Continentale Edison and the lobby of the Union pour la Protection de la Propriété Industrielle – generally referred to by Mouton as 'friends of patents'. For example, the 1882 edition of *La Lumière Electrique*, in addition to dealing at length with the freedom from patents in the Netherlands, contained an exhortation to French manufacturers: 'N'allez pas exposer à Amsterdam!' With its patriotic tinge, this appeal, the signatories to which included Paul Jablochkoff, urged diplomatic pressure and a boycott, and haughtily qualified the Netherlands, Greece, Switzerland and Turkey equally, as Balkan states.[46] This contrasts strongly with the verdict reached in 1890 by the electrical fraternity in England, where, after years of incessant conflict, the monopolistic effect of the administration of justice in patent suits was denounced not only as 'a legal terrorism over small traders', but also as having proved disastrous for the progress of the British electrical industry:

We say 'disastrous' advisedly, because few circumstances could be more prejudicial to the welfare of the industry as a whole than that entire branches should fall into the hands of monopolists who use their position to crush out all progress in hands other than their own.

Thus the leading technical and economic journal, *The Electrician*, 'A Weekly Illustrated Journal of Electrical Engineering, Industry and Science',

[42]  *De Economist*, 1879, Vol. 1, 123 ff.    [43]  *Journal des Economistes*, May 1878.
[44]  Thus described by d'Aulnis de Bourouill; cf. note 42 above.
[45]  Machlup and Penrose, 'The patent controversy', 4; also Report of the APMCI, 1890, 127.
[46]  *La Lumière Electrique*, 1882, Vol. 7, 637 ff.

in its issue of 20 June 1890. This emotive view might well have been expressed by the APMCI; but because no comparable *casus belli* existed in the Netherlands, it was then of purely academic interest to the majority of Dutch manufacturers.

Among those directly concerned was Gerard Philips, who had lived and worked in Britain and, perhaps better than anyone else, had observed the interests which were involved, and who also saw that the incandescent lamp industry in France was in decline.[47] In the Netherlands, on the other hand, the very absence of patent legislation afforded the aspiring lamp manufacturer ample scope. While negotiating on behalf of AEG, it must have become abundantly clear to him that the monopoly of lamp supply demanded by Rathenau, which stemmed from the principle of the 'complete electric lighting system', was no longer publicly acceptable. It led to the disintegration of a monopolistic market situation and to the creation, for a manufacturer specializing solely in lamps, of a virtually unlimited market – albeit this provisionally excluded Great Britain and the United States of America.

In the summer of 1889, while still in London, Gerard Philips had been a close observer of the case brought by Edison & Swan against the Anglo-American Brush Electric Light Corporation.[48] He and Emile Garcke had then turned their thoughts to the possibilities offered by the Netherlands as a base for the manufacture of incandescent lamps. Coming so soon after his experience in the British capital, the discussions on the subject of patents which took place at the Palace of Industry in Amsterdam will have been of immediate interest to him. Mouton was again the principal speaker. Replying to the arguments put forward by supporters of patents, such as solidarity with other countries and fairness towards inventors, he dealt at length with the conflict which existed in Europe concerning the form which a patent system should take. He contended, among other things, that in Germany, in contrast to other countries, the term 'invention' was not enshrined in law but was left to scientific or judicial interpretation. But despite being exemplary by reason of its high degree of selectivity, the German system was adjudged by interested parties in America, who were accustomed to no more than a brief preliminary investigation, to be 'a perfect system of spoliation'. They maintained that 'eight out of ten applications are refused, and of the other two, one is withdrawn after three

---

47  *The Electrician*, 5.12.1890: 'The protection of the electrical industry in France'.
48  Cf. Chapter 2, pages 73 ff and 82.

years'.[49] This conception, Mouton felt, was exaggerated, but understandable in view of the stance adopted by the *Patentamt*, namely that too many patents hampered industrial progress. He contested the classic argument that patents advanced the cause of industry, pointing, for example, to his extensive treatise on the subject, which had appeared in the review *Vragen des Tijds* a few months previously.[50] Among his findings was that in the space of fifteen years – the life of most patents – a greater number of margarine factories had come into existence in the Netherlands than could ever have been the case had patent protection existed. It was not until 1883 that Messrs Jurgens, of Oss triumphed in England, their principal export market, in a patent case which threatened them and their competitors alike with extinction. Mouton, who as chairman of the Association of Dutch Margarine Manufacturers[51] was well informed, concluded with the observation that every technical innovation soon found its way into all these factories. This he saw as a reason for urging the meeting to continue to judge the patent issue on its own merits and not in the light of extraneous factors such as solidarity with other nations in working towards an institution which 'is mainly felt to be wrong'. Philosophizing, a member, M. A. Caspers, an underwriter by profession, posed the question, 'What is intellectual property?', adding immediately, 'We do not know.' Until this was established, he maintained – though not all agreed with him – discussing a patent law was an unrewarding task.

The proponents, too, were more vociferous than in previous years. They included the Amsterdam chemist C. D. Nellensteijn and the young lawyer R. J. H. Patijn,[52] Clerk of the Lower House of Parliament. Both claimed that opinion was swinging in favour of the reintroduction of patent legislation and that this was a result partly of the work of the Association of Supporters of a Dutch Patent Law, to whose aims they subscribed, but equally of foreign pressure. They cited a French proposal to exclude the Netherlands from the international agreement to protect trademarks. 'It boils down to the fact that we have no choice;' Patijn declared, 'the wisest course for Dutch industry is to accept a patent law as a present-day requirement.'[53]

[49] Report of the 39th General Meeting of the APMCI, 1890, 120.

[50] *Vragen des Tijds*, Vol. 2, 1890, 93–116: 'Octrooien'.

[51] J. Th. Mouton, *Margarine Boter*, 1881; by the same author, *Butterine, a good, useful, wholesome and cheap article of food*, 1885.

[52] Rudolf Johan Hendrik Patijn (1863–1936); rose through the ranks of the civil service to become Secretary-General for Foreign Affairs; a member of the Supervisory Boards of the Dutch State Railways, Unilever and other companies.

[53] Report of the 39th General Meeting of the APMCI, 1890, 126.

With this, he allied himself with the view expressed shortly beforehand by the conservative statesman, J. Heemskerk Azn.,[54] a member of the Hague branch of the Society for the Promotion of Industry. His approach to the subject was more akin to a governmental viewpoint and, in principle, indicative of the social contrast between the Society and the more middle-class APMCI, both of which were patrons of Dutch industry. This contrast, which can broadly be characterized as one between conservatives and liberals,[55] also applied to their respective approaches to the social reforms referred to earlier in this chapter.

On the cardinal issue, the desirability of introducing a patent law in the Netherlands, the meeting ultimately voted, by a majority of six, in favour of such a step. But as it was felt that the question had not been thoroughly debated, the members refrained from voting on the second clause of the motion, which proposed that the executive committee be authorized to take active steps to promote the relevant Bill. The meeting thus again aligned itself with the old, uncommitted policy pursued by Mouton, who put practicability above the desirability which was frequently based on ideal-ism. Twenty years were to pass – years in which the fortunes of both camps ebbed and flowed – before a Dutch Parliament approved such a Bill. This became law in 1912, by which time the advances made by Dutch industry rendered it imperative to establish order in this area. In the Netherlands, as in other countries, the emphasis was thereupon seen to have shifted from the personal 'intellectual property', to which Caspers had referred as recently as 1890, to industrial property.

We have already mentioned that, given the state of Dutch industry in the 1880s, the introduction of patent legislation could have seriously hampered the commencement of incandescent lamp production.[56] With his modest capital and small-scale operation, and combining the roles of manufacturer and merchant, the Dutch entrepreneur was no match for companies such as Edison & Swan, Siemens and AEG. Nevertheless, the manufacture of incandescent lamps got off the ground in the Netherlands, a paradoxical development which was primarily attributable to the rigid patent regimes in industrially more developed countries, notably Britain! The Boudewijnse works and those of Goossens & Pope are the outstanding examples; and

54  Heemskerk was among the fervent supporters of a patent law; cf. J. J. Huizinga, *J. Heemskerk Azn. (1818–1897), Conservatief zonder Partij*, 1973, 109.
55  Report of the 28th General Meeting of the APMCI, 1879, 86: 'Our Association takes a liberal view of economic matters; the Society formerly followed, and continues to follow, a different path.'
56  Cf. pages 247 ff.

this was also the source of inspiration for Gerard Philips' plans, initially in association with Brush. In 1890, Mouton, who was extremely well acquainted with this subject, and while closely involved had retained a sense of reality, characterized the confusing lawsuits concerning Edison's basic patent which were being prosecuted in England and Germany as follows: 'The big companies fight each other, then join forces to obstruct others in the performance of their industrial activities.'[57] He went on to describe the fate which had befallen several electrical companies in other countries and added that many engineers in the Netherlands – including one with an outstanding background – had shown themselves to be opposed to patents.[58]

As far as legal vulnerability and commercial expediency were concerned, his observations coincided with those of Gerard Philips and his counterpart, Hugo Hirst (1863–1943), who emigrated to England from Germany in the 1880s. Hirst was the founder of the English GEC concern.[59] As soon as Edison's basic patent expired, he set up a small incandescent lamp works in England and this, under the technical management of Charles John Robertson, who had meanwhile returned to his native country, soon became the largest British producer. Robertson was 'well known as one of the most experienced incandescent lamp makers in England and on the Continent'.[60] Hirst and his associates were obliged to wait four years for their opportunity; Gerard Philips had no such problem. Not for nothing did Professor J. A. Snijders, the first professor of electrical engineering at Delft University, refer at that time to 'a fortunate country where no patents exist'.[61]

Gerard's partner in the plan to establish an incandescent lamp works in the Netherlands, Jan Jacob Reesse (1853–1910), was a chemical technologist.[62] He studied at the Delft Polytechnic, and in 1878 took up a technical post at the Beuker and Hulshoff sugar refinery on the Lauriergracht in Amsterdam, which was owned by his father. The Reesse family had for several generations been involved in the prosperous sugar trade in Amsterdam and was regarded as well-to-do. But in 1880 the refinery was destroyed by fire,[63] and this, on top of the prospect of a decline in fortunes

---

[57] *Vragen des Tijds*, 106 ff.
[58] Report of the 39th General Meeting of the APMCI, 1890, 116, 128.
[59] Byatt, *British Electrical Industry*, 189; also Jones and Marriott, *Anatomy of a Merger*, 73 ff.
[60] *The Electrician*, 29.9.1893, 595.        [61] Snijders, *De vorderingen der Electrotechniek*, 85.
[62] A. Heerding, 'J. J. Reesse', in *Biografisch Woordenboek van Nederland*, 1979, Vol. 1, 483 ff.
[63] *Eigen Haard*, 1880, 66 ff.

following the abolition of export subsidies and changes in the tax on sugar, led Reesse to leave that branch of commerce. In 1883, after a sojourn in Germany, where he made a thorough study of the manufacture of Portland cement, he took over the Sybrand Hoven cement works at Farmsum, near Delfzijl, which he renamed Nederlandsche Portlandcementfabriek J. J. Reesse & Co. His lectures to the Vereeniging tot Bevordering der Bouwkunst (Association for the Advancement of the Art of Building) are both noteworthy and indicative of his industrial vision. In these he drew attention to the fact that although marl, the principal raw material for the manufacture of cement, was present in the province of Limburg in quantities which matched those in Germany, the Dutch reserves remained unexploited while the German cement industry prospered.[64] He was one of the few who recognized this paradox. It was to be another fifty years before this source of wealth was successfully developed by a Belgo-Swiss consortium, Enci.[65]

In spite of modernizing the works at Farmsum[66] and producing a grade of Portland cement which could compete with foreign products, the price of which was kept artificially high, Reesse's efforts to interest the trade in domestic cement, in place of the established English and German brands to which it was accustomed, did not entirely succeed. In 1888 he left the company and accepted a post as technical adviser to the Tjibodar cement works, which was to be built near Buitenzorg, on the island of Java. His knowledge and interest, particularly in the technological aspect of cement manufacture, in which the laboratory is the nucleus of the company, are revealed in several of his contributions to De Ingenieur in 1888 and 1889. In the spring of 1890 he returned to his native land, where he sought a suitable opportunity to deploy his entrepreneurial talent in the chemical field. Through his work in connection with the safety exhibition referred to earlier, but more specifically as a result of his friendship with F. J. Lugt,[67] the architect of the Amsterdam electricity concession, he came into contact with Gerard Philips and became his partner in a challenging project: the manufacture of a scientifically designed product. His experience as a laboratory technician and his familiarity with high-temperature experiments – this time aimed not at producing cement but at carbonizing filaments – must have been an added reason, and an incentive in itself, for joining Gerard.

[64] De Ingenieur, 1886, 137.
[65] A. Heerding, Cement in Nederland, 1971, 103 ff.
[66] De Ingenieur, 1887, 114 ff.
[67] According to various documents in the archives of the Lugt family, The Hague.

The two men produced and tested their earliest filaments at Number 220 Herengracht, Amsterdam, the seventeenth-century home of the Reesse family, which Jan Jacob then shared with his three sisters, who like himself were unmarried. With a little imagination, one can still see in the basement of this canalside house the rudiments of their laboratory, with its old-fashioned taps and the sculleries which then existed. The building now houses the Association 'Het Nederlandsch Economisch-Historisch Archief' and the Economisch-Historische Bibliotheek. In the summer of 1890, when Gerard's commission from AEG came to an end, he and Reesse embarked on their experiments to change chemically the structure of cellulose in order to obtain a substance from which a fine filament could be produced. Their work was based on an 'English invention' which, according to Gerard, gave a thread 'more homogeneous than the bamboo fibre which Edison used'.[68] Their starting material was cotton wool (cellulose), which they purified chemically before dissolving it in concentrated zinc chloride which was gradually heated over a steam bath;[69] while dissolving, the cellulose was constantly stirred. The syrupy liquid thus obtained was diluted to the desired consistency by the addition of water and hydrochloric acid before being stored in a glass vessel. This was closed at the bottom by a stopper having a fine ground aperture. With the aid of compressed air, the liquid was forced through the aperture and collected in a tray containing alcohol. Not being soluble in the excess of alcohol, the cellulose immediately coagulated to form a strong, smooth, uniform thread, the diameter of which corresponded to the aperture in the stopper. A number of stoppers with apertures of various sizes were made, enabling threads with predetermined diameters to be produced. This method eliminated the risky and unreliable technique of drawing the thread through dies, which was a necessary part of the processes used by Edison (for bamboo) and by Swan (with parchmentized cotton thread).[70] However, great care had to be taken to ensure that the cellulose solution did not contain particles of dust or waste material which could clog the aperture. Nor might it contain air bubbles which could interfere with, or even prevent, the uniform flow of material; to prevent this, the vessel was connected to a vacuum pump prior to squirting, in order to extract air present in the solution. The squirted thread was then washed in water or hydrochloric acid to remove zinc or zinc oxide residues adhering to it, and finally wound on to drums for drying.

[68]  *Nieuwe Rotterdamsche Courant*, 28.3.1916: an interview with Gerard Philips.
[69]  C. F. Cross et al., *Cellulose, an Outline of the Chemistry of the Structural Elements of Plants*, 1895, 8.
[70]  G. S. Ram, *The Incandescent Lamp and its Manufacture*, 1893, 16 ff.

Early experiments in the manufacture of filaments from cellulose, Amsterdam, 1890. (The handwriting is that of Gerard Philips.)

This trial and error method, which in part was dictated by the variety of materials used, led to the following results:

Today we took Chlzn with an s.q. of 1.87, namely 4000 × 200 [by this is meant 4,000 grams of zinc chloride with 200 grams of cotton wool]. The cotton wool became thicker at outset owing to higher concentration. At the end, however, as thin as usual. Added 270 grams of water instead of 330. Boiling now takes longer, namely half an hour. Whereas we formerly boiled the zinc chloride solution with a small amount of water, with the result that it remained thin for a longer period, the solution is now stiffer, has a skin on it and is more difficult to squirt.[71]

We have found no detailed written evidence of the research conducted at the house on the Herengracht. Only a few pointers, in telegram style, appear in a notebook kept by Gerard Philips, which relates to the period from 31 January to 6 March 1893 and thus dates from the early days in Eindhoven. This shows that while the main problems concerned with the preparation of the cellulose thread had been solved, even though new questions kept arising, considerable difficulty was still being experienced in achieving a strong, uniformly carbonized filament:

On Saturday, for the first time, we put a crucible containing carbons [pieces of cellulose thread] near boiler. For five hours in the middle opening. The filaments were beautifully shiny, but still not completely free of indentations. The resistance still far too high, more than 100,000 ohms.

At the point of fracture, the filament is shiny black, the thickness of a 72/32 [a filament for a 72-volt, 32-candlepower lamp] made from 36 diameter material is 26–27, so the shrinkage with heavy carbonization after 5 hours must be small.

The filaments were further carbonized with three baskets [of coke] in the normal manner. They become nice and shiny. One piece gives very fine carbon, very shiny but brittle; this was material with a diameter of 22. Will certainly be due to slow carbonization. The material for 72/16 [for a 72-volt, 16-candlepower lamp] was of 16/2 and 10/2; both supported 11 kilograms; that of the 10s was slightly more transparent than that of the 16s.

As far as the carbonization is concerned, the big question is: To get rid of the indentations, must I carbonize at even lower temperature than in the middle opening, or will this make the carbon more brittle; is it then better to carbonize at a given, higher temperature?

As far as the material is concerned, the main problems are:

Can I obtain a tough carbon with a shiny surface by carbonizing a denser substance in any special way?

Can I obtain this by squirting material made from a dilute cellulose solution at low pressure? See notes on my earlier experiments with Reesse.

Can I obtain this by using molten or polished agate dies?

[71] Notebook of Gerard Philips, 1893, page 13; Philips Archives, Eindhoven.

Can I obtain it by taking a 10% or 15% cellulose solution and allowing this to heat up over a very long period, thus by using a lot of dilute zinc chloride? Earlier, when I used small quantities...[72]

These extracts illustrate some of the difficulties encountered in the carbonizing process, which even after two years of experimentation had not been completely overcome and, in Gerard Philips' own words, boiled down to the fact that: 'The thread which we succeeded so well in making on a small scale, we were unable to make on a large scale.'[73] With this comment, made twenty-five years after the event, Gerard touched upon the essence of the manufacturing problem which he was called upon to solve in Eindhoven, even though in December 1890, while working with Reesse, he had been able to produce 'a fine, clean chemical thread'.[74] His observation also shows how long was the road which he had to travel between the preparatory stage in 1890 and the commencement of incandescent lamp manufacture in Eindhoven. It is probable that neither Gerard nor Reesse realized just how arduous that journey would be. They commenced in Amsterdam by manufacturing, on a laboratory scale, a cellulose thread which had then to be carbonized. In November 1890 they placed an order with Thomas Fletcher & Co., London, for the necessary laboratory furnace and the associated Morgan graphite crucibles and bellows, requesting that these be despatched direct to the Herengracht. 'We require this set for making experimental carbonized filaments for incandescent lamps', Gerard added in his letter.[75] With the filament which they thus obtained – the cellulose thread was carefully laid in the crucible, covered with graphite, gently compressed and then heated to 2,000°C – Gerard and Reesse took their first, faltering steps on the road which led to the profession of incandescent lamp manufacturer.

With the choice of this process, they joined the ranks of modern manufacturers in their branch of industry, who were endeavouring to replace the early, often craft-based working methods by industrial methods. Gerard had learned the essence of this concept in the second half of 1889, during 'the negotiations with Messrs Philips for the establishment of an incandescent lamp factory in Holland'.[76] At the Brush works in London,

[72] Notebook of Gerard Philips, page 56.
[73] *Nieuwe Rotterdamsche Courant*, 28.3.1916: an interview with Gerard Philips.
[74] Copy-book of Gerard Philips, 30.12.1890.
[75] Copy-book of Gerard Philips, 21.11.1890.
[76] Minute Book No. 1, 23.10.1889, Board of the Anglo-American Brush Electric Light Corporation, Ltd.

where production had meanwhile ceased, he was able to obtain details of the manufacture of squirted cellulose thread by the zinc chloride method devised by Wynne and Powell.[77] Frank Wynne was the engineer with responsibility for the technical aspects of Brush's 'continental business' and a colleague of Emile Garcke, who was in charge of the general and commercial affairs of the company. Gerard, of course, had been closely associated with both men during the negotiations aimed at establishing a company in the Netherlands to take over the production of the Brush lamp. As stated earlier, this method was ideal for the manufacture of extremely homogeneous and uniform cellulose thread on an industrial scale. After experiments lasting about two years, Brush was ready to replace the Lane-Fox system by the Wynne and Powell process for its entire production of incandescent lamps. In an article which appeared in *The Electrician* of 4 February 1887 and contained a reference to this process, Swinburne wrote that 'Very good lamps are said to be made by the Anglo-American Brush Corporation, who own this patent.' We know Swinburne as the technician and entrepreneur to whom Gerard once gave credit for having aroused in him 'more than usual interest in the manufacture of incandescent lamps'.[78] The new process inspired Brush to greater efforts to set about incandescent lamp manufacture in Britain. There was therefore every reason for Garcke to announce to shareholders on 3 October 1888 that his company was in a position to produce a lamp which 'in terms of price, efficiency and life' was superior to any other British or foreign lamp.[79]

As an engineer, Gerard Philips, who was conversant with the mechanically complex method of processing bamboo fibre employed by AEG (the Edison system) and the difficulty involved in the manufacture of the Seel filament,[80] must have recognized the important advantages of the Brush method. The attraction of trying to obtain an option on the process, or to emulate it, must have been all the greater after it was shelved in Britain in 1889 as a result of the Edison & Swan monopoly. That monopoly stifled the development of the British lamp industry at the very moment when manufacturers, faced with a sharp decline in prices and a rapid rise in consumption, had no choice but to adopt efficient mass-production methods. To Brush, the process was no longer of significance except in relation to the Vienna works. The value of filaments made from colloidal cellulose was also recognized in Germany. In 1889 these were the subject of

[77] British Patent 'A.D. 1884, 22nd December, No. 16805'.
[78] Cf. Chapter 2, page 63.    [79] Cf. Chapter 2, page 79.
[80] German Patent No. 36206 dated 6.9.1885, granted to Carl Seel, Charlottenburg.

a case brought by AEG against De Khotinsky. The latter employed the Weston process, but his right to do so was contested by AEG, which held the patent but until then had made no use of it.[81] The reason for this was that shortly beforehand AEG had commenced to manufacture the tried and tested Edison lamp, and with its high volume of sales – then about 650,000 lamps a year and rising rapidly – it hesitated to undertake the technically difficult changeover to the Weston system. Here we see one of the advantages of the greater dynamism possessed by the smaller, specialist lamp manufacturers who were then emerging, such as Goossens & Pope and De Khotinsky.

Gerard's father, the solid businessman Frederik Philips, who would certainly have taken note of the results achieved by the existing Dutch factories and their viability, also recognized the potential of such a competitive enterprise. He had been a party to the plan to set up a lamp works in the Netherlands in association with Brush, and he remained a partner now that Gerard and Reesse were pursuing their joint goal. We have no evidence of his commercial assessment and are therefore obliged to seek indications in his immediate circle of acquaintances. We are struck by the example of his merchant colleagues Schöffer and Goossens, who in 1889 and 1890 respectively proceeded substantially to enlarge their successful lamp factories.[82] It may be assumed that Frederik and Gerard duly noted these developments; indeed, the latter observed: 'The lamps made in Venlo are very widely used here; the factory doubled its production last summer.'[83]

We may take it for granted that Frederik Philips had complete confidence in his son Gerard and not only in technical matters. After all, the latter, in the course of his lengthy travels abroad and his personal relationships with leading entrepreneurs such as Rathenau and Garcke, had amassed almost unrivalled experience and knowledge of electrical engineering. From a business point of view, it can be said that the experience which Gerard obtained from the joint project with Brush provided, if not the stimulus to a modern enterprise, at least the notional basis for his later lamp factory. His choice of filament, in particular, is indicative of a very keen appreciation of matters commercial and technical – but also of self-confidence in tackling the highly complex problems inherent in manufacturing, despite having

---

[81] Patentblatt und Auszüge aus den Patentschriften, No. 14, Berlin, 8.4.1891.
[82] Cf. Chapter 4, pages 176 ff and 173.
[83] Copy-book of Gerard Philips: a letter to E. Woschke, 28.2.1891.

ELECTRISCHE GLÜHLAMPEN-FABRIK "WATT,"

## VIENNA, AUSTRIA.

# INCANDESCENT LAMPS

OF THE

# HIGHEST QUALITY ONLY.

Technical Director: Mr. CHARLES J. ROBERTSON.

## PRICES ON APPLICATION.

# PHILIPS & CO.,

## EINDHOVEN, HOLLAND.

*Telegrams: "PHILIPS, EINDHOVEN."*

# INCANDESCENT LAMP MAKERS.

PERFECTION IN ALL DETAILS. QUICK DELIVERY.

## FIRST-CLASS ANGLO-AMERICAN REFERENCES.

Advertisement in *The Electrician, Electrical Trades' Directory and Handbook*, 1893

little or no practical experience in that field. The circumstances which led to the birth of the Eindhoven lamp works are thus seen to have been principally of a technical-historical nature; but this fact was overlooked in later years. The assumption that Gerard Philips himself had invented a new process[84] must accordingly be rebutted. Nor was there any booty in the sense in which the term was once used by Mouton in connection with two 'respected Dutch industrialists' who, dressed as labourers, travelled to a neighbouring country and pulled off a piece of industrial espionage.[85] On the contrary, the establishment of the factory was the logical consequence of the fact that the manufacture of incandescent lamps in Britain, even under the Wynne and Powell patent, constituted an infringement of Edison's basic patent as this was interpreted by the English courts. The *raison d'être* of the Eindhoven works was thus identical to that of the Boudewijnse and Goossens & Pope works, which also produced a lamp with British origins. The continued relationship between Gerard and Brush suggests that there were no complications; certainly there were no legal grounds for any. Indeed the opposite is more likely, for when the Philips lamps first arrived in England, the advertisement bore the cryptic recommendation 'First-class Anglo-American references'. Here we observe a typical example of the involuntary transference of a production process which has been brought to a halt by external factors. In this case it was made possible by a policy of expediency, in the shape of freedom from patent restrictions, which, as has been explained, was defended in the interests of the country's still young industries.

We have already described how Brush ceased the manufacture of incandescent lamps in Great Britain. This was a severe blow to Emile Garcke.[86] The factory at Brook Green, in London, which had been completed in 1889 with the aim of introducing the Wynne and Powell process 'on a very large scale', never went into production. After standing empty for four years, it was sold to GEC.[87] It was at about this time that the manufacture of incandescent lamps in Eindhoven had passed the experimental stage. Frederik Philips judged the time ripe to recall his youngest son, Anton Frederik, who was then a trainee with a London firm

---

[84] Bouman, *Growth of an Enterprise*, 37.
[85] Report of the 32nd General Meeting of the APMCI, 1883, 62.
[86] Cf. Chapter 2, page 83.
[87] Minutes of the Board of Brush, 1893.

**ZURICH INCANDESCENCE LAMP CO.**

**47,**

**VICTORIA ST., WESTMINSTER, S.W.**

*Director :*

**C. H. STEARN,**

Joint Inventor

with

Mr. J. W. SWAN,

of the modern

Incandescence

Lamp.

Lamps delivered by

postal packets to all

parts of the

United Kingdom.

Lamps of Long
Duration with
larger consumption
of power, or of
greater economy
and Shorter
Duration, delivered
as required.

Terminals affixed
as ordered,
to suit any
holders of the
current types.

The Lamps are
manufactured under
Mr. STEARN'S
Personal Direction
by an English Staff.

**ALL LAMPS ACCURATELY CLASSIFIED IN VOLTAGE & CANDLE-POWER**

The Company are now supplying

**STEARN'S NEW CENTRAL STATION LAMPS**

at 2·6 to 2·9 watts per candle, "for use where Economy of Current is the first consideration." These Lamps effect a saving of **10s. 2d.** per 1,000 hours on a 16-c.p. Lamp as compared with the ordinary 4-watt Lamps, price of current being 7d. per Board of Trade Unit.

**ORDERS FOR LARGE QUANTITIES OF LAMPS PROMPTLY EXECUTED.**

Advertisement in *The Electrician, Electrical Trades' Directory and Handbook,* 1893

of stockbrokers, and entrust him with the task of selling the lamps. In later years Anton was to recall the difficulties with which Gerard had to contend in the initial period:

The year '91 was spent in equipping the factory, '92 in getting things running more smoothly, and in '93 production and sales commenced in earnest. I joined in January '94 and when we drew up the balance sheet in '95 we found that even with a few small items of depreciation we had covered our costs in '94.[88]

The task which confronted Gerard Philips was a great deal more onerous than one might infer from Anton's comments. Although conversant with electrical engineering, he was not acquainted with the myriad facets of a lamp factory in full daily production. His experience could certainly not be compared with that of a foreman or electrician who had absorbed every detail of the manufacturing process and applied his knowledge in practice. It was this which distinguished Gerard's position from those of Robertson in Middelburg, Pope in Venlo and Alewijnse in Nijmegen, all of whom had worked for years in lamp factories before starting out on their own. Even De Khotinsky had needed two years (the generally accepted period)[89] to get into his stride, for he, too, was initially lacking in the necessary skill. Knowledge of a process, therefore, was by no means the same as mastery of the secret in which lay the art of successful lamp manufacture in both technical and economic terms. As Swinburne put it, there were all too many instances of an 'inventor' producing a couple of dozen lamps in his laboratory and then taking it for granted that all he had to do was to go on and manufacture in large quantities. In reality, that was only the beginning; often the costly preparations went wrong and the aspiring lamp manufacturer later discovered that he had omitted to design and build 'the apparatus for manufacturing on a large scale with uniformity'.[90]

Hidden behind the apparent simplicity of the incandescent lamp was a complex manufacturing process in which, besides knowledge of electricity, mastery of a wide range of subjects, including vacuum technology, metallurgy, glass-forming, chemical techniques and photometry, and the use and maintenance of instruments, played an important part. Furthermore, installers demanded that the lamps should conform as closely as possible to predetermined technical specifications covering light intensity, current

---

[88] Address given by Dr A. F. Philips in Eindhoven, 1949; Philips Archives, Eindhoven. According to our information, Anton Philips did not arrive in Eindhoven until 1895.

[89] *Electrical Review*, Vol. 19, No. 454, 6.8.1886: Swinburne, 'The Edison filament case': 'A factory takes about two years to get into swing'.

[90] *The Electrician*, 26.11.1886, 60 ff.

consumption and voltage (resistance). Standardization based on a pattern of manufacturing regulations was therefore necessary from the outset. In addition to these factors, consumers demanded a choice of lamps, which meant producing and stocking a wide range of different types. The production process chosen therefore had to meet the following requirements:

the lamp had to be capable of being manufactured in large numbers and to a uniform standard, and
various combinations of power, resistance and physical shape had to be supplied.

To comply with these, it was necessary to develop in advance a uniform method of manufacture; the uniformity, in turn, required far-reaching subdivision of the labour process. An organizational system was therefore called for which, by reason of the variety of individual operations, appealed to unskilled workers, but at the same time met the stringent demands imposed by the scientific and technical concept which lay at the root of the mass production of incandescent lamps. This, in its entirety, was already then the distinctive feature of the incandescent lamp industry. To prevent miscalculation in this area, which was all too easy, Swinburne, the insider, succinctly reiterated the peculiar quality of the incandescent lamp in 1893:

The incandescent lamp is simple, but its manufacture is one of the most intricate and difficult examples of scientific industry, and it is understood by very few people, as it is seldom that anyone has both the necessary scientific knowledge and ability and the opportunity for acquiring practical experience.[91]

With these words he characterized the specific qualities which distinguished Gerard Philips and his work, then and for the remainder of his life.

But we must return to the preparations which Gerard and Reesse were making in Amsterdam. In order to calculate the cost price, Gerard sent enquiries to several suppliers of lamp parts in November 1890. For lamp caps he sought a quotation from the Vitrite Works in Middelburg, and for bulbs he invited offers from German glass manufacturers. On 17 November 1890, the former replied to 'Mr G. L. F. Philips, Hotel Mille Colonnes, Amsterdam', offering to supply:

Vitrite caps No. 17 at ƒ 45 per 1,000 net
Vitrite caps No. 23 at ƒ 35 per 1,000 net (the cheapest type).

---

[91] *The Electrician*, 22.12.1893; J. S[winburne], referring to G. S. Ram, *The Incandescent Lamp and its Manufacture*.

'Be so kind as to determine your requirements in advance,' the company requested, 'for this [the autumn] is our busiest time of the year and the volume of orders does not allow us to maintain large stocks.'[92] Later correspondence reveals that Gerard was also interested in Brush lamp caps, and these the Vitrite Works was also able to supply.

Nalder Bros. & Co. of London were asked to quote for ampère, volt and watt meters, but, remarkably, the letter found its way to the offices of Boudewijnse in Middelburg, who represented this manufacturer in the Netherlands. The latter's conclusion was as rapid as his reply: 'As you presumably require the instruments for an incandescent lamp factory, I would also invite your attention to galvanometers, resistance boxes, etc.'[93] Boudewijnse went on to say that if his surmise were correct, Gerard would probably require special volt and ampère meters, and he offered to go to Amsterdam to provide details of these. To the writer, as both an incandescent lamp manufacturer and a supplier of electrical instruments, the matter was one of conscience, the more so as he had unpleasant memories of a similar transaction when he was setting up his own lamp works: 'My voltmeter was made by one of my competitors, who knew what it was to be used for and deliberately introduced a fault.'[94] Thus did Boudewijnse seek to justify himself in the face of complaints of voltage errors from potential clients. This was a pretty serious accusation, but he also used it to explain the troubles which initially beset his own factory, when some of the first lamps produced glowed red instead of white-hot.

A rumour that an unnamed lamp factory was to be established in Amsterdam had reached Boudewijnse several weeks previously. In all probability he heard about it from the electrical suppliers, Fred. Stieltjes & Co.[95] of 745 Keizersgracht, with whom he did business. Prior to this, on 19 August 1890, he had supplied this Amsterdam company, at its request, with a complete specification, together with a number of drawings, showing the workings of mechanical and mercury pumps of the types used in incandescent lamp factories.[96] 'You will doubtless be familiar with the mechanical pump,' Boudewijnse had written, 'but drawings of mercury pumps, such as those of Geissler and Sprengel, are found only occasionally in scientific books, because there are no specific manufacturers: each incandescent lamp manufacturer has his pumps made by his own glass-

[92] Copy-book of the Vitrite Works, 17.11.1890.
[93] Copy-book of Boudewijnse, 16.1.1891.
[94] Copy-book of Boudewijnse, 7.2.1888.
[95] Cf. Chapter 4, page 160.
[96] Copy-book of Boudewijnse, 19.8.1890.

blowers.' He had then described the various combinations of pumps. 'Formerly, I employed Geissler + Sprengel,' he explained, 'but now I use the mechanical pump plus the Sprengel, for this is much more satisfactory than the first, as will be clearer to you when you are familiar with the enclosed Sprengel model [...] You can thus certainly recommend the combination described above, since your client is bound to have a mechanical pump.'

The inference is that the unsuspecting Boudewijnse, and possibly an equally naive Stieltjes, anticipated supplying a pump installation to a laboratory or an educational institution in Amsterdam. 'The installation', Boudewijnse suggested, 'could probably be carried out by a laboratory assistant under my supervision.' A month or two later, it appears, he was in possession of the facts, and in a letter in English to Cadiot, his agent in Paris, he said: 'You know that the factory in Amsterdam does not yet exist, but if it is erected then it is just now the right time to work that firm in the ground.'[97] The disillusionment led him to adopt a tone which, while admittedly more and more prevalent among powerful German manufacturers at that time, is extremely difficult to reconcile with someone of Boudewijnse's modest position and can only be ascribed to lingering indignation. The disturbed relationship led Gerard in 1892 to make fresh enquiries, via the representative of the Vitrite Works, Middelburg, concerning Boudewijnse's pump installation:

We should be pleased to receive further details of the air pumps used by B. & Co. We presume that our mercury pump system differs little from theirs. The rise and fall of the mercury in our system, too, occurs automatically as a result of the application of atmosphere and vacuum. One boy can manage 200–300 lamps per day. We are meanwhile interested in learning a little more about the pumps used by the company concerned, and we should therefore be pleased to receive a sketch of these. Our pump is not a Westinghouse, but of another American make, and is meanwhile becoming too small for flashing and pumping. Can you find out what type the new pump is? It is surely not the Berrenberg pump? We should also be pleased to receive a sketch of the Corburier apparatus (benzine for enriching the carbon gas).[98]

A friendly gesture was made by Roothaan & Alewijnse of Nijmegen, who invited Gerard to inspect their works and even allowed him to make sketches of vital pieces of equipment, including the pumps.[99] The Nijmegen works employed a replica of the ingenious pumping system which De Khotinsky had designed and which, as early as 1887, had been praised by

---

[97]  Copy-book of Boudewijnse, 15.11.1890.
[98]  Copy-book of Gerard Philips, 16.4.1892.
[99]  Ibid., 30.12.1890.

Zacharias for its high efficiency. It had meanwhile been further improved.[100] With this system, Roothaan & Alewijnse succeeded in exhausting bulbs in less than half an hour, and this fitted in excellently with Gerard's manufacturing plan, which was based on welding electrically and under vacuum the connections between the filament and the two platinum wires in the glass stem. Gerard also obtained information about the equipment and operation of the Goossens & Pope factory. In December 1890 he was aware that in Venlo, too, the pumping took no more than half an hour. The strong emphasis on saving time and labour is among the characteristic features of Gerard's factory design. It represents a deliberate search for competitiveness, the importance of which he had recognized as early as 1889, when he pointed out to Garcke that lamp prices on the Continent were falling rapidly and that there were already four competitors in the Netherlands. As he had then put it, 'The question is whether we shall be able to manufacture the lamp so cheap as to leave a considerable margin, even at prices ranging from Mark 1.50 to say, Mark 1.'[101] Just how intrigued Gerard was by the question of the pumping operation is revealed in the correspondence which passed between him and Emile Woschke, who at the time was foreman of the Seel works in Brussels, but whom Gerard engaged a few months later. In this, besides referring to the quality of the lamp – 'The lamps from Venlo are well known' – he gave a detailed description of the Sprengel pump installation at the Goossens & Pope works.[102] Only one man is needed to exhaust 500–600 lamps a day, he informed Woschke. All he had to do was to operate an air valve because, with the pneumatic method used there, the heavy work of raising the weights (an operation which had to be repeated to raise the level of mercury in the pump) had become a thing of the past. This is further evidence that from the outset the Dutch factories, in this case the one at Venlo, employed the latest improvements in production methods. 'As you will understand,' Gerard advised Woschke, 'there is a great deal of difference between working with this method and with the abnormally slow equipment used by Seel.' The German lamp manufacturers employed the much less efficient pump system devised by the Edison Lamp Company.[103] The economic significance of the labour saving which could be achieved in this area is apparent if one compares the situation in the Siemens & Halske[104] and

[100] Cf. Chapter 4, page 144.
[101] Copy-book of Gerard Philips, 16.12.1889.
[102] Ibid., 28.2.1891.        [103] Hammond, *Men and Volts*, 93.
[104] 'Die Entwicklung der Glühlampenfabrikation'; internal study carried out by Siemens & Halske, 24.9.1930; Siemens Archives, No. 68 Li 188, Munich.

Seel[105] factories with that at the Goossens & Pope works. With a production of 1,000 lamps a day, the former employed eighteen and forty men respectively for exhausting bulbs, against two or three at Venlo. The method chosen determined the rate of production, and thus exerted a major influence not only on labour costs but also on the capacity of the factory.

The realization of the plan to establish an incandescent lamp works, of course, also involved engaging a technically skilled manager and determining the magnitude of the production. In an advertisement which appeared in the 17 October 1890 issue of *The Electrician*, Gerard and Reesse invited applications for the post of electrician, and this drew quite a large number of replies from England and Germany.[106] To one of the English applicants, M. E. Bailey of London, Gerard explained that they were looking for a man capable of organizing and equipping a modern incandescent lamp factory 'on thorough business principles' – in other words, making first-class lamps, on a sound industrial base, as cheaply and efficiently as possible.[107] From the record of the conversation with this applicant it is clear that the works which was then envisaged would have a capacity of 1,000 lamps a day, but that production would commence on a smaller scale and gradually rise to the target figure. An interesting aspect of the conversation is Gerard's statement that he was in a position 'to manufacture exceptionally homogeneous and uniform cellulose filaments on an industrial scale'. He made it plain that his interest lay not so much in any particular technical detail or patent, of which all who were engaged in the manufacture of incandescent lamps 'as a rule have quite a number', but rather in the cost price aspect. Even though it was not uncommon in the Netherlands to attribute only a limited value to patents, it is clear from Gerard's words that he was aware that his process was among the best. Moreover, he was anxious to guard against what he was later to describe as the 'dangerous game of playing inventor'.[108] He found Bailey's claim to be able to make a lamp for fourpence three-farthings immensely significant, but at the same time incredible. 'How do you arrive at that price?' he asked the applicant. 'Can you confirm, and even guarantee, that this is a net price, including London wages and salaries, interest, depreciation and so on?' It would be fairly safe to assume that Bailey was referring solely to the labour cost, for in Boudewijnse's records and those of a British and a German factory we have

[105] Zacharias, *Die Glühlampe*, 159.
[106] The advertisement pages of *The Electrician* have not survived and thus the exact text cannot be reproduced; the same applies to ETZ No. 43, 1890.
[107] Copy-book of Gerard Philips, 14.11.1890.      [108] *Nieuwe Rotterdamsche Courant*, 28.3.1916.

found cost price calculations in which labour accounted for roughly the sum quoted by him. Bailey apparently ignored material costs and over-heads, which represented more than half of the cost price of a lamp.[109] In questioning Bailey's assertion, Gerard referred, among other things, to the very high price of platinum – more than threepence three-farthings per lamp – and the high cost of mercury pumps, two obstacles which the Americans were trying to overcome.

On that note, this English applicant disappears from the scene. It is known that Gerard would have liked to hear his views on the cost of setting up a factory with a capacity of 1,000 lamps per day, and this lends support to the belief that he was still largely groping in the dark as far as the financial aspect of the enterprise was concerned. To him, and perhaps even more so to Reesse, a clearer picture was a prerequisite for the further elaboration of the plan. The more so as Gerard, since the breakdown of the negotiations with Brush – 'under those circumstances you would object to give me any outcome regarding the prospects of continental lamp trade, cost prices of your lamps, etc.'[110] – possessed no certainty in this respect. Unlike his Dutch colleagues, who employed experienced English managers, he was obliged to discover these and other details for himself in order to substantiate his plan.

The most interesting response to the advertisement placed by Gerard and Reesse was from Charles John Robertson,[111] the electrician at the Boudewijnse works since 1887. His intention was not simply to change his job, but to obtain a partnership in the projected company. In his appli-cation, he hinted that the qualities required were to be found, not in an electrician, the generic term for the all-round electrical technician, but rather in an electrical engineer, which he was. With this expression of emancipation, he demonstrated that, as an actual lamp-maker 'in the factory', he desired a role in the overall management. He lost no time in voicing the opinion that the capacity of the works should be 2,500 lamps per day, which was so far above the initial figure of 500 contemplated that it probably aroused uncertainty in the mind of Reesse, who was largely guided by Gerard's knowledge of affairs. For such an increase, in addition to demanding a much larger investment, raised the question, who would then have to carry the final responsibility for technical matters, Gerard or the practically much more experienced Robertson? This, of course, was a

[109]  Cf. Chapter 4, page 157.
[110]  Copy-book of Gerard Philips, 16.12.1889; a letter to Emile Garcke.
[111]  Cf. Chapter 4, pages 153 ff.

complication, albeit unvoiced, which already existed in the association between Gerard and Reesse, both engineers and of whom the latter was the elder by five years and had earlier held the position of factory manager.

Needless to say, Gerard himself was determined to engage an electrician, a man 'able to plan and fit up the factory and to manage the works'.[112] And he made it very plain to Robertson that there were numerous applicants for the post, including highly qualified men. We may assume that Robertson sought to emulate the status of his compatriot, Frederic Roberts Pope, who in 1889 had been offered a partnership by Messrs Goossens on the grounds of his knowledge and skill. We would, however, make the point that at the Venlo works Pope was alone in possessing technical know-how. It seems to us that, prior to the interview in Amsterdam, Robertson anticipated finding a situation similar to that in Venlo; but he was mistaken.

Influenced by the suggested advantages of manufacturing on a large scale from the outset, Gerard and Reesse proved willing in principle to consider enlarging the scale of the plan and accepting Robertson as a partner. 'Our plans have indeed not yet been fully elaborated,' Gerard informed him, 'and your knowledge of Dutch factories and prices can certainly be of value to us. Moreover, you are familiar with the language.' At this point, Gerard revealed to Robertson that it was proposed to build a factory – 'we will probably choose Breda' – of sufficient size and machinery capacity to produce 1,000 lamps a day. 'We can provide the capital necessary for a factory of that size', he added. Naturally, Gerard depended upon his father, Frederik Philips, to finance the venture. The total investment was put at ƒ75,000, comprising ƒ37,000 for the building and equipment, and ƒ38,000 to cover current assets. Gerard recognized that it might be necessary to increase the working capital at a later date, and 'in the light of our excellent contacts' it was quite conceivable that a syndicate could be formed for that purpose. Were this course to be adopted, Robertson might be offered a certain sum in shares in recognition of goodwill and patents. Everything points to Gerard having consulted his uncle, August Philips, the Amsterdam lawyer, as well as his father. Having obtained advice, he informed Robertson that such an arrangement would require a separate contract, 'since the Dutch laws don't allow such seemingly gratuitous allotments to be incorporated with the articles of association'.[113]

Before the question was examined in detail, it was agreed that Robertson

---

[112] Copy-book of Gerard Philips, pages 149 and 150 (date illegible); a letter to Robertson written on or about 9.11.1890.
[113] Copy-book of Gerard Philips, pages 149 and 150.

should draw up a calculation showing the net return and report on the comparative advantages of plans providing for:

an output of 1,000 lamps per day, commencing with 500 but with a
   building and machinery large enough for 1,000, and
an output of 2,500 lamps per day.

Gerard went on to explain that the company envisaged making lamps in all common ratings up to 100 candlepower and that they therefore had to base their calculations on standard costs for materials, fuel and labour. Where costing was concerned, he had taken a lesson from Garcke's handbook, 'Factory Accounts – their Principles and Practice', which had been published in 1887. The most subtle pointer came with a request to Robertson to prepare two distinct cost estimates, the first ignoring any remuneration of the partners, the second including such payments to the management as he considered appropriate. Robertson was thus called upon to put a value on his own services.

Robertson's attention was temporarily distracted from this task by a fierce but short-lived dispute which concerned the reputation of the lamps made in Middelburg, and which patently offended him. Gerard, who had investigated various lamps and criticized the quality of German brands as well as the one from Middelburg, probably based his remarks on information supplied by Mijnssen & Co., the Amsterdam agents for the Boudewijnse lamp, who just then had cause to complain about caps parting from lamps. Incidentally, the factory replaced the faulty lamps, but Boudewijnse enquired of Mijnssen whether the damage was not perhaps caused by carelessness, observing that he had seldom if ever received a complaint of this nature from his other customers. He had evidence that all the lamps had burned, so that 'the fault cannot have occurred when they were being fitted'.[114]

At about the same time, but from quite a different angle, Boudewijnse reiterated his views on the quality of incandescent lamps. He was moved not by a complaint from a customer, but by the growing anxiety which he, as a manufacturer, felt on this score. Under the pressure of steadily declining prices and keen competition, it was becoming 'ever more difficult to make lamps which are as nearly perfect as possible'.[115] Apart from the manufacturing problem, he was hinting at the growing popularity of the incandescent lamp, which implied that it could no longer be treated as a

114  Copy-book of Boudewijnse, 20.10.1890.
115  Ibid., 15.11.1890; a letter to Th. van Doesburg, Rotterdam.

showpiece costing a guilder or more, but had become a consumer item which had to be turned out, profitably, for thirty or forty cents. Thus, like others, the Boudewijnse works, which had gone into production in 1887, saw itself obliged to change drastically the largely craft-based methods which it had so far employed. To express the situation in economic terms, the market demanded that the entrepreneur perform his classic role and adopt the required, new approach to manufacturing and marketing – an approach for which Gerard Philips, among others, was preparing himself, and in which Boudewijnse and Robertson also recognized that their future lay. The last two, in Middelburg, not only faced the problem of cheap labour, but also a financial hurdle in the shape of unwillingness on the part of local capitalists[116] to invest in modernization just when the market was falling.

On 12 November 1890, Robertson submitted the cost estimates to Gerard and Reesse.[117] He demonstrated that a factory producing 500 lamps a day could at best cover its operating costs, and that only with a higher output could any real profits be anticipated. He had computed the trading result at 500 lamps a day on the basis of his experience at the Boudewijnse factory and related this to current market prices. For higher levels of production, he based his figures on his own alternative concept of a modern operation, which he termed 'the manufacture of lamps under improved conditions of labour and improved methods of manufacture'. This shows once again that the project in which Robertson sought to become involved was in fact the same as was envisaged by Gerard Philips, but with the vital distinction that the latter was still in the development stage and therefore preferred to advance step by step along his own, necessarily longer, road. The actual cause of the breach between these two, each of whom was to become a very large manufacturer of incandescent lamps, thus lay not in differences in assessment, but in the recognition that their goals were basically identical. Viewed objectively, the delicate question put to Robertson concerning the conditions on which he would join the firm was superfluous, for he was not interested in the vacant position of factory foreman, and a partnership did not fit in with Gerard's plans or, in all probability, with those of Frederik Philips, who will certainly have demurred to such a proposition. He, too, must have favoured cautious progress alone above the sudden acceptance

---

116  Copy-book of Boudewijnse, 20.11.1894.
117  Neither the cost estimate nor the related documents from Reesse were among the material at our disposal. The quotations are drawn from letters written by Gerard Philips.

of the risks inherent in a larger-scale operation, and this under the guidance of a third party. Gerard's action in writing to Robertson on 14 November 1890, informing him that: 'We think that the business is too small to allow three partners'[118] is therefore completely understandable. He went on to explain that he and his partner(s) felt that such a structure would be so heavy and so risky as to make it impossible to attract the additional capital required for a larger operation. We may assume that Frederik Philips, and perhaps Reesse also, imposed limits in this respect. They thus deliberately opted, partly on financial grounds, for the small incandescent lamp scheme. The original plan, not 1,000 or 2,500 lamps a day to start with, but a 'pilot plant' producing about 500, whether profitable or not, was maintained.

As for Robertson, he continued his quest, stimulated by Boudewijnse's action in reducing his salary, which he considered too high. To Robertson, who anyway was anxious to improve his position, this step was as sudden as it was unpalatable. 'I thought that you would not make this change, as our orders have made a large increase of late', he informed his employer.[119] In March 1891 he left the factory in Middelburg and travelled to Vienna where, on the instructions of Messrs Latzko & Scharf, he set up the Electrische Glühlampen-Fabrik 'Watt', of which he became technical manager and partner. This modern works, which by about 1895 was producing 5,000 lamps a day, would continue to play an important role for many years.[120] In 1894 Robertson returned to England, where he supervised the commissioning of an incandescent lamp factory for the General Electric Company, Ltd. This was housed in the buildings at Brook Green, in London, which Brush had earlier built but was unable to use owing to the Edison & Swan monopoly.

With the lapsing of the Edison patents in 1893 came Mr Robertson's opportunity. Why should not the electric lamp-making industry, as yet in its infancy, and capable of giving employment to so many thousands of workers, be as successfully carried on in England as abroad?

The same idea had long been present in other minds, and by a fortunate combination of circumstances Mr Robertson found the field fully prepared for him.[121]

Until the appearance of the metal-filament lamp, Robertson was a household name in incandescent lamps in Britain. As entrepreneurs, he and the

---

[118] Copy-book of Gerard Philips, 14.11.1890.
[119] C. J. Robertson to C. Boudewijnse, 3.1.1891; archives of the Vitrite Works, Middelburg.
[120] In 1902 they sold 2.5 million lamps.
[121] Cf. Henry Loring, *From the Beginning* (Story of the 'Robertson' Electric Glow Lamp), 1905, 21.

first generation of lamp manufacturers in that country had paid dearly for national patent legislation.

To fill the post of electrician in their projected factory, Gerard and Reesse chose Emile Woschke,[122] a German citizen and the foreman of the Seel works near Brussels. Gerard had earlier made thorough enquiries of the Berlin engineer Grünwald, whom he had met at Seel, concerning Woschke's possible suitability for the post of production engineer. Woschke was also informed of the plan to set up an incandescent lamp factory with a daily output of 500 lamps and of the vacancy for an experienced man to equip this and take charge of the production. He must have felt less than secure at Seel. The company, whose affairs were discussed in an earlier chapter,[123] was in financial difficulties. Its former chief engineer, J. Zacharias, informed Wilhelm von Siemens on 15 April 1890 that the factory 'has dismissed its entire staff and now operates solely with master foremen'.[124] During the period of experimentation in Amsterdam, Gerard had journeyed to Brussels to see Woschke, and during their meeting had consulted him on certain details of filament manufacture.[125] In December 1890, Woschke received an invitation to visit Zaltbommel, where he was to come face to face with Frederik Philips. 'You may be certain that you are dealing with reputable people', Gerard reassured him in a letter which also contained exact details of the rail connections through to Zaltbommel, where he would board an omnibus. The visit led to Woschke, as the first employee of the nascent enterprise, being engaged with effect from 1 February 1891 at a salary of $f$120 per month.[126] Gerard, with obvious satisfaction at this decisive step, proceeded to bring him up to date with the preparations which had already been made, after which the two men exchanged information, mainly of a technical nature. While the company was still without a factory, Woschke was obliged to remain in Brussels; but on 2 May the moment of departure for Eindhoven arrived. In the interim, contact was maintained by letter, and it is this exchange of correspondence[127] which enables us to throw a little more light on a number of events which occurred on the eve of the formal establishment of the

---

[122] According to the Civil Register, Eindhoven: Ernest Auguste Emile Woschke, engineer, born at Stargard, Germany, on 11.9.1856.

[123] Cf. Chapter 2, page 70.

[124] Siemens Archives, No. 21 Lg 315, Munich.

[125] *Nieuwe Rotterdamsche Courant*, 28.3.1916.

[126] Current Account Book of Frederik Philips, folio 8, 1891; Philips Archives, Eindhoven.

[127] Copy-book of Gerard Philips; four letters in all.

company. Various extracts have appeared in previous chapters. As a product of the months leading up to the founding, the letters afford a picture of Gerard's intense and simultaneous occupation with all the facets of incandescent lamp manufacture, notably the preparation of the filament, the equipping of the factory and the estimation of the sums to be invested and the cost prices of the finished products. The statement by Gerard in one of the letters, 'I am far from satisfied with many details of the manufacturing process',[128] leaves no doubt that the technical preparations were far from complete when Woschke arrived.

As the shape of the company became clearer, its founders were moved to review the implications of their plan and also their individual aims. Whereas they had merely set out on a reconnaissance, more specifically in the field of chemical technology, by the end of 1890 they had an indication of the size of the factory, the time which this would take to get into production and the financial risk involved. The last two factors may have caused Reesse, whose industrial ambitions had earlier been dashed, to doubt the wisdom of participating in a new company which as yet offered no prospect of a suitable reward for enterprise. At the very least, this was a reason to bring up the question of formalizing his partnership. Viewed objectively, could the company, with its deliberately small scale, afford the luxury of two highly skilled engineers from the start? The technical and economic information furnished by Robertson would have caused both men to think again. Quite by chance, something then occurred which could not fail to be noticed in that small environment: C. D. Nagtglas Versteeg,[129] the only engineering graduate from Delft to be employed in the Dutch incandescent lamp industry in 1890, left the Boudewijnse factory.

These factors, together with the sharp fall in lamp prices and its effect on the market, then obliged Reesse, or rather Gerard and Reesse together, to make a crucial choice. But clearly the issue was one which also had to be judged on its commercial merits by Frederik Philips, whose involvement in the preparatory phase of the incandescent lamp project was much closer than has ever been revealed. In December 1890, Frederik Philips travelled to Amsterdam, where he studied the situation in company with Gerard and Reesse. Before the month had elapsed, the decision was reached and Gerard informed Woschke: 'I shall not be running the business in company with Mr Reesse, but alone with the support of my father.'[130] In this context, we

128  Ibid., 30.12.1890.
129  Copy-book of Boudewijnse, 3.10.1890.
130  Copy-book of Gerard Philips, 30.12.1890.

would reiterate that it had always been the intention that Frederik Philips should be a partner and co-financier, irrespective of any role which Reesse might play; this would also have been the case if the proposed association with Brush had come about. Now only he and Gerard were left.

Reesse, having withdrawn from the project, went to the Dutch West Indies, where at the request of the Municipal Archivist of Amsterdam he spent several years writing a history of the Amsterdam sugar trade from the early seventeenth century until 1813. In 1899 he was invited to take charge of the Noord-Nederlandsche Beetwortelsuikerfabriek, a beet sugar refinery, at Vierverlaten, near Groningen, where he remained until 1907. After his death in 1910, his friend F. J. Lugt completed the manuscript of the second volume of the history of the sugar trade.[131] Lugt had been a director of the Maatschappij 'Electra' since 1892; he, too, remained on friendly terms with Gerard for many years. The experiments in the house by the Herengracht continued until the end of February 1891. On the last day of the month Gerard informed Woschke: 'I leave for Zaltbommel today.' The 'Amsterdam period', which was so important a phase in the life of Gerard Philips, had come to an end.

To some extent, the choice of location for the factory was still open. At the same time, all the signs point to a preference for one of the industrial regions of North Brabant, in view of the availability of labour there.[132] The first possibility to be discussed, in November 1890, was the baronial town of Breda. A less predominantly Roman Catholic town, yet set within the labour catchment area of Brabant, Breda almost certainly represented a personal preference on the part of Reesse, who was drawn to the Protestant faith and felt more at home in a Protestant environment. Had his association with Gerard continued, these factors could have played a part, but no more than that. More significantly, but of less appeal to a company considering settling there, 'senior army officers, senior civil servants, landowners and merchants' held sway in Breda,[133] a fact which scarcely offered any guarantee of flexibility. Furthermore, as Van den Eerenbeemt points out, a section of the working class in the town (and this applied also in 's-Hertogenbosch) was not well equipped mentally to perform regular work at a high tempo in a factory, which was precisely what was required in

---

[131] *Algemeen Handelsblad*, 11.10.1910, 13.10.1910 and 3.10.1911.

[132] Cf. Chapter 4, page 173.

[133] H. F. J. M. van den Eerenbeemt and R. M. A. A. Geuljans, in 'Breda mét en Eindhoven zonder Philips'; jubilee issue of the *Philips Koerier*, 3.9.1966, 39 ff.

an incandescent lamp works. From this point of view, rural Eindhoven was a more suitable location. In 1891, Breda had just over 20,000 inhabitants, compared with 4,500 in Eindhoven. If, however, we include the surrounding villages of Gestel, Blaarthem, Stratum, Strijp, Tongelre and Woensel – which until 1920 remained separate municipalities – the population of the Eindhoven region at that time numbered about 19,000.[134] In quantitative terms, the supply of labour was thus virtually on a par with Breda. The lamp factory established in Eindhoven in 1891 was followed a year later by one in Breda;[135] this was owned by Rogier, Smagghe & Co., whose existence was relatively brief, though this was not governed to any significant extent by its choice of location. We shall revert to this company in the next volume.

In the choice of location, the views of Frederik Philips, who had spent several decades in the tobacco trade in North Brabant, naturally carried a great deal of weight. With his involvement in the coffee market, and partly through his banking activities, he was oriented towards 's-Hertogenbosch; however, the emphasis of his principal occupation, the trade in tobacco and cigars, lay more on Eindhoven and its environs. External sources admittedly contain references to negotiations in Den Bosch,[136] but our information concerning Frederik and Gerard Philips does not confirm this. Nor has any document which explains the choice of location, if indeed this was considered in detail beforehand, come to light. There have been attempts at reasoning whether it was coincidence or predestination which pointed the way to Eindhoven, but as far as locational factors are concerned – if this is not too modern a term to apply to a comparatively small factory in the process of gestation – there is no firm evidence of an overriding consideration save the availability of the right type of labour. On 28 March 1891, a site of just over 1,200 square metres, situated on the former Westbinnensingel in Breda,[137] was purchased by Gerard Philips. However, a month earlier, in a reference to the factory in Eindhoven, Gerard had informed Woschke:

I am at the moment still negotiating for the purchase of an existing factory building. I have been offered a nice, square, single-storey building, not many years old, complete with a steam engine and boiler, but the building is entirely of brick and

[134]  Brand, *Eindhoven*, 19.
[135]  Council Report, Breda, 1892.
[136]  H. F. J. M. van den Eerenbeemt, *Ontwikkelingslijnen en scharnierpunten in het Brabants industrieel bedrijf, 1777–1914*, 1977, 121; see also K. Spierings, *Wij waren nog een stadje*, 1966, ch. 62.
[137]  Deed enacted by P. C. A. Kuypers, notary of Breda, on 28.3.1891; the purchase price was *f* 2,500. The land was resold for the same price in 1895.

iron, and I am afraid that the iron will affect the instruments. I should be pleased to hear your opinion. The building measures 18 × 20 metres.[138]

One possible explanation is that the negotiations for the purchase of the factory broke down, and that the land was purchased irrespective of any real intention to settle in Breda; but that no further action was taken in anticipation of fresh developments in the more favoured Eindhoven. If so, this would indicate that Frederik Philips, the merchant, correctly assessed the situation, with all its far-reaching consequences. We cannot escape the impression that Frederik Philips preferred Eindhoven from the outset, and that even when Breda was mentioned he stuck to his own choice, which was also the more favourable in relation to the German hinterland. This would explain Gerard's letter to the impatient Woschke, informing him that 'various circumstances have resulted in the matter being postponed'.

The dénouement came on 27 April 1891 at Stoot's coffee-house, which was situated in the hall in the Stratumseind used by the Eindhoven Male Voice Choir. There, Josephus Johannes Fens, notary of Eindhoven, publicly auctioned the factory which had been described to Woschke. It was purchased by the mechanical engineer Gerard Leonard Frederik Philips for the sum of ƒ12,150.[139] Of a serious intention to build a factory on the land bought in Breda, there is no evidence.

The factory in Eindhoven, which had been unoccupied for some time, stood in an old district which was nicknamed Kateknip. It had previously belonged to J. F. Schröder & Co., manufacturers of buckskin. It stood in the Vrijstraat, and was bounded on the western side by the Vest canal, which at that time was not linked to the 'Knip', later the Emmasingel, by a bridge. The 45 h.p. steam engine and the associated facilities, including a chimney, had been installed in 1869 by the original owners, the 'Stoom-Fabriek van Draadnagels, Springveren Enz., de Gebroeders Raijmakers', whose principal manufactures were wire nails and leaf springs. The factory was large enough to accommodate sixty workers and met the needs of Philips & Co. until about 1896, when the first extension was built. The refurbishment of the steam engine, the preparations for the electrical installation and the procurement of instruments, apparatus and other requisites took up the whole of Gerard's time in the remaining months of 1891.

By the time the works was ready to go into production and all the necessary materials were in stock, the list of assets and the related costs were

---

[138] Copy-book of Gerard Philips, 28.2.1891.
[139] Deed enacted before J. J. Fens, notary of Eindhoven, 27.4.1891.

The Eindhoven lamp factory, 1891

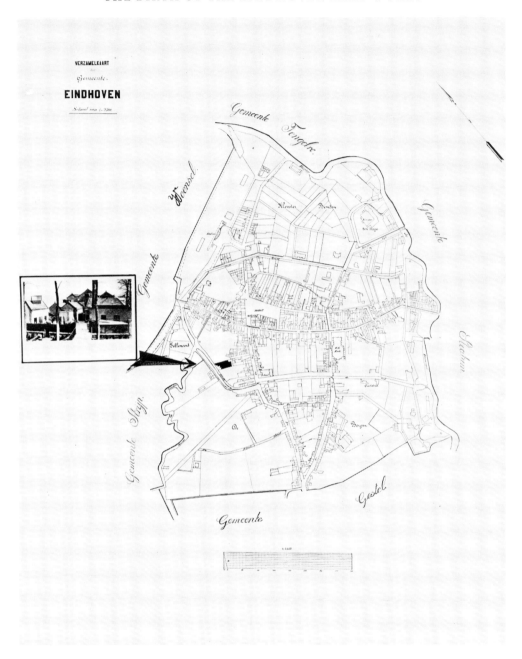

Plan of Eindhoven, c. 1890

Table 23. *Summary of the assets of Philips & Co., Eindhoven, 1892*[a]

| | |
|---|---|
| Factory buildings at Emmasingel | ƒ12,650 |
| Steam engine, boiler, transmission system, etc. | 5,885 |
| Electrical installation, cables, dynamos | 4,250 |
| Equipment for glassblowing department | 445 |
|    pump installation | 2,205 |
|    flashing apparatus | 300 |
|    capping equipment | 340 |
| Annealing furnace | 100 |
| Equipment for chemical laboratory | 510 |
| Instruments and measuring apparatus | 1,835 |
| Tools | 1,110 |
| Equipment for stores, furniture | 1,855 |
| Factory stocks | 4,745 |
| Total | ƒ36,230 |

*Note:*
[a] Copy-book of Gerard Philips, 5.2.1892; a letter to the Amsterdam underwriters, C. B. J. Mijnssen

as shown in Table 23. The initial capital of Philips & Co., which amounted to ƒ75,000,[140] was greater than that of any other Dutch incandescent lamp manufacturer, but this was not immediately apparent from the scale of investment. Even in the longer term, neither Gerard nor Frederik Philips could have anticipated a business of the magnitude to which their initiative was eventually to lead. Their object was a healthy enterprise – a specialized incandescent lamp works – which could stand up well to comparison with others like Goossens & Pope in Venlo or Schöffer in Gelnhausen. Nothing more need be said about Gerard Philips' knowledge and experience in the field of electrical engineering. In this respect, the Eindhoven company differed greatly from most of its Dutch rivals, who were highly dependent upon foreign, largely British, experts. To compensate for his lack of specific experience in the manufacture of incandescent lamps, Gerard deliberately set off at a slow pace, giving himself time to acquire the necessary knowledge before embarking on mass production. The clearest evidence of this is to be found in the production figures for 1892 and 1893: 11,000 and 45,000 lamps respectively, which was exceptionally small in comparison with the other factories in the Netherlands. The success of this policy was manifested in 1894, when the company made a modest profit in spite of a dramatic fall in lamp prices. The suggestion of failure, leading Frederik and

[140] Current Account Book of Frederik Philips.

Gerard to decide in that year to sell the business,[141] must therefore be viewed as just another legend. It is noteworthy in this context that the 's-Hertogenbosch agent of De Nederlandsche Bank wrote in his report for 1893 that the lamps from the Eindhoven factory were 'selling well'.[142]

As the fifth entrant into the field of incandescent lamp manufacture in the Netherlands, Philips & Co. were relatively late starters. They arrived on the scene just as the craft-based method of manufacture was making way for the industrial process. The incandescent lamp had become an article of mass consumption and consequently had to be an article of mass production. By commencing at that juncture, Philips & Co. were spared the difficult and costly conversion which was forced upon their forerunners, and benefited greatly from a level-headed approach to the economic and technical realities. But the company's greatest strength perhaps lay in the fact that it rested on the firm foundations of the Philips family business, generations old and in 1891 personified in the merchant, Frederik Philips, without whose enterprising spirit and active interest in technical progress the lamp factory in Eindhoven would not have been established. On 15 May 1891, he and his son Gerard appended their signatures to a private partnership agreement. Eight days later, the document, the text of which is reproduced below, was lodged with Pieter Jacobus van der Feen, Clerk of the Divisional Court in Eindhoven.

The party of the first part, Benjamin Frederik David Philips, merchant, residing at Zaltbommel
and the party of the second part, Gerard Leonard Frederik Philips, mechanical engineer, residing at Eindhoven,
hereby declare that they have entered into a partnership with the object of manufacturing incandescent lamps and other electrical articles, and also engaging in trade therein, and this on the following conditions:
    Article One: The partnership is entered into for a period of five successive years commencing on the fifteenth of May eighteen hundred and ninety-one and therefore ending on the fourteenth of May eighteen hundred and ninety-six, but shall be deemed to have been extended from year to year unless six months' notice of termination has been given.
    Article Two: The partnership shall be domiciled at Eindhoven and shall trade under the name Philips & Co.
    Article Three: Both the partners are authorized to sign documents as agents of the aforementioned company, but solely in matters which concern this partnership.
    Both partners are authorized to act on behalf of the partnership, to pay and

141  Bouman, *Growth of an Enterprise*, 26.
142  Report 1892/93 by Van Lanschot to the Board of De Nederlandsche Bank, Amsterdam; archives of De Nederlandsche Bank, Amsterdam.

receive monies and to enter into obligations, with the proviso that for the acceptance of loans and the granting of suretyship their joint signatures shall be required.[143]

Gerard's share in the company amounted to $f$ 18,500, which sum was advanced by his father, who thus took upon himself the whole of the financial risk pertaining to the venture.

Gerard Philips, the working partner and technical architect of the Eindhoven lamp works, stood on the threshold of an illustrious career as an engineer and entrepreneur. He was convinced that he was on the right road, and would succeed.[144] The silent partner, Frederik Philips, merchant, manufacturer and banker, turned his attention back to his own affairs. In June 1891 he took over the tobacco trading and manufacturing firm of J. W. van Nouhuys in Zaltbommel.

[143] The agreement was registered at Eindhoven on 26.5.1891.
[144] *Eindhovensch Dagblad*, 31.5.1916: an interview with Gerard Philips.

# EPILOGUE

In the preceding chapters we have sought to explain how the incandescent lamp industry in the Netherlands came into being. In this context we have examined, in some cases in detail, a wide range of matters in the area of electrical engineering. This excursion into the territory surrounding our subject, the history of N.V. Philips' Gloeilampenfabrieken, was not part of a well-considered plan, but came about as a result of our researches. Had we been unwilling to divert our eyes from the chosen path, fascinating questions concerning the origin of the enterprise, both in the narrower sense and when set against the wider background of technical and economic developments, would have remained unanswered. Much of the material necessary for a sound insight into the principal subject had to be sought abroad, and this, too, broadened the area of investigation and immediately drew attention to the international character possessed by the incandescent lamp industry from its earliest beginnings. This, as we have seen, enabled Dutch entrepreneurs – who had previously made no contribution to the development of the incandescent lamp – to grasp the commercial opportunity which its appearance presented and, by importing the technical knowledge which they lacked, quickly to get on equal terms with the established manufacturers. This inborn flexibility was the starting point for the development of an independent lamp industry in the Netherlands; independent in the sense that it came into being not only without links with major electrical engineering concerns, but even at their expense.

Closer study of the incandescent lamp industry in Britain reveals that the patent problems which existed there helped, albeit unintentionally, to eliminate the early lack of specialist knowledge on the part of the Dutch. Germany and France, and beyond them the remainder of Europe, represented a very substantial market at close range. Those who secured an *entrée* to this international field of activity found themselves in a market in which the growth of demand at times exceeded even the wildest expectations. Apart

from the individual ability of the entrepreneurs attracted by this new phenomenon to react adequately to it, the Netherlands' favourable position – which in economic and geographical terms allowed of a very wide choice of markets – should not be underestimated. These basic conditions are seen to have been fully applicable to the birth of Philips & Co. and to the incandescent lamp factories earlier established in the country. By 1890 the Netherlands had the second largest lamp industry in Europe, after Germany,[1] a fact which acted as a beacon and reinforced confidence among Dutch producers in the future of this branch of industry.

Mass production, which was Gerard Philips' aim from the outset, was the product of, and the commercial answer to, this development. It was also the only basis for a lamp factory capable of competing in the long term. Indications that he was indeed striving in this direction[2] were found in a number of documents, but their precise implications could be determined only after a thorough analysis of the manufacturing methods employed at the time. The investigation also provided an answer to the question of which procedure Gerard employed to make his filaments. It showed that Bouman was in error in assuming that the filament was 'a slight improvement' on the one made by Edison.[3] Moreover, it showed that Bouman's description of the homogenization of the filament in an atmosphere of hydrocarbon gas as if this were a new method of manufacture devised by Gerard Philips,[4] was in fact the flashing process which almost all lamp manufacturers had been using for many years. These and other discoveries necessitated a reappraisal of the traditional image of Gerard Philips as an inventor rather than a businessman – a misconception which also lurks in the inference that he had little understanding of 'the economic problems associated with the running of a modern industrial undertaking'[5] and, to give a concrete example, that with his figure of 500 lamps per day he had underestimated the unfulfilled demand on the lamp market. The considerations which led Gerard to set the initial capacity of his works, having rationally weighed the various technical and economic factors, indicate precisely the reverse; these were dealt with at length in Chapter 6. His decision to commence with 500 lamps a day, on a small scale, stemmed not from any estimate of unfulfilled demand,[6] but from the realization that he

[1]  Cf. Chapter 4, page 176.          [2]  Cf. Chapter 6, pages 258 ff.
[3]  Schiff, *Industrialization*, 59.
[4]  Bouman, *Growth of an Enterprise*, 34.
[5]  Ibid., 21.
[6]  In 1890, the annual consumption of lamps in Europe was approximately 5 million; between then and 1900 the figure increased by an average of 2 million annually.

had to master the art of manufacturing incandescent lamps before embarking on production on an industrial scale. Only after a year or two was he
able to pluck the first fruits of his cautious approach. The older Dutch lamp
companies which failed to make the transition to industrial production
soon disappeared from the scene. It was thus not a miscalculation on the
part of a man poorly versed in business matters, but a course carefully
charted by an accurate researcher and capable entrepreneur who knew
exactly what he was doing. A similar attitude must be attributed to Frederik
Philips – the first to introduce mechanization in the manufacture of cigars in
the Netherlands – whose role in the establishment of the lamp factory went
far beyond that of a financier.

Round about 1890, profound technological changes occurred in the
manufacture of incandescent lamps, chiefly as a result of the introduction of
mass production. Beside the necessary skills, lamp manufacture called for
scientific ability,[7] and even at that time was described as 'one of the most
intricate and difficult examples of scientific industry',[8] a description which
it was to retain as far as manufacturing methods were concerned. It says
much that, under the influence of patent protection in the more advanced
industrial countries of Europe, this manufacturing process should have
been undertaken in a land which had a lot of ground to make up in the
economic and technical fields, and where, certainly at that time, the
conditions for the establishment of an electrical engineering industry were
completing lacking, as were facilities for the training of electrical engineers.
Five years abroad helped Gerard Philips to acquire knowledge and
experience which the Netherlands could not provide, but for which it
offered scope for development. Gerard, of course, opted for electrical
engineering in order to deploy his own talents. But in doing so he chose a
very different path from that hitherto taken by graduates of mechanical
engineering in the Netherlands. The results can be put on a par with the
lasting impulses towards industrialization in this country after 1890.
Together with a handful of contemporary engineering graduates who were
similarly obliged to seek their training abroad, he paved the way for the
remarkably viable electrical engineering industry in the Netherlands. A
similar claim to the role of pioneer is made by those young men, many of
them without adequate secondary or advanced education, who
accumulated the necessary knowledge while working for electrical firms
and later put this to practical use, in many cases as installation contractors.

---

[7] Cf. Chapter 2, page 65.          [8] Cf. Chapter 6, page 265.

Research into this aspect was also among the reasons for not keeping our eyes fixed on the lamp factory in Eindhoven.

The need for a wider insight into the factors which motivated producers and the consumer aspect of electric lighting was another reason for broadening the base of this study. This led us to the problem of classifying the categories of producers and consumers at the time of the earliest applications for electricity. If we disregard low-voltage applications, the electrical industry was largely synonymous with electric lighting until about 1890. Three main types of undertaking existed in the Netherlands: electric lighting companies, which generated and distributed current; installation contractors, most of whom were also importers and traders in electrical articles; and the producers of such articles, which included incandescent lamps, lamp bases and small dynamos.

The coming of arc lighting and incandescent lighting round about 1880 marked a new application for which, if it was to be widely exploited, an operational basis had to be devised. The creation of demand presupposed the construction of central generating stations which, within comparatively small areas, could as it were bring electric lighting to every home. We refer here to the initial demand, and definitely not to the subsequent moves towards the mass consumption of electricity. The leading electrical manufacturers, such as Siemens & Halske and AEG, turned their attention to this new market and found themselves faced with the dilemma of having to build central stations in order to stimulate demand, but without tying up their resources for an unlimited period. To this end they encouraged the establishment of independent lighting companies in which they participated, albeit in a limited way. In the majority of instances, the aim was that local bankers or other interested parties should take over the shares once the company was operating. In the case of the Nederlandsche Electriciteit-Maatschappij in Amsterdam, which was founded in 1882 to represent the Compagnie Continentale Edison, of Paris,[9] the majority of the partners were local capitalists who saw a future in the new style of lighting. By this entrepreneurial activity, they also sought to acquire a stake in a modern urban amenity which, like gas lighting before it, promised a sound investment at a calculable risk – provided, that is, that it was covered by the guarantee of a long-term monopoly. This was accordingly the principal aim, though in the Netherlands the efforts met with only limited success. At the outset, the early English and French electric lighting companies – many

[9]  Cf. Chapter 3, page 114; the NEM also attempted to obtain a concession in Rotterdam in 1882.
[10]  Cf. Chapter 3, pages 126 ff.

of which are now seen to have had but a brief existence – served as a model
for Dutch investors; but fairly soon after the Paris Electricity Exhibition of
1881, a climax, their hopes were dashed by the financial disasters in
England and France, for which a combination of unbridled speculation and
stagnation was to blame.[10] After this, Germany, where electric lighting was
introduced somewhat later and developed in a much more stable manner,
served as the example. Those in the Netherlands who in 1885 made a fresh
attempt to secure concessions based their plans on the German situation,
both in technical matters and as regards the terms on which a concession
should be granted.

We have shown how fierce competition grew between the candidates for
a concession in Amsterdam. Because the demand for electric lighting there
did not really manifest itself until the late 1880s, it was only then that the
political dialogue concerning the integration of electricity into the social
pattern arose. In 1889, the secessionist group of radical liberals headed by
Treub checked the advance of the conservative forces in the capital, most of
whom favoured a private monopoly.[11] As a result, the view prevailed that
the terms of the electricity concession should accord more closely with the
common interest than did those of the gas concession granted a few years
earlier. Electricity thus brought about a reversal of policy at the City Hall;
at that juncture, the Council had no choice but to grant a concession, albeit
on very rigorous conditions. With this the illusion, in Amsterdam and
elsewhere, of a long-term future for privately owned electricity undertakings was shattered. Where it mattered most, in the principal towns, they had
fulfilled their historical role of promoting electric light and creating a
demand for it. After the events in Amsterdam, no town of any size in the
Netherlands granted an electricity concession to a private company.

The ending of the struggle for long-term concessions did not delay the
introduction of electrical applications.[12] It did, however, relieve the central
stations of the implicit obligation to place construction, installation and the
supply of materials and lamps in the hands of a single manufacturer. What
in fact occurred, on political grounds, was the dismantling of the economic
framework of Edison's 'complete electric lighting system', which rested
upon a strong patent position, or on the creation of monopolies. The effect
of this was to create a wider, separate market for numerous electrical
articles, including the incandescent lamp; a market in which comparatively

[11] Cf. Chapter 5, pages 291 ff.
[12] De Jonge, *Die Industrialisatie*, 180: after 1891, the electrification proceeded rapidly in the
Netherlands.

small, specialist manufacturers could, subject to the rules of competition, find a niche. The complete systems, the supply of which had hitherto been the prerogative of full-line producers, were separated into their individual components, and on the markets for these, new suppliers with varying degrees of industrial and commercial strength appeared.

For Gerard Philips, who had been confronted with similar developments while acting as agent for AEG in Amsterdam and, earlier still, when he worked in the electric lighting department of Brush in Berlin, the decentralization provided an economic basis on which to found his own lamp factory and to engage in competitive trade free of any concentration of power in the international electrical industry. It also enabled the leading independent lamp makers in Hungary and Austria to operate freely.[13] Interestingly, the competitive struggle was often of a mainly technical nature, waged between specialized incandescent lamp manufacturers and the managers of incandescent lamp departments of firms which, at least in the period with which we are concerned, attached much more importance to heavy electrical equipment than to lamps.

To the Dutch installation contractors, for whom the period round about 1890 was one of major expansion, the diversification meant a larger market and more freedom of action than would have existed if so important an area as the lighting of a city had been the subject of a monopoly and all installation work had been carried out by one party, and a foreign party at that. Gerard Philips had good reason for advising Rathenau that his demand for the sole right to carry out house-to-house installations in Amsterdam was politically unacceptable and should be abandoned.[14] The Amsterdam contractors, who had started out in business only a short while before, were not slow to react to the threat of exclusion. Not as a serious gesture, but rather to prolong the debate, two of their number, G. Groeneveld and P. H. ter Meulen, promptly submitted applications for a concession. Their action was typical of the incisiveness of this group of entrepreneurs, about whom we know little as individuals. Their backgrounds differed, a few having studied at Delft while the majority were craftsmen, but they set up in business and thus gave rise to a new branch of industry.

The growth of the installation sector was not limited to the large towns,

[13]  Basch, *Die Entwicklung*, 78: 'In Oesterreich-Ungarn und Holland war die Glühlampenindustrie zu Hause, und hatte in der kurzen Zeit ihres Bestehens stark an Ausdehnung gewonnen und war sogar exportfähig geworden.'

[14]  Minutes of Council meeting, 23.1.1889, pages 52 and 53.

but extended to other parts of the country. In the early days, modernization in the shape of electric lighting in factories and workshops in such industries as diamond processing, textiles and food products provided the greater part of the work. From 1891 onwards, when electric motors and electric traction were increasingly used, electrical engineering and those responsible for its introduction – the installation contractors – can be said to have played an active part in the nation's industrial development. During the 1890s, a number of installers in small towns and villages became private suppliers of electricity, in some cases using a separate generator, in others by taking current from an industrial power supply. Systems of the latter type operated in Terborg and Vreeland, the sources being an iron foundry and a dairy plant respectively. With the severing of the ties inherent in the 'complete electric lighting system', the installation contractors commenced to trade in incandescent lamps of various makes, eventually becoming the main channel of distribution. We have already shown how, when production at the Eindhoven factory was just getting into its stride, Gerard Philips looked mainly to the installation contractors, who were the principal link with the domestic market.[15] He had already established contact with Van Rietschoten & Houwens in Rotterdam, and in 1890 he approached Mijnssen & Co. in Amsterdam. Both were leaders in their field and had been among the pioneers. Gerard used his good offices on behalf of the latter firm to obtain orders for electrical installations at the Heineken brewery and at 'Prins Hendrik Oord', the country seat of Adolph Bois-sevain, at Lage Vuursche.[16] This formed the prelude to a mutually beneficial business relationship.

The available data do not reveal the exact number of firms operating in the installation sector in the years round about 1890, but we estimate this to have been approximately fifteen. It is, however, known that in 1895 some forty persons engaged in the installation sector were members of the Nederlandsche Vereeniging voor Electrotechniek, which was established in that year. The founder members of this national electrical association numbered 146 in all, and this gives some indication of the broad spectrum of skilled men who at that time were involved in the introduction of electricity in the Netherlands.[17] The years which followed brought growth in all sectors, and even before the turn of the century the electrical industry as a whole, i.e. manufacturers, installation contractors, central stations and the telephone service, provided work for more than a thousand people.

[15] Cf. Chapter 6, pages 240 ff.     [16] Copy-book of Gerard Philips, 16.5.1890 and 19.7.1890.
[17] Cf. Chapter 4, page 177: a breakdown of the number of members from each branch of industry.

We have seen how, in the late 1880s, the tide of opinion swung against private concessionaires, including those in the field of electric lighting. This was not an isolated phenomenon. Lambers showed that the term 'De Tachtigers' (the Men of the Eighties) applies not only to the literary innovators, but also to a transformation which occurred in the socio-economic life of the country.[18] In this period, alongside the emergence of symptoms of cultural and social change, Dutch industry commenced to be a factor of importance.[19] This applied not to any one branch in particular but to a wide variety of manufacturing activities. We have already referred to the Association for the Promotion of Manufacturing and Craft Industries, a national organization which embraced industrial interests in the widest sense of the term. Like many who sought to bring about change, the organization pursued a progressive liberal policy. Its membership in the 1880s numbered more than a thousand, drawn from a surprisingly wide field of activity. In 1890, the members included more than two hundred manufacturers, a similar number of traders, about 165 craftsmen and seventeen bankers. In its approach to society, this body differed signifi-cantly from the Association of and for Dutch Industry, founded by Petrus Regout in 1862. The latter only accepted industrialists into membership, was exclusive by reason of the high membership fee, and had far fewer members.[20] It also favoured the reintroduction of patent legislation, which was described by the association of manufacturers and craftsmen as a 'reactionary principle' and, rightly, unsuited to a country which lagged behind in the industrial sense.[21] To digress for a moment, this may explain why neighbouring Belgium, an industrially more advanced country with a patent law, and also many more trained electrical engineers, was unable to develop its own incandescent lamp industry in the 1880s.

In addition to the two associations mentioned above, there were in the Netherlands the Society for the Common Weal and the Society for the Promotion of Industry. By about 1890 the latter – 'in worse health than we had believed' – faced a crisis.[22] In his history of industrialization in the Netherlands, De Jonge establishes that while both organizations counted a

---

[18] H. W. Lambers, 'De industriële ondernemer in een bewegende economische orde', in *Ondernemend Nederland 1899–1959*, edited by M. Rooij, 1959, 99.

[19] De Jonge, *Die Industrialisatie*, 267.

[20] According to Article 2 of the Articles of Association; Archives of the Department of Justice, The Hague.

[21] Report of the 27th General Meeting of the Association, 1878, 142.

[22] J. A. van Lanschot Hubrecht, 'Tweehonderd jaar geschiedenis van de Maatschappij, 1777–1977', in *De economische geschiedenis van Nederland*, edited by J. H. van Stuijvenberg, 1977, 364.

number of industrialists among their members, they were primarily societies of well-to-do citizens 'who considered it part of their duty to promote the material and moral interests of the less fortunate classes and of the nation as a whole'. As De Jonge rightly says, they were not militant bodies claiming to defend common interests.[23]

Nevertheless, and indicative of things to come, the executive committee of the Society for the Common Weal voted in 1885 for an overt change of course. The measures which it proposed included the publication of a magazine, the 'Social Weekly', which by 'stimulating, encouraging and supervising' would dispel the lethargy that gripped the various sections of the organization. Such a revival on the part of the society, however, was not welcomed in domestic political circles. Not only did it aggravate the differences of opinion within the Conservative–Liberal Party, but it also met with opposition from the Social Democrats and the Anti-Revolutionary Party in the person of its leader, Abraham Kuyper, who charged the liberals with trying to steal a march on his party.[24] W. C. Mees, who has described this development in detail,[25] states that the cumbersome sections of the organization were unable to follow the progressive ideas put forward by the executive committee or those propounded by the editorial staff of the 'Social Weekly', who included Van Marken and Mouton, both prominent figures in the APMCI. These two men, who in their more practically oriented association of manufacturers and craftsmen were far less concerned with ideological discussions on class warfare and class distinction, represented a current of opinion which genuinely sought to bring the interests of industry as a whole, including the electrical sector, to the fore.

If we are to remain within the confines of our subject, the initial development of the electrical industry, we can do no more than to refer to the reports of this Association. In the period with which we are concerned, it sought to promote the interests of industry within the overall pattern of social progress. We have examined only one moment in its history in detail: the patent debate which took place at the annual meeting in 1890. The agenda for the meeting also included social, administrative and technical issues.[26] In the last of these categories were three subjects in the electrical field: rights pertaining to the installation of intercommunal telephone lines, the dangers of overhead electricity cables and the relative merits of electric

[23] De Jonge, *De Industrialisatie*, 331.
[24] *Sociaal Weekblad*, 1887, 12.
[25] W. C. Mees, *Man van de daad – Mr Marten Mees en de opkomst van Rotterdam*, 1946, 619–26.
[26] Cf. Chapter 6, pages 239 ff.

and gas lighting in terms of safety and economy. The fact that these issues were raised and the comprehensive reports on them, produced by experts among the membership, show clearly that the Association and its supporters were also interested in *technical* innovation. To those in the newly created profession of installation contractor, it offered a perfect framework at exactly the right moment. In 1890, for example, during the battle for the concession in Amsterdam, their interests were defended by fellow members such as Alderman Serrurier and Councillor Treub.

From which sections of society did the various types of entrepreneur in the electrical industry stem? The majority of installation contractors were from the middle class and had one thing in common, namely that with at best a secondary education behind them, they had made themselves proficient in the science of electricity. As self-made men they had set out to become entrepreneurs.[27] The traditional branches of industry experienced strong growth in the period, but this came about within the framework of existing positions and a reticence to admit newcomers. Electrical engineering provided a modern vehicle in which there were places free for young businessmen who could 'pay the fare'. The majority of the opportunities lay in the installation sector, for there the need for initial capital was relatively modest. It would be a disaster, Professor J. A. Snijders of Delft observed in 1888, if the places in electrical engineering had to be given to foreigners, and 'our young men had to be satisfied with the crumbs which fall from the table'.[28] That such a situation did not arise was due in part to the fact that the opportunities which occurred in the installation sector in the development phase, between 1880 and 1890, were grasped; orders, however, were initially few and far between.

The innovations introduced by the contractors called for a system within which the freedom to engage in trade was a recognized principle. However, the elevation of installation to a profession simultaneously demanded stricter rules and official regulations than existed in most other areas; indeed these were vital if the profession was to be accepted. Just how difficult this could be was shown by the Electric Lighting Act of 1882 in Britain, which produced years of stagnation.[29] Although Britain had a substantial lead, electrification there did not get under way until 1889. The Netherlands, where the process commenced somewhat later and proceeded at a steady pace, was spared any repetition of this.

[27]  Cf. Chapter 3, pages 115–19.
[28]  J. A. Snijders, *Electrotechnisch Onderwijs aan de Polytechnische School te Delft*, 1888, 42.
[29]  Cf. Chapter 1, page 26, and Chapter 2, page 72.

As was the case with the installation contractors, a number of manufacturers were spurred on by a desire for greater social standing, albeit their
individual objectives were more varied. Willem Smit, the dynamo manufacturer, is an exception by reason of his family ties with an existing
shipbuilding company and of the 'Fabriek van Materiëel voor Electrische
Verlichting' which he established.[30] Among the incandescent lamp
manufacturers in the Netherlands, De Khotinsky, who was more of a true
inventor than any of his rivals, primarily sought social recognition. He
based his early plans on the original concept of a complete electric lighting
system, which embraced the manufacture of a source of electrical energy
and the associated lamps, and the installation of these. In 1883 his method
of working impressed the Rotterdam merchant Wilhelm Schöffer, to whom
industrial activity was vital for the progress of society. The expectations on
the part of the two men, which were closely allied to those of the electric
lighting companies of the day, were not to be fulfilled. Moreover, the
partnership between merchant and inventor did not endure. In the end,
their joint enterprise, a limited liability company, depended mainly on the
manufacture of incandescent lamps for its survival.

In the lamp producers Boudewijnse, Roothaan and Alewijnse, all very
young businessmen, we were unable to discern the idealistic motives which
inspired Schöffer. They entered the electrical industry in search of a
personal goal, hoping to find full scope for their talents. But such was their
diligence that besides setting up a lamp factory they installed electric
lighting and engaged in trade in electrical articles. They were, above all,
practical men. Like most installation contractors, they stemmed from the
middle class and set up their businesses with the aid of family capital. Their
manufacturing methods scarcely progressed beyond the craft stage, and for
this reason their future ultimately lay not in the incandescent lamp, but in
installation and the supply of components. The success which they all
achieved in these fields testifies to their adaptability as businessmen and also
to the mobility which, then and later, existed in the electrical industry.

Lastly there were Emile Goossens and Gerard Philips, each of whom
established a factory for the mass production of a single article, the
incandescent lamp. They, too, relied on family capital to finance their
ventures, which enjoyed the patronage of merchant-entrepreneurs of an
older generation with experience of the processing industry and the
European produce trade. These *hommes d'affaires* grasped opportunities

[30] Cf. Chapter 3, page 119.

for expansion which were presented by the advance of technology. For the two established houses, situated in Venlo and Zaltbommel respectively, 1889 was a turning point, for it was then that they developed an active interest in the manufacture of incandescent lamps. In that year great strides were made in the introduction of electric lighting, not only in the Netherlands but also elsewhere.[31] Members of the Goossens family established a separate company in partnership with the Englishman, Pope; at almost the same moment, the Philipses commenced discussions with Brush in London.

The formation of the two enterprises, which although similar in their industrial aims differed in their method of achieving these, has been described in detail. It is noteworthy that in both cases the process involved traditional businessmen diverting investment from commercial and craft-based activities to industrial production – a transition to the factory system which, as Brugmans has explained, was an essential element in the industrial development that occurred in the Netherlands at the end of the nineteenth century.[32] The Goossens and the Philipses took this step, not in the familiar environment of coffee and tobacco processing, but with a new product for which there was a demand and which came within the scope of their entrepreneurial skills. With the financial, technical and commercial means at their disposal, they thereby laid the foundations for the modern incandescent lamp industry in the Netherlands. Although the rates of growth of the enterprises differed, both proved capable of withstanding the war of competition which was unleashed during the 1890s, and each made its own, growing contribution to national and international lamp manufacture. Thus was created a manufacturing sector which fitted into the overall pattern of industrialization in the Netherlands after 1890 and which employed new concepts of production made possible by advances in natural science and fundamental changes in the socio-cultural and political climate.[33]

[31]  Cf. Chapter 1, page 32.
[32]  I. J. Brugmans, *Paardenkracht en mensenmacht*, 1961, 315.
[33]  De Jonge, *De Industrialisatie*, 358.

# APPENDICES

# ELECTRIC LAMPS

SPECIFICATION OF THOMAS ALVA EDISON
A.D. 1879, 10th November No. 4576

*Letters patent* to Thomas Alva Edison, of Menlo Park, in the State of New Jersey, United States of America, for the Invention of *Improvements in Electric Lamps, and in the Method of Manufacturing the same.*
Sealed the 6th February 1880, and dated the 10th November 1879.
*Provisional specification* left by the said Thomas Alva Edison at the Office of the Commissioners of Patents on the 10th November 1879.

THOMAS ALVA EDISON, of Menlo Park, in the State of New Jersey, United States of America. *Improvements in Electric Lamps, and in the Method of Manufacturing the same.*

It is necessary to practically subdivide the electric light into a great number of luminous points, so that lamps connected in multiple may be employed without the necessity of using conductors of great size for the current to the lamps. It is essential that the lamps should be of great resistance. In the Provisional Specification of Patent dated June 17th, 1879, No. 2402, I have set this forth, and obtained lamps of great resistance by employing long lengths of platinum or metallic wires pyroinsulated, and wound in such a manner that but small radiating surface is exposed to the air, although a great length of wire is used.

My present Invention relates to lamps of a similar character, except that carbon threads or strips are used in place of metallic wires. I use a block of glass, into which are sealed two platinum wires. These wires serve to convey the current to the electric lamp within a bulb, which is blown over the lamp and united to the glass block. The bulb is exhausted of air to about one millionth of an atmosphere. Upon the ends of these wires are two clamps that secure two other platinum wires. The burner consists of a filament or thread of carbon, preferably coiled, with the ends secured to the platinum wires, the whole being made as follows: –

Fibrous material, such as paper, thread, wood, or any vegetable or animal matter which can be carbonized, has the ends secured to platinum wires, the fibre is wound in such a shape as to expose the least amount of surface to radiation, such as in a helix or spiral. The helix is secured to the platinum wires by plastic carbon, and the

---

[1] See Chapter 1, page 3.

whole is placed in a closed vessel free from air, and subjected to a heat sufficient to fully carbonize the fibre, and leave nothing but carbon. At the same time the effect of the carbonization is to lock the carbon to the platinum wire, and make a good connection.

These wires are secured by the clamps to the two platinum wires in the bulb, and the bulb is exhausted of air and sealed. Lamps of one hundred ohms resistance may be made in this manner, from which light from the incandescent carbon is obtained. The destruction of the fragile carbon by oxidation is prevented by the high vacuum, which is obtained before sealing the glass bulb.

Previously to my Invention carbon sticks have been used, but they have only had a resistance of three or four ohms, and none have been used in vacuum bulbs composed entirely of glass, except the leading wires, hence the difficulties of sealing leading wires into glass, which would convey a current of sufficient strength to a lamp of but three or four ohms resistance is too great to make such a lamp successful, but when the resistance of the lamp is 100 ohms or more the leading wires can be very small, as they will then be a small factor in the total resistance of the lamp, and will not heat so as to crack the glass.

Lamp black, which has been placed in sealed crucibles, and subjected to a white heat for several hours, may be kneaded with tar until it reaches such a consistency as to allow its being rolled out on flat plates to very thin wires, which are sufficiently flexible to allow of coiling into helices; after they are rolled out to the proper length and size they are coated with a non-carbonizable powder of liquid, and wound or coiled.

The two ends are increased in size and secured to platinum wires, the whole is then subjected to heat in a closed tube, and the volatile constituents of the tar driven off and the balance carbonized, thus making a solid and homogeneous coil, which can be then united to the leading wires of the lamp, and a glass bulb blown over it and exhausted of air, and the lamp is then ready for use. The non-carbonized material prevents the spirals from touching each other until the whole has so stiffened sufficiently to remain in its position.

To assist in more rapidly manufacturing these spirals I sometimes wind the flexible carbon wires between metallic spirals, which after the carbonization of the tar are eaten away by acids, thus leaving the carbon intact. I also sometimes roll a thread within the compound of carbon and tar, so as to allow of greater convenience in handling the same, and the flexible carbon filament is not so liable to crack by its own weight in the act of winding.

To increase the resistance of the lamp black tar compound I sometimes work it into a volatile powder, such as powdered camphor, oxide zinc, but to make the light insensitive to variations of the current a considerable mass of matter should be used, in order that the specific heat of the lamp may be increased, so that it takes a long time to reach its full brilliancy, and also to die away slowly. To do this it is better to have the carbon as homogeneous as possible, and obtain the requisite resistance by employing a filament several inches long, and winding the same in a spiral form, so that the external radiating surface shall be small.

*Specification* in pursuance of the conditions of the Letters Patent filed by the said Thomas Alva Edison in the Great Seal Patent Office on the 10th May 1880.

THOMAS ALVA EDISON, of Menlo Park, in the State of New Jersey, United States of America. *Improvements in Electric Lamps, and in the Method of Manufacturing the same.*

The object of this Invention is to produce electric lamps giving light by incandescence, which lamps shall have high resistance so as to allow of the practical subdivision of the electric light.

The Invention consists in a light giving body of carbon wire, or sheets coiled or arranged in such a manner as to offer great resistance to the passage of the electric current, and at the same time present but a slight surface from which radiation can take place.

The Invention further consists in placing such light giving body of great resistance in a nearly perfect vacuum, to prevent oxidation and injury to the conductor by the atmosphere.

The current is conducted into the vacuum bulb through platina wires sealed into the glass.

The Invention further consists in the method of manufacturing carbon conductors of high resistance, so as to be suitable for giving light by incandescence, and in the manner of securing perfect contact between the metallic conductors or leading wires, and the carbon conductor.

Heretofore light by incandescence has been obtained from rods of carbon of one to four ohms resistance placed in closed vessels, in which the atmospheric air has been replaced by gases that do not combine chemically with the carbon. The vessel holding the burner has been composed of glass cemented to a metallic base. The connection between the leading wires and the carbon has been obtained by clamping the carbon to the metal.

The leading wires have always been large, so that their resistance shall be many times less than the burner; and in general the attempts of previous persons has been to reduce the resistance of the carbon rod. The disadvantages of following this practice are, that a lamp having but one to four ohms resistance cannot be worked in great numbers in multiple arc without the employment of main conductors of enormous dimensions, that owing to the low resistance of the lamp the leading wires must be of large dimensions and good conductors, and a glass globe cannot be kept tight at the place where the wires pass in and are cemented, hence the carbon is consumed because there must be almost a perfect vacuum to render the carbon stable, especially when such carbon is small in mass, and high in electrical resistance.

In the use of a gas in the receiver at the atmospheric pressure, which, although not attacking the carbon, serves to destroy it in time by 'air washing' or the attrition produced by the rapid passage of the air over the slightly coherent highly heated surface of the carbon.

I have reversed this practice. I have discovered that even a cotton thread properly carbonized, and placed in a sealed glass bulb exhausted to one millionth of an

atmosphere, offers from one hundred to five hundred ohms resistance to the passage of the current, and that it is absolutely stable at very high temperatures; that if the thread be coiled as a spiral, and carbonized, or if any fibrous vegetable substance which will leave a carbon residue after heating in a closed chamber be so coiled, that as much as two thousand ohms resistance may be obtained without presenting a radiating surface greater than three sixteenths of an inch; that if such fibrous material be rubbed with a plastic compound composed of lamp-black and tar, its resistance may be made high or low according to the amount of lamp-black placed upon it. I have also discovered that carbon filaments may be made by a combination of tar and lamp-black, the latter being previously ignited in a closed crucible for several hours, and afterwards moistened and kneaded until it assumes the consistency of thick putty. Small pieces of this material may be rolled out in the form of wire as small as seven one thousandths, 7/1000, of an inch in diameter, and over a foot, in length, and the same may be coated with a non-conducting non-carbonizable substance, and wound on a bobbin, or as a spiral, and the tar carbonized in a closed chamber by subjecting it to high heat, the spiral after carbonization retaining its form. I sometimes roll a thread within the compound of lamp-black and tar, so as to allow of greater convenience in handling the same; and the flexible carbon filament is not so liable to crack by its own weight in the act of winding.

To increase the resistance of the compound of lamp-black and tar I sometimes work into it a volatile powder, such as powdered camphor, oxide zinc, but to make the light insensitive to variations of the current a considerable mass of matter should be used in order that the specific heat of the lamp may be increased, so that it takes a long time to reach its full brilliancy and also to die away slowly.

To do this it is better to have the carbon as homogeneous as possible, and obtain the requisite resistance by employing a filament several inches long and winding the same in a spiral form so that the external radiating surface shall be small. All these forms are fragile and cannot be clamped to the leading wires with sufficient force to ensure good contact and prevent heating. I have discovered that if platinum wires are used and the plastic lamp-black and tar material be molded around it that in the act of carbonization there is an intimate union by combination and by pressure between the carbon and platina, and nearly perfect contact is obtained without the necessity of clamps, hence the light giving body and the platina wires are connected and ready to be placed in the vacuum bulb.

When fibrous material is used the plastic lamp black and tar is employed to secure it to the platina wires before carbonizing. By using the carbon wire of such high resistance I am enabled to use fine platinum wires for leading wires, as they will have a small resistance compared to the light giving body, hence will not heat and crack the sealed vacuum bulb.

Platina can only be used, as its expansion is nearly the same as that of glass. By using a considerable length of carbon wire and coiling it in such a manner that only a small portion of its entire surface radiates light, I can raise the specific heat of the whole and thus prevent the rapid reception and disappearance of the light, which on a plain wire is prejudicial as it shows the least unsteadiness of the current by the

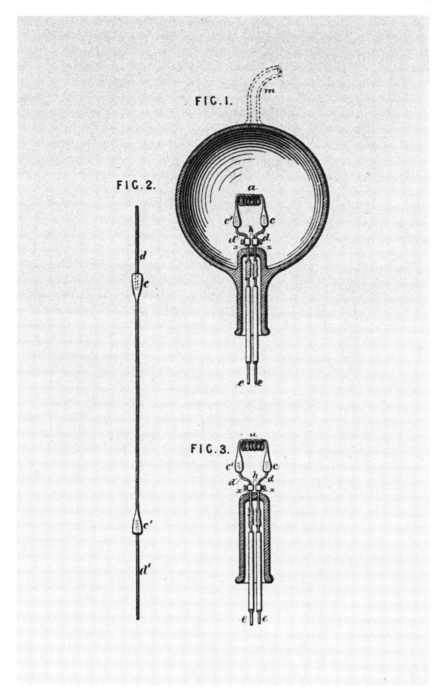

FIG. I.

FIG. 2.

FIG. 3.

flickering of the light, but if the current is steady the defect does not show. I have carbonized and used cotton and linen thread, wood-splints, paper coiled in various ways, also lamp-black, plumbago, and carbon in various forms mixed with tar and kneaded so that the same may be rolled out into wires of various lengths and diameters, each wire however is to be uniform in size throughout. If the carbon thread is liable to be distorted during carbonization it is to be coiled between a helix of copper wire. The ends of the carbon or filament are secured to the platina leading wires by plastic carbonizable material and the whole placed in the carbonizing chamber. The copper which has served to prevent distortion of the carbon thread is afterwards eaten away by nitric acid, and the spiral soaked in water and then dried and placed in the glass holder, and a glass bulb blown over the whole with a leading tube for exhaustion by a mercury pump. This tube when high vacua has been reached is hermetically sealed.

With substances which are not greatly distorted in carbonizing they may be coated with a non-conducting non-carbonizing substance, which allows one coil or turn of the carbon to rest upon and be supported by the other.

In the Drawing Fig. 1 shows the lamp sectionally. $a$ is the carbon spiral or thread; $c, c^1$, are the thickened ends of the spiral formed of the plastic compound of lamp-black and tar; $d, d^1$, are the platina wires; $h, h$, are the clamps which serve to connect the platina wires cemented in the carbon with the leading wires $x, x$, sealed in the glass vacuum bulb; $e, e$, are copper wires connected just outside the bulb to the wires $x, x$; $m$ is the tube, shown by dotted lines leading to the vacuum pump, which tube is hermetically sealed near the glass bulb after the bulb has been exhausted of air, as aforesaid.

Fig. 2 represents the plastic material before being wound into a spiral.

Fig. 3 show the spiral after carbonization ready to have a bulb blown over it.

I claim as my Invention, –

First. An electric lamp for giving light by incandescence consisting of a filament of carbon of high resistance, made as described and secured to metallic wires, as set forth.

Second. The combination of a carbon filament within a receiver made entirely of glass, through which the leading wires pass and from which receiver the air is exhausted, for the purposes set forth.

Third. A coiled carbon filament or strip arranged in such a manner that only a portion of the surface of such carbon conductor shall radiate light, as set forth.

Fourth. The method herein described of securing the platina contact wires to the carbon filament and carbonizing of the whole in a closed chamber, substantially as set forth.

In witness whereof, I, the said Thomas Alva Edison, have hereunto set my hand and seal, this 20 day of April, A.D. 1880.

Witnesses,                                              THOMAS ALVA EDISON. (L.S.)
*Cha$^s$. H. Smith*, 140, Nassau St., N.Y.
*Geo. T. Pinckney*, 140, Nassau St., N.Y.

# PATENT APPLICATION BY FREDERIK PHILIPS

TO HIS MAJESTY THE KING

With due respect, Benjamin Frederik David Philips, merchant, residing in Zalt-Bommel in Gelderland, declares that, by reason of an agreement entered into with the foreign inventor or his successors in title, he is the first and only person to introduce into this country a machine for the manufacture of cigars, of which an accurate and detailed description in the petitioner's own hand and bearing his seal, together with a drawing, accompanies this petition; and for which machine an application has been submitted by or on behalf of the inventor for a patent in the Kingdom of Belgium for a period of fifteen years, and for which patents have already been obtained in the Kingdom of Hanover, Saxony, the Grand Duchy of Baden and the Kingdom of Prussia.

On these grounds, the petitioner respectfully requests that it may please Your Majesty to grant the petitioner a patent pertaining to the introduction of the said machine for the manufacture of cigars for a period of fifteen years.

Zalt-Bommel, 21 July 1857.                              (*Signed*) FRED. PHILIPS

# KARL MARX TO LION PHILIPS

*(translated from German)*

9, Grafton Terrace,
Maitland Park,
Haverstock Hill,
London.

*6 May 1861.*

Dear Uncle,

First I must thank you most sincerely for the great friendship which you again demonstrated and for the warm hospitality extended to me in your house. Not wishing to lay myself open to a charge of flattery, I shall mention only *en passant* how great a pleasure it was to be associated with a man of your experience who takes so human, unprejudiced and original a view of world events, yet has retained to the full the fire and tempestuousness of youth.

My journey from Bommel went completely according to plan. In Rotterdam I found Jacques on the platform, spent a couple of hours chatting with him, and then travelled on to Amsterdam, where on the following day I quickly got through my business. August and his family – this time accompanied by his wife's cousin from Rotterdam – were well and in good spirits. August particularly instructed me, upon my return to Rotterdam, to try to inject some life into Monsieur Jacques who is suffering in greater or lesser degree from *Weltschmerz*, a condition which can be recognized simply by the fact that he, in contrast to the great majority of people, is self-critical and has so far been unable to find a satisfactory attitude towards politics. On the return journey I reached Rotterdam at half-past nine in the evening, from where I was to catch the London boat at 7 o'clock on the following morning (Sunday). In the short time which I spent with Jacques, it was, of course, impossible to answer all the questions which he put to me, or to deal more than briefly with all the points which he raised. Jacques decided that our conversation should be continued in London, and proposed to discuss the visit with his employers. I arrived in the world metropolis on Monday, where I found the whole family fit and well. Jacques surprised us by arriving last Wednesday. He left yesterday morning, much to the sorrow of my family and myself, who would have liked him to stay longer. We arranged to enter into a sort of political correspondence.

You will recall, dear Uncle, that we often jested about the breeding of human beings these days being so far behind the breeding of animals. I have now seen your entire family, and I must say that you are a virtuoso in the breeding of humans. Never in my life have I known a better family. All your children are self-reliant,

---

[1] Cf. Chapter 2, page 56.

each is an individual, each has outstanding intellectual characteristics, and all have developed a common understanding of their fellow human beings.

Here in London, there is great consternation following the events in America. The acts of violence, to which not only the seceded states have contributed but also some of the central or border states, have ruled out any possibility of a compromise. And there are fears that those eight border states, namely Virginia, Kentucky, Missouri, North Carolina, Tennessee, Arkansas, Maryland and Delaware, will side with the secessionists. At first the struggle will doubtless tend to go in favour of the South, where the unpropertied white adventurers provide an inexhaustible source for a bellicose militia. In the long run, of course, the North will triumph, for if necessary they can play their trump card, a revolution by slaves. The big question facing the North is how to get their forces to the South? Even an unopposed march, on which at this time of year they could cover 15 miles per day, would be something trying; but Charleston, the next point which can be attacked, is 544 miles from Washington, 681 from Philadelphia, 771 from New York and 994 from Boston, and the last three of these are the main bases for operations against the South. And the distances from these places to Montgomery, the seat of the Secessionist Congress, are even greater – 910, 1,050, 1,130 and 1,350 miles respectively. Marching overland therefore appears to be out of the question. (The use by the Northern invaders of the railways would promptly lead to the destruction of the lines.) All that remains is the sea and naval warfare, but this could lead to complications with foreign powers. The attitude which the British Ministry would adopt towards such a development will be announced in the House of Commons this evening.

To me, personally, the events in America are of course rather damaging, because for the time being newspaper readers on the other side of the Atlantic have eyes and ears only for what is happening there. I have, however, received profitable offers from the Vienna *Presse*, which I propose to accept when one or two ambiguous issues have been cleared up. I must write to them from London.

My wife is still very much against moving to Berlin, for she does not wish our daughters to be introduced into the Hatzfeldt Circle and feels that, once there, it will be difficult to keep them out. I received a very friendly letter from Lasalle today. He has not heard any more from the Commissioner of Police at Zedlitz regarding my renaturalization. The confrontation between the police and the public in Berlin, Lasalle informs me, has now entered a new phase.

With kindest regards to you and yours from myself and the whole family,

Your faithful nephew

K. MARX

*Appendix 4*[1]

# HONOURS GRADE

[Not more than *seven* questions to be attempted.]

1. State the laws of current distribution in divided circuits. Twelve wires, each of one ohm resistance, are joined up to form a skeleton cube. Show that the resistance between diagonally situated corners is five-sixths of an ohm.

2. If currents are flowing in a network of conductors, explain the means by which the dissipation of energy in horse-power can be calculated. Explain fully what rule should, according to Sir W. Thomson, determine the size of the conductors in any system employed for distribution.

3. Define the term *specific resistance*. Explain fully how you would proceed to determine the specific resistance of carbon of such quality as is used in arc lighting. Is it possible by any means to construct a resistance which is unaffected by moderate change of temperature?

4. Give a careful explanation of what is meant by *self induction*. Is the self induction of a circuit the same for steady currents and for rapidly alternating currents? If not, state how it is different. Are there any facts which would lead you to prefer a copper rather than an iron wire for telephonic purposes?

5. You are required to report on some samples of iron furnished to you as intended for field magnets of dynamo machines. State the experiments you would make, and what is the special quality you would desire to find present in order to approve of a sample as good.

6. Explain the structure of any practical form of *secondary generator*, and say whether, and why, you would design a secondary generator with a closed rather than an open magnetic circuit.

7. Give an explanation of a method for determining the commercial efficiency of a continuous current dynamo. Describe the principle of Dr. Hopkinson's method of measuring the combined efficiency of a dynamo and identical motor, or any modification of the method since suggested.

8. You are given a commercial ampère-meter to test and standardize. Explain how you would propose to do it.

9. The secondary current from an induction coil is passed through a long helix of wire, and through a Bell telephone in series with it. The telephone emits a

---

[1] The examination paper which Gerard Philips took for the City and Guilds of London Central Institution; see Chapter 2, page 66.

continuous sound. What effect, if any, should you expect to be produced by introducing a bundle of iron wires into the helix, and why?

10. Explain the construction of a Pilsen arc lamp. How can arc and glow lamps be run on the same circuits?

11. How is pure copper prepared electrolytically?

12. Explain the principles of any form of practical power-meter for measuring electric power expended in any circuit.

13. Explain the reasons for the counter electromotive force developed by a motor when running. If a shunt-wound motor is being worked at constant potential, describe some means by which the direction and speed of revolution may be controlled by an operator using it; according to the nature of the work being performed.

14. Can one alternate current dynamo be driven as a motor by another identical machine? if so, state how you would arrange and join up the machines. Give a full reason for your reply.

# CONTRACT ENTRE E. H. CADIOT ET JOHAN BOUDEWIJNSE

*Paris le 16 juin 1888*

Contract entre M. E. H. Cadiot Paris et Johan Boudewijnse à Middelbourg.

Monsieur Cadiot s'engage à prendre au moins 50.000 lampes à incandescence de Johan Boudewijnse dans le temps du 1 septembre 1888 jusqu'à le 15 décembre 1889 et Johan Boudewijnse s'engage à les lui livrer; la quantité par semaine n'excédera pas 2500 lampes.

Moyennant ce contract M. Cadiot aura l'agence exclusive pour la vente des lampes de sa fabrication pour la France et l'Alsace et la Lorraine avec liberté à lui de vendre dans tous les autres pays pourvu que ce soit avec sa marque.

Pour l'Espagne Johan Boudewijnse ne nommera pas un agent avant le 15 décembre 1889. M. Cadiot donnera les noms de ses clients qui devront ne pas être sollicité par Johan Boudewijnse ou ses agents.

Johan Boudewijnse donne une garantie de trente jours de 10 heurs de marche des lampes de 3 et 3,5 Watts par candle dans quel temps les restes des lampes seront retournées et les lampes remplacées aussitôt que possible.

Pour avoir le contrôle que la brise des lampes ne sera pas causée par une faute de machine de dynamo M. Cadiot fera toutes les instructions possibles et prendra les moyens de s'en assurer

Le prix des lampes sera pour des lampes de moins de 8 candles prenant moins de 2 ampères Fr. 2,20

> pour celles moins de 8 candles prenant plus de 2 ampères Fr. 2,50
> pour celles de 8, 10, 16, 20 et 25: Fr. 2,50 et,
> pour celles de 30, 40 et 50: Fr. 2,75 par lampe

En cas d'un rabais déloyale de la part d'autres fabricants connus MM Cadiot et Boudewijnse devront s'entendre loyalement pour soutenir la concurrence en cas que possible.

Johan Boudewijnse ne peut pas vendre dans les autres pays à moins de Fr. 2,50 par lampe mais pas franco porte, droit d'entrée et emballage, pour quantités moins de 50.000 par an à une firme et il s'engage aussi à stipuler dans les contracts qu'il ferait à l'étranger que ses acheteurs ne devront pas faire la concurrence à M. Cadiot en France ou pays où M. Cadiot a la vente.

[1] See Chapter 4, page 159.

Johan Boudewijnse mettra sur les lampes les marques que M. Cadiot lui demandra pourvu qu'elles ne soient pas des contrefaçons.

Ces marques seront monopolisées entre les mains de Johan Boudewijnse qui prendra les mesures nécessaires pour leur protection en Hollande pendant toute la durée de ce contrat à l'expiration duquel elles deviendront la propriété de M. Cadiot.

Le payement se fera deux mois et demi après mois de date de délivré des lampes en traite acceptée dans les dix jours de leur envoi par M. Johan Boudewijnse.

En cas de force majeure comme un interdit d'introduction des lampes en France ou autre pays M. Cadiot devra aviser Johan Boudewijnse et les parties contractantes devront s'entendre loyalement pour régulariser leurs interests.

Il ne se fera jamais un procès quelconque en cas de différence on tachera à s'accorder amicalement.

En cas qu'une ou plusieurs personnes desireraient à acheter les lampes directement de la firme Johan Boudewijnse elle s'y mettra en correspondance avec M. Cadiot qui d'accord avec Johan Boudewijnse fera le prix et les conditions de vente et l'ordre obtenu le surplus de prix sera divisé 2/3 pour M. Cadiot et 1/3 pour Johan Boudewijnse.

La base de ce contract sera avant tout une interpretation loyale de part et l'autre.

Les lampes se feront à oeillets ou à montures Système Vitrite, Edison, Cruto, Siemens, Lane-Fox et Victoria.

Fait à Paris le 16 juin 1888 en doubles.
w.g. Johan Boudewijnse
E. H. CADIOT

# ELECTRIC LIGHTING:
# DANGERS FOR THE INDIVIDUAL

To the Editor

The accidents which occurred in America, notably in the latter part of 1889, and in which a number of people lost their lives have shaken the confidence of those who at first were well disposed towards electric light, and led to the view that the new form of lighting, if indeed it can ever be employed with the requisite degree of safety, is still at a stage where it would be inadvisable to use it on a large scale in a well-regulated city. Fortunately, however, these fears are completely without foundation. What do people know about the method of installation in America? Are they aware that, there, wires with little if any insulation, and carrying a voltage which can kill a human being, are being taken through the streets of densely populated towns, and are often attached to the poles which support telephone and telegraph lines? Some time ago the British magazine, *The Electrician*, gave an accurate description of the lack of care exercised with high voltages in America, and anyone who reads this must be amazed that there have not been many more accidents.

The authorities have not reached complete agreement on the limits of dangerous and safe voltages. But then these depend largely on the individual and the circumstances. In the meantime, it is very necessary to distinguish between *alternating currents* and *direct currents*. Alternating currents derive their name from the fact that the direction of the current in the wires alternates very rapidly – usually between 40 and 200 times per second. At a given voltage, such a current has a greater effect on the human body than one whose direction and magnitude remain constant. The electrical apparatuses which one can enjoy at the fairground, and which are used by doctors for electric therapy, commonly deliver alternating currents.

It may be assumed that a direct current of 1,000 volts is a *danger to life*, while an alternating current at the same potential is definitely *lethal*. A direct current of 500 volts *can* be injurious; an alternating current at the same potential *is* injurious. To be completely safe, a direct current must not exceed 300 volts and an alternating current must be of less than 150 volts.

(A note concerning the term *volt*, which causes alarm to many: it is merely a unit of electrical potential, just as a *kilo* is a unit of steam or water pressure.)

But in spite of all that has been said, someone recently stated in *The Electrician* that he had several times received a shock from a current of 1,000–1,500 volts

---

[1] Cf. Chapter 5, page 212.

without injury; and he offered to repeat the test in the presence of others interested in such experiments.

Greater care is taken to protect human lives in Europe than in America; situations such as exist in the latter country in the area of electric light and electric power simply could not occur here. In Britain, many more precautions are taken to make installations safe, and better materials are used. Yet even there, more than one case of carelessness has occurred and things have been done which would never have been permitted here or in Germany.

In London, a number of cables run above the streets and houses, carrying alternating current at 1,800 volts. A number of lives have been lost in Britain, but recently far greater caution has been exercised: new cables in the major towns and cities are mainly being laid underground; in London this is now compulsory.

Yet in Germany, the country which seems destined to set the example where electricity supplies are concerned, *not a single human life has been lost*. More significantly, it is absolutely impossible for anyone in Germany to suffer injury as a result of contact with electric current. If only people would not look for an example to America, where human lives count for little, but to our eastern neighbours who, where the sound, lasting, rational lighting of cities is concerned, not only set the tone in Europe, but also outdo America, and in the area of safety are far ahead of that country. Since visiting Berlin last summer, Edison has repeatedly stated that the electric lighting there, both in terms of the quality of the light and the standards of safety, is better than anywhere else in the world. He said this not only in Berlin – under the pressure of hospitality – but later in London and in an interview with the *Evening Reporter* in New York. Nowhere in the entire Berlin system, with its 70,000 lamps, is the potential greater than 220 volts.

The solution to the problem of safety in installing electric lighting on a large scale in towns and cities boils down to this:

Lay your cables properly, underground; the higher the voltage passing through your cables, the greater the care needed in laying them.

*Never* allow high voltages to come within reach of individuals; in houses, keep to low voltages, i.e. no more than 300 volts direct current, or 150 volts alternating current.

Make sure that your installation is of high quality throughout; so for heaven's sake avoid provisional permits! One thing or the other: either grant a sound concession – with, of course, the necessary guarantees, etc.– which gives the contracting parties an opportunity to create something sound, something good, or grant absolutely nothing and let Amsterdam continue to be deprived of the advantages of electricity. The latter course is naturally not without its drawbacks, especially in a city which takes a pride in not lagging too far behind. For in the major cities abroad, the consumption of electricity is rising sharply: in many of them the question of general electricity supplies has been solved, and in numerous others, including some smaller ones, the issue is already on the agenda.

Will those in power here wait until perfection is achieved?

Such waiting has already cost the Netherlands dear on many occasions, and seriously harmed our reputation abroad!

*Amsterdam, 8 March 1890.*                                          INGENIEUR

# LETTER OF SIEMENS & HALSKE TO THE AMSTERDAM CITY COUNCIL

To the Amsterdam City Council

*Berlin, 24 March 1890*

We have the honour to inform the Amsterdam City Council that we have withdrawn the tender, submitted on our behalf by the Nederlandsche Maatschappij voor Electriciteit en Metallurgie of The Hague, for the concession for an electric lighting system in the City of Amsterdam. We have been informed by the Allgemeine Elektricitäts-Gesellschaft here that they have already submitted a tender, and in view of our close ties with that company it is our intention to carry out the installation in the City of Amsterdam in association with them. In the matter of the concession to be sought in that city, we are in contact only with the Allgemeine Elektricitäts-Gesellschaft here and with no other competitor.

Yours respectfully,

(*Signed*)   Siemens & Halske

[1]  See Chapter 5, pages 214–15.

# ELECTRIC LIGHT

To the Editor,                                                    26–3–1890

In the article entitled 'Electricity before the Council', which appeared in the evening edition on the 15th inst., it was observed that it was no easy task to draw up the terms for a concession for the supply of electricity, particularly for a Council in which the law is so much better represented than industry. All who attended the last meeting of the Council and who have any understanding of the technical aspects of the matter will concur fully in the latter comment. But even where non-technical issues are concerned the arguments put forward by the learned counsel were far from unassailable. The situation is indeed not very encouraging: if the Council had more faith in the advice and the policy of the alderman and the technical officers of the Municipality, who, if we are not mistaken, by considering the proposals and seeking the advice of others, have given clear evidence of careful preparation in this matter, a solution would be forthcoming. Yet there has been little evidence of such faith, at least at the last meeting of the Council, and not entirely without reason, for the alderman was not particularly enthusiastic in his defence of the proposals.

Last summer, prior to taking his seat on the Executive, the alderman sent two memoranda to the Council, setting out his principal objections to the proposals tabled by the Executive on 21 May 1889. These objections were overcome in the new proposals: the alderman, who is completely familiar with the technical side of the matter, thoroughly revised the old proposals. Yet one nevertheless gets the impression that the alderman continues to regard the new proposals as something dating from before his time, the defence of which does not call for any special effort on his part.

This, it seems to us, is the wrong way to go about settling an issue which is indeed very important. Admittedly, it is stated in the explanatory notes that the Executive shares the view that 'it is almost impossible to word the terms of the concession in such a way as to make it even probable that all subsequent events will be covered'. This has already been established; long-term contracts, like these concessions, can give rise to difficulties for both parties, but of this the members of the Council are also fully aware. The problem is to prevent as far as possible these difficulties arising at a later stage, and it seems to us that the proposals tabled by the Municipal Executive represent a serious attempt in this direction.

[1] Cf. Chapter 5, page 217.

Anyone who compares the proposed conditions with those applying to the gas concession cannot fail to observe the considerable distinction: the proposals for the new concession leave the Municipality completely free and give it considerable power over concessionaires. We need only cite the provision whereby prices can be revised every five years, a very stringent provision which leaves one amazed that there should still be any concessionaires. It is true that there remains a possibility of a *de facto* monopoly at a later date, but one cannot guard against this; in any case, as the chairman observed, the possibility would remain even if ten concessions were granted simultaneously.

Rightly, you point out in your article that the cost of a *short-term* concession will be *high*.

For example, a concession for a period of twelve years, as was proposed in certain quarters, would be *very costly*, and would never appeal to a company of standing. Concessionaires, that is possible! Who knows, before the next meeting of the Council, a 'bargain' offer on those lines may be forthcoming from one or other company. It is easily made and need cost nothing.

.[. . .]

In the majority of cities in Europe, the minimum period for a concession is thirty years. In Britain, concessions for the supply of electricity were limited to twenty-one years by the 1882 Act, and the result was complete stagnation in the electric lighting of the cities. That situation lasted until 1888, when the law was amended and the period extended to forty-two years, and soon afterwards the supply of electricity from power stations increased by leaps and bounds. Today, the councils there cannot take over electricity supplies for forty-two years from the date of the concession.

The provision in the proposals tabled by the Municipal Executive which prevents the Council from taking over the electricity supply companies until twelve years have elapsed met with opposition from several councillors. Mr Heineken tabled an amendment on this point, the effect of which would be to give the Council the power of compulsory acquisition from the outset.

If, however, we look back to the terms of the gas concession, we see that there is really no need for such haste. And due regard should be paid to the gas concession, as the Council was recently, and so painfully, reminded. In Article 3 of the conditions of that concession we read:

For the duration of this concession, the Council waives its right to undertake the provision of lighting, heating or the generation of motive power for the benefit of individual persons by a system other than is envisaged in these conditions; the Council, however, is at all times authorized to grant concessions for these activities, for the whole of the parish or a part thereof.

That obligation thus remains until 1918.

And Article 29, clause 1, of the same conditions states:

The Council shall have the right to withdraw the concession on or after 1 August 1897, subject to at least two years' notice of such action being given to the concessionaire.

This is followed by details of the compensation to be paid.

Now, there is really no need for anyone to fear that the Council would wish to take over the supply of electricity within twelve years, for firstly it will have no opportunity to do so until 1897, and secondly it would afterwards have to take over the gas company. In the five years which remained, it would be necessary to take over both the gasworks and the electric lighting company, and organize and run both. This strikes us as a somewhat fanciful notion. Alternatively, it might be possible to persuade the gas concessionaire to waive the conditions referred to, but that would be a costly affair.

One could conceive of the Council desiring to acquire the electric lighting company compulsorily and then transfer it to a third party; but the terms proposed really do give the Council sufficient power to force concessionaires to meet their obligations or, if they fail, to withdraw the concession.

[. . .]

Those who are at present seeking concessions in Amsterdam are in anything but a favourable position. Often in the past, the Council has given too much to concessionaires and allowed its hand to be tied in all manner of ways. Now, the natural reaction to this has reached its peak under the pressure of public opinion, or what is taken to be public opinion. As with all reactions, the pendulum has swung completely the other way. Concessions are almost unavoidable – even the anti-monopolistic councillors recognize this – but the ideal appears to be to keep all the advantages for the city and leave the concessionaire with all the risks. Obviously, this is untenable and would lead from the frying pan into the fire. In the above-mentioned article, you rightly point out that little good can be expected from applying the thumbscrew too tightly.

Time will show that the right course lies somewhere between the two extremes, and therefore one might wish that, in this context, more advice was sought in the major cities abroad, especially those where, the authorities not having burned their fingers on earlier concessions, a moderate approach may be anticipated and not, as in Amsterdam, a reaction.

The country would do well to pay more heed to this advice in other areas as well. It is lagging behind in many fields, yet when it comes to introducing a modern development, people act as if they were dealing with something completely new. First they examine it from all angles, then they venture to test it on a very small scale, and only after that do they proceed, slowly and hesitantly, to its introduction. But the days of Jan van der Heyden and the first fire engines and street lamps are well and truly past; today, by the time a new development comes along, you can be sure that in most large cities abroad it has already been tried out, energetically applied and proved successful.

*Amsterdam, March 1890*                                    INGENIEUR

# LETTER OF GERARD PHILIPS TO THE AMSTERDAM CITY COUNCIL

To the Council of the Municipality of Amsterdam

The Allgemeine Elektricitäts-Gesellschaft, domiciled at Berlin, which Company, in the name of the Nederlandsche Electriciteits-Maatschappij of this city, has entered into negotiations with the Municipal Executive concerning a concession for the supply of electricity within this Municipality, respectfully states:

that it has taken cognizance of the most recent proposal regarding this matter submitted to the Council by the Municipal Executive;

that it feels obliged to invite the attention of Your Council to the fact that, in the opinion of the petitioner, the period within which the Executive is authorized to terminate the concession under the terms of the proposal is much too short; that no serious and honest operator will invest the large amount of capital necessary for such an operation in a company when there is a fear that, when the difficult years have passed and the capital has scarcely become productive, the concession will be withdrawn; and, moreover, that with such a short period he is unable to include the legitimate amortization as a factor in calculating the price;

that in the unexpected event of the approval by Your Council of the proposal of the Municipal Executive, in its present form, the petitioner, albeit with reluctance, would feel obliged to withdraw as a candidate for the supply of electricity within this municipality;

that, on the grounds of the foregoing, the petitioner urges most strongly that the afore-mentioned proposal should be rejected, or that the discussion of it should be postponed for up to one month, during which the petitioner envisages making other proposals which take account of the objections raised in connection with this matter during recent meetings of Your Council.

On these grounds, the petitioner respectfully requests Your Council:

(a) to reject the proposal of the Municipal Executive
(b) or to postpone discussion of the electricity question for up to one month for the reasons set out above.

And your petitioner will ever pray, etc.
On behalf of the Allgemeine Elektricitäts-Gesellschaft

*Amsterdam, 22 April 1890.*

G. L. F. PHILIPS
*Representative*

[1] See Chapter 5, page 221.

# LETTER OF HARTSEN AND BOEING TO THE AMSTERDAM CITY COUNCIL

To the Council of the Municipality of Amsterdam

Your Worships

Jonkheer Jacob Hartsen and Ernest Boeing, in their capacity as Directors of the Partnersnip, 'Electra' Maatschappij voor Electrische Stations, whose registered office is situated at Kalverstraat No. 36, Amsterdam, would respectfully inform you:

that they have noted with interest the amended proposal of the Municipal Executive dated 17 April 1890 (No. 233) for establishing the conditions on which a concession will be granted for the use of municipal land and municipal waterways for the laying of electricity cables;

that they have no objection to concession without monopoly or to the stipulations set out in the draft resolution, but only to the notice of termination;

that according to the proposal the concession may be terminated simply by notice being given;

that it is impossible to obtain capital for a large undertaking for so short a period, and it is abundantly clear that if the intention were to cover the investment in the space of ten years, this could be achieved only by inordinately high profits such as the Company does not intend to make and could not make, since at the price charged for electricity no consumers could be found;

that there should be a guarantee that the entrepreneurs will in any case be able to operate for thirty or twenty-eight years, subject to the power of the municipality to acquire the undertaking compulsorily, albeit at the end of the period and on the terms set out in Art. 13 of the draft resolution;

that the objection on the part of the petitioners is not to the power of the municipality to acquire the undertaking after ten years compulsorily, but to the possibility that the concession will be terminated after ten years *without compensation*, and that in view of these contingencies it is impossible to establish a solid enterprise, since this requires a concession of thirty or at least twenty-eight years.

On these grounds, the petitioners respectfully request Your Worships to amend Art. 2 and if necessary related articles in such a way that the concession is granted for at least twenty-eight years.

And your petitioners will ever pray

*Amsterdam, 22 April 1890*                    J. HARTSEN   E. BOEING

[1] See Chapter 5, page 223.

# LETTER OF AEG AND SIEMENS & HALSKE TO THE AMSTERDAM CITY COUNCIL

To the Council of the City of Amsterdam

*Berlin, 26 August 1890*

The undersigned companies have the honour to confirm that they are willing to accept in full the 'Conditions for the granting of a concession for the use of council land and waterways in connection with the laying of electric cables for lighting and power', published by the City Council on 25 June 1890.

We venture to set a maximum price of *60 cents* (*sixty cents*) for the unit of current of 1,000 volt–ampères stipulated in Art. 7, and we enclose a *cahier de charges* in which we have inserted Art. 7 and which bears our signatures.

The conditions imposed on concessionaires are in many respects onerous. Nevertheless, we feel that we can accept them, on the one hand because we are convinced that the Council will show goodwill and co-operation towards the undertaking which we propose to establish for the common weal, and on the other hand because we hope that the considerable experience which we have gained in building and operating Europe's largest generating stations will enable us gradually to make the undertaking profitable in spite of the low tariff.

We make no secret of the fact that this profitability can be achieved only after years of operation, and we therefore trust that the Council will approve the granting to us of an exclusive concession for at least five years.

The undersigned believe that it is unnecessary to furnish evidence of their ability to construct and operate generating stations, for the installations of this type manufactured by them are known all over the world. One of the co-signatories, Allgemeine Elektricitäts-Gesellschaft, was able on a number of occasions during earlier negotiations to demonstrate its achievements in this field.

We undertake to deposit, within eight days of being requested to do so by the Mayor and Aldermen, a sum of *f* 100,000 by way of surety that the concession, if granted to us, will be transferred within six months to a company limited by shares, which will be established and will meet the conditions set out in Art. 32.

---

[1] Cf. Chapter 5, page 227.

We recognize the right of the Mayor and Aldermen to declare this security forfeit in the event of our failing to comply with this obligation within the stated period of six months.

We remain respectfully yours

*Allgemeine Elektricitäts-Gesellschaft*
*Siemens & Halske*

# BIBLIOGRAPHY

ARCHIVES

General Government Archives, The Hague
Government Archives, Arnhem
Government Archives, Middelburg

Municipal Archives, Amsterdam
Municipal Archives, Eindhoven
Municipal Archives, Haarlem
Municipal Archives, The Hague
Municipal Archives, Middelburg
Municipal Archives, Nijmegen
Municipal Archives, Rotterdam
Municipal Archives, Utrecht
Municipal Archives, Venlo
Municipal Archives, Zaltbommel

AEG-Telefunken Archives, Brunswick
Archives of Johan Boudewijnse, Middelburg
Archives of the Brush Electrical Engineering Co., Ltd, Loughborough
Archives of De Nederlandsche Bank N.V., Amsterdam
Archives of N.V. Philips' Gloeilampenfabrieken, Eindhoven
Archives of N.V. Pope's Draad- en Lampenfabrieken, Eindhoven
Archives of the Vitrite Works, Middelburg
Siemens Archives, Munich

Archives of the Association for the Promotion of Manufacturing and Craft Industries in the
    Netherlands, The Hague/Middelburg
Archives of the City and Guilds of London Institute, London
Glasgow University Archives
Archives of the Institution of Electrical Engineers, London
Nederlandsch Economisch-Historisch Archief, Amsterdam
Strathclyde Regional Archives, Glasgow

Alewijnse family Archives, Ubbergen
Lugt family Archives, The Hague
Nagtglas Versteeg family Archives, Amsterdam, Haarlem, The Hague

Economisch-Historische Bibliotheek, Amsterdam
KEMA Library, Arnhem
Koninklijke Bibliotheek, The Hague
Library of the Delft University of Technology, Delft
Library of the Eindhoven University of Technology, Eindhoven
Library of the International Institute for Social History (I.I.S.G.), Amsterdam
Library of the VEG Gas Institute, Apeldoorn
Patent Office Library, Rijswijk
PTT Library, The Hague

D. H. Aldcroft (ed.), *The Development of British Industry and Foreign Competition 1875–1914*; London, 1968.

G. B. Barham, *The Development of the Incandescent Electric Lamp*; London, 1912.

C. J. Basch, *Die Entwicklung der elektrischen Beleuchtung und der Industrie elektrischer Glühlampen in Deutschland*; Berlin, 1910.

H. Baudet, 'De dadels van Hassan en de start der Nederlandse industrialiteit' in: *Bedrijf en Samenleving*, a collection of essays presented to Professor I. J. Brugmans; Alphen a.d. Rijn, 1967.

L. D. Belkind, *Aleksandr Nikolaevitch Lodygin*; Moscow, 1948.

L. Bernard, *Die Entwickelung und Bedeutung der elektrotechnischen Industrie in Oesterreich*; Munich, 1908.

Boissevain Walrave, *Mijn Leven 1876–1944*; Bussum, 1950.

J. H. Bolland, *Slepende Rijk – Het ontstaan van de Nederlandse zeesleepvaart*, 1968.

F. J. M. Bothe, *75 Jaar AEG-Telefunken Nederland N.V.*; Amsterdam, 1977.

C. Boudewijnse, *Eenige beschouwingen over Electrische Verlichting naar aanleiding van de brochure van Polet*; Middelburg, 1889.

P. J. Bouman, *Growth of an Enterprise; The Life of Anton Philips*, second edition; Macmillan, London, 1970.

W. Brand, *Eindhoven, Sociografie van de Lichtstad*; Amsterdam, 1937.

A. A. Bright, *The Electric-Lamp Industry: Technological Change and Economic Development from 1800 to 1947*; New York, 1949.

S. Brouwer, *De Amsterdamsche Bank 1871–1946*; Amsterdam, 1946.

J. J. Brugmans, *De arbeidende klasse in Nederland in de 19e eeuw 1813–1870*; Utrecht, 1958.
   *Paardenkracht en Mensenmacht. Sociaal-economische geschiedenis van Nederland 1795–1940*; The Hague, 1961.

I. C. R. Byatt, *The British Electrical Industry 1875–1914: The Economic Returns of a New Technology*; Oxford, 1979.

P. van Cappelle, *De Electriciteit, hare voortbrenging en hare toepassing in de industrie en het maatschappelijk verkeer, naar Arthur Wilke*; Leiden, 1893.

C. M. Cipolla (ed.), *The Fontana Economic History of Europe – The Emergence of Industrial Societies, Part One*; Glasgow, 1973.

J. H. Clapham, *The Economic Development of France and Germany 1815–1914*; Cambridge, 1923.

C. F. Cross et al., *Cellulose, an Outline of the Chemistry of the Structural Elements of Plants*; London, 1895.

G. Doorman, *Het Nederlandsch Octrooiwezen en de techniek der 19e eeuw*; The Hague, 1947.

Th. Dumoncel, *l'Eclairage Electrique*; Paris, 1879.

F. L. Dyer and T. C. Martin, *Edison, his Life and Inventions*; New York, 1910.

H. van Eeden, *Zestig jaar Electrostoom 1892–1952*; Wageningen, 1952.

H. F. J. M. van den Eerenbeemt, *Ontwikkelingslijnen en Scharnierpunten in het Brabants industrieel bedrijf 1777–1914*; Tilburg, 1977.

J. G. Einhart, *Die Wirtschaftliche Entwicklung und Lage der Electrotechnik in der Schweiz*; Zürich, 1906.

H. H. Emck et al., *Ridderkerk, herdenking 500 jaar*; 1946.

F. N. van Es, *100 Jaar Elektrotechnische Installaties – De Eeuw van Croon & Co. 1876–1976*; Rotterdam, 1976.

J. Escard, *Les Lampes Electriques*; Paris, 1912.

J. Feith, *N.V. Philips' Gloeilampenfabrieken 1891–1916*; Eindhoven, 1916.

L. Figuier, *Het Elektrische Licht*, Dutch-language adaptation by A. van Oven; The Hague, 1886.

E. de Fodor, *Das Glühlicht, sein Wesen und seine Erfordenisse – Erfahrungen über Herstellung, Dauer und Leuchtkraft der Lampen. Berechnungen und Ausführung der Anlagen, praktische Lichtvertheilung im Raume und ausserordentliche Betriebsverhältnisse*; Vienna, 1885.

A. Fürst, *Emil Rathenau – der Mann und sein Werk*; Berlin, 1915.

J. W. Hammond, *Men and Volts; The Story of General Electric*; Philadelphia, 1941.

N. van Harpen, *De gemeentelijke electrische centrale en Electra*; Amsterdam, 1903.

T. W. Heather, *The G.E.C. Its History, Structure and the Future*; London, 1953.

A. Heerding, *Cement in Nederland*; Amsterdam, 1971.

A. Heggen, *Erfindungsschutz und Industrialisierung in Preussen 1793–1877*; Göttingen, 1975.

M. Heiman Gans, *Memorboek*; Baarn, 1971.

Th. Heuss, *Robert Bosch, Leben und Leistung*; Stuttgart, 1948.

J. Heyn Jr, *Mijlpaal 60, 1889–1949*. Biography published to mark the Sixtieth Anniversary of N.V. Pope's Draad- en lampenfabrieken te Venlo; Venlo, 1949.

E. J. Hobsbawm, *Industry and Empire. An Economic History of Britain since 1750*; London, 1968.

F. Holthof, *Das elektrische Licht in seiner neuesten Entwickelung*; Halle, 1882.

E. J. Houston and A. E. Kennelly, *Electric Incandescent Lighting*; New York, 1906.

J. W. Howell and H. Schroeder, *History of the Incandescent Lamp*; New York, 1927.

J. J. Huizinga, *J. Heemskerk Azn. (1818–1897), Conservatief zonder Partij*; Harlingen, 1973.

F. Jehl, *The Manufacture of Carbons for Electric Lighting and Other Purposes*; London, 1899.

R. Jones and O. Marriott, *Anatomy of a Merger, A History of G.E.C., A.E.I., and English Electric*; London, 1970.

A. M. de Jong, *Geschiedenis van de Nederlandsche Bank*; Amsterdam, 1967.

J. A. de Jonge, *De Industrialisatie in Nederland tussen 1850 en 1914*; Amsterdam, 1968.

S. de Jonge-Mulock Houwer, *C.D. Nagtglas Versteeg*; Heemstede, 1956.

M. Josephson, *Edison A Biography*; New York, 1959.

M. Keyser, *Komt dat zien, de Amsterdamse Kermis in de 19e eeuw*; Amsterdam, 1976.

A. de Khotinsky, *Der De Khotinsky-Accumulator und der Weg seiner Entstehung*; Gelnhausen, 1891.

G. H. Knap, *Mens en Bedrijf. 75 jaar electrotechniek, 75 jaar Smit-Slikkerveer*; Slikkerveer, 1958.

W. Koch, *Die Konzentrationsbewegung in der deutschen Elektroindustrie*; Berlin, 1907.

G. A. de Kok, *De Koninklijke Weg. Honderd jaar geschiedenis Koninklijke Maatschappij De Schelde te Vlissengen 1875–1975*; Middelburg, 1975.

E. A. Krüger, *Die Herstellung der Elektrischen Glühlampe, nach in den verschiedenste Glühlampen-Fabriken gesammelte praktischen Erfahrungen*; Leipzig, 1894.

G. C. P. Linssen, *Verandering en verschuiving, industriële ontwikkeling naar bedrijfstak in midden- en noord-Limburg, 1839–1914*; Tilburg, 1969.

H. Lintsen, *Ingenieurs in Nederland in de negentiende Eeuw, een streven naar erkenning en macht*; The Hague, 1980.

H. Loring, *From the Beginning – Robertson Electric Lamps*; London, 1905.

D. McLellan, *Marx' leven en werk*; Amsterdam, 1975.

G. Maier, *Erinnerungen aus dem Leben von Wilhelm Schöffer*; Zürich, 1901.

W. C. Mees, *Man van de daad – Mr. Marten Mees en de opkomst van Rotterdam*; Rotterdam, 1946.

W. Meinhardt, *Entwicklung und Aufbau der Glühlampenindustrie*; Berlin, 1932.

J. Meijer, *Zij lieten hun sporen achter, Joodse bijdragen tot de Nederlandse beschaving.*

J. Th. Mouton, *Margarineboter, Hare bereiding, verteerbaarheid en bestrijding – uitgegeven door en voor rekening van de Vereeniging van Margarineboterfabrikanten in Nederland*; Oss, 1884.

H. J. G. Mijnssen, *Het gloeilicht, zijn wezen en vorming; berekiningen en uitvoering van installaties, practische lichtverdeeling in lokalen en bijzondere buitengewone opmerkingen bij de toepassing in 't algemeen, naar E. de Fodor*; Gouda, 1886.
*Practische vraagstukken over electrische verlichting, naar R. E. Day*; Gouda, 1883.

C. D. Nagtglas Versteeg, *De wenschelijkheid eener betere Controle van Electrische installatiën*; Bussum, 1900.

W. J. van Overbeek de Meijer, *Eenige opmerkingen over Octrooien en Octrooiwetten*; Utrecht, 1891.

H. C. Passer, *The Electrical Manufacturers 1875–1900; A study in Competition, Entrepreneurship, Technical Change, and Economic Growth*; Cambridge (Mass.), 1953.

G. A. Percival, *The Electric Lamp Industry*; London, 1920.

Ed. Philips, *Gedachten en Herinneringen*; The Hague, 1957.

F. Pinner, *Emil Rathenau und das elektrische Zeitalter*; Leipzig, 1918.

P. Polet, *Middelburg Electrisch Verlicht*; Middelburg, 1889.

F. L. Pope, *Evolution of the Electric Incandescent Lamp*; Elizabeth, N.J., 1889.

G. S. Ram, *The Incandescent Lamp and its Manufacture*; London, 1893.

E. Rebske, *Lampen, Laternen, Leuchten: eine Historie der Beleuchtung*; Stuttgart, 1962.

A. W. Ressing, *De levering van Electriciteit te Amsterdam*; Amsterdam, 1900.

W. Ringnalda, *De Rijkstelegraaf in Nederland, Hare opkomst en ontwikkeling, 1852–1902*; Amsterdam, 1902.

A. Roelvink, *De gemeente Amsterdam en de electriciteit*; Amsterdam, 1900.

H. Roodhuijzen, *Mijn ontslag als Curator van de Latijnsche School te Zaltbommel*; Zaltbommel, 1879.

M. Rooij (ed.), *Ondernemend Nederland, zestig jaar ontplooiing, 1899–1959*; Leiden, 1959.

B. Russell, *The Autobiography of Bertrand Russell*; London, 1971.

M. A. Satelen, *Russkie elektrotechniki vtoroj poloviny XIX Veka*; Moscow, 1950.

W. E. Sawyer, *Electric Lighting by Incandescence*; New York, 1881.

H. J. Scheffer, *Henry Tindal – een ongewoon heer met ongewone besognes*; Bussum, 1976.

E. Schiff, *Industrialization without National Patents – The Netherlands 1869–1912, Switzerland 1850–1907*; Princeton, N.J., 1971.

C. Schöffer, *Het huis Hofmann Schöffer & Co., eene schets bij gelegenheid van het vijftigjarig bestaan der Firma, aan hare vrienden opgedragen door C. Schöffer*; Rotterdam, 1888.

G. Sciama, *Rapport présenté au nom de la commission des douanes de la chambre Syndicale des industries électriques*; Paris, 1890.

J. D. Scott, *Siemens Brothers, 1858–1958; An Essay in the History of Industry*; London, 1958.

R. Seth, *The Russian Terrorists: The Story of the Narodniki*; London, 1966.

G. Siemens, *Geschichte des Hauses Siemens*; Munich, 1947.
*History of the House of Siemens, Vol. 1. 1847–1914*; Munich, 1957.

J. A. Snijders, *Electrotechnisch Onderwijs aan de Polytechnische School te Delft*; Delft, 1888.
*De vorderingen der Electrotechniek in de laatste jaren en de stand van het electrotechnisch onderwijs*; The Hague, 1894.

K. Spierings, *Wij waren nog stadje*; 's-Hertogenbosch, 1966.

E. Star Busmann, *Over octrooijen van uitvindingen*; Groningen, 1867.

J. Stellingwerf, *Inleiding tot de Universiteit*; Amsterdam, 1971.

J. M. van Stuijvenberg (ed.), *De economische geschiedenis van Nederland*; Groningen, 1977.

J. W. Swan, *Electric Lighting, A Lecture delivered by J. W. Swan before the members of the literary and philosophical society of Newcastle*; Newcastle-upon-Tyne, 1880.

K. R. Swan, *Sir Joseph Swan and the Invention of the Incandescent Lamp*, published for the British Council; London, 1946.

M. E. Swan and K. R. Swan, *Sir Joseph Wilson Swan – A Memoir*; London, 1929.

M. W. F. Treub, *Herinneringen en overpeinzingen*; Haarlem, 1931.

A. Urbanitzky, *Die elektrische Beleuchtung und Ihre Anwendung in der Praxis*; Vienna, 1890.

Joh. de Vries, *Een eeuw vol effecten – Historische schets van de Vereniging voor de Effectenhandel en de Amsterdamse Effectenbeurs 1876–1976*; Amsterdam, 1976.

J. Wegner, *Siemens in den Niederlanden, Geschichte des Hauses Siemens im Ausland*; Erlangen, 1970.

G. Werkman, *Kras = 100/100 = Kras*; Amsterdam, 1966.

K. Wilhelm, *Die A.E.G.*; Berlin, 1931.

J. W. Willemsen, *De ontwikkeling en toepassing van electriciteit aan boord van schepen*; Amsterdam, 1931.

C. Wilson, *Geschiedenis van Unilever*; The Hague, 1970.

L. von Winterfeld, *Entwicklung und Tätigkeit der Firma Siemens & Halske in den Jahren 1847–1897*; Leipzig, 1913.

J. Zacharias, *Die Glühlampe, Ihre Herstellung und Anwendung in der Praxis*; Leipzig, 1890.

S. Zadoks, *Geschiedenis der Amsterdamsche Concessies*; Amsterdam, 1899.
G. P. Zahn Jr, *De Geschiedenis der verlichting van Amsterdam*; Amsterdam, 1911.
A. C. Zoethout, *Handboek voor den electriciën*; Dordrecht, 1908.

BIBLIOGRAPHY
(without name of author)

Allgemeine Elektricitäts-Gesellschaft, *50 Jahre AEG*. Collection of essays to mark the Fiftieth Anniversary of the company on 19 April 1933; Berlin, 1956.
*Algemene Geschiedenis der Nederlanden*, Vol. 13; Haarlem, 1978.
*Bol'saja Sovetskaja Encyklopedija*, Vol. 25; Moscow.
*Catalogue Général Officiel* of the International Electricity Exhibition held in Paris, 1881.
*Electro-technische Opstellen*, presented to Professor C. Feldmann upon his retirement from the Delft University of Technology on 8 June 1937; Delft, 1937.
*Elektrizität*, offizielle Zeitung der Internationalen Elektrotechnischen Ausstellung Frankfurt am Main, 1891.
Elektrotechnische Gesellschaft, *Geschichtstafeln der Elektrotechnik 1831–1931*; Frankfurt am Main, 1931.
The General Electric Co. Ltd, *The Story of the Lamp*; London, 1924.
N.V. Groeneveld van der Poll & Co., *Commemorative Book 1887–1937*; Amsterdam, 1937.
N.V. Hazemeyer, *Gouden Schakel* – Commemorative Book marking the Fiftieth Anniversary of N.V. Hazemeyer; Hengelo, 1957.
Ketjen, *Honderd Jaar Zwavelzuur-Fabricatie, 1835–1935*; Amsterdam, 1935.
Mijnssen & Co., *De Eerste 50 Jaren*, internal study, unpublished.
*The National Cyclopaedia of American Biography*, Vol. 25; New York, 1936.
Nationale Levensverzekerings-Bank N.V., *Honderd Nationale Jaren*; Rotterdam, 1963.
Nederlandsche Maatschappij voor Nijverheid en Handel, Jubilee Issue, 1778–1928; Amsterdam Branch, 1928.
Van Rietschoten & Houwens, *Honderd Jaar Techniek*; Rotterdam, 1960.
W. Schöffer & Co., *Ein Beitrag zur Geschichte des Kaffeehandels, aus den 'Lebens-Erinnerungen von Wilhelm Schöffer'* – den Freunden der Firma W. Schöffer & Co. in Rotterdam gewidmet anlässlich deren 50-jährigen Bestehens; 1905.
Stork & Co., *De machinefabriek van Gebroeders Stork & Co. te Hengelo* – Memoir marking the 25th Anniversary on 4 September 1893; The Hague.
*Vereeniging tot behartiging van de belangen van het personeel aan de Machinefabriek van Gebr. Stork & Co., Hengelo 1881–1906*; The Hague, 1908.
Vereeniging tot Bevordering van Fabrieks- en Handwerksnijverheid in Nederland, Annual Reports, 1878–92.
*Is gas of electriciteit voor verlichting van fabrieken en werkplaatsen het meest aan te bevelen?*; The Hague, 1893.
Vereeniging van Directeuren van Electriciteitsbedrijven in Nederland, *De Ontwikkeling van de Electriciteitsvoorziening van Nederland tot het jaar 1925*; Amsterdam, 1926.
Vereeniging van Directeuren van Electriciteitsdrijven in Nederland, *De ontwikkeling van onze electriciteitsvoorziening 1880–1938*; Arnhem, 1948.

PERIODICALS

*The Electrician: A Weekly Journal of Electrical Engineering, Industry and Science*; 1878–1900.

*The Electrician, Electrical Trades' Directory and Handbook*; 1889–1900.

*Elektrotechnische Zeitschrift. Herausgegeben vom Elektrotechnischen Verein*; 1879–1900.

*De Ingenieur. Orgaan der Vereeniging van Burgerlijke Ingenieurs*; 1886–1900.

*La Lumière Electrique. Journal universel d'Electricité*; 1879–90.

*Natuur. Populair geïllustreerd maandschrift gewijd aan de natuurkundige wetenschappen en hare toepassingen*; 1887–91.

*Telegraphic Journal and Electrical Review*; 1877–90.

*Tijdschrift der Nederlandsche Maatschappij ter Bevordering van Nijverheid*; 1876–1900.

*Zeitschrift für angewandte Elektricitätslehre mit besonderer berücksichtigung der Telegraphie des elektrischen Beleuchtungswesens der Galvanoplastik und verwandter Zweige*; 1879–1900.

*Zentralblatt für Elektrotechnik*; 1879–89.

# INDEX

161, 163, 175, 176, 178, 240, 242, 243,
245, 246, 248, 291–4, 296
Netherlands Institute of Accountants, 169
Netherlands–Israelite Poor Relief Board, 204
Newcastle Chemical Society, 13
Newcastle-upon-Tyne, 11, 34
New York, electric lighting, 25, 93
*New York Herald*, 14
*New York Sun*, 13
*New York Tribune*, 56
Nierop, F. S. van, 188
Nierstrasz, Technisch Bureau, 219
Nihilists, 93, 93n, 142
Nijmeegsche Bankvereeniging, Van Engelenburg
& Schippers, 169
Nijmegen, 53, 167, 173
electric lighting, 122, 123
incandescent lamp factory, 32, 34, 132, 150,
164, 166–9
Noord-Nederlandsche Beetwortelsuikerfabriek,
277
North Brabant, 42
Norway, 102
Notten, C. van, 114
Nouhuys, J. W. van, tobacco factory, 42, 284

Oberbruch, incandescent lamp factory at, 149
O'Connel, Maurice W., 172
Octrooiwet, Vereeniging van Voorstanders
eener Nederlandsche, 245, 251
Oesterreichische Schuckertwerke, A. G., 80
Offenbach, 38, 52
Olland, H., 101, 104
Oudschans, Dr S., 185
Oyens, G., 95, 101, 104n

Paets van Troostwijk, A., 103
Palais de l'Industrie, Paris, 86–9
Palace of Industry, Amsterdam, 235–9, 250
pantheism, 138
parallel connection, 19, 22, 25
parchmentized thread, 17
Paris, 41, 87, 88, 92
electric lighting, 88, 89, 92–9, 140, 196,
197, 200
incandescent lamp factories, 27, 34, 132,
140, 157, 158
Park Theatre, Amsterdam, 110
Passer, Harold C., 18
patent agents, 5, 28, 245, 247
patent conflicts, incandescent lamp industry,
19, 26, 27, 30, 31, 71, 73–5, 77–100,
127, 143, 146, 150, 153, 154, 163, 253,
260
patent laws, 19, 27, 80, 126, 127, 243–53,
262, 292
Belgium, 292
France, 146, 249

Germany, 146, 244, 247, 250, 253
Great Britain, 7, 29, 80, 127, 146, 153, 163,
164, 176, 244, 247–9, 252, 253, 262, 274,
285
Netherlands, 29, 164, 165, 238, 240,
242–53, 261, 292
Switzerland, 31, 246, 249
U.S.A., 150, 245, 248, 250
patents, Dutch, 5, 41–2, 244, app. 2
patents, incandescent lamp, 3, 17ff, 22, 25–8,
30, 69, 75, 77, 79, 97, 259, 260, 262,
269, 274, 289, app. 1
Patijn, R. J. H., 251
Peerbolte, L., 44ff
Peletier, Gerlachus, *see* Ribbius
Peletier & Philips, 37–40, 42–4, 46, 48, 49,
147
Perry, Prof. J., 153
Pesters, Jonkheer C. A. de, 114
'Phaëton', Electriciteits-Maatschappij,
incandescent lamp manufacturers, 169
Philippart Frères, incandescent lamp
manufacturers, 34
Philips, Abraham, 52
Philips, Alexander, 52
Philips, Dr Anton Frederik, 35, 49–50, 52–3,
59, 262
Philips, August, 45ff, 53, 55–7, 210, 271,
app. 3
Philips, Benjamin, 50–2
Philips, Benjamin Frederik David, *known as*
Frederik Philips, 2, 33, 36–49, 50, 52, 55,
60, 82, 84, 147, 171, 260, 261, 271,
273–9, 282, 283, 284, 287, 296, app. 2
Philips, Eduard, 46, 52
Philips, Eduard J., 49, 52, 58
Philips, Frederik (Maastricht), 52
Philips, Frederik (Zaltbommel), *see* Philips,
Benjamin Frederik David
Philips, Dr Gerard Leonard Frederik, 2, 33, 37,
44, 46, 50, 52, 60–73, 82–4, 112, 127,
165, 173, 178, 184, 202–10, 212, 214,
217–21, 224–8, 238–41, 243, 250,
253–84, 286, 287, 290, 291, 295, 296,
app. 6, 8
Philips, Henri L., 49, 52
Philips, Isaac, 38, 52
Philips, Jacques, 49, 52
Philips, Johannes, 52
Philips, Joseph, 37, 52
Philips, Karel S., 52
Philips, Leonard I. H., 52, 55, app. 3
Philips, Lion, 37–40, 44, 51, 52–9, app. 3
Philips, Louis, 49
Philips, Nannette, 56, 58–9
Philips, Philip (Maastricht), 37, 52
Philips, Philip (Veenendaal), 42, 50, 52, 53
Philips, Fred., bankers, Zaltbommel, 45, 47, 49
Philips, De Gebroeders, Maastricht, 37
Philips Juniores, Gebrüder, Aachen, 38

Wertheim, A. C., 45, 241
Wertheim, L. B., 114
Wertheim & Co., Leon, 114
Wester Sugar Refinery, 115
Weston, Edward, 27, 260
Weston Electric Light Company, 17
Wetteren, N. van, 101, 104
Wheatstone, Charles, 9
White Vitrite and Luminoid Company, 163
Wigels, P. tobacco factory, 42
Wijsman, G. L., 188
Wilde, H., 9, 57
William III, H. M. King, 41
Willemstijn, H., 47
Willeumier, C. M. J., 222
Wisse, Willem J., 108–11, 203, 213, 214, 227, 229–31
Wisse Piccaluga & Co., Electrische Verlichting-Maatschappij, 101, 107–11, 117, 166, 185, 249
Wittop Koning, D. A., 192, 194, 195
Wolff, L. & S., bankers, 70
Woodhouse & Rawson, incandescent lamp manufacturers, 26, 28, 74, 78, 81, 153, 159
workers, 15, 26, 31, 38, 41–3, 111, 112, 117, 124, 144, 148, 153–5, 164, 164n, 167, 172, 176, 207, 278, 279, 291
working conditions, 42, 156, 157, 235, 237
working hours, 42, 44, 156, 172, 239
World Exhibition, 245, 247
  Paris, 1878, 100, 245
  Paris, 1889, 33n
  Philadelphia, 1876, 92
Woschke, Emile, 71, 173, 275–9
Wurfbain, A. L., 188
Wynne, Frank, 19, 259
Wynne & Powell, zinc chloride process, 19, 259

Zacharias, Johannes, 33, 67, 70, 72, 144, 157, 172, 268, 275
Zaltbommel, 1, 37–40, 42–9, 51–6, 58–9, 239, 275, 277, 296
  gas works, 44, 47–8
  tobacco industry, 37–43, 52, 284
Zanni, Deodati, 71
Zanni-Shippey lamp, 71
Zevenbergen, 106
zinc chloride process, 19, 96, 255–60
Zürich Incandescent Lamp Company, 31, 35